Nervous People

and OTHER SATIRES

MIKHAIL ZOSHCHENKO

Nervous People

and OTHER SATIRES

Edited, with an Introduction by
HUGH McLEAN
Translated from the Russian by
MARIA GORDON *and* HUGH McLEAN

INDIANA UNIVERSITY PRESS

Bloomington and Indianapolis

This book is a publication of

Indiana University Press
601 North Morton Street
Bloomington, Indiana 47404-3797 USA

www.indiana.edu/~iupress

Telephone orders   800-842-6796
Fax orders   812-855-7931
Orders by e-mail   iuporder@indiana.edu

ACKNOWLEDGMENTS
The translators wish to express their thanks to Fruma Gottschalk for helping to find approximate English equivalents for some of Zoshchenko's saltier colloquialisms, and to George Siegel for bibliographical assistance.

The paper used in this publication meets the minimum requirements of American National Standard for Information Sciences—Permanence of Paper for Printed Library Materials, ANSI Z39.48-1984.

Manufactured in the United States of America

Library of Congress Cataloging-in-Publication Data

Zoshchenko, Mikhail Mikhaĭlovich,   1895–1958.
    Nervous people, and other satires.
    (A Midland book ; MB-192)
    Reprint of the ed. published by Pantheon Books, New York.
    I. Title.
PZ3.Z79Ne5 [PG3476.Z7] 891.7'3'42   75-9131
ISBN 0-253-20192-6

6   7   8   9   10   10   09   08   07   06   05

CONTENTS

AUTOBIOGRAPHY

INTRODUCTION

ONE of the paradoxes of post-Revolutionary Russian literature has been the remarkable vitality of comedy and satire. After all, revolution is a grim and bloody business, and its aftermath is often grimmer and bloodier than the revolution itself, as totalitarian fanaticism with its program of planned happiness and its machinery of planned terror undertakes the task of compressing a nation's life into a predetermined mold. The consequences are material hardship, social dislocation, and omnipresent fear—all of which have been features of Russian life since 1917. Whatever the economic, social, and military achievements of the Soviet regime, it is hard to see how its subjects have found much in it to laugh at. Indeed, it would almost seem as if laughter were forbidden them altogether—public, literary laughter at any rate. Most laughter is by nature irreverent, and irreverence is by definition subversive: it is "unfear" (*in-re-vereri*). If fear is the chief emotional instrument of rule, then laughter becomes a danger to the state. What the Soviet regime has therefore sought from its literary servants has been not laughter but reverent, "epic" celebrations of its own greatness, choruses of everlasting yeas.

But the nay-saying strain in human nature is a strong one, and somehow laughter manages to survive a surprising amount of prohibiting pressure. In any event, it is a fact that some of the greatest comic works of modern times have been written by Soviet Russians:

the two satirical plays by Vladimir Mayakovsky, the two picaresque novels *The Twelve Chairs* and *The Golden Calf*, as well as the short stories and *feuilletons* by Ilya Ilf and Evgeny Petrov, and the stories, tales, and sketches of Mikhail Zoshchenko.

Since it extends all the way from the Revolution to 1958, Zoshchenko's literary career offers a vivid illustration of the vicissitudes of a Soviet humorist during those forty turbulent years. He was born in 1895, in the Ukrainian town of Poltava, but spent most of his life in St. Petersburg. His Ukrainian father was a mediocre painter of historical subjects. His mother, a Great Russian, had been an actress. The family appears to have been comfortably off, distinctly upper-class in mores and tastes. Zoshchenko attended a good Gymnasium and later enrolled in the Faculty of Law at Petersburg University, but did not complete the course. In 1914 he volunteered for military service and after a special indoctrination course was commissioned a sublieutenant and shipped off to the front. He saw a great deal of action, was wounded several times and also gassed—an experience which left him with permanent damage to his heart and liver.

Doubtless the satirist's mocking, derisive, generally negative view of human beings and their pretensions was already ingrained in Zoshchenko by the time of the Revolution. It showed itself partly in the extreme restlessness which led him through an extraordinary series of jobs and occupations during the revolutionary period, and it was probably a factor in his decision to side with the Reds in the Civil War. He joined the Red Army in 1918, more from negative than from positive motives, as he later confessed: "I am not a Communist, and I entered the Red Army to fight against the nobility and the landlords, a milieu I know quite well enough." Because of his war injuries he was released from the Red Army as physically unfit for service and spent the next few years acquiring a varied storehouse of potential literary material. "In three years I changed cities twelve times and professions ten. I was a policeman, a bookkeeper, a cobbler, an instructor in aviculture, a telephone operator for the border patrol, a detective, a court secretary, and a government chief clerk."

But during this kaleidoscopic succession of experiences Zoshchenko was clearly preparing himself for his true calling, literature. He began writing professionally in 1921, and his first volume of collected stories appeared in 1922. It was an immediate success with the reading public—a success Zoshchenko was to repeat and maintain for many years to come, in fact for as long as he was allowed to publish. During the twenties and thirties he was, next to Gorky, the most popular living Russian writer. Huge editions of his works were reprinted again and again, and the name Zoshchenko became a household word among persons who could hardly have mentioned another contemporary writer. At the same time, this mass popularity was not purchased at the price of any loss of artistic integrity or even of the esteem of the literati; indeed, Zoshchenko is one of the few writers of modern times who have successfully bridged the gap between the elite and the average reader. The most astute and discriminating critics, like Viktor Shklovsky and Viktor Vinogradov, were as entranced by his stories as any philistine in the street.

From the very beginning of his literary career Zoshchenko showed an unusual independence and boldness of attitude—a sturdy refusal to see the world through any glasses but his own. In the early 1920's he was associated with a remarkable group of young writers who called themselves the "Serapion Brothers," taking their name from the hermit hero of one of E. T. A. Hoffmann's stories. Despite their vast differences over literary principles, forms, and subjects, the group shared a common conviction that art should maintain its independence from politics and its freedom to follow its own devices. It was for a collection of autobiographical pieces, *The Serapion Brothers About Themselves*, that Zoshchenko wrote his own manifesto of independence. This was an unusually bold piece even for such a bold company, but the boldness was ostensibly tempered by the offhand tone of sly banter which was to become Zoshchenko's trademark:

> . . . Being a writer is sort of hard . . . Take ideology —these days a writer has got to have ideology.
>
> Here's Voronsky* now (a good man) who writes: "It is necessary that writers should have a more precise ideology." Now that's downright disagreeable! Tell me, how can I have a "precise ideology" when not a single party among them all appeals to me?
>
> I don't hate anybody—that's *my* precise ideology.
>
> Still more precise, if you please. Well, in their general swing the Bolsheviks are closer to me than anybody else. And so I'm willing to bolshevik around with them . . . But I'm not a Communist (or rather, not a Marxist), and I think I never will be.

Needless to say, this damaging document was unearthed by heresy-hunting literary detectives of later years and hurled back at Zoshchenko with the customary cries of outraged admonition, and it was to constitute one of the main points in the bill of particulars against Zoshchenko drawn up by Comrade Zhdanov in 1946. By that time such a pledge of qualified allegiance sounded as seditious as a bomb hurled at the Kremlin walls.

During the relatively liberal twenties and even later Zoshchenko somehow managed to get away with his

* Aleksandr Voronsky was a noted Communist critic, for many years editor of the leading Soviet literary magazine *Red Virgin Soil*. As an editor, he advocated a policy of tolerance and understanding toward non-Communist writers. Voronsky disappeared during the purges of the 1930's.

irreverences. To be sure, there were warnings—rumbles, snarls, and even an occasional nip—from the regime's literary watchdogs, but as yet no all-out assault. No doubt Zoshchenko's persistence in the face of these repeated danger signals was a demonstration of his determination and courage. But that he succeeded for so long in displaying his boldness in print was one of the advantages of his peculiar artistic method—a combination of irony, ambiguity, and camouflage which for many years bewildered his censors. It was discouragingly hard to pin him down.

Zoshchenko's method of artistic camouflage was not actually invented by him, but rather adapted from certain nineteenth-century Russian writers who had faced similar problems in evading the Czarist censorship, particularly Gogol and Leskov. The basic ruse is to create uncertainty in the reader's mind about the author's relation to his work and in particular about his emotional attitude toward the events and characters presented. One way of doing this is to interpose a narrator between the author and the story, preferably a narrator sharply distinguished in some way—origin, status, education, or sex—from the author himself. The author then ostensibly figures merely as a transmitting agent and presumably cannot be held responsible for the narrator's statements. If the narrator expresses heretical ideas or reprehensible attitudes, they cannot be charged to the author; indeed, if the narrator is presented in a negative or satirical manner, the author may well maintain that his own position is diametrically opposed.

From the artistic point of view the important thing in "camouflage" narrative of this kind is to establish the distinction between author and narrator, not merely by stating it explicitly, but by embedding it in the texture of the story itself. In other words, the narrator must be set apart from the author not only socially and morally, but also stylistically. This is easiest to do, even in Soviet Russia, if the author and narrator belong to different social classes. Clearly, for speakers of a given language, geographical region and class constitute the chief social determinants of linguistic behavior; and for purposes like Zoshchenko's, class is the more satisfactory basis for "motivating" a stylistic distinction between author and narrator. Two individuals who come from the same region but belong to different classes will share many of the same experiences but see them from different points of view and, most important, express their views in different natural styles. The satirist can then provide, so to speak, a simultaneous double commentary on the events presented: one, the narrator's, explicit, and the other, his own, implicit. Of course, this distinction in styles may have artistic functions other than camouflage. The mode of narration is an effective means of characterizing the narrator himself, who is frequently a prominent actor in his own tale; and often the narrator's style, if colorful enough, has artistic value in its own right, a diverting display of picturesque linguistic behavior.

In a series of stories written in the early twenties, Zoshchenko used a narrator very close to the Leskovian archetype: Gospodin Sinebryukhov (Mr. Bluebelly), an ex-peasant and ex-sergeant in the Czar's army, who regales us with tales of his experiences in the war and its aftermath. These experiences are varied and entertaining enough, but Bluebelly's greatest artistic distinction lies in his use of language, which is somehow symbolic of the whole disrupted era of war and revolution. Though fundamentally a "dumb" peasant, he has become semiliterate during his years in the army and has picked up bits and pieces of linguistic "civilization," rather poorly assimilated, in the form of newspaper jargon, foreign words, often distorted and imperfectly understood, and "officialese." This peasant in a state of transition toward urban mass culture is a pathetic and often ludicrous creature, and the incongruous hodge-podge of his language is intrinsically funny. And of course, in this bizarre language Bluebelly can make all sorts of dubious judgments about the world he lives in without anyone's dreaming of attributing these views to Mikhail Zoshchenko.

Before long, Zoshchenko found less obvious stylistic masks than Bluebelly. In most of the stories written after the mid-twenties Zoshchenko took a somewhat better educated narrator than Sinebryukhov, though one still socially and intellectually distant from the author. The language of this new narrator approaches normal Russian, though not normal literary Russian. It is highly colloquial in tone and often in vocabulary, and its forays into literariness are usually tinged with parody, mostly unconscious. It represents the language of the urban man-in-the-street, the semi-educated mass man. This language is distinguished from Zoshchenko's own not so much by obvious grotesqueries like Sinebryukhov's—though there are some of these—as by its sheer colloquial informality, its deviation from accepted norms of literary discourse. Reading it, we inevitably conclude that a person who speaks this way must belong to the lower orders of society; he could not have passed through the taboo-imposing experiences of a traditional Gymnasium and university education. Further, this informality of language symbolizes and blends with the ideas and sentiments it communicates —"everyman's" reflections, sometimes apt, often ignorant, almost always naïve, on life and the world around him. "Debased" language combined with naïveté of thought implies that the author's attitude toward his apparent spokesman is tinged with irony, and we naturally conclude that the narrator's ideas are to be regarded with skepticism. But we cannot always be sure. Sometimes "naïve" remarks, like the child's observation about the emperor's clothes, have a way of striking taboo targets. The reader's uncertainty—is the author being serious or not?—proved extremely useful to Zoshchenko throughout his entire career.

Besides his value as a mask for a censor-shy author, this man-in-the-street narrator with a taste for armchair philosophizing is a remarkably vital creation in his own right. There is a satisfying, down-to-earth humanness about him, a kind of philistine vigor which helps us to see things in their proper proportions. He is the voice of the philistine in all of us. In an era of ringing words and cataclysmic events, when empires are toppling and the advent of a new epoch in human history is being proclaimed, he asserts the eternal verities of what the Russians call *byt,* a rather pejorative term for the mundane aspects of everyday life. Socialism, communism, world revolution, the end of the exploitation of man by man, the five-year plan in four years—all this is very well, Zoshchenko's hero seems to say, I'm for it and take pride in it, and so forth. But our real lives are not lived on this plane. Striped socks, sausages, sofas, bedbugs, bathrooms, and sex: these are the things that really stir our souls. There is more human passion in some housewives' squabble in a communal kitchen or in a bridegroom's quest for a second-hand armoire than in a hundred *Pravda* pep talks.

In a collection of novelettes called *Sentimental Tales* which he published in 1929 Zoshchenko "lays bare," to use a favorite term of the Russian formalists, the ambiguous relationship between himself and his narrator; he calls attention to it, makes it explicit. The book has three prefaces, supposedly to three successive editions. The first two are signed by the putative author, one I. V. Kolenkorov (the name comes from the Russian word for "calico," a cheap, mass-produced material doubtless symbolic of Kolenkorov's social and cultural standing). In both his prefaces Kolenkorov expresses his gratitude to "the well-known writer Mikhail Zoshchenko" for his kind assistance in putting the tales into publishable form. In the third preface this well-known assistant comes out from behind the scenes and speaks in his own name:

> In view of previous misunderstandings, the author informs his critics that the person who tells these stories is, so to speak, an imaginary figure. He is the middling type of intellectual who happened to live on the border line between two epochs. We were forced to endow this upstart of ours, I. V. Kolenkorov, with such things as neurasthenia, ideological waverings, gross contradictions, and melancholy. The author himself, M. M. Zoshchenko, the writer, is, it is true, the son and brother of such unhealthy people, but he has long since surmounted all that. At the present time he has no contradictions. If he may occasionally lack complete peace of mind, it is for entirely different reasons, which the author will tell about sometime later. In this instance it is a literary device. And the author implores his esteemed critics to remember this particular fact before they open fire on a defenseless writer.*

Of course, such ostensible revelations of the author's true face are in fact only sleight-of-hand tricks with the "calico" mask. The "true" author, though he calls himself M. M. Zoshchenko, proves to be almost as questionable a figure as Kolenkorov, whose "son and brother" he admits he is. The tongue-in-cheek claim to freedom from "contradictions" is proof enough in itself. If more were needed, there is evidence enough, in *Before Sunrise* and elsewhere, that the real Zoshchenko had more than his share of unsurmounted "contradictions," including ideological waverings and especially melancholy. But the bantering, "naïve" philosopher who appears as the "author" in many of Zoshchenko's stories

---

* A modified version of this Introduction, without Kolenkorov, appears in "The Lilacs Are Blooming" in this volume.

is in fact another mask behind which the true Zo-shchenko can only be glimpsed darkly.

In the late twenties and for a time thereafter this system of ironic camouflage worked quite well. Some critics threatened Zoshchenko, urging him to declare himself unequivocally for the regime and to give up his irritating ambiguity, which was misleading the masses. But for the most part Zoshchenko only smiled and quickened the conjuror's patter that accompanied his tricks. During the thirties, however, he seems to have thought it politic to throw the critics a bone in the form of a few irreproachably "correct" Soviet stories. For once he laid aside his mask of irony and wrote like the serious, dedicated servant of the communist ideal that the regime expected its "engineers of human souls" to be. In 1934 he did his stint for a particularly unpleasant propaganda volume entitled *The White Sea–Baltic Canal*, edited by the former literary *Gauleiter* Leopold Averbakh (later purged). This work was designed to show that the Soviet forced labor camps, far from being a brutal travesty of the regime's "socialist" ideals, were actually beneficent institutions, something like psychological blacksmith shops, where convicts engaged in digging the White Sea–Baltic Canal under the fatherly supervision of the NKVD were "reforged" into useful Soviet citizens. Zoshchenko's piece, "The Story of One Reforging," purports to be a truthful record of one of these spiritual metamorphoses. It is entirely serious in tone and lacks any of the familiar Zoshchenko flavor. It also lacks any literary value. Other "bones" were a satirical biography of Alexander Kerensky and a saccharine series of *Stories About Lenin* written for children.

Having thus openly rendered unto Caesar, Zoshchenko apparently felt that he had won the right to pursue his own artistic bents. First, he continued to produce regularly works in his "trade-mark" genre, the short-short story or sketch, only two or three pages long, which he had made peculiarly his own. These little satires, which often made their first appearance in newspapers, were largely responsible for Zoshchenko's enormous popularity. They seemed to strike a responsive chord in the hearts of Russians of every description. Seemingly innocuous anecdotes illustrating what used to be called "defects in the mechanism," that is, disparities between official mythology and the stubborn facts of everyday life, they appealed to people as an expression of their irrepressible, unofficial human needs. No matter how unabated his Communist enthusiasm, no one could deny that for most Russians life was pretty hard; and to laugh about hardship made it easier to bear. Zoshchenko had a keen eye for the comic incongruities that cropped up constantly to bedevil people's lives. For instance, at one time in the thirties it was apparently impossible to find any but very high-powered light bulbs in Soviet stores. A trivial circumstance, no doubt, but one of the many small annoyances that caused so much human wear and tear for ordinary Russians. Zoshchenko transforms irritation into comedy in "A Clever Little Trick," as his hero complains to the meter reader, who has commented on what a lot of current he is using, that he cannot summon courage to venture into a bathroom illuminated by a dazzling 500-candlepower bulb.

The building of the Soviet Utopia required not only a complete change in the economic and social conditions of life, but also a basic transformation in the behavior patterns of its citizens. To be sure, according to the Marxist formula, "being determines consciousness", fundamental changes in the economic and class structure of society will in time automatically produce changed human beings. But this process takes time, and in the meantime the majority of Russians had been psychologically shaped under capitalism and carried with them into the new society obnoxious "capitalist

survivals in the human consciousness." Official critics
friendly to Zoshchenko interpreted his satires as directed against these "capitalist survivals"; he was thus
playing a historically progressive role in helping the
new Soviet man to throw off these unwanted relics of
the past. Zoshchenko never openly objected to this useful interpretation, but one cannot escape the impression
after reading many of his stories that he hardly shared
it; he did not believe that all the antisocial tendencies
of Soviet citizens were attributable to capitalism. Human nature, Zoshchenko seems to be saying, is much
more intractable than the Utopians think.

For instance, one of the attributes of the new socialist
man was supposed to be a sense of collective responsibility. The new society was no longer the capitalist
jungle where men fought one another for the necessities of life, but a co-operative enterprise where all strove
together for a common goal. Zoshchenko displays his
skepticism in an anecdote called "The Bottle." A
young man accidentally drops a bottle on the sidewalk
and walks away in disgust, making no effort to pick up
the pieces of broken glass. Other passers-by likewise
fail to take any socially responsible action against this
dangerous hazard. The narrator, who is watching these
events while sitting on the opposite curb, bemoans
such appalling evidence of bourgeois-individualistic survivals in the popular mind:

> What do I see? I see people walk on the broken glass.
> They curse, but still they walk. What lack of culture!
> There's not a single person who will fulfill his social ob-
> ligations. . . . No, my friends! I think. We do not yet
> understand our social responsibilities. We traipse along
> over broken glass.

The narrator, of course, accepts the "capitalist survivals"
theory. But does Zoshchenko?

With his elusive, innocent manner Zoshchenko got

away with themes few other writers would have dared
to touch; he even skirted some of the really forbidden
topics of Soviet literature, such as the Party purges.
One unsettling phenomenon of Soviet life in the thirties (and also recently)was the rapid changes in the
names of institutions, streets, and whole cities as the
stars of leading Party personalities rose or set. In "An
Incident on the Volga" Zoshchenko succeeded in making this ominous feature of the permanent purge petty
and ridiculous. During a single excursion trip on the
Volga a steamer's name is changed, much to the confusion of its passengers, from *Comrade Penkin* to
Storm to *Korolenko*. The name *Korolenko* was likely to
last, the narrator observes, " . . . since Korolenko was
dead. Whereas Penkin was alive. And this was his basic
shortcoming, which led to his name's being replaced."

In most of these stories Zoshchenko's method might
be called "reverse idealization": he debases, degrades,
vulgarizes, trivializes the material. Nothing is too sacred
for his mocking irony. In "Poverty" even Lenin's far-
sighted program for the electrification of Russia, which
had inspired so many poets to write hymns to planning
and progress, is brought down to the setting of a petty-
bourgeois bedroom, now lit up by electricity for the
first time:

> You couldn't see much by kerosene light. But now that
> we're all lit up, what do we see? Over there, someone's
> torn slipper lying around; in another place the wallpaper
> is ripped off and hangs in tatters; here a bedbug races
> along, running away from the light; or you see some in-
> describable rag, a gob of spittle, a cigarette butt, and a
> flea capers about . . .

The reason these irreverences were tolerated as long
as they were lay partly in the magic word "petty bourgeois." The petty bourgeoisie was the repository of capitalist survivals in their most squalid form. The aris-

tocracy and big bourgeoisie had been scattered by
the Revolution to the four corners of the earth, but the
artisans, the petty tradespeople, the minor civil servants
and clerks had mostly stayed on, adapting themselves
as best they could and carrying on their vulgar and
materialistic existence in the midst of Soviet cities. As
a class the petty bourgeoisie was doomed by history:
it would either be cast aside or else be transformed and
transfigured by society's victorious march toward socialism. Therefore, if Zoshchenko's satires were aimed
at the petty bourgeoisie, so much the better, ran one
official interpretation. But even in the writings of official Soviet critics the term "petty bourgeois" is sometimes used as if it describes, not a concrete sociological
category, but an attribute of human nature—the petty,
self-seeking, vulgar, and mundane element in everyone.
But of course, "we are overcoming these things," and
in the future Communist society there will be no room
for them. In Zoshchenko, however, belief in the uni-
versality of petty-bourgeoisdom is often quite explicit,
and only slightly less so are his doubts about the possibility of overcoming "these things."

> There exists an opinion [he wrote in an appendix to
> *Youth Restored*] that I write about the petty bourgeoi-
> sie. However, people often say to me, "Isn't there some
> mistake in your work? With us the petty bourgeoisie
> does not exist as a separate class. That mournful category
> of people is not characteristic of our country. For what
> purpose do you depict the petty bourgeoisie and lag be-
> hind the types and tempos of contemporary life?" . . .
> There is no mistake [Zoshchenko replies]. I do write
> about the petty bourgeoisie . . . For the most part I
> create a synthetic type. In all of us there are certain traits
> of the petty bourgeois, the property owner, the money
> grubber. I write about the petty bourgeoisie, and I sup-
> pose I have enough material to last me the rest of my
> life.

Besides his familiar "short-short" stories, Zoshchenko also worked in the somewhat longer form known in Russian as the *povest'* or short novel. Zoshchenko's *povesti* tend to be more serious, more intellectual, more conventionally literary than the shorter stories. The most substantial of them is probably "Michel Sinyagin" (1930), which has the range of a full-fledged novel, treating with a remarkable combination of understanding and ironic detachment the gradual disintegration of a representative of the pre-Revolutionary literary intelligentsia under the conditions of Soviet life. Here too Zoshchenko strives for an ambiguity of mood. The melancholy overtones of Sinyagin's wretched life are offset by "the author's" quasi-personal digressions on all sorts of irrelevant subjects, often involving abrupt shifts from the tragic to the ludicrous. The effect is to short-circuit our sympathy for the hero and make him shrink into the emotional distance.

During the thirties Zoshchenko produced two books in still another form, an experimental one which seemed to suit his peculiar purposes. In *Youth Restored* (1933) and *The Blue Book* (1935) he sought a means of combining fictional and nonfictional material, essentially by organizing the fiction within a nonnarrative, expository framework. *Youth Restored* is allegedly a serious treatise on senescence as a physiological and psychological phenomenon and possible ways of avoiding or retarding it. Zoshchenko's narrator-philosopher undertakes, as it were, a research project on the problem of aging (or rejuvenation). He does so, however, not as a scientist, but as a "naïve" layman, somewhat overconfident, perhaps, and unabashed by the complexities and difficulties of the problem. In a rambling, bantering Introduction, he presents his subject and gives us some random speculations about it. The core of the book is a novel, but its theme has to do with senescence. Finally, a good half of the book consists of a voluminous series of "commentaries" on the narrative in which Zoshchenko, writing "straight" this time, gives all sorts of additional tidbits of information and further speculations on points raised in the course of the story. Both the "naïve" tone of the Introduction and the ambiguous nature of the story itself—an aging executive achieves very temporary "rejuvenation" by running away with his neighbor's young wife—may be taken as clues that the author is hardly serious about his "problem." On the other hand, the commentaries seem quite straightforward, and the matter of rejuvenation was at that time very much publicized in Soviet science, as Professor Bogomolets—according to rumor with Stalin's personal support—was experimenting with a wonderworking "youth serum" designed to abolish old age forever. Curiously enough, the ambiguity of *Youth Restored* seems to have escaped many readers, including some learned scientists who took part in public discussions of Zoshchenko's hypotheses. Much later, in *Before Sunrise* (1943), Zoshchenko told how surprised he was at these developments.

In *The Blue Book* the technique is basically the same, although the subject has shifted from science to history. Zoshchenko's new "problem," which he proceeds to analyze and illustrate with both fictional and historical examples, is the role played in history by such "forces" as Money, Love, and Perfidy. Again there is a vast apparatus of introductions, commentaries, and footnotes along with the narratives, and again one is unsure how seriously it is all meant. No doubt the ambiguity was necessary, since the fundamental idea is the same one that may be deduced from Zoshchenko's stories in general, namely, that the imperfections of human nature are pretty much a constant. The contrast between the historical illustrations and the fictional stories from the Soviet present is supposed to show how man has been transformed by social conditions for the first time;

but in fact it seems to show just the opposite: that the pettiness and triviality of human life are as firmly entrenched as ever in the new society.

During the war Zoshchenko made a third experiment with the "fictional treatise" form, the autobiographical *Before Sunrise*. This time he turned to psychology, or more specifically, to the causes of his own unhappiness. Once again the "investigation" is presented from the point of view of the "naïve" layman, the author himself, who uses his own case material to explore the whole subject of unhappiness and its cure. This time, however, the irony and banter of *Youth Restored* and *The Blue Book* are virtually absent. The poignant subjectivity of much of the material seems to have led Zoshchenko to do away with the protective distancing and trivialization of the earlier books. The author tells us that all his life he has been a victim of depression. "Laughter was in my books, not in my heart." He has undergone various kinds of (physical) treatment at the hands of doctors, all unsuccessful, and at last he has decided to seek for himself the causes for his melancholy. Again with seeming artlessness he decides to recollect his life in order to determine the cause. These recollections take the form of ultra-short stories, often only a paragraph or two in length, but astonishingly complete as artistic units. They range over his entire experience: first his adult life, and then, as his quest leads him further and further back into the past, his childhood as far back as the age of two. But here, at the point where all memory fails, he feels he must pursue his search still further. He hopes that through dreams he can uncover even earlier experiences which he suspects are at the root of his difficulties.

The subject of dreams leads him to an investigation of dream theory, and thus, inevitably, he arrives at the name of Freud—a somewhat risky name for a Soviet Russian to be conjuring with in 1943. Ostensibly, however, with the typical indignation of the layman, he rejects the Freudian interpretations of his dreams as too obsessed with sex. Patriotically, he tries to construct a rival hypothesis based on Pavlov's theory of conditioned reflexes. Furthermore, no doubt suspecting that this highly subjective work, about as remote as it can be from the usual patriotic war novel, might not be favorably received in official quarters, Zoshchenko tries to link Freud with fascism, on the ground that Freud had advocated a reversion to barbarism as a means of overcoming the "discontents" of civilized man. It is probable that this bit of misrepresentation was quite deliberate on Zoshchenko's part. After all, public advocacy of psychoanalytic theory would hardly have been permitted him, even in the relatively liberal war period. Unfortunately, the trick did not work very well. Despite all Zoshchenko's subterfuges, the ideological overlords, though belatedly, seized upon this piece of wartime heresy and proceded to vent their wrath on Zoshchenko. How dare he muck about in his own nasty little soul in the midst of the national holocaust? Further publication of *Before Sunrise* was stopped, and the editors who had permitted the first installments to appear were reprimanded. It was a premonition of far worse things to come.

As one of the relatively few victims of ideological whip-cracking over literature during the war, Zoshchenko was to be singled out as one of the major targets for the great crackdown which the bosses decided upon in 1946. During the war the Party had somewhat relaxed its insistence on the ideological purity of Soviet culture: in its hour of peril it had found a broad-based patriotic appeal more effective than Communist slogans in rallying popular support for the war, and a good deal of miscellaneous heterodoxy had slipped under the wire along with the patriotism. Doubtless most Russian intellectuals hoped that the end of the war would bring still more liberalization. In the aftermath of victory they longed for an era of good feeling, of relaxation and expanded contacts with the West. But the leaders had very different ideas. Now that the fascist invader had been expelled, it was time to quicken the march toward communism. Russia must grab the fruits of victory and prepare for a new, prolonged struggle with her ex-allies in the capitalist West. And literature, along with other forms of culture, must be made to do its part in the fight. The writers needed an object lesson: wartime laxity was a thing of the past, and all dreams of postwar liberalization were harmful heresies. A new and tougher era had begun.

Along with the distinguished poet Anna Akhmatova, Zoshchenko was selected as the sacrificial victim for a demonstration of the Party's new line. Incidentally, both of them lived in Leningrad, where a kind of Soviet Fronde was felt to exist. First, the Central Committee itself issued an angry decree reprimanding the Leningrad magazines in which Akhmatova and Zoshchenko had frequently published. One was abolished altogether; the editors of the other were dismissed and new Party watchdogs installed. Shortly afterwards Andrei Zhdanov, the "culture specialist" in the Politburo, enlarged on the Central Committee resolution with a vituperative attack in the characteristic style of Stalinist invective. Zoshchenko was a "philistine," a "vulgarian," an "unprincipled literary hoodlum," whose works were a "crude slander on Soviet life," a deliberate attempt to "disorient our youth and poison their minds." For some reason the rather innocuous story "The Adventures of a Monkey" was singled out for special attention. Zhdanov's interpretation—an odd one, to say the least—was that Zoshchenko's intention was "to make the monkey utter the foul, poisonous, anti-Soviet statement that it is better to live in a zoo than outside it, that one can breathe more freely in a

cage than among Soviet people." Zhdanov then enumer-
ated a whole catalogue of Zoshchenko's sins dating back
to the Serapion Brothers' declaration of 1922. He concluded: "In twenty-five years he not only has learned
nothing and has not changed, but on the contrary he
continues to remain . . . an unprincipled and con-
scienceless hoodlum . . . He is alien and inimical to
Soviet literature."

Such words from on high were swiftly translated
into action. Zoshchenko and Akhmatova were officially
expelled from the Union of Soviet Writers and their
works banned. During the grim twilight years of Stalin's
reign Zoshchenko published only a few insignificant
Party-line pieces that one can hardly believe were written by the author of *Before Sunrise*. Perhaps he considered them more "bones" to be thrown to the wolves.
Even after 1953 Zoshchenko remained a taboo figure
for some time. In 1954 a visiting British delegation
managed to arrange a public meeting at which Zoshchenko was present. They asked him what he thought
of Zhdanov's criticisms of him. With courageous candor,
Zoshchenko replied that what Zhdanov had said in
1946 was false then and was still false. Whatever the
feelings of the then ruling "collegium," Malenkov,
Khrushchev, Bulganin *et al.*, may have been about
their late colleague, such open defiance of Communist
authority was hardly prudent, and Zoshchenko's re-
habilitation may have been postponed by this act.

None the less, Zoshchenko did begin publishing
again in magazines such stories as "An Extraordinary
Incident" (1955) which were not unworthy of his
earlier work. Finally, in the great "de-Stalinization"
year, 1956, when the "thaw" reached its highest tem-
peratures, it became possible at last to bring out a
whole retrospective volume of Zoshchenko stories. The
edition was carefully selected and "cleansed" here and

there of offensive passages (such as some excessively pro-American remarks in "The Bathhouse"), but at least it was a book. And it quickly sold out. But alas, Zoshchenko was not to enjoy his public vindication for long. He died two years later, in 1958.

By way of posthumous tribute, new editions of Zoshchenko's selected works were brought out in 1959 and 1960 totaling 300,000 copies. Their immense success was testimony enough of how little the years of disgrace and the abuse of Zhdanov and his satraps had dampened Soviet readers affection for Mikhail Zoshchenko.

I have tried in this collection of translations to give a representative selection of Zoshchenko's work throughout his career, including the various genres in which he worked. Unfortunately, limitations of space required many regrettable omissions, but from *Before Sunrise*, the three novellas, and the forty-seven short stories presented here the reader can get a good idea of the range and variety of Zoshchenko's talent. Although some of the translations were made from recent Soviet reprints, where one sometimes finds evidence of political editing, these have been checked against earlier editions published in Zoshchenko's lifetime, and original readings restored in cases where changes are obviously nonartistic in motivation. In many instances, however, stylistic revisions seem to have been made by Zoshchenko himself, who had a habit of tinkering with his texts on every republication; these have been left intact.

The translations were made from the following editions: Mikhail Zoshchenko, *Rasskazy i povesti* (Leningrad, 1960); *Povesti i rasskazy* (New York, 1952); 1935-37: *Rasskazy, povesti, fel'etony, teatr, kritika* (Leningrad, 1937), and "Pered voskhodom solntsa," *Oktiabr'*, Nos. 6-7, 8-9 (1943).

NOTE TO THE MIDLAND BOOK EDITION

The concluding portions of *Before Sunrise* were finally published, but not until 1972, under the title "A Tale About Reason"; and even then no mention could be made of this "tale's" connection with the work suppressed in 1943. A translation by Gary Kern of the complete text of *Before Sunrise* was published in 1974 by Ardis Publishers (Ann Arbor). H. MCL.

Nervous People

and OTHER SATIRES

WHAT THE
NIGHTINGALE SANG

How people will laugh at us some three hundred years from now! How weirdly those characters, they will say, used to live! They had some sort of money, passports, registrations of civil status and living space measured in square meters . . .

Well, let them laugh!

There is one problem—they won't understand half of it, those devils. And how can they, if their life will be something we can't imagine, even in our dreams?

The author does not know and does not wish to guess what their existence will be like. Why harry one's nerves and shatter one's health? It's all useless. He will never see that beautiful future life.

And will it be beautiful? That's still a question. For his own peace of mind the author supposes that even in the future there will be a lot of stuff and nonsense.

But perhaps it will only be small-sized nonsense. For instance, somebody—if you will excuse the poverty of the thought—has been spat upon from a passing dirigible. Or some ashes in the crematorium get mixed up and instead of your deceased relative, you are handed someone else's low-grade remains . . .

These things, of course, are unavoidable—there will be small everyday unpleasantnesses. But otherwise, life will probably be fine and wonderful.

Perhaps people won't even have money. Everything

may be free. Fur coats and scarfs may be handed out gratis in department stores . . . "Here, citizen," someone will say, "take this marvelous fur coat." And you will pass on. Your heart won't even flutter. "No, honored comrade," you will reply, "what the devil do I want with a fur coat? I have six of them already."

Whew! What a gay and attractive future life the author has conjured up!

But here you have to stop and think. If you eliminate all monetary calculations and selfish motives, what astounding forms life will assume! And human relationships, what marvelous qualities they will acquire! For instance, love! How luxuriantly will blossom that most delicate of emotions!

What a life it will be! What a life! With what sweet joy the author contemplates it, even at this distance and without the slightest guarantee of ever attaining it! . . . Let us take love.

Of that we should speak particularly. There are many learned men, even men belonging to the Party, who are inclined to belittle that emotion. "Excuse us," they say, "love? There is no love. And there never was. It's just one of those ordinary statistics of civil status, like funerals."

The author cannot agree.

He has no desire to make his confession to a casual reader, and he does not wish to reveal his intimate life to certain (for him) very unpleasant critics, but just the same, harking back, he remembers a certain girl from the days of his youth. She had such a silly white face, hands and pathetic shoulders. And into what calf's raptures the author used to fall! What voluptuous moments he experienced when, from an overflow of all kinds of noble sentiments, he used to fall on his knees and like a fool kiss the earth!

Now that fifteen years have passed and the author is graying slightly from different illnesses and jolts dealt by life, from worrying about the next bite to eat; when he simply does not want to lie and has no reason to lie; when, finally, he wants to see all of life as it is, without falsehoods or embellishments, he still submits, without fear of appearing a ridiculous relic of the last century, that the learned and Party circles are very much mistaken on this account.

The author can see that these lines about love will call forth a volley of cruel rebuttals on the part of public leaders.

"Comrade," they will say, "your own person is no example. Why do you shove your own amorous escapades under our noses? People like you are not in harmony with our age and have somehow survived to the present day only by chance."

You see? By chance!

"What do you mean, may I ask, 'by chance'? What do you want me to do? Throw myself under a streetcar?"

"That's as you please," they will answer. "Under a streetcar or off a bridge, but your existence has no foundation. Look at simple, unsophisticated people, and you will see how differently they think."

Ha! Excuse me, reader, for this weak little laugh. The author read recently in *Pravda* of a young barber's apprentice who, out of jealousy, bit off the nose of a girl citizen.

Isn't that love? Would you say it was the same as a beetle dropping his dirt? Or was the nose, in your opinion, bitten off for savory satisfaction? You can go to hell! The author has no wish to upset himself and stir up his blood. He still has to finish writing this story. Then he has to take a train for Moscow and make some unpleasant calls on several literary critics to ask them to take their time about writing critical articles and essays about this story.

Well, then—Love!

Let everyone think what he wishes about this refined sentiment. The author, however, acknowledging his personal insignificance and incapacity for life—even admitting, damn you, that he may have the wheels of a streetcar in his future—will nevertheless stick to his opinion.

He only wants to acquaint the reader with one little amorous episode that took place in these times. Again people will say, "Little episodes! Say, young man, have you lost your wits? Who, on a cosmic scale, needs your little episodes?"

The author honestly and openly requests: "Please don't hinder, comrades. Let a fellow have his say even if it's only for the sake of argument."

2

Phew! What a job it is to write literature! Perspiration will roll off you while you wade through the impenetrable jungle.

And for what purpose? To relate some love affair of citizen Bylinkin.

He is neither friend nor brother of the author's. The author has never borrowed money from him, and has no ideological connections with him.

If one were to speak the truth, the author is profoundly indifferent to him and has no desire to paint him in strong colors. Besides, he doesn't even properly remember the face of Bylinkin, Vassily Vassilyevich.

As for the other persons who figure in some way or other in this story, even their faces pass before the author's gaze without arousing his curiosity. With the exception, perhaps, of Lizochka Rundukov, whom the author remembers for quite special and, shall we say, subjective reasons.

Mishka Rundukov, her brother, a Young Communist,

he remembers much less vividly. He was an extremely aggressive and impudent fellow. As to his physical appearance, he was an ash blond with a meaty face.

The author has no desire to enlarge upon his appearance. He had reached an age of transition. Describe him now and the son-of-a-bitch will grow up by the time this story is published. Then where are you with Mishka Rundukov? And where did this mustache come from, when at the time of the events described he had no mustache at all?

As for the old woman, Mama Rundukov, the reader will hardly make any protest if we pass over the old woman entirely in our description. Especially since it is in general pretty difficult to describe old women artistically. An old woman, that's all. Who cares what she looks like? Who would want a description of her nose, for instance? A nose is a nose, and to describe it will not make life any easier for the reader.

Of course, the author would not have undertaken to write an artistic tale if he had only such meager and worthless information about his heroes. He does indeed have enough material and can depict their lives very clearly. Their small Rundukovian house. It was a dark one, with only one story. On the front, Number 22. A bit higher up a boat hook is painted on a little board. That's in case of fire. Who must carry what? The Rundukovs, it seems, must bring a boat hook. But do they have a boat hook? What if they haven't? . . . Well, it's not the business of literature to find out and draw the facts to the attention of the provincial administration.

And the interior of the Rundukov house—its material shape, so to speak, in the sense of furnishings—stands sufficiently outlined in the author's memory . . . Three smallish rooms. A crooked floor. A Bekker piano. Such a terrible piano. But you can play on it. Some other bits of furnishings. A couch. A cat, male or female, on the couch. On the mirrored mantelpiece a clock under a glass bell. The glass bell is dusty. And the mirror itself is murky—will tell you lies about your face . . . A large chest . . . smells of naphthalene and dead flies . . .

What a bore it would be for citizens from the capital to live in that house! What a bore, too, to enter the kitchen, where wet laundry hangs on a line. At the stove the old woman is cooking victuals, peeling potatoes, for instance. The peelings coil from under the knife like a ribbon.

The reader must not imagine, however, that the author is describing these petty details with any love or rapture. Not at all. There is no sweetness or romanticism in these trifling reminiscences, none whatsoever. The author knows these houses and their kitchens. He's been in them. Has lived in them. Perhaps even lives in one now . . . There's nothing good in that: just utter misery. You step into that kitchen and you will surely stick your nose into some wet underwear. It wouldn't be so bad if it were some nobler part of the wardrobe, but it's likely to be a wet stocking. Lord, it's disgusting to put your face in a stocking! Damn it all! Such filth!

For reasons which had nothing to do with literature, the author was called upon to visit the Rundukovs several times. And he was always surprised that in such rot and paltriness there could live such an exceptional young lady, such a lily of the valley and nasturtium as was Lizochka Rundukov.

Not that the author exalts the human being too much. It's about time, citizens, to refrain from this senseless pride in ourselves. The author reckons that if a cuttlefish can live in wet slime, a human being should be able to live amid wet wash.

Just the same, the author always felt very, very sorry for Lizochka Rundukov.

In due time we will speak of her fully and in detail.

At present, however, the author has to say something about citizen Vassily Vassilyevich Bylinkin. Where he came from. And whether he is politically reliable. What is his connection with the Rundukovs? Is he related to them?

No, he is no relative of theirs. Only accidentally and temporarily did he become entangled in their lives.

The author has already warned the reader that he does not remember any too well the physiognomy of Bylinkin. Nevertheless, if he shuts his eyes he can visualize him as if he were alive.

This Bylinkin always walked slowly, even thoughtfully. Kept his hands behind his back. Blinked his eyes terribly often. And had a posture somewhat stooped, as if bent by worldly cares. Bylinkin wore his heels down on the inside, right to the insole.

As for his education, he gave the impression of being educated at least up to the fourth grade in the old Gymnasium.

His social origin—unknown.

The man arrived from Moscow at the height of the Revolution and did not give out excess information about himself.

Why he came was also unclear. Did the provinces seem to him better supplied with food? Or was he a person who could not stay put, who was attracted by the lure of faraway places and adventures? To hell with him and his psyche. You can't climb into everybody's soul.

But it seems most likely that he thought there was more food in the provinces. Because, those first days, the man used to walk around the open market and stare hungrily at the loaves of fresh bread and the mountains of produce.

How he managed to eat was an unsolved mystery to the author. He may even have begged. Or perhaps he gathered corks from bottles of mineral and fruit water

and then sold them afterwards. Such desperate speculators were known in the town.

But it was obvious that the man did not live well.
He looked ragged and had begun losing his hair. And he
walked timidly, looking on all sides and dragging his
feet. He even stopped blinking his eyes and looked
before him immovably and without interest.

But later on, inexplicably, he took a turn for the
better. At the moment of the unfolding of our love
story, Bylinkin had a sure social position, a government
job with a salary of the seventh class plus overtime.

By that time Bylinkin's figure had somewhat rounded
out; he had, so to speak, been refilled with the lost
sap of life, and again he blinked his eyes carelessly.

He walked the streets with the solid gait of a man
thoroughly steeled by life, a man with the right to
existence and knowing his own worth. Indeed, at the
beginning of this episode, he was in his thirty-second
year and in the very prime of life.

He took frequent walks through the streets and,
brandishing his cane, beat the flowers along the road,
or grass, or even leaves.

Sometimes he sat down on a bench and breathed
deeply and vigorously, smiling happily.

What he was thinking about and what exceptional
ideas crowded into his head, nobody knows. Possibly
he thought of nothing at all. Possibly he was simply
imbued with the ecstacy of his lawful existence. Or,
most probably, he thought of the fact that he absolutely
had to change his living quarters.

He lived with Volosatov, a deacon of the Living
Church,* and, in view of his government position, was
very much worried about staying in the house of a
person so besmirched politically.

He kept asking whether anyone knew, for God's

* A government-sponsored, pro-Soviet wing of the Orthodox
Church. *Ed.*

sake, of some miserable apartment or a room, as it was getting beyond his strength to live any longer with a votary of a certain cult.

Finally someone, out of the goodness of his soul, procured him a small room, about two square meters in size. It happened to be in the house of the esteemed Rundukovs.

Bylinkin moved right then and there. One day he took a look at the room and the very next morning he took off, hiring Nikita the water-carrier for the moving.

The reverend deacon had no use whatsoever for this Bylinkin, but, obviously wounded in his vague but estimable feelings, he reviled him in the most terrible manner, and even threatened to beat him up when he got the chance.

When Bylinkin was piling his belongings onto a cart, the deacon stood at the window and guffawed loudly and deliberately, hoping thereby to show his complete indifference to the departure.

The deacon's wife, however, kept running out from time to time and throwing some of the things into the cart, calling out, "Good riddance! Drop like a stone in the water! We're not keeping you!"

The people and neighbors who had gathered around laughed with pleasure, throwing transparent hints as to their possible amorous relationship. The author will not affirm the truth of this. He doesn't know. And doesn't care to engage in unnecessary gossip in *belles lettres*.

3

The room had been rented to Bylinkin, Vassily Vassilyevich, without any view to profit or any particular necessity. Rather, old Darya Vassilyevna Rundukov was afraid that, because of the housing crisis, their nice little apartment might become crowded through the forcible intrusion of some rough and unwanted element.

Bylinkin even took advantage of this. Passing the Bekker piano, he squinted at it angrily and remarked with displeasure that such an instrument was, generally speaking, quite superfluous, and that he, Bylinkin, was a quiet man, a man shaken by life, who had been on two fronts and under fire of heavy artillery, and could not stand unnecessary petty-bourgeois sounds.

The old woman, offended, replied that the piano had stood there forty years, and that they could not break it up or pull the strings and pedals out of it to satisfy Bylinkin's whims, especially since Lizochka Rundukov was learning to play the instrument, which might even become the chief aim of her life.

Bylinkin angrily waved the woman aside, saying that his words had been uttered in the form of a delicate request and not at all as a strict command.

Here the deeply hurt old woman began crying, and came near refusing him the room altogether, had she not thought of the possibility of enforced tenantry from another quarter.

Bylinkin moved in in the morning, and until evening grunted in his room as he fixed up everything according to his big-city tastes.

Two or three days passed quietly and without any special changes.

Bylinkin went to work, returned late, and walked for a long time about his room, shuffling over the floor in his felt slippers. In the evening he chewed something and finally fell asleep, snorting slightly and twisting his nose.

Lizochka Rundukov went about quietly these two days and asked her mother and Mishka Rundukov several times what sort of man this Bylinkin seemed to be; whether he smoked a pipe, and had he ever had any affiliations with the naval commissariat.

At last, on the third day, she herself saw Bylinkin.

It was early in the morning. Bylinkin, as usual, was getting ready to go to work.

He was walking along the corridor in his nightshirt, with the collar open. The suspenders of his trousers hung behind him, waving to and fro. He walked slowly, carrying in one hand his towel and cake of scented soap. With the other he was smoothing his hair, ruffled during the night.

She was standing in the kitchen busy with her domestic duties, blowing the charcoal in the samovar or tearing a bit of kindling from a dry log.

On seeing him, she gave a soft cry and darted aside, ashamed of her disorderly morning toilette.

But Bylinkin, standing in the doorway, eyed the maiden with some amazement and even with rapture.

And, truly, that morning she was very pretty.

The youthful freshness of a slightly sleepy face. The careless stream of blond hair, slightly tilted nose, clear eyes. And the figure, slight in stature, but well-rounded. They were all extraordinarily attractive.

There was the enchanting carelessness, you might even say slovenliness, of the type of Russian woman who jumps out of bed in the morning and unwashed, with felt slippers on her bare feet, begins to bustle about her house.

The author, perhaps, even likes such women. He has nothing against them.

On the whole there is nothing good about them, these full-bodied women with lazy eyes. There is no vivaciousness in them, no sprightliness, no coquetry. They just move about slowly, in soft slippers, uncombed . . . Generally speaking, if you like, it's even repulsive. Well, there you are.

A strange thing it is, reader.

Some doll-like lady, the product, so to speak, of Western bourgeois culture, is not at all after the author's heart. Lord knows what you call her hair-do—

Greek, maybe—anyway, don't dare touch it! And if
you do there's no end of cries and scandal. Such un-
natural clothing. Again, don't come near. You'll either
tear or soil it. And who, tell me, wants that? Where's
the charm or joy of existence?

Now, ours—when she sits down you see clearly that
she is sitting, and not stuck on a pin, like that other
one. The other one sits as if she were on a pin. Who
wants that?

The author is thrilled by many features of foreign
culture; as regards women, however, he sticks to his
national prejudices.

Bylinkin also seemed to like that kind of woman.

At any rate, he stood now before Lizochka Rundukov
and looked at her with joyful amazement, slightly opening his mouth from ecstasy and not even picking up his
hanging suspenders.

But that lasted only a moment.

Lizochka Rundukov gasped softly, darted about the
kitchen, and went out, arranging her toilette and disheveled hair on the way.

Toward evening, when Bylinkin returned from work,
he walked slowly to his room, hoping to meet Lizochka
in the hall. But he didn't meet her.

Later on in the evening he meandered into the
kitchen five or six times and finally met Lizochka Rundukov, to whom he bowed ever so politely and gallantly,
slightly bending his head to one side and making an indefinite gesture with his hands which expressed en-
chantment and extreme pleasure.

A few days of such encounters in the passage and
the kitchen brought them considerably closer to one
another.

Bylinkin came home now and, listening to Lizochka
pick out some tra-la on the piano, asked her to play
more and more such pieces that make you tingle.

So she played some lousy waltz or shimmy or

sounded a few loud chords from the second or third, maybe—God knows which one—even the fourth rhapsody by Liszt.

And he, Bylinkin, who had been twice on all the fronts and had been under fire by heavy artillery, listened as if for the first time to those quavering sounds of the Bekker piano. Sitting in his room, he leaned back in his armchair and meditated on the beauties of human existence.

A gorgeous life began for Mishka Rundukov. Twice Bylinkin gave him a ten-kopeck piece, and once even a fifteen, asking Mishka to whistle softly through his fingers when the old woman was in the kitchen and Lizochka alone in her room.

Why Bylinkin needed to know is not at all clear to the author. The old woman regarded the amorous couple in absolute ecstasy, planning to marry them off not later than autumn and get Lizochka off her hands.

Nor did Mishka Rundukov try to figure out Bylinkin's psychological subtleties, but on his own initiative whistled some six times a day, inviting Bylinkin into this room or that.

Bylinkin would enter the proper room, sit down beside Lizochka, first exchange a few inconsequential words with her, then ask her to play one of her favorite pieces on the instrument. And there, by the piano, whenever Lizochka stopped playing, Bylinkin put his knotted fingers, the fingers of a man with philosophical leanings, seared by life and fired upon by heavy artillery, on Lizochka's white hands and asked the young lady to tell him of her life, taking a lively interest in the details of her previous existence. Sometimes he asked her whether she had ever before felt the palpitation of real, true love, or was it happening to her for the first time.

The maiden smiled enigmatically and, softly fingering the piano keys, said, "I don't know."

4

They fell in love with each other passionately and dreamily.

They could not see each other without tears and tremors.

Every time they met they experienced new floods of ecstatic joy.

However, Bylinkin inwardly regarded himself with some fear, and thought with amazement that he, who had twice been on all the fronts and had paid very deeply for his right to life, would now readily surrender his life for one trifling whim of this rather pretty young lady.

And, passing over in his memory all the women who had crossed his life—even the last one, the deacon's wife, with whom he did have an affair after all, the author is sure of it—Bylinkin was convinced that only now, in the thirty-second year of his life, had he discovered true love and the genuine tremor of emotion.

Whether life's juices were simply bursting out in Bylinkin, or whether human beings in general have a predisposition and inclination to abstract romantic feelings—this remains for the time being a mystery of nature.

At any rate, Bylinkin realized that he was a different person now from what he had been before, that the composition of his blood had changed, and that all life was insignificant and ridiculous in the face of the extraordinary power of love.

Bylinkin, this near-cynic, a man hardened by life, who had been deafened by shellfire and come face to face with death more than once, this grim Bylinkin even took to writing poetry, tossing off half a score of different verses, and one ballad.

The author is not acquainted with his verses, but one poem, entitled "To Her and to the Other Girl . . ." sent by Bylinkin to the newspaper *Dictatorship of Labor* and rejected by the editors as being incompatible with the socialist era, became known to the author accidentally and through the kindness of the technical secretary, Ivan Abramovich Krantz.

The author has his own ideas about verses and amateur poetry, and therefore he will not fatigue the readers and typesetters with the complete poem, which was fairly long. He offers for the attention of the typesetters only a couple of the last, most sonorous stanzas:

> *Insignia of my beating heart,*
> *My love I progress called;*
> *The dainty image of thy face*
> *Alone my eyes enthralled.*
>
> *Oh, Liza, darling, I have burned,*
> *Burned up, like ash from fire,*
> *Our friendship is that fire.*

From the point of view of the formalist school those verses don't seem so bad, after all. But in general they are pretty scabby verses, and are in fact out of rhythm and harmony with the age.

Later, Bylinkin resisted the call of poetry and deserted the hard road of the bard. Always rather inclined to American practicality, he soon tossed aside his literary achievements, buried his talent in the earth without regret, and resumed his former life without committing his mad ideas to paper.

Bylinkin and Lizochka, meeting now in the evenings, went out and walked about the deserted streets and boulevards far into the night. Sometimes they descended to the river and sat above the sandy bank, watching with deep and silent joy the swift waters of the river Kozyavka. And sometimes they held hands

and sighed softly, enraptured by the extraordinary col-
orings of nature or by a light, airy cloud racing across
the skies.

All this was new to them and enchanting, and it
seemed to them that they were seeing it all for the first
time.

Sometimes the enamored couple left the town and
walked to the forest. And there, with fingers entwined,
they walked about as if stunned, stopping before some
pine or spruce to gaze at it with amazement, sincerely
marveling at the astonishing and bold flourish of nature
that had brought forth from beneath the earth a tree
so useful to humanity.

Then Vassily Bylinkin, shaken by the astonishing fact
of our existence on the earth and by its remarkable laws,
gave way to his abundant emotions, fell on his knees
before the young lady, and kissed the earth around her
feet.

All about them, the moon. All around, the mystery
of the night, the grass, the chirping of glowworms, the
silent forest, the frogs, the insects. All around in the air,
sweetness and contentment. All around that sheer delight in one's existence. The author too is loath to renounce such delight altogether and therefore in no
way can consider himself a superfluous figure against
the background of our surging life. Like any human being, however insignificant, he maintains his right to live
somehow or other, despite all the hue and cry of aus-
tere and impatient critics.

Well, then, Bylinkin and Lizochka liked best of all
those walks out of town.

But on one of those charming walks, probably on a
damp night, the incautious Bylinkin caught cold, and
took to his bed. He developed an illness somewhat
akin to mumps.

By evening he felt a slight chill and a stabbing pain
in his throat. By night his face began swelling.

Crying softly, Lizochka came to his room, and with loosened hair and soft slippers darted from the bed to the table, at a loss what to undertake, what to do, and how to alleviate the lot of the invalid.

Mama Rundukov—even she—rolled into the room several times during the day to inquire whether the sick man wanted some cranberry jelly, which, she considered, was indispensable in all cases of infectious disease.

Two days later, when Bylinkin's face had swollen until he was no longer recognizable, Lizochka ran for a doctor.

After examining the sick man and prescribing some medicines, the doctor left, apparently cursing to himself because he had been paid in small change.

Lizochka Rundukov ran after him and, overtaking him in the street, began wringing her hands, jabbering and asking, "How is he? What's wrong? Is there any hope?" The doctor should know that she could not survive the loss of this man.

Then the doctor, whose profession had accustomed him to such scenes, said indifferently that mumps were mumps and that unfortunately no one died of them.

Somewhat vexed by the slightness of the danger, Lizochka returned home sadly and took to nursing the invalid with self-abnegation, not sparing her feeble strength or her health, nor even fearing to contract the same mumps through contagion.

The first few days Bylinkin was afraid to sit up in bed. Feeling his swollen throat with his fingers, he asked Lizochka with terror whether she would continue to love him after the illness, which had enabled her to see him in such a hideous and loathsome condition.

But the young lady begged him not to worry, saying that in her eyes he had become an even more imposing man than he had been before.

Bylinkin laughed quietly and gratefully, replying that

this illness had proved better than anything else the strength of their love.

5

It was an absolutely extraordinary love. After Bylinkin rose from his sickbed, and after his neck and face had resumed their former shape, he began to think that Lizochka Rundukov had rescued him from the arms of death.

Through this, their amorous relationship acquired a certain solemnity, and even nobility.

One day soon after his illness Bylinkin took Lizochka by the hand and, in the tone of a man who had made up his mind about something, asked her to listen carefully to him and not to put to him, for the time being, any unnecessary questions or break in with any of her dumb remarks.

In a long and solemn speech, he said that he knew full well what life was, knew how difficult it was to exist in this world, and that earlier, when still an unfledged youth, he had taken life with criminal levity, for which he had paid dearly in his time; but now, having passed his thirtieth year, made wise by worldly experience, he knew how one should live—he knew the stern and inviolable laws of life. And, taking all that into account, he was considering some changes in the life he had mapped out.

In short, Bylinkin made a formal proposal to Lizochka Rundukov, entreating her not to worry about her future well-being, even should she, Lizochka Rundukov, continue to be unemployed and incapable of adding her mite to the modest common pot.

She acted coy for a moment and, to make the experience seem more refined, talked a little about free love; nevertheless, she accepted his proposal with rapture, adding that she had been expecting it for a long time, and that if he had not made it she would have considered him the worst sort of crook and swindler. As for free love, though it is fine and dandy in its own way, it is not the same thing as the other, and so on.

Lizochka Rundukov right away ran to her mother and then to the neighbors with her glad news, inviting them to come to the wedding, which would take place in a very short time and would be a modest family affair.

The neighbors congratulated her warmly, saying that she had been hanging on the vine long enough suffering from the hopelessness of her position.

Mama Rundukov cried a bit, of course, and went to Bylinkin to make sure that it was really true.

Bylinkin reassured the old woman, solemnly asking her permission to call her Mother from that day on. She, weeping and blowing her nose in her apron, said that she had lived fifty-three years in this world, but that this day was the happiest of her life. And, in turn, she asked if she could call him Vassya, to which Bylinkin graciously gave his consent.

As for Mishka Rundukov, Mishka took the change in his sister's life rather indifferently, and at that moment was running headlong through the streets somewhere, sticking out his tongue.

The enamored couple no longer took walks out of town. For the most part they sat at home, talking late into the night and discussing plans for their future life.

During one of these discussions, Bylinkin, a pencil in hand, began to sketch out on paper the plans for their future rooms, which would be like a separate small but comfortable apartment.

Breathlessly disputing with each other, they argued about where it would be best to put the bed, and where the table, and where to place the dressing table.

Bylinkin tried to persuade Lizochka not to be so foolish as to put the dressing table in the corner.

"It's so common," said he, "to put a dressing table in the corner. Every young girl does that." It was much better and more imposing to put the chest of drawers in the corner and to cover it with a lace cloth, which her mother, he hoped, would not refuse to give them.

"A bureau in the corner is also very common," replied Lizochka, almost in tears. "Besides, the bureau belongs to Mama, and will she let us have it? That's the question."

"Nonsense," said Bylinkin, "how can she refuse it? We can't keep our underwear on the window sill. That's utter nonsense."

"You talk to Mother, Vassya," Lizochka said severely. "Talk to her as you would to your own mother. Say, 'Please, Mother, give us the chest of drawers.'"

"What nonsense!" cried Bylinkin. "However, if you want me to so badly, I'll go right now."

And he went into the old woman's room.

It was rather late. The woman was asleep.

Bylinkin shook her for a long time, and she, kicking at him in her sleep, refused to wake up and understand what it was all about.

"Wake up, Mother," he said sternly. "Can't Lizochka and I count on some sort of small comfort? Must our underwear lie around on window sills?"

Understanding with difficulty what was wanted of her, the old lady set to talking. The chest had stood in its place for fifty-one years, and now, in the fifty-second year, she had no intention of moving it all over the lot and throwing it around right and left. She was no maker of chests of drawers. And it was too late for her, at her age, to learn carpentry. It was about time they understood that and stopped affronting an old woman.

Bylinkin tried to shame her, saying that he, who had been on all the fronts and twice under fire from heavy artillery, at last had the right to a peaceful life.

"Shame on you, Mother!" he cried. "You begrudge us the chest. You can't take it with you into your coffin. Try to realize that!"

"I won't give you the chest," whined the old woman. "When I'm dead you can take all the furniture."

"Yes, you'll die," said Bylinkin with indignation. "Wait! . . ."

Seeing that the affair had begun to take a serious turn, the woman began to weep and wail, saying that in such a case the lips of an innocent child, Mishka Rundukov, should say the final word, the more so because he was the only male representative of the Rundukov clan, and because by rights the chest of drawers belonged to him and not to Lizochka.

Mishka Rundukov, wakened, was extremely unwilling to give up the chest.

"Ye-yes," said Mishka, "some people are pretty generous with ten-kopeck pieces, but now they want to take people's bureaus. Chests of drawers cost money, too."

Thereupon Bylinkin, slamming the door, went into his room, and, bitterly scolding Lizochka, told her that without a bureau he was like a man without arms, and that he, hardened by fighting, knew what life was, and would not retreat one step from his ideals.

Lizochka literally flitted back and forth between her mother and Bylinkin, entreating them to reach an agreement in some way, and proposed that from time to time they drag the chest of drawers from one room to the other.

Then, asking Lizochka to stop flitting, Bylinkin suggested that she go to bed immediately and gather strength to take up this fateful question early the next morning.

The morning brought no improvement.

The angry old woman said with desperate resolution

that she saw him, Vassily Vassilyevich Bylinkin, through and through, and that today he demanded the chest, and tomorrow he would roast her and eat her up alive. That's the kind of man he was.

Bylinkin yelled that he would report her to the criminal investigation department and have her arrested for propagating obviously false and injurious rumors.

Lizochka ran from one to the other with low cries, begging them at least to cease yelling and try to discuss the question quietly.

Then the old woman said that she was past the age for yelling and that without yelling she would tell one and all that Bylinkin had to date dined with them three times and had not even had the courtesy to offer some small compensation for at least one of the dinners.

Terribly excited, Bylinkin said sarcastically that, as to that, he had many times bought Lizochka candy and pastilles while out walking with her, and twice bouquets of flowers, and that, nevertheless, he was presenting no bills to her mother.

To which Lizochka, biting her lips, replied that he should stop such shameless lying; that there had been no pastilles, only some gumdrops and a small bouquet of violets, worth a few kopecks, which had faded the next day, what was more.

Having said that, Lizochka ran sobbing from the room, leaving everything to the will of fate.

Bylinkin wanted to chase after her and present his apologies for his incorrect statements, but he got into a new squabble with the old woman, called her an old bitch, spat at her, and ran out of the house.

Bylinkin left the house and for two days his whereabouts were unknown. When he reappeared, he announced in an official tone that he found it impossible to remain in the house.

Two days later he moved to another apartment, in

the Ovchinnikovs' house. During those two days Lizochka demonstratively stayed in her room.

The author is ignorant of the details of his moving and of the bitter moments experienced by Lizochka. Did she experience them? And did Bylinkin regret it all, or did he act with complete assurance and deliberation?

The author only knows that for a long time after his departure Bylinkin kept visiting Lizochka Rundukov, in fact even after his marriage to Marusya Ovchinnikov. Shaken by their misfortune, they sat side by side exchanging meaningless words. Sometimes, however, evoking the memory of one or another happy episode or event of the past, they spoke of it with sad and pitiful smiles, keeping back their tears.

Sometimes the mother entered the room and then all three of them bemoaned their fate.

Later on, Bylinkin stopped going to the Rundukovs. And if he met Lizochka on the street, he bowed to her politely and with reserve, and passed by . . .

6

Thus ended their love.

Of course, at another time, some three hundred years later, this love would not have ended in such a manner. It would have blossomed, dear reader, into a glorious and rare flower.

But life dictates its laws.

At the conclusion of this story the author wishes to say that in the act of unfolding this simple love story, and somewhat carried away by the experiences of his characters, he lost sight of the nightingale that was so mysteriously mentioned in the title.

He fears that an honest reader or a typesetter, or

even some carping critic, who reads this story, will become upset.

"Excuse me," he will say, "but where is the nightingale? What is the idea of making a fool of me, of luring the reader with a pretty title?"

It would be absurd to begin this whole love story again. The author is not trying to do that. He only wishes to recall certain details.

It was at the very height, the climactic moment of their affection, when Bylinkin and the young lady used to go out of town and walk in the woods, far into the night. And there, listening to the chirp of insects or the singing of the nightingale, they stood for long spells, immovable. And then Lizochka, gesturing, used to ask, "Vasya, what do you think the nightingale sings about?"

To which Vasya Bylinkin used to reply reservedly, "His belly is empty. That's why he sings."

Only later on, when he had grown better acquainted with the psychology of the young lady, Bylinkin answered in a more detailed and mysterious manner that he supposed the bird sang about some splendiferous future life.

Such also is the opinion of the author: about an excellent life, say some three hundred years hence, perhaps even less.

Yes, reader, if only those three hundred years would pass like a dream, then how we would live!

And if things are bad even then, the author will agree, with a cold and empty heart, that he is indeed a useless figure against the background of our surging life.

There is always time to throw yourself under a streetcar.

1925

THE LILACS ARE BLOOMING

INTRODUCTION

In view of previous misunderstandings, the writer wishes to inform his critics that the protagonist of this story is, so to speak, an imaginary character. He is one of those run-of-the-mill intellectuals who happened to live on the border line between two epochs.

Neurasthenia, ideological wavering, gross inconsistencies, and melancholia—this is what we have been forced to ascribe to our "self-made man." But the author himself—the writer M. M. Zoshchenko, the son and brother of similar unhealthy people—he has left all this far behind. At present he has no contradictions. In his soul there is complete clarity and roses unfold. And if at times these roses fade and his heart is not really at peace, that is for many other reasons, which the author will try to tell about sometime later.

In this instance it is a literary device.

And the author begs his esteemed critics to remember this peculiar fact before they start slashing away at a defenseless writer.

Moreover, the author feels it his duty to reassure the reader: despite the fact that the protagonist is an imaginary character, the story as a whole is far from imaginary—everything in it was taken completely from life, and the main events took place literally before the author's eyes.

1

And now people are going to rebuke the author again for this new artistic creation.

They'll say it's another crude slander on man, isolation from the masses, and so forth. And, they'll say, the ideas he chose are pretty insubstantial ones.

The heroes aren't nearly as impressive as we naturally wish they were. Somehow, they'll say, their social significance isn't very noticeable. And in general their actions won't arouse much, well, fervent sympathy on the part of the toiling masses, who, they'll say, won't follow such characters unreservedly.

Of course, there's really nothing to argue about—it's true the characters are not of the highest caliber. There's no denying that they aren't leaders. They are, in fact, only ordinary citizens doing ordinary things and having ordinary worries.

As for slander against the human race, there is definitely none of that here.

Perhaps at one time the author could have been criticized, if not for slander, then for a certain excess of melancholy and for wanting to see various dark and crude sides of nature and man. And actually, he did once go pretty far astray on certain basic questions and came close to out-and-out obscurantism.

Some two years ago, the author didn't like this and didn't like that. He subjected everything to the most extreme criticism and destructive conjectures. Now, of course, it is awkward to confess this to the reader, but the author carried it so far that he even began to be offended by the flimsiness and impermanence of the human organism and by the fact that a man, for example, consists mainly of water, of liquid.

"Forgive me, but what is this, a mushroom or a

berry?" the author used to exclaim. "Why so much water? It's downright offensive to know what a man consists of." Even in such a sacred matter as man's external appearance he began to see only what was
coarse and unpleasant.

"It's only that we have got used to man," he used to
say to his close relatives. "But if you draw back a little
or, for example, don't see a human being for five or
six years, you'll be amazed at what flagrant ugliness can
be observed in our appearance. Well, take the mouth—a
kind of slap-dash hole in the puss. The teeth stick out
from it like a fan. Ears hang from the sides. The nose—
a kind of curlicue, put right in the middle of the face
as if on purpose. Well, it's unattractive! Not interesting
to look at!"

These were the kind of foolish and unhealthy ideas
the author had.

He even criticized such an unquestionable and fundamental thing as the human mind in the most desperate way.

"The mind," he said, "well, let's suppose there is
such a thing. There's no disputing that people have discovered many curious and amusing things with the
mind: the microscope, the safety razor, photography,
and so on, and so on. But to discover how to make
every man live in complete happiness—we certainly
haven't done that yet. And, by the way, centuries are
passing, ages are passing. The sun has started to get covered with spots already. It's cooling off, you know. Let's
say the year is nineteen twenty-nine; you see how much
time we've already let slip by."

These were some of the unworthy thoughts that
flashed through the author's mind.

But such thoughts were, no doubt, due to his illness.

His severe depression and irritation with people drove
him absolutely to desperation, blotted out horizons
and prevented him from seeing many things, includ-

ing everything going on around us right now.

But now the author is boundlessly happy and pleased that he did not write any stories during those two or three wretched years. Otherwise he would have been roundly disgraced. They would really have been malicious slanders, coarse and boorish calumnies against world order and human organization.

Now all this turbulent melancholy has abated and the author once more sees things as they are with his own eyes.

Yet in no way did the author cut himself off from the masses during his illness. On the contrary, he lived and ailed, you might say, in the very thick of humanity. And he describes events not from the planet Mars, but from our accursed little earth, from our eastern hemisphere, where there just happens to be, in a certain building, a communal apartment in which the author resides and as it were, sees people face to face, without any adornments, fancy clothes, or coverings.

In this kind of life the author observes what's what, and why. To rebuke him now for slander and for insulting people simply won't do. The more so since he recently began to feel especially intense love for people, with all their defects and inadequacies.

It is true, of course, that other intellectuals at other times will say something else. People, they'll say, are definitely still trash. We'll have to straighten them out, put them in order. We'll have to shake all the coarseness out of them. They need to be ironed out. Only then can life shine forth in all its marvelous brilliance. It's only a small hitch, as it were. But the author is not at all of this opinion. He definitely stands apart from such views. Though we should absolutely outgrow such defects in the machinery as bureaucracy, vulgarity, government red tape, underworld activity, and so on.

But for the time being everything else can more or less stay put; it doesn't hinder us.

And if someone asked the author, "What do you

want, dear friend? To what changes in the people close
to you would you assign top priority, besides the shortcomings listed above?" he would be hard put to answer at once.

No, besides these things he doesn't want to change
anything. Only a trifle, perhaps. Such a thing, maybe, as
greediness. Such a thing as the daily vulgarity of material calculations. So that people would start to pay visits
just for the sake of pleasant, sincere sociability, without any hidden motives and calculations.

Of course, all this is nonsense, idle fantasy, and the
author has probably turned overfastidious from soft living. But he has such a very sentimental nature that he
wishes violets would grow right on the sidewalks.

2

All the things we have just said may have no direct relation to our work of art, but, you know, they are very
up-to-date, agonizing questions. And the author has
such a difficult nature that until he has said his say to
the reader, he's just not up to writing a story.

But it so happens that in this particular case all these
words do have a certain bearing on our story. Moreover, we have been talking about certain mercenary
calculations; and it just happens also that the hero of
this story is a man who came up against these same
problems and stood open-mouthed, overwhelmed by
the veritable whirlwind of events stirred up by them. In
the splendid years of his youth, when life seemed to be
a morning stroll, as if along a boulevard, the author did
not see many of its darker sides. He simply did not notice them. He had eyes for other things. He looked for
all sorts of cheerful things, all kinds of beautiful objects
and experiences. How flowers grow and buds unfold
and how clouds float along and how people love one
another dearly. But how all this happens and what

makes the wheels go round he failed to see because of his youth, the foolishness of his character, and the naïveté of his outlook.

But later the author began to look around. And suddenly he saw various other things.

Let's say he sees a gray-haired man press another man's hand, gaze into his eyes, and say something. Previously he would have watched this and rejoiced from the bottom of his heart. "Look," he would have thought, "how nice, how special everyone is; how much people love one another and how splendidly life is arranged."

Well, now he doesn't believe in his visual hallucinations. Doubts gnaw at him. He worries that maybe that graybeard presses the other man's hand and gazes into his eyes to bolster his shaky position in his job, or to be named to a professorial chair from which he will give lectures on beauty and art.

The author will remember for the rest of his life a trivial event which happened recently. And this event really cut him to the quick. There's this nice house. Company is always dropping in. They stay there day and night. They have little games of cards. They guzzle coffee with cream. They pay the most respectful attentions to the young hostess and kiss her hand. And then the husband, an engineer, is arrested. The wife gets sick and, naturally, almost bursts from hunger. And not one of that crew appears to testify. And nobody kisses hands any more. There's a general panic that this former acquaintanceship might cast a shadow on them.

But afterwards the engineer is released—they don't find him guilty of anything special. And the same whirl begins again. It's true, though, that the engineer becomes morose and doesn't always come out to greet the guests, or, if he does come out, stares at them with a certain fear and astonishment.

Well, what about it? Perhaps it's some kind of slander? Perhaps it's a malicious invention? Ha! No, that's the way it is; we can see things like this every moment of our lives. And it's high time to speak of it straight out. Otherwise, you know, everything is beauty and grandeur, and "that has a proud ring." * But when it comes down to the facts, you simply get nonsense.

The author is not giving way to dejection, though. Especially because sometimes, say once in five years, he meets odd characters who stand out sharply from their fellow citizens.

Still, all this is theoretical speculation, while what the author wants to tell is a true story, taken from the very wellspring of life. Before describing the actual events, however, he would like to pass on a few more doubts.

The thing is, that in the course of the story there appear two or three ladies who are depicted as not overly nice.

The author did not spare himself any pains and tried to give them a fresh and up-to-date appearance, but his conscience did not let him try too hard. So that each of the three came out worse than the next and, in general, not much like heroines. Many people, especially women readers, may be extremely offended by these female characters and may try to convict the author of a reactionary attitude and of unwillingness to let women have equal rights with men. The more so since several women acquaintances of his have already taken offense. "To hell with you," they say, "your lady characters are always perfectly nasty."

But the author implores his readers not to scold him for this. He himself is amazed that his pen produces such uninteresting ladies.

It is all the more strange since all his life the author has seen, for the most part, only quite nice, good-natured, and not-at-all mean ladies.

* An allusion to a famous line from Gorky's *Lower Depths:* "Man,—that word has a proud ring!" *Ed.*

And in general, the author is of the opinion that women are probably even better than men. They somehow seem more warm-hearted, softer, more responsive, and pleasanter.

Because of such views, the author will never allow himself to offend a lady.

So that if uncertainties on this score do occur sometimes in his story, they're only misunderstandings, and the author begs his readers not to pay any attention to them and, more important, not to upset themselves over trifles. To the author all people are absolutely equal.

It's a different matter if, for the sake of curiosity and amusement, you take the animal kingdom.

There differences do exist. There are even differences among birds. There the male is always a little more expensive than the female.

A male siskin, for example, costs two rubles by present calculations, whereas a female costs fifty, forty, or even twenty kopecks. But to look at, the birds are as alike as two drops of water. That is, you literally can't figure out which one is worth something and which isn't.

But say the two birds are put into their cages. They peck bird seed, drink water, hop about on their perches, and so on. Suddenly the male stops drinking. He settles himself more firmly, lifts his avian gaze to the heavens, and begins to sing. This is why he's so expensive. This is why you have to produce the cash. For singing, for artistic performance.

But what is proper in the bird kingdom just isn't suitable among people. With us, ladies are the same price as men. Furthermore, with us, women, as well as men, sing. So all questions and doubts in this matter fall to the ground. Besides, in our story all the rude attacks on women and suspicions concerning their greed emanate from our main hero—a man who is definitely hypercritical and sick. A former ensign in the Czar's army, he received slight contusions about the head and got generally battered by the Revolution.

In 1919 he spent the night in the reeds countless times —he was afraid the Communists would arrest him, seize him, and use him as a hostage.

And all these terrors sadly affected his character.

Even in the 1920's he was a nervous and irritable fellow. His hands shook. He couldn't even put a glass on the table without knocking it over with his trembling hand.

Nevertheless, in the battle of life his hands did not tremble.

For this very reason he did not die, but survived with honor.

3

It's certainly not so easy for a man to die. That is, the author thinks it's not that simple for a man to die of hunger. If he has some sense, if he has arms and legs and a noggin on his shoulders, then he can certainly make an effort and find sustenance, even if he has to resort to begging.

But in this case things did not go so far as begging, although Volodin was in a pretty tight spot, to say the least.

Moreover, he had spent many years at the front, had completely lost touch with ordinary life, and could not do anything especially useful except shoot at a target or at people. So he did not know yet what he could turn his hand to.

And, of course, he had no relatives. And he had no apartment. Literally nothing.

He had had only a mama, but she had died of old

age during the war. On her death her little apartment passed swiftly into other hands. And our ex-soldier citizen was left on his arrival completely out of touch with things and, so to speak, without portfolio.

Nevertheless, he did not let himself panic too badly in this critical moment of his life. He took a clear-eyed look at what was what, and why. He saw the city spread out before him. He took an eagle's view of the city and he saw life going on in much the same way as ever. People walking along the street. Citizens hurrying here and there. Young girls with parasols walking along.

He looked around to see what was what and what made the wheels go round.

Well now, he thought, I can't throw myself into the lake, and it's obviously necessary to sell people pronto some product which will have a circulation equal to that of government bank notes.

In short, he thought, I've got to sell something people will buy.

And he saw that they would buy anything that was worth money. The things that are worth money, of course, are strength, cleverness, and various forms of beauty, and, naturally, all sorts of talents and capabilities.

Well, then, he thought, as a last resort I can load firewood or move fragile furniture, or maybe take up petty trading. Or else, finally, it's possible to marry with some profit, though you can't make a tremendous profit in that last way any more, but, let's say, you can certainly get yourself a place to live, fuel for heating, and food.

Of course, he was not such a worthless man as to let a lady support him; but to let her give the first helping hand at a difficult moment of life—that was no disgrace.

Besides, he was young rather than old. He was a little over thirty.

And although his central nervous system had been somewhat battered by the storms and agitations of life, he was still a pretty fair specimen of a man. He had an attractive and pleasing appearance. Even though he was a blond, he was still a fairly masculine-looking blond, and he wore small Italian sideburns on his cheeks. This improved his face still more and added something demonic and bold, which made women shudder with their whole bodies, drop their eyes, and quickly tug their skirts over their knees.

These were the assets and strong points which he had when he set out to meet his destiny. After his military service he came to the city and settled temporarily in an anteroom in the apartment of an acquaintance of his, the photographer Patrikeyev, who, although he took him in out of the goodness of his heart, counted all the same on making a little profit out of the deal. He listed him as official occupant of part of the living space in the apartment* and, besides, he expected that Volodin, out of a sense of acute gratitude, would sometimes greet his customers for him, open doors for them, and write down their names.

But Volodin did not fulfill these entrepreneurial hopes—he ran around for whole days at a time, God knows where, and several times even rang the bell loudly late at night, causing great disquiet and disturbance in the house.

The photographer Patrikeyev grew very unhappy over these events. His health suffered, and sometimes, after jumping up at night in his drawers, he even became terribly abusive, calling Volodin a good-for-nothing and a ragamuffin ex-nobleman.

But anyhow, not more than six months later Volodin did begin to bring his patron a tangible profit.

* Each person was officially allowed so many square meters of "living space" in city apartments. *Ed.*

It's true that this was already at the end, when he had moved out of the apartment and made an advantageous marriage. The fact was that when he was still very small he had had a certain inclination and love for sketching. And when he was a tiny little boy he had liked to scribble all sorts of pictures and drawings with pencils and paints.

Now, unexpectedly, his artistic gifts came in handy.

At first as a joke, but later more seriously, he began to help Patrikeyev the photographer by retouching his photos and plates.

All sorts of young ladies who came in demanded a respectably photographed face without folds, wrinkles, pimples, or other annoying features which unfortunately were present in the individual's natural appearance.

Volodin drew over these pimples and bumps with a pencil, skillfully adding shading and highlights to the photographed likenesses.

In a short time, he became pretty successful in this field and began to earn himself some money, rejoicing heartily at this turn of events.

And, having mastered this ingenious art form, he realized that he had arrived at a definite position in life and that it would be rather difficult and even close to impossible to dislodge him from it. To do so it would be necessary to destroy all photography shops and categorically prohibit all inhabitants to be photographed, or else for photographic paper to disappear completely from the market. But, alas, life took so favorable a turn only after Volodin had taken a decisive step—he had married a certain lady citizen before he had the slightest notion that his art would make it possible for him to stand on his own feet.

Living at the photographer's and not having any special prospects, he naturally began to look at the surrounding populace and particularly at ladies and women who could give him a friendly, sympathetic, helping hand. Such a lady was found to respond to the perishing man's cries for help.

She was a woman from the next house, Margarita Vassilyevna Hopkiss.

She had an entire apartment, where she lived with her younger sister Lelia, who was married to a male nurse named Comrade Sypunov.

These two sisters were still fairly young and worked at sewing shirts, underpants, and other items of civic utility.

Necessity had forced them to take up this occupation. They had not counted on such an insignificant fate before the Revolution, when they had finished their higher education at a girls' Gymnasium.

Having acquired such a proper education, they had naturally dreamed of living in a worthy manner, marrying exceptional men or professors, who would fill their lives with luxury, indulgence, and pleasurable pastimes.

But meanwhile life was passing. The stormy years of the NEP and the Revolution did not give one much time for getting one's bearings and dropping anchor just where one would like.

And so the younger sister, Lelia, after lamenting the uncertainty of fate, hastily married Sypunov, a thoroughly coarse, unshaven character, a male nurse or orderly at the city hospital. While the older sister Margaritochka, sighing for the impossible, had lamented away her best years, and as she approached thirty, had pulled herself together and begun casting about here and there, hoping to get at least some kind of shopworn man for a husband.

It was into her outspread net that our friend Volodin fell. He had long dreamed of a more suitable life, of a certain family coziness, of not living in a passageway, of a bubbling samovar, and all the little comforts of this sort which certainly do adorn life and give it the quiet charm of petty-bourgeois existence. And here all these factors were present, in addition to a stable situation and independent earnings, which were something in the order of a dowry and unquestionably made the bargain even more interesting.

Of course, had the acquaintance come later, Volodin, having his own earnings, would not have taken this step so precipitously. The more so since Margarita Hopkiss, with her boring, lusterless face, did not attract him at all.

Volodin was attracted and aroused by girls of an entirely different kind—those with tiny dark mustaches on their upper lips. Girls who were very gay, flashy, and quick in their movements and knew how to dance, swim, dive, and babble all sorts of nonsense. Whereas his Margarita, thanks to her profession, was sedentary and too timid in her movements and actions.

But the die had been cast, and the spring kept unwinding without stopping.

Now when he passed by the house next door, Volodin always stopped by the windows and talked a long time, chatting about this and that. Standing before her in profile or three-quarter face and tugging at his sideburns, he made many allegorical remarks concerning a decent life and a happy fate. And from these conversations with her he found out definitely that a room in her apartment was at his disposal, provided he did not limit himself to hints. After he had mulled the whole thing over and looked at his lady with a more attentive and demanding eye, he charged into battle with a cry of victory. And so the celebrated marriage took place.

Volodin moved to the Hopkiss apartment, adding to the common pool his all too modest, lonely pillow and other meager belongings. Patrikeyev the photographer saw Volodin off, shook his hand, and advised him not to throw away his newly acquired know-how in the retouching business.

Margarita Hopkiss made a gesture of annoyance and said that it wasn't very likely that Volodin would ever need such a picayune occupation.

Thus Volodin began a new life, figuring that he had made a fairly profitable deal, based on precise and correct calculations. He rubbed his hands vigorously and mentally slapped himself on the back, saying, "Well, brother Volodin, I guess life has started to smile on you, too."

But that smile wasn't exactly a fond one.

4

Our Volodin's life had unquestionably changed for the better. From the uninviting passageway he had moved into a wonderful bedroom with all kinds of what-nots and cushions.

Furthermore, whereas he used to eat poorly and modestly, feeding on all sorts of scraps and tripe, he was much better off in this respect, too. Now he ate all manner of respectable dishes—soups, meat, dumplings, tomatoes, and so on. Besides that, once a week he now drank cocoa with his family, feeling amazed and ecstatic at this rich drink whose flavor he had forgotten during his eight or nine years of comfortless existence.

However, Volodin was not being kept by his lawful wife. He did not give up his work in the field of photography but made a great success of it and began to receive not only gratitude but hard cash for his efforts.

The good fresh food enabled Volodin to throw himself into his work with particular inspiration. And, since he was not exceptionally happy with his young spouse, he buried himself in his work. He did this work so skillfully and artistically that all the ugly faces they photographed came out looking completely angelic, and their owners were so sincerely amazed at such unexpected luck that they became more and more eager to have their pictures taken, didn't care how much it cost, and kept sending in more and more new customers to the studio.

Patrikeyev the photographer now set great store by his employee, and gave him a raise every time a client was exceptionally delighted at his artistry.

At this point Volodin felt solid ground beneath his feet and realized that it was now unthinkable for anyone to dislodge him from the position he had won.

He began to get fat and chubby and to adopt a calmly independent manner. He wasn't turning into a butterball; his organism had simply begun prudently storing up fats and vitamins against an evil day, just in case.

Yet, Volodin was not exceptionally tranquil or contented.

After he had stuffed himself full of food, talked over household matters with his wife, and ordered the following day's dinner, he would remain in melancholy solitude, grieving sincerely at his lack of tender feeling for his young wife—the kind of feeling which properly beautifies life and makes all the subhuman nonsense of every day into the events and beautiful details of a happy life. Thinking such thoughts, Volodin would put on his hat and go out into the street, having first, of course, shaved, powdered his elegant nose, and trimmed his Italian sideburns.

He would walk along the streets and look the passing women over, taking a lively interest in what they were like, how they walked, and what kind of faces or kissers they had. He would stop, look after them, and whistle some special tune. And so time passed imperceptibly. Days, weeks, and months went by. Three years passed imperceptibly in this way. The young wife, Margarita Hopkiss, couldn't get enough of admiring her remarkable husband.

She went on working like an elephant, literally without resting for a minute. She wanted to make things as nice as possible for her lord and master. Wishing to beautify his existence, she used to buy all sorts of nice and diverting trifles: handsome suspenders, watch straps, and other domestic notions. But he looked gloomy and charily presented his cheeks for his wife's abundant kisses. Sometimes he simply snarled rudely and waved her away like an annoying fly.

He began to feel plainly and openly sad, grew pensive, and cursed his existence.

"No, my life didn't work out," muttered our Volodin, trying in vain to understand what mistake he had made in his life and his plans.

Then, in the spring of 1925, if our memory doesn't fail us, some important events took place in the life of our friend, Nikolay Petrovich Volodin. He was courting a certain rather pretty girl and fell passionately in love, or, to put it more simply, he went wild over her and even started to think about a fundamental change in his life. Now that his earnings were more respectable, he could think about a new and happier life.

Everything about this girl seemed attractive and charming to him. In a word, she fulfilled all his spiritual requirements, since she had just the kind of appearance he had dreamed about all his life. She was a thin, poetic little thing with dark hair and shining eyes like stars. Her tiny little mustache especially delighted Volodin and made him consider the situation more seriously.

But various homely details and a premonition of loud scenes and blows made him cool off and drive away any decisive thoughts.

Not wanting to sully his higher feelings and sensations yet, he tried not to think of bad things and lived literally like a butterfly, fluttering from flower to flower.

Just in case, he even became a little politer to his wife, and when he left the house he used to make up something about friends he was hurrying to visit and, slapping her on the back, he made various amiable and inoffensive remarks. Madame Volodin, understanding that something exceptionally important was going on, blinked and didn't know how to act—whether to shout and make a scene or to wait a little while and first gather incriminating material and evidence.

Volodin would leave the house, meet his little girl friend, and lead her triumphantly through the streets, full of clever phrases, inspiration, and turbulent, seething life.

The girl would hang on his arm, twittering about her innocent little interests and about the fact that many married men who go out with girls entertain impossible fantasies and try to get the devil knows what, but that she herself, regardless of the complete moral laxity at present, looked at the matter quite differently. And only serious circumstances could incline her to anything more definite. Or perhaps a love that was too strong might also be able to make her waver. Sensing a confession of love in these words, Volodin pulled his lady along with exceptional energy, and pressed her to him, muttering all kinds of irresponsible thoughts and wishes.

But they hardly spoke of crude material things.

They carried on more elevated conversations, kissing each other at every corner and under every tree.

In the evenings they would go to the lake and there, on the high bank, on a bench, or simply on the grass, they would sit beneath the lilacs, tenderly embracing one another and conscious every second of their happiness. It was the month of May, and that wonderful time of year, with its beauty, fresh colors, and light, intoxicating air, particularly inspired them.

The author, to his regret, does not possess a substantial poetic gift and is not capable of gracefully employing the poetic vocabulary. Not being an imagist, he is sincerely sorry that he has little talent for word painting and artistic prose in general. Otherwise, he would have produced grand universal pictures, describing these fresh emotions of hearts in love against a marvelous background of a spring landscape, our wealth of natural beauties, and sweet-smelling lilacs.

The author admits that he has more than once attempted to penetrate the secret of word painting, that secret which our contemporary giants of literature command with such enviable ease. However, the pallor of his words and the vagueness of his thought have not permitted him to enter deeply into the virgin thickets of Russian ornamental prose.

In presenting the enchanting picture, full of poetic melancholy and heart-throbs, of our friends' rendez-vous, the author nevertheless cannot resist the temptation to plunge into the sweet, forbidden waters of literary craftsmanship. And he dedicates a few lines describing a nocturnal scene to our lovers, with love. Only let us hope that experienced literary artists won't be too severe in their judgment of this modest exercise. This is not an easy occupation. This is hard labor.

Just the same, the author will try to take a dip into highbrow artistic literature.*

The sea gurgled . . .

Suddenly, around something there was a curling, scurrying, and prickling.

---

* The following passage is a parody of the "ornate prose" popular in Russia in the 1920's. It stemmed from the prose of Andrey Bely, which was imitated by such Soviet writers as Boris Pilnyak and the early Leonid Leonov. Zoshchenko uses here a great many strange words—dialecticisms and coinages—the precise flavor of which it is almost impossible to reproduce in English. *Ed.*

It was a young man uncinching his shoulders and cinching his hand into his side pocket.

In the world there was a bench.

And so there suddenly entered this world a

ci-

gar-

ette,

which

the

man

thoughtfully

and

s   l   o   w   l   y

caught with his even, dull yellow, slightly protruding teeth (was it with his teeth?), for this purpose opening his eater a half-centimeter and twelve millimeters. In doing this, he exposed his pale red, or rather pink, or more correctly, bluish gums, solidly bespeckled with teeth, as if with mold. On the upper gum there was a small (barely visible) dark dot, which hardly glimmered in the moonlight, and which only the experienced, keen eyes of the artist could see for the use and glory of our national literature.

The sea gurgled . . . The grass rustled ceaselessly. The clay and sand had sifted long before beneath the lovers' feet. The girl shamblingly and cross-eyedly hatted, hooking the lilac. (The girl smiled mischievously and merrily, sniffing the lilac.)

Rushya, Rushya, my mother Rushya! Aw, the devil take you!

The sea, that is, I should say, the lake, gurgled, reflected opal and turquoise, nodded and vomited. Again around something there was an artistic prickling, scuttling, curling. And suddenly the colors of the spectrum lit the undulating landscape with their unutterably wondrous radiance . . .

Oh, to hell with it! It doesn't come off. The author has the manliness to confess that he has no gift for so-called highbrow literature. People have different gifts. The Lord gives one man a simple rough sort of tongue and another a tongue which can execute all kinds of subtle artistic ritornellos every minute.

But the author does not set himself up as a literary master and will again attempt to describe events in his clumsy language.

In a word, without striving for artistry of diction, we will say that our lovers sat by the lake and conducted long and unending amorous conversations, from time to time sighing and silently listening to how the sea gurgled and the vegetation rustled.

The author is always very much astonished when people talk of things without thinking about their natures and causes.

Many of our well-known men of letters and even our strong satirists habitually and thoughtlessly write words like these, for example: the lovers sighed.

But why sighed? Why did they sigh? For what reason do lovers have such a definite habit of sighing? Explain this, elucidate it to the inexperienced reader, if you call yourself a writer. But they don't. They say it, and so long—with criminal negligence they're off to another subject.

The author will undertake to meddle in this matter, which is also none of his business. According to the popular description of a certain German dentist, a sigh is simply a holding back. That is, he says, in your organism there takes place, so to speak, a kind of braking, a holding back of some kind of forces which are prevented from directly following their assigned courses, and so a sigh takes place.

A man sighed—that means the man is prevented from fulfilling his desires. And hitherto, when love was not very attainable, lovers were obliged to sigh most cruelly. But, by the way, this sometimes happens even now.

This is how simply and splendidly the course of our

life goes, and how the modest, imperceptible workings of our organism are carried on.

But all this does not prevent the author from feeling love and admiration for many excellent things and desires.

And so our young couple conversed and sighed. But by the month of June, when the lilacs were blooming by the lake, they sighed more and more rarely and finally stopped sighing altogether and sat on the bench leaning toward one another, happy and ecstatic.

The sea gurgled. The clay and sand . . .

Oh, the hell with it!

At one of these nice sentimental meetings, when Volodin was sitting with his young lady and uttering various poetic similes and rhymes to her, he let slip a rather beautiful phrase which he had without any doubt swiped from some anthology, although he insisted he hadn't. However, it is unlikely that he could have formulated such a picturesque and poetic phrase, worthy of the pen of a powerful imagist.

Bending toward the young lady and smelling a branch of lilac with her, he said, "Lilacs bloom a week and fade. So will your love." The young lady swooned in utter rapture, demanding that he repeat these wonderful musical words again and again.

And he repeated them for the whole evening, reading in the intervals Pushkin's poem "The bird is hopping on the branch," Blok, and other responsible poets.

5

When he returned home after this exalted evening, Volodin was met with wild cries, wails, and coarse words.

The entire Hopkiss family, together with the noto-

rious male nurse Sypunov, fell upon Volodin and reviled him with all the bad names they could think of,
calling him a swindler, a scoundrel, and a skirt-chaser.

The male nurse Sypunov literally turned handsprings
all around the apartment, shouting that if women were
weak he could very easily bash someone's head in for
him if he had to and if such an ungrateful creature as
Volodin was going to run around at night with his
tail in the air and wreck a family idyll.

Margarita herself, sensing inevitable disaster, bawled
as piercingly as a whistle and shouted through the
whistling and moaning that such an unfeeling and
disgraceful beast ought to be thrown out by the scruff
of his neck, and that only love and, most important,
her wasted youth, held her back from such a step.

It struck Volodin with special unpleasantness that
the younger sister, Lelia, who one would think had no
need of him anyway—she was howling too. With her
howling she only created an atmosphere of strain and
aggravated the misfortune into a big family scandal.

This crude and uncouth little scene put an end to
all Volodin's exalted thoughts. After having come
home full of the most profound and refined experiences,
noble thoughts, and the scent of lilacs, he now clutched
his head and mentally cursed his haste in marrying
this crazy woman who was now irrevocably ruining his
youth. Without raising his voice, in reply to the wailing
and outcries he sent his whole family to the kind of
places you can't come back from and locked himself in
his room. And in the morning, just as soon as it
started to get light, he quietly gathered his belongings
and wardrobe and prepared his departure. And when
the male nurse had left for work, Volodin took his
bundles and left the apartment despite his better half's
groans and the hysterical and fainting attacks she was
having every minute.

He went to his photographer, who greeted him with

open arms and unfeigned happiness, supposing that
Volodin would now begin to retouch on a more economical basis, if not for nothing.

Unnerved by the step he had taken, Volodin promised
friendly and gratuitous services, without thinking what
he was saying. He was burning only with the desire to
see his little girl friend as soon as possible in order to
report to her the happy new turn of events.

And at two in the afternoon, he met her, as always,
by the lake, near the little chapel.

And, clutching his tiny one's hands, he excitedly
began to tell her about it, embellishing his act with
heroic details and flourishes. Yes, he had left home,
having torn off his hated chains and pushed the male
nurse's face in.

The young lady was extremely delighted by this communication. She leaped around him like a little nanny
goat in the spring and, pressing close to him, kept
saying that at last he was a free citizen and at last he
would be able to call his little fish his real wife for
ever and ever amen. And how enchanting everything
would be when they had begun to live together in one
apartment, under one roof—he working like an elephant, never taking rest, she bustling about doing the
housework, the sewing, throwing out the trash, and so
on, and so forth. This all too obvious desire to take
possession of him as a husband and put him in harness,
making him a breadwinner to the end of his days—
this struck Volodin disagreeably.

He gazed a bit gloomily at the young lady and began to say that all this was very fine, but that they still
had to examine all sides of the matter, since he wasn't
used to having a loved one subject herself to privation
and poverty.

To tell the truth, he said this simply out of a wish
to pull the girl up short in her materialistic schemes
and raise the discussion to a higher plane. It seemed

insulting to him that a young lady could regard him from such a practical, mercenary point of view.

As he remembered in an instant his own marriage and his own calculations, Volodin began to look at the girl more inquiringly, wishing to penetrate her thoughts and her heart.

And it seemed to Volodin that in the girl's eyes there burned greedy calculation, self-interest, and the desire to arrange her life as soon as possible.

"And then, I simply don't have any money," he said.

Suddenly, in a flash he thought of a plan of action: he decided to pretend he was poor and out of work.

"Yes," he repeated, already more firmly and even, so to speak, solemnly, "I have no money, no money at all, and unfortunately I can't give you security with my work and my means."

This was, of course, untrue: he lived well and re spectably. But he wanted to hear fine and unmercenary words from the girl's lips: "Well, really, indeed, what kind of calculations are these," and so on, and "Really, what do we want with money when such a wonderful emotion is blooming in our hearts?"

But Olenka Sisyaeva, unhappily, was struck not so much by his assurances as by his tone and, wrinkling up her little nose, she muttered some incoherent words which could be taken rather for irritation and shattered dreams.

"How is it," she said finally, "that previously you said completely different things and, on the contrary, described all sorts of plans, and now it comes out just the opposite. Well, why is that?"

"Very simple," he answered rudely. "You know, dear comrade, I don't have a government job and my position is too insecure and isolated. And, perhaps, I have almost no work right now. I'm almost desperately in need of work, dear comrade. And I don't know myself how I'm going to make ends meet in the future.

Maybe I'll have to walk along the roads barefoot and beg subsistence, dear comrade."

The young woman gazed at him with protruding, glassy eyes, dimly realizing what was going on. But he went on talking nonsense and overwhelmed his lady with pictures of poverty, lack of comforts, and imminent need.

Afterwards, before saying good-bye, they both tried to smooth over this rude little scene and walked together for about ten minutes, chatting about the most impersonal and even poetic things. However, the conversation lagged and they parted, she astonished and uncomprehending, and he all the more convinced of her subtle female designs and reflections.

Returning to his empty passageway, Volodin lay down on the couch and tried to figure out his young lady's feelings and desires.

Cleverly done, he thought. She tried to play the simpleton. She must have been pretty horrified when she heard about poverty.

No, he was not playing tiddlywinks. He'd take another look at what kind of love she felt.

And although he was not precisely and completely certain about her calculations, he went on thinking in this way, hoping that he would quickly hear her words and assurances to the contrary.

Certainly, unquestionably, she had been stunned by his unexpected disclosure and couldn't reveal her true feelings right away, but now, having thought it all over, she would have to decide on the basis of complete and sincere unselfishness. Real love does not cease when confronted with poverty and want. And if she loved him, she would take him by the hand and say various things—"Really, what are you talking about? What's bothering you? Your poverty doesn't frighten me; we'll work and strive for something."

Pondering in this way, he lay in worry and indecision. Suddenly someone rang from the hall. It was the male nurse Sypunov, who asked him in a stern voice to follow him to neutral territory in the yard, where they could freely discuss the actions and deeds that had passed.

Agitated and not daring to refuse, Volodin put on his hat and went down into the yard.

The whole family was already standing there, engaged in a lively and heated discussion.

Not wasting precious time or words, the male nurse Sypunov went up to Volodin and hit him with a cobblestone which probably weighed something over a pound.

Volodin didn't jerk his head away in time, but only ducked to one side and so weakened the blow somewhat. The cobblestone slid down his hat, slightly scraping his ear and the skin on his cheek.

He covered his face with his hands and dashed back, and there immediately flew after him two or three stones, hurled by the weak hands of the esteemed women.

Volodin darted up the stairs in one breath and hastily closed the door after him.

The male nurse rushed after him and from sheer rowdiness kept kicking the door for quite a while, inviting Volodin to come out and talk again, only this time more peacefully and without fighting.

Volodin, covering his injured ear with his hand, stood on the other side of the door, holding his breath. His heart was beating desperately. His legs were frozen with fear. The male nurse, still pounding on the door, said that if things went on like this, then the whole family would grab his scoundrelly body and pour sulphuric acid on him. That is, if he wouldn't change his mind and return to fulfilling his duties.

Beaten and shaken, Volodin lay on his couch thinking that everything had crashed and was ruined. He could find no consolation. Even his love was now in doubt. His own feelings had been deceived and wounded by crude calculation and speculation.

But after thinking about this, Volodin again began to doubt whether it was so.

Well, and if it wasn't so, then he would go to her and be convinced once and for all.

Yes, he would go and tell her everything. He would tell her that life was taking a sharp turn for the worse, that at the risk of his life he was pursuing the ideals he had set himself, and that she should know once and for all that he had literally nothing.

He was naked and a beggar, without a piece of bread and without any work. If she liked, she could take the chance of marrying such a person. If she didn't want to, they'd shake hands and part like ships in the night.

He wanted to run to her right away and confront her with these last words, but it was already late, and after taking off his bloodstained jacket, he rinsed his mangled ear under the faucet and, wrapping a towel around his head, went to bed.

He slept badly, tossed, and bleated so loudly in his sleep that the photographer had to call out to him twice to stop his bleating.

6

The male nurse Sypunov—that rude and uncouth fellow—really did get hold of a bottle of sulphuric acid somewhere.

He set it on the window sill and gave both sisters a lecture on the usefulness of this liquid.

"It never does any harm to splash a little bit of it," he said to the sisters, vividly acting out the moment of pouring it over someone. "You don't really have to burn out the eyes, but," he went on, "you can definitely mess up the nose and other features. The more so that with a red mug the victim won't be a very attractive little guy, girls will no doubt stop throwing themselves at him and, like a nice fellow, he'll come back to his own stall. The law will, of course, find various extenuating circumstances and let you off with a suspended sentence."

Margarita Hopkiss gasped, sighed, and wrung her hands, saying that if that was the way it had to be, she'd rather shrivel up the puss of that mustachioed, dark-skinned little wench who had ruined her happiness and driven her loved one away from her.

However, figuring that there wasn't any possibility of getting him back with his countenance intact, she gaspingly agreed and said that from humane considerations the poisonous liquid ought to be diluted a little.

The male nurse thundered and banged the bottle against the window sill, saying that, in any event, if it came to that, he could splash the hell out of both of them, that he was sick and tired of them both—they were disturbing his character. And that he would even splash a third person, perhaps that dark-skinned girl's mother—why did she let her daughter run around like that, getting herself tangled up with a man who was already taken? As for diluting the liquid, that wouldn't get them anywhere, because chemistry is an exact science and demands a specific formula. It wasn't for people with their kind of education to change formulas.

The younger sister, Lelia, who had a premonition of great new upheavals, accompanied this whole family scene with intense sobbing.

The author hastens to reassure his dear readers that nothing especially serious came of this. Everything ended, if not completely happily, then nearly so. But the scare was terrific. And our friend Volodin had to experience a lot of grief in connection with this upheaval. The next day, when he had shaved and had powdered his damaged ear, Volodin went out on the street and hurried to his little girl friend.

He went along the street gesticulating stormily and talking to himself out loud.

He was thinking up all kinds of tricky questions to put to her, which would reveal the young lady's mercenary, undercover game.

She was poor, she was completely dependent on her mama, she wanted to make a life for herself. But she was cruelly mistaken. Yes, he didn't have a kopeck to his name. He had only the clothes on his back. These were his only tie and his only trousers. And he was out of work too, without any prospects for the future. She should know that his photographic business didn't bring in anything. Except for heavy expenditures for pencils and erasers, he saw nothing in the future. And if he worked at this business, it was solely out of kindness and friendship for the photographer Patrikeyev, who had let him use his couch and room.

That was how he would talk to her and see what was going on. Let her definitely give her own opinion about this. He walked hurriedly, noticing no one and hearing nothing. From the corner by the vacant lot, his former wife, Margaritochka Hopkiss, was approaching.

Seeing her, Volodin turned deathly pale and, as if bewitched, gazed fixedly at her and walked slowly toward her.

When he was three paces away, Margarita softly cried out something, gave a wave of her hand, and splashed Volodin with acid upwards from below.

The distance was great and the flask had a narrow neck, so that only a few drops fell on Volodin's suit.

Volodin ran to one side, yelping piercingly, and kept slapping his palms against his face, wanting to assure himself that his mug was still whole.

When he had convinced himself that it had come

through all right, he turned around and rushed toward Margarita Hopkiss, who was standing like a shadow by the fence. Volodin grabbed her by the throat and began to shake her, hitting her head against the fence and shouting some incoherent phrases. All this took place on the deserted lonely street along which Volodin usually walked to meet his little one.

People began to come over from other streets, however, eager to see the show that was being performed for their benefit.

But the show was coming to an end. Afraid that he would be dragged off to the police station, Volodin stopped shaking his missus and went quickly home without looking around.

He felt shaken and agitated. His teeth were chattering like a drum roll.

He went home almost at a run and locked himself in his apartment.

Naturally, he couldn't go to see his little one in such a state.

He was in a fever. His legs trembled and his teeth were chattering.

Volodin lay on the couch for a while. Then he started walking about the room, glancing fearfully out the window and listening for sounds. He didn't go out all day, fearing that the male nurse would finish him off in the yard or cripple him by breaking his arms and ribs.

He spent the day in extreme anguish, without any food. He only drank incredible quantities of water, trying to cool off and quench the fever within him. All night, without shutting his eyes, he thought over the situation that had developed, trying to find some respectable and face-saving way out. And he did find such a way out, coming to the conclusion that he had to make a truce with his former wife and her guardian angel Comrade Sypunov. He wouldn't sue them for attempted murder, and in return they could stop beating him within an inch of his life.

Having settled this, he turned his mind to the other, no less important battleground and began to consider for the hundredth time what new and decisive words he would say to his little girl friend and how he would say them so that he could be sure of getting a real human being with unmercenary feelings instead of a wily female with her practical tricks. For the sake of attaining this goal he would not stop at any difficulties or expense. Yes, he would say he was unemployed and at first he would work at his photographer's without her knowledge to assure himself once and for all that his young lady had no calculations or selfish considerations.

Volodin pictured in his mind's eye scenes in which he would work in secret, with his coat collar turned up and the curtains carefully drawn, never resting, retouching photographs day and night. He would work like this a whole month or two months or even a year and put away the money, spending absolutely nothing. Then at last, sure of his little one, he would lay a pile of money at her feet and beg her to forgive him for doing such a rude and impudent thing.

The young lady, with tears in her eyes, would push aside his money with her pale little hand, saying, "Really, what are you doing, what is it for, why so much? This really spoils our relationship."

And then unclouded happiness and a wonderful, unique life would begin.

Tears of joy would come into Volodin's eyes when he thought of such an outcome to the matter. And he would turn over energetically on his couch, making all the springs creak and wiping his eyes with his shirt sleeve.

But then he would again think of his sorrows, of the beatings and all the recent dark doings. And then he would literally grow cold and, fearing in retrospect that he might have been disfigured after all, he would jump up from his tattered couch and run again, now to the mirror to make sure his face was all right, now to his suit to examine the burned-through fabric.

He spent the whole night in this disturbed and difficult way, dozing off a little only toward morning.

In the morning, gray-faced and dull-eyed, he began hurriedly to go about his business, having decided first of all to visit his young lady in order to put his plan into action as soon as possible. After that, he would unfurl the white flag and begin negotiations with his dear relatives.

Going out onto the stairs, Volodin began to clean his boots, as was his custom, polishing them with a buffer to a blinding shine.

He had already cleaned one boot when suddenly, very likely from the coldness on the stairs, he hiccuped. He hiccuped once, then again, then, after a few seconds, a few more times.

Clearing his throat and doing the same little setting-up exercise, Volodin began energetically rubbing the other boot. But since his hiccups did not go away, he went into the kitchen and, taking a piece of sugar, began to suck it, because it is very awkward to talk to the woman you love with such a defect in your speech.

However, the hiccups still did not go away. And he now hiccuped regularly, like a machine, after a definite interval of time, every half-minute.

A little upset by this new and unexpected impediment which prevented him from seeing the person dear to him, he began to walk about the room, singing gay and comic songs at the top of his voice, so as not to give way to inner anxiety and worry.

After walking like this for about an hour, he sat down on the edge of the couch and suddenly realized with horror that his hiccups had not only not lessened but, on the contrary, had become heavier and more resonant, although the interval between the spasms had increased to nearly two minutes.

During these intervals, Volodin sat motionless, almost holding his breath, awaiting with terror another convulsion in his throat. And when he hiccuped he would jump up, wave his arms, and look straight ahead with a stricken and other-worldly gaze, seeing nothing.

He suffered in this way until two in the afternoon, and then informed his roommate, the photographer, of his misfortune. The photographer Patrikeyev frivolously burst out laughing, calling it an absolute trifle, a matter of no consequence which happened to him almost every day. Then Volodin summoned what was left of his manliness and set off to see his Olenka Sisyaeva.

He hiccuped all the way, jerking his whole body and abandoning all decorum.

As he was approaching the girl's house, he unhappily started to hiccup so frequently and energetically that passers-by turned around and called him a donkey and other unflattering terms.

Summoning the girl with a knock on the window, Volodin prepared himself for a showdown, forgetting, it's true, all his tricky questions because of his new calamity.

He excused himself for his purely nervous hiccups, which were apparently caused by a severe cold and anemia, and elegantly kissed Olenka's hand, hiccuping a couple of times in the course of this simple procedure.

Thinking that he had got drunk from grief, Olenka Sisyaeva fluttered her eyelashes, preparing to give him a stern reply. But he, thinking more about his illness, incoherently stammered a few words to the effect that he was down and out, unemployed, and that his only capital consisted of one tie and a pair of drawers. And for this reason Olenka had better say at once whether she was willing to marry such a ragamuffin whose future looked black and with whom she might have to go begging as if he were a blind man, asking for food. Or whether she, dear comrade, really loved him no matter what.

Olenka Sisyaeva blushed a little and said that it was unfortunately too late to ask questions of that sort. The more so that, as had been ascertained yesterday, she was in a certain condition, and it was rather strange and silly in her special condition to hear talk and statements like these. And that a husband was a husband, and his duty was to feed his future family somehow.

Astounded by this new disclosure, and receiving no definite answer to his thoughts and doubts, Volodin, thrown for a loop, irrevocably lost the thread of his plan and now stared amazedly at the young woman, hiccuping from time to time.

Then he seized her by the hands and said in a thin, cockroach-like voice that, for God's sake, even if she was in this situation she should tell him whether she loved him and whether she was taking this step willingly.

The girl, smiling sweetly, said that of course, without doubt she loved him, only he would have to make a serious effort to cure his nervous hiccups, because she didn't fancy a husband with a strange defect of that kind.

And here, after saying good-bye, they parted, she sure of herself, he full of uncertainty and even despair because he had not been able to find out about the girl's feelings with any surety.

7

It was very strange and surprising, but Volodin's hiccups did not go away.

When he returned home, he went to bed early, secretly hoping that they would be all gone by morning and that a simple, splendid human life would begin again. When he woke up, however, he discovered that his misfortune had not passed. It was true that he now hiccuped seldom, once in three minutes on the average, but he hiccuped, nevertheless, and could see no signs of recovery.

Without getting up from his couch, and turning cold at the thought that his indisposition would remain with him for ever and ever, Volodin lay there for a whole day and night, now and then running into the kitchen to drink some cold water.

In the morning, when he raised his head from the pillow again and found that he still had his hiccups, Volodin's spirits sank completely. He stopped resisting nature and, humbly giving in to his fate, lay like a corpse, only occasionally jerking his body from the effect of his nervous hiccups.

The photographer Patrikeyev was worried by his lodger's strange condition and began to be afraid that he might be saddled with an invalid who would hiccup day and night and scare away his customers and visitors. So without saying anything to Volodin, he ran to see the fatal Olenka Sisyaeva to ask her to come to the sick man's bedside, hoping in this manner to relieve himself as quickly as possible of all moral and material responsibility and of the trouble of caring for Volodin. He went to her and began to beg her to come, saying that her friend, if not absolutely dying, was in a very bad way and, most important, was repeating her name after every two words, probably longing intensely to see such a darling young lady as soon as he could.

The girl, embarrassed by such an unusual illness on her fiancé's part, could not properly express her unhappiness and anxiety.

Since she wasn't as exceedingly stupid as she seemed, she tried to see the funny side of the trouble, saying that it was nothing, nonsense, and altogether a purely nervous occurrence which would certainly go away before their wedding.

Conversing in this manner, they arrived at the sick man's apartment together.

A bit upset by the poor and uncomfortable appearance of the room and the scantiness of his possessions, the young lady stopped on the threshold, unable to make up her mind to approach the sick man, who lay looking completely abstracted, with his head thrown far back and his arms outspread.

When he saw the young woman, the sick man leaped up from the couch and then lay down again, hastily covering his torn apparel.

The young woman moved a stool over to the couch and sat down on the edge of it, dejectedly watching the illness convulse her fiancé.

The news that a man had been hiccuping for three days and nights had somewhat excited the inhabitants of the nearby houses. Word of the nightmarish drama increased the citizens' curiosity. The apartment literally became the object of a pilgrimage, which one photographer was not strong enough to stop. Everyone wanted to see how the bride-to-be acted with her fiancé and what she said and how he, with his hiccups, answered her.

Here, too, putting on airs among the visiting citizens was our male nurse Sypunov, but he didn't risk going into the room lest he frighten the sick man.

As the closest relative and a medical worker, surrounded by a crowd of curious people, he spoke authoritatively about the sick man's condition, explaining what was what and what was the matter.

He really had not intended such an outcome. He had unquestionably frightened the man, but he had been motivated by a feeling of fairness and also by his family ties with Margarita Hopkiss, who would now be left without a man in her declining years.

However, the melancholy picture of illness moved him deeply, the more so that he took into account the emotion of love, and he now allowed no one to touch his former relative, Nikolay Petrovich Volodin. If worse came to worst, Margaritochka could dance away her life somehow. As for the illness, it was most likely a purely nervous complaint growing out of a cold. In the hospital where he worked, the devil knows what illnesses grew out of colds, and it was all right. If the person didn't die, there were no dangerous after-effects for the rest of his life.

The photographer Patrikeyev, afraid that in the crush and confusion someone might steal his photographic equipment, began to shout, urging the crowd to disperse or else he would call the militia* and forcibly put a stop to the disgraceful goings-on.

The male nurse, taking orders from the photographer, began to push out the intrusive public, waving a tripod and crowding the visitors into the kitchen or out onto the stairs. He asked them to get out peaceably and not make him take stronger measures.

Seeing such a shameful scene—public exposure of everything and open disgrace—the young lady, Olenka Sisyaeva, began jumping up from her stool, gasping and acting nervous.

She began to babble that the sick man ought to be taken to the hospital, or that at least the communal doctor, who would be able to get rid of the crowd of superfluous people, ought to be called.

Among the visitors, by the way, was a kind of former intellectual, a certain Abramov, who announced that there was absolutely no need for a doctor, that a doctor would soak you three rubles and make such a sad mess of things that the sick man could probably never be cured after that.

* The word "police" being redolent of czarist or capitalist associations, ever since the Revolution the word "militia" has been used to signify the ordinary civil police. *Ed.*

And that it would be better to let him, Abramov, try an experiment which would tear out the illness by its roots.

This fellow Abramov was not a doctor or a scientist, but he had a deep understanding of many questions and liked to treat citizens for various illnesses and infirmities with his home remedies. Here he said that the illness was all too clear to him; that it was an incorrect movement of the organism, and that it would be necessary to interrupt this movement as soon as possible. The more so that an organism has, so to speak, its own momentum, and when it forms a firm habit of moving in one direction, it's a serious matter. It's from this that almost all our illnesses and ailments come. And you have to treat these things energetically, giving a vigorous shake and a push in the opposite direction to the whole organism, which is working blindly, unaware what direction its wheels are turning in and what will come of its workings.

He ordered them to seat the sick man on a chair while he, mocking loudly at doctors and medicine, went into the kitchen to begin his scientific preparations. There he filled a pail full of cold water, cautiously ran out on tiptoe, stood behind the door and, with a cry, suddenly poured all this water over the head of the sick man who, understanding little of what was going on, had been until then sitting unconcernedly on the chair like a sack of potatoes.

Forgetting about his illness, Volodin was on the point of starting a fight, and in general, after this procedure, began to act rowdy, chasing people out of the apartment and tearing after his home-grown doctor to beat him up. But Volodin calmed down quickly and, after changing his clothes, dozed off with his head on his little girl friend's lap. The next morning he arose completely well and, after shaving and tidying himself up, began to live in his usual manner.

Of course, the author is not about to declare that this

home remedy effected the cure. Most likely, the illness went away by itself. The more so because three or four days is quite a long time for such an attack, although, of course, even more protracted attacks of this illness are known to medicine. But, all the same, the nice cool water might have had a positive effect on our sick man's tormented brains and in this way hastened the cure.

8

A few days later, Volodin registered his marriage to his little girl friend and moved into her modest abode.

Their honeymoon went smoothly and quite uneventfully.

The male nurse had completely changed his anger to good will and even dropped in twice to visit the newlyweds, once graciously borrowing three rubles, not promising, however, to return them. On the other hand, he made a solemn promise not to try to kill Volodin any more under any circumstances.

As for his earnings and finances in general, Volodin had to confess his slander. Well, yes, he had lied a little, wanting to test her love. There's nothing insulting about that.

And speaking of this, he begged her to tell him once more whether she had known that he had lied intentionally, or whether she hadn't known and had married him out of disinterested feeling.

The little lady, laughing thoughtfully, assured him that the latter was the case, saying that at first, of course, she hadn't known about his lying and was afraid that he really didn't have a kopeck. But afterwards she had definitely seen through his overly transparent behavior. Well, she didn't have any reproaches—it was his lawful right to find out about a girl.

Listening to this feminine speech, Volodin raged

mentally and called himself an ass and a sheep for not having been able really to trap the girl.

Besides, of course, what could he have done? Moreover, his malignant illness had made a fool of him—had deprived him of his energy and will and altogether addled his brains. Because of this, he had not been able to solve the problem properly. Then too, the young lady had outplayed him, since she held the ace of trumps—her condition. But in the future everything would somehow come clear by itself.

As for Margaritochka Hopkiss, she went on being angry and once, when she met Volodin on the street, did not respond to his dignified bow, but turned her profile to the side. This trivial incident nonetheless affected Volodin unpleasantly, for he had lately begun to wish that everything in life would be smooth and nice and that doves would flutter through the air.

That day he got a little upset again, remembering the latest events of his life.

At night he couldn't sleep. He tossed in his bed and gazed morosely and inquiringly at his missus.

The young lady was sleeping with her lips parted, smacking them and whimpering.

She had it all figured out, thought Volodin. She really knew everything, damn it. And of course she wouldn't have married him if he had really had nothing. In his pain and agitation, Volodin got out of bed, walked around the room, went over to the window and, pressing his burning forehead to the glass, watched for a long time the wind swaying the trees in the dark garden.

Then, afraid that the nighttime coolness would bring on his illness again, he hurried back to bed. He lay for a long while with his eyes open, tracing the pattern of the wallpaper with his finger.

She really knew that I lied, damn it, Volodin thought again, falling asleep.

But in the morning he got up like a nice little fellow and tried not to think about crude things any more. And if he did think about them, he would sigh and wave his hand, reflecting that no one had ever done anything without selfish motives.

MICHEL SINYAGIN

PREFACE

THIS story is a memoir about a certain person, about a
certain, shall we say, little-known minor poet, with
whom the author rubbed shoulders for quite a number
of years.

The fate of this man impressed the author exceedingly, and for this reason he decided to write a kind of
memoir or, shall we say, biographical story about him,
not for the edification of posterity, but just for its own
sake.

We can't all go on writing biographies and memoirs
about wonderful and great people, about their instructive lives and about their brilliant thoughts and attain-
ments. Someone has to respond to the experiences of
other, let's say, more average, people, who are not, so
to speak, listed in life's velvet-covered book.

And in the author's opinion, the lives of people like
this are also quite instructive and curious. The extent of
a man's mistakes, missed opportunities, sufferings and
joys does not diminish because, let's say, he didn't paint
on canvas some delightful chef-d'oeuvre called "Girl
with a Pitcher," or didn't learn to hammer away at the
keys of a piano, or, let's say, didn't discover some extra
star or comet in the firmament for the welfare and
tranquillity of mankind.

On the contrary, the lives of such ordinary people are
even more understandable, even more deserving of

wonder, than, let's say, the exceptional and extraordinary actions or eccentricities of some genius of an artist, pianist, or piano-tuner. The lives of simple people like this are even more interesting and even more readily understandable.

The author does not mean by this that you are about to see something which is exceptionally interesting and impressive for sheer intensity of experience and passion. No, it will be a life lived out modestly, and recounted, moreover, somewhat hurriedly, carelessly, and, no doubt, with many mistakes. Of course, the author tried as hard as he could, but he didn't have, shall we say, the necessary peace of mind or the love for various trivial subjects and experiences to give the description its full luster.

You won't feel here the quiet breathing of an author whose destiny is protected and pampered by a golden age. You won't find any beautiful phrases, daring turns of speech, or ecstasy at the grandeur of nature.

You will simply find a life truthfully set forth. In addition, the author's somewhat fidgety character, his restlessness and concern with other trifles oblige him at times to abandon the easy flow of narrative in order to deal with some current question or other or resolve some doubt.

As for the title of the book, the author agrees that it is dry and academic—it offers little to the mind and heart. But he is keeping this title for the time being. The author wanted to call the story something else, like "In Life's Clutches," or "Life Begins the Day After Tomorrow." But he didn't have enough self-confidence or impudence for this. Moreover, these titles were very likely already in literary circulation, and he didn't have the wit or inventiveness to think up a new one.

1

In a hundred years. Concerning our time. Concerning adaptability. Concerning duels. Concerning socks. The prologue to the story.

Now, in the distant future, in some hundred years or a little less, say, when everything has finally been shaken down and settled into place and life shines forth with untold brilliance, let's suppose some citizen, some citizen with a little mustache, in some kind of, well, little sandy-colored chamois suit or, say, in silk, evening lounging pajamas, will pick up our modest book and lie down with it on a sofa. He'll lie down on a morocco-leather sofa or on some sort of soft *causeuse* or chaise longue, and resting his perfumed head on his lily-white hands and musing a bit about beautiful things, he will open the book.

"Interesting," he'll say, munching some candy, "to see how they lived in their time."

His beautiful young wife, or, let's say, the helpmeet of his life, is sitting there beside him in one of her extra-special peignoirs.

"Andreus" (or maybe it's Téodore), she'll say, adjusting her peignoir, "why do you bother reading all kinds of unintelligible junk? You'll only upset your nerves at this late hour."

And she herself will perhaps take from the shelf a small volume in a colored silk binding—the works of some famous poet—and begin to read:

> *Outside my window swayed a lily,*
> *A fever burns me through . . .*
> *Love, O love, it's so idyllic*
> *Now I'll come to you . . .*

Whenever the author pictures to himself for a minute such a water color as this, his pen simply drops from his hand—he just can't go on writing, that's all.

Of course, the author doesn't claim that life in the future will contain scenes exactly like this. No, that would be quite unlikely. That was just a momentary supposition. Most likely, on the contrary, there will be a very, shall we say, healthy and vigorous generation.

They'll be sunburned people bursting with health, dressed modestly but simply, without any special pretensions to luxury and elegance.

Then too, they may not even read such wretched little lyric verses at all, or read them only in exceptional circumstances, preferring our prose works, which they will take in their hands with great inner trembling and with complete respect for their authors.

But as soon as the author thinks of real readers like these, he becomes perplexed again, and again the pen falls from his hand.

Well, what can he give such wonderful readers?

The author sincerely acknowledges all the greatness of our time, but nonetheless lacks the ability to produce a suitable work fully describing our epoch. Maybe he has wasted his talent on petty, everyday, vulgar things, on all sorts of personal afflictions and cares, but in any event he is not capable of producing the kind of epic work which would interest the respected readers of the future even a little. No, it's better to close one's eyes to the future and not think about the generations to come. It's better to write for our tried and tested readers.

But here again doubts appear, and the pen drops from the author's hand. At present, when the most current and even essential theme is the scarcity of packing materials or the construction of silos, it may be that it's simply improper to write any old way, and in general to write about the experiences of people who in the main don't even play a role in the complex mechanism of our times.

The reader may simply call the author a pig.

"Look at what another one of these guys is writing," he'll say. "He's describing personal experiences, damn him. Just wait, in a minute he'll start turning out epic poems about flowers."

No, the author won't start writing about flowers. He will write a story, in his opinion an extremely necessary story, which will be a summing-up of the old way of life —a story about a certain insignificant poet who lived in our time.

Of course, he foresees harsh criticism of it from young and thoughtless critics who take a superficial view of such literary creations.

But the author's conscience is clear. He is not forgetting the other front and does not disdain writing about absenteeism, ensilage, or the fight against illiteracy. On the contrary, modest work of this kind is even to his taste.

But besides this, the author has an exceedingly strong urge to write his memoir of this man as soon as possible, since before long life will have jumped over him, everything will be forgotten, and grass will cover the path along which passed our modest hero, our acquaintance and, we'll say it straight out, our relative, M. P. Sinyagin.

The latter circumstance enabled the author to see the man's whole life, all the trivial details of his existence, and all the events which took place in his final years. His entire private life took place, as if on a stage, before the author's eyes.

And if that fellow with the little mustache and the chamois suit should, God forbid, slip through into the next century, he will probably be a bit surprised, and will begin thrashing about on his morocco-leather *causeuse*.

"Darling," he'll say, stroking his mustache, "it's interesting. They had," he'll say, "some kind of personal life."

"Andreus," she'll say in a throaty voice, "don't bother me, for God's sake, I'm reading poetry . . ."

But actually, reader, some fellow like the one with the little mustache will be quite unable in his peaceful time to form a correct picture of our life. He will probably think that we spent all our time in mud huts, ate sparrows, and lived some kind of unthinkable, primitive life, full of daily catastrophes and horrors.

One must admit, it's true, that many people really haven't had any so-called personal life—they have sacrificed all their strength and will for the sake of their ideas and the pursuit of their goals.

And those who were a bit shallower—they maneuvered as best they could, adapted themselves, and tried to get in step with the times in order to live out their lives decently and eat more heartily.

And life followed its course. There were love, and jealousy, and childbirth, and all sorts of great maternal emotions and all sorts of beautiful experiences. We went to the movies with girls. And went rowing. And sang and played the guitar. And ate waffles with whipped cream. And wore stylish striped socks. And danced the fox trot to the music of the family piano . . .

No, that so-called personal life went on its own little way, as it always does under any kind of circumstances.

And those who liked this kind of life adapted themselves and adjusted as well as they could.

Every epoch has, so to speak, its own psychology. And in every epoch so far it has been equally easy, or, more correctly, equally difficult, to live.

Let's take, for example, a really troubled century, let's say the sixteenth. If we look at it from a distance, it seems simply unthinkable. At that time they fought duels almost every day. They threw guests from towers. And it was all right. It was all in the natural order of things.

For us, with our psychology, it's simply terrifying to picture a life like theirs. For example, some feudal son-of-a-bitch of theirs, some kind of viscount or ex-count,* goes out for a walk, for example.

He's setting out for a walk, and that means he fastens his sword to his side—who knows whether in a minute someone won't, God forbid, push him with his shoulder or curse at him, and he'll have to fight at once. So it's all right.

He goes for his walk, and there's not even any sadness or panic written on his mug. On the contrary, he goes along and even, maybe, smiles and whistles. And he'll carelessly kiss his wife good-bye.

"Well," he'll say, "*ma chère,* I'm going for a walk."

Nothing bothers her. "Fine," she'll say, "don't be late for dinner."

Whereas in our time a wife would sob and cling to his legs, begging him not to go out on the street or, at the very least, would ask him to assure a comfortable existence for her. But here it's simple, without any fuss. He takes his little sword, whets it if it has been dulled in a previous skirmish, and goes out to wander around until dinnertime, with an excellent chance of getting into a duel or a skirmish.

It must be admitted that if the author had lived during that epoch, they couldn't have smoked him out of his house by force. So he would have lived out his life locked up until our time.

Yes, from our point of view life was uninteresting. But at that time they didn't notice this, and lived swim-

* In early post-Revolutionary days it became habitual to attach the adjective *byvshii* ("former") to all aristocratic titles. Here, of course, the extension of the practice to the sixteenth century has a comic effect. *Ed.*

mingly. They even went to parties given by owners of towers.

So that in this sense man is very magnificently made. Whatever kind of life is going on, he lives splendidly in it. And those who can't do so doubtless go off to one side so as not to get trampled underfoot. Life has very strict rules in this respect, and not everyone can lie down across the path and disagree.

At this point we will turn to the main narrative, for the sake of which this book was really written. The author apologizes if he has blurted out anything superfluous which has nothing to do with the matter at hand. These are all very vital problems and questions that demand immediate solutions.

And as for what we said about psychology, it's very true. It's borne out completely by history.

And so at this point we will begin with a clear conscience our memoir of a man who lived at the beginning of the twentieth century.

In the course of the story the author will be obliged to touch on many painful subjects, sad experiences, deprivations, and poverty. But he asks his readers not to jump to hasty conclusions about them.

Certain complainers are capable of ascribing all these misfortunes to the Revolution, which was going on at that time.

You know, it's very strange, but the Revolution had nothing to do with it. It's true that the Revolution knocked this man off his course. But actually—how shall I say it?—such a life is possible and even likely at any time. The author suspects that a memoir just like this could have been written about some other man living during some other epoch.

The author begs his readers to note this circumstance.

The author once had a neighbor living in the room next to his. A former drawing teacher. He had taken to drink, and he led a wretched and improper life. And this teacher always liked to say, "It wasn't the Revolution that ruined me. Even if there hadn't been a Revolution, I would have taken to drink all the same, or ruined myself through stealing, or I would have been shot in the war, or I would have been taken prisoner and had my face beaten out of shape. I knew in advance," he said, "what I was in for and what kind of life was before me."

These were golden words.

The author is not trying to make a melodrama out of this. No, the author believes in the victorious march of a life which will make it possible for everyone to live in clover. A great many people are thinking about this now and racking their brains in the effort to make things easy for man in this way.

Of course, this is still, so to speak, the prologue to history. Life hasn't settled down yet. They say that two hundred years ago people had just begun to wear socks.

So that everything is all right. The good life isn't far off.

2

The birth of our hero. His youth. A contemplative mood. Love of beauty. Concerning gentle souls. Concerning the Hermitage and a wonderful Scythian vase.

Mikhail Polikarpovich Sinyagin was born in 1887 on the estate of "Pankovo" in the province of Smolensk. His mother was a noblewoman and his father an hereditary honorary citizen.*

But since the author is about ten years younger than

* In pre-Revolutionary Russia this title was given to individuals of non-gentry origin as a reward for achievement or for attaining a certain level of education. *Ed.*

M. P. Sinyagin, he can't say anything particularly relevant about his early years until 1916.

But since he was always called Michel, even at the age of forty, it is evident that he had a tender upbringing, attention, love, and affectionate care. They called him Michel, and really, he couldn't have been called anything else. No coarser name would have gone with his face, his slender body, or his elegant movements, which were executed with grace, dignity, and a sense of rhythm.

I think he graduated from the Gymnasium, and that he studied somewhere or other for two or three more years. In any case, he had an exceptionally fine education.

In 1916 the author happened to be in the same town with him and, from the height of his eighteen years, involuntarily observed his life and was, so to speak, an eyewitness to many important and significant changes and events.

M. P. Sinyagin was not at the front because of a strangulated hernia. And at the end of the European war he was sauntering around town in a civilian raincoat with a flower in his buttonhole and a smart ivory-handled walking stick in his hand.

He walked along the streets, always a bit melancholy and languid, completely alone, muttering to himself verses which he composed in great abundance, having considerable talent, taste, and a sensitive instinct for everything beautiful and elegant.

He was enraptured by the melancholy and monotonous natural scenes around Pskov—birch trees, brooks, and all sorts of little insects circling above the flower beds.

He would walk into the country and, taking off his hat, would watch the play of birds and mosquitoes with a sensitive and understanding smile.

Or, gazing at the moving clouds with his head

thrown back, he would on the spot compose suitable rhymes and verses about them.

In those years there were still a good number of highly cultivated and intelligent people with sensitive spiritual make-up and a gentle love of beauty and of the various decorative arts.

It must be recognized that in our country there has always been an exceptional stratum of intellectuals to whom all Europe and even all the world listened.

Truly, they were very fine judges of art and ballet and the authors of many remarkable works, and they inspired many distinguished deeds and great doctrines.

They were not *spetses* in our sense of the term.*

They were simply intelligent, cultivated people.

Many of them had tender hearts. Some simply wept at the sight of a superfluous flower in a flower bed, or a little sparrow hopping on a dung heap.

It is all in the past now, but, of course, one must say that there was even a certain kind of abnormality in this. And such a luxurious flowering was no doubt at the expense of something else.

The author is not too experienced in the art of dialectic and is unacquainted with various scientific theories and trends, so he does not undertake to look for causes and effects in this matter. But reasoning crudely, you can still dig up a little something, of course.

Let's suppose that in a certain family there are three sons. And if we suppose that one son is taught, fed sandwiches with butter, given cocoa, washed in a bathtub daily, and has his hair combed with brilliantine,

* In the 1920's and 1930's those members of the old pre-Revolutionary professional classes, such as engineers, who had skills needed by the new regime and who, though avowedly non-Communist, were not anti-Communist, were allowed to take responsible jobs in Soviet industry, agriculture, and commerce under the supervision of Party watchdogs. In the slang of the day they were called *spetsy*, short for *spetsialisty*. But they tended to be technicians rather than people with general literary and artistic interests, such as those Zoshchenko is talking about here. *Ed.*

while the others are given worthless trifles and frustrated in all their needs, then the first son can easily make great strides in his education and in the development of his spiritual qualities. He'll begin to put together little verses, be moved to compassion by the sight of sparrows, and talk on various elevated subjects.

It happens that the author was recently in the Hermitage. He was looking through the Scythian section, and there is a wonderful vase there. They say that that vase is more than two thousand years old, if they're not lying. Such an elegant golden vase. Exceptionally delicate Scythian work. Actually, they don't know what the Scythians made it for. Maybe it was for milk, or to put wild flowers in for the Scythian king to smell. No one knows; scholars have failed to clear up this point.

They found this vase in a burial mound.

Well, on this vase he suddenly saw drawings—Scythian peasants are sitting there. One middle peasant* is sitting down, another is picking at the first one's tooth with his fingers, and the third is fixing his bast shoes.

The author looked a little closer. Good heavens! They're exactly our pre-Revolutionary peasants. Let's say from the year 1913. Even the attire is the same— the same loose, belted shirts. Long, tangled beards.

The author somehow felt shaken by this. What the hell is this? You look in the catalogue—the vase is two thousand years old. You look at the drawings—fifteen hundred years less. That means that either this is an out-and-out hoax on the part of the scientific workers at the Hermitage, or that clothes and bast shoes like these actually survived until our Revolution. And if this is so, then it means that for fifteen hundred years people couldn't manage to dress any better. They were too busy being exploited.

* Again a humorous anachronism. Marxist theoreticians had classified the twentieth-century Russian peasants into rich (*kulaki*), middle (*seredniaki*), and poor (*bediaki*). *Ed.*

By all these remarks the author, of course, doesn't in the least want to disparage the former intellectual stratum he was talking about. No, here he simply wants to find out what's what, and who is to blame for what.

But the stratum itself, one must admit, was simply splendid—you can't say anything against it.

As concerns M. P. Sinyagin, the author, of course, doesn't want to put him on the same level with the people we were talking about. But, nevertheless, he was also an intellectual and cultivated to a considerable degree. He understood a great deal, liked pretty baubles, and went into ecstasies every minute over literary art. He adored such wonderful, distinguished poets and prose writers as Fet, Blok, and Nadson.*

And since he was not distinguished for exceptional originality, he was strongly influenced in his own work by these famous poets; and especially, of course, by the most brilliant poet of those years, A. A. Blok.

3

The mother and aunt of M. P. Sinyagin. Their past. The purchase of the estate. Life in Pskov. Clouds gather. The character and inclinations of Aunt M. A. Ar——v. A meeting with L. N. Tolstoy. The poet's verses. His spiritual condition. Infatuation.

Michel Sinyagin lived with his mother, Anna Arkadyevna Sinyagin, and her sister, Marya Arkadyevna, about whom we will later have to speak in detail, giving her a special description and characterization, since this esteemed lady, the widow of General Ar——v,

* Afanasii Fet (1820-92), a distinguished lyric poet, and Aleksandr Blok (1880-1921), the greatest of the Russian symbolist poets, are here rather incongruously linked with Semyon Nadson (1862-87), a sentimental neo-Romantic—demonstrating the eclecticism of Sinyagin's tastes. *Ed.*

plays a role of no little importance in our story.

And so, in 1917 the three of them were living in Pskov like fortuitous guests, having got stuck in that nice little town because of events beyond their control.

The Sinyagins had come there during the war to move in with their sister and aunt, Marya Arkadyevna, who had chanced to buy a small estate not far from Pskov.

On this estate both old ladies wanted to live out their lives close to nature, in complete quiet and tranquillity, after rather turbulent and gaily spent lives.

This ill-starred estate was suitably named "The Quiet Spot."*

And Michel, that somewhat morose young man, susceptible to vague melancholy and a bit wearied by his poetic work and the noisy life in the capital with its restaurants and singers and fist fights, also wanted to live in peace and quiet for a while in order to gather strength and then plunge onward again at full speed.

Everything, however, turned out very differently from what was intended.

"The Quiet Spot" had been purchased just before the Revolution, something like two months before, so that the family had not even had a chance to move there with their things and trunks. These trunks, feather beds, couches, and beds were temporarily and hurriedly stored in the city apartment of some Pskov acquaintances. And it was in this very apartment that Michel would be obliged in the future to live for several years with his elderly mother and aunt.

Remarkable for their liberalism and having a certain, well, fascination and love for revolutions, the sisters did not lose their senses because of the revolutionary upheaval and the confiscation of landowners' property. However, the younger sister, Marya Arkadyevna, who had sunk nearly sixty thousand rubles in the estate,

* Title of a story by Turgenev. *Ed.*

would sometimes gasp and sigh, saying that the devil knew what it was when you couldn't move into an estate bought with your own hard-earned money.

Anna Arkadyevna, Michel's mother, was a rather inconspicuous lady. She had not distinguished herself in any particular way in life, except by giving birth to a poet.

She was a fairly quiet and peaceable old woman, who liked to sit by the samovar and drink coffee with cream.

As for Marya Arkadyevna, she was an altogether different type of woman.

The author did not have the pleasure of seeing her in her younger days, but it was common knowledge that she had been an extremely pretty and appealing girl, full of life, fire, and high spirits.

But at the time we are concerned with here, she was already a shapeless old woman, nearer to ugly than to beautiful, although still very mobile and energetic.

In this respect her former profession had left its mark on her. In her youth she had been a ballerina and had been a member of the *corps de ballet* in the Mariinsky Theater.*

She had even been a celebrity, after a fashion, since the former Grand Duke Nikolay Nikolayevich had been in love with her. It's true that he soon left her, after giving her some kind of unusual moleskin stole, some beads, and something else or other. But the career she had begun was now assured.

Both these old women will play fairly significant parts in the life of Michel Sinyagin, so the reader should not be affected or annoyed by the fact that the author has dwelt so long on the description of two such, well, decrepit and withered heroines.

The poetic atmosphere which was present in the

* The Mariinsky Theater was the principal operatic theater in St. Petersburg. *Ed.*

house thanks to Michel somewhat affected our ladies as well. And Marya Arkadyevna was fond of saying that she would soon begin writing her memoirs.

Her turbulent life and her meetings with many well-known people would have made them worth writing. She had seen in person, perhaps twice, L. N. Tolstoy, Nadson, Koni, Pereverzev,* and other famous people, her impressions of whom she wished to convey to the world.

Thus the family came to Pskov at the beginning of the Revolution and got stuck there for three years. M. P. Sinyagin said every day that he had absolutely no intention of sticking around there and that he was going to Moscow or Petrograd at the first opportunity. However, subsequent events and changes in his life delayed this departure.

And our Michel Sinyagin continued his life beneath the Pskov heavens, occupying himself for the time being with his verses and with his temporary infatuation with a certain local girl, to whom he dedicated a great many of his poems.

Of course, these poems were not works of genius; they were not even as original as they might have been, but their freshness of emotion and their straightforward, uncomplicated style made them noticeable in the general run of poems of that time.

The author does not remember these verses. Life, cares, and disappointments have crowded the elegant lines and poetic rhymes out of his memory, but a few fragments and single stanzas he has retained because of their genuine feeling.

* Anatoly F. Koni (1844-1927), a famous lawyer, friend of writers, and himself the author of an important book of memoirs; Valerian F. Pereverzev (1882-?), a literary historian, founder of a Marxist-sociological school of criticism subsequently denounced as "vulgar" and "Menshevik." A furious campaign against Pereverzev was going on in the Soviet press just at the time *Michel Sinyagin* appeared. *Ed.*

> *Petals and forget-me-nots*
> *Drifted by the windowpane* . . .

The author cannot recall this entire poem "Autumn," but he does remember that the end was full of civic melancholy:

> *Oh, please tell me why and how*
> *Nature was created so*
> *Ordered sternly, so that now*
> *There's no happiness to know.*

Another poem of Michel's spoke of his love of nature and of its stormy elemental manifestations:

> THE THUNDERSTORM
> *The storm has passed*
> *A white rose branch appears—*
> *My window is ajar—*
> *Exhaling scent.*
> *The grass has now amassed*
> *Transparent tears*
> *The thunder booms afar*
> *Its power spent.*

By the way, this poem is so well written that there is a suspicion that the novice poet may have copied it from somewhere.

In any event, Michel Sinyagin said it was his, and we do not consider it our right to burden the reader with our opinions on this score.

Anyway, this poem was memorized by the whole family, and every day the old ladies would recite it to the author in a sing-song chant.

When there was company, Anna Arkadyevna Sinyagin would usher them into Michel's room and there, pointing to the Karelian birch writing table, she would sigh and say with moist eyes, "It was at this table that Michel wrote his best things: 'The Storm,' 'Petals and Forget-me-nots,' and 'Ladies, Ladies.'"

"Mama," Michel would say in embarrassment, "Stop it . . . Why do you . . . You're really such a . . ."

The guests would wag their heads and touch the table with their fingers as if in admiration or perhaps regret and then say vaguely, "Mm—yes, not bad."

A few crass souls would ask at this point how much the table had cost, and thus sidetrack the conversation into other topics, less pleasant for the mother and Michel.

The poet was also interested in women.

However, since he was under the powerful influence of the famous poets of that time, especially Blok, he did not throw away his feelings on any particular woman. He had an ideal love for some unknown woman who shone with beauty and mystery.

One wonderful poem, "Ladies, Ladies, Why Do I Love to Gaze at You," is an excellent illustration of his attitude. That poem ended like this:

> That is why I worship a woman unknown.
> And when the woman unknown becomes
>   known to me
> I'll be reluctant to gaze on a face that is
>   known,
> Reluctant to give her the ring of betrothal.

Nevertheless, the poet did become infatuated with a certain girl, and in this respect his poetic genius took a course somewhat contrary to that of his natural requirements.

Yet in all fairness, we are obliged to note that Michel felt oppressed by his earthly infatuation, finding it somewhat vulgar and trivial. The main thing that frightened him was that he might be caught somehow and forced to get married and in that way be lowered to the level of ordinary, everyday activities.

Michel counted on a different, more remarkable fate, and he thought of his future wife as some kind of astonishing lady with no resemblance whatsoever to the Pskov girls.

He did not have an exact mental image of what kind of wife he would have, but when he thought about it he would see in his mind's eye some kind of little dog, and furs, harnesses and carriages. She steps out of a carriage with a luxuriously dressed woman, and a footman, bowing respectfully, opens the door. This was the kind of picture he would draw when he thought of his future wife.

But the girl he was interested in was a more ordinary sort of girl. This was Simochka M., who had graduated from the Pskov Gymnasium that year.

4

Infatuation. Short-lived happiness. Her passionate love of the poet. The widow M——v and her character. An unexpected visit. An ugly scene. A marriage agreement.

Though he treated Simochka somewhat carelessly, Michel was nevertheless quite infatuated with her. But he never for a moment admitted the idea that he might marry her.

This was simply an infatuation, it wasn't serious and was, so to speak, a first draft of love, with which it would have been wrong to occupy one's heart completely.

Simochka was a sweet and even pretty girl, but her little face was, alas, excessively covered with freckles.

But since she did not enter deeply into Michel's life, he didn't protest against this manifestation of nature and even found it quite pleasant and not out of place.

They would go to the woods or the fields and read

poetry aloud or run races like children, frolicking and enjoying the sunshine and fragrance.

Nevertheless, one fine day Simochka discovered that she was to become a mother and informed her friend of this. She loved him with the first feeling of womanhood, and could even gaze at his face for a long time without looking away.

She loved him passionately and touchingly, understanding very well that she, a provincial girl, was not a suitable match for him.

Simochka's news profoundly stunned and even frightened Michel. He was not afraid so much of Simochka as he was of her mother, the Citizeness M., well known in the town as a very energetic, lively widow, burdened with a large family. She had something like six daughters, whom she was rather successfully and energetically marrying off, resorting for this purpose to all sorts of tricks, threats, and even assault.

She was a very dark-skinned, somewhat pockmarked lady. In spite of this, all her daughters were blond and even had white brows and lashes, probably resembling their father, who had died two years earlier.

At that time there was no alimony or divorce law, and Michel thought of the possible consequences with horror.

He definitely could not marry her. This was not the wife he had dreamed of, nor had he planned to lead a provincial life like this.

It had all seemed to him temporary, casual and ephemeral. It had seemed to him that soon he would begin a different life, full of wonderful joys, raptures, heroic deeds, and undertakings.

Looking at his friend, he thought that this girl with white eyebrows and freckles must under no circumstances become his wife. Besides, he knew her older sisters: after marriage all of them had soon withered and aged, and this too did not please his poetic soul.

He already wanted to pull up stakes and move to

Petrograd, but subsequent events kept him in Pskov.

The dark-skinned and pockmarked lady, the widow M., came to his apartment.

She came on a day and at an hour when there was no one else in the apartment, and Michel was forced willy-nilly to receive the full impact of the blow alone.

She came to his room, and at first even with some embarrassment and timidity told him the purpose of her visit.

The modest, dreamy, and delicate poet tried at first to reply just as politely, but all his words were unconvincing and failed to penetrate the consciousness of the energetic lady.

Soon the polite tone was replaced by a more animated one. Gestures and even ugly words and cries followed. They both shouted at the same time, trying to drown one another out and at the same time morally crush the other's will power and energy.

The widow M. had been sitting in an armchair, but when she grew heated she began to stride around the room, moving chairs, bookcases, and even trunks to emphasize her points. Michel, like a drowning man, tried to scramble out of the abyss. He did not surrender, but yelled and even tried to push the widow forcibly out into the next room and the anteroom.

But the widow and loving mother suddenly and unexpectedly jumped onto the window sill and said in a solemn voice that she would immediately jump out of the window onto Soborny Street and be killed if he didn't agree to the marriage. And opening the window wide, she rocked back and forth on the window sill, looking as if she might plunge to the ground at any minute.

Michel stood stunned and, not knowing what to do, began running around, first to her, then to the table, and then into the hall, clutching his head, to call for help.

Down on the street, people had already begun to

gather, pointing their fingers and giving voice to the boldest suppositions about the lady who was screaming and jumping up and down on the window sill. Anger, injured dignity, fear of scandal, and horror paralyzed Michel, and he stood crushed by the lady's extremely energetic character.

He stood by his table and with horror watched his guest, who was screeching piercingly, like a fishwife, and demanding a positive answer.

Her feet were slipping on the window sill and any careless move could result in her falling from the third floor.

It was a beautiful August day. The sun shone in a blue sky. The open window made a sunbeam dance on the wall. Everything was familiar and wonderful in its pleasant, everyday quality, and only the shouting and screeching woman disrupted the habitual order of things. Agitated and begging her to stop her outcries, Michel consented to marry Simochka.

Madame got down from the window sill quickly and willingly, and quietly asked him to excuse her somewhat, perhaps, noisy behavior, alluding to her maternal feelings and sensations.

She kissed Michel on the cheek and calling him her son, sobbed from unfeigned emotion.

Michel stood there glumly, not knowing what to say or what to do or how to get himself out of the mess. He saw the widow to the door and, crushed by the force of her will, found himself kissing her hand to his own surprise; then, in a state of total embarrassment, he said good-bye and that he hoped he would see her soon, stammering some incoherent words having little to do with the matter at hand.

The widow silently, triumphantly, and radiantly left the house, having first powdered her face and penciled in her eyebrows, which had been knocked somewhat askew.

5

*A nervous upset. Literary legacy. A meeting. The wed-
ding. Aunt Marya's departure. The death of Michel's
mother. The birth of a child. Michel's departure.*

The evening of that unlucky day, after the departure
of his uninvited guest, Michel wrote his famous poem,
afterwards set to music, "Pine trees, pine trees, answer
me . . ."

This calmed him somewhat; however, the upset had
been so significant and serious that during the night
Michel suffered from violent palpitations, causeless terror, nausea, and dizziness.

Thinking that he was dying, with trembling hands
and wearing only his drawers, the poet leaped out of
bed and, clutching at his heart, in anguish and terror
awoke his mama and aunt, who had not yet been told
the story. Without explaining anything, he began to
stammer about death, telling them he wanted to give
final instructions concerning his manuscripts. He staggered to the desk and began to pull out piles of manuscripts, looking them over, sorting them, and indicating
what, in his opinion, should be published and what
should be put aside until a later date.

Both elderly ladies, who had lost their taste for nocturnal adventures, fluttered miserably around the room,
dressed in petticoats and with their hair down. Wringing their hands, they tried to persuade Michel to go to
bed and even attempted to put him to bed by force,
considering it necessary to put a compress over his heart
or to paint iodine on his side and thus draw away the
blood which had rushed to his head.

But Michel, asking them not to bother about his,
after all, insignificant life, told them they would do bet-

ter to remember what he was saying on the subject of his literary remains.

After he had sorted out his manuscripts, Michel ran about the room dictating to his aunt Marya Arkadyevna a new version of "Petals and Forget-me-nots," which he had not yet had a chance to write down.

Weeping, and choking on her tears, Aunt Marya, writing by candlelight, smudged the paper, mixing up and miscopying stanzas and rhymes.

The feverish work distracted Michel to some extent from his illness.

The palpitations continued, but were milder, and the dizziness was replaced by utter sleepiness and apathy.

Michel, to everyone's surprise, quietly fell asleep curled up in an armchair.

After they had covered him with a blanket and made the sign of the cross over him, the old ladies went away, fearing for the poet's exceedingly nervous organism and unstable psyche.

The next day Michel arose refreshed and cheerful. But yesterday's terror had not left him, and he informed his relatives of his upsetting experience.

A tearful, dramatic scene was just at its peak when a note from Simochka arrived begging him to come see her.

He went to meet her with haughty dignity, never thinking, by the way, because of a certain decency he had, that he might use some ruse and wriggle out of his promise.

The infatuated woman begged him to excuse her mother's unworthy behavior, saying that although she personally had dreamed of joining her life with his, she would never have risked making such brazen demands.

Michel replied with dignity that he would do what he had promised, but that he did not guarantee that they would live together in the future. Perhaps he would go on living in Pskov a year or two, but ultimately he would most likely go off to Moscow or Petrograd, where he would continue his career or, in any event, try to find the kind of life he wanted.

Without insulting the girl by what he said, Michel nevertheless gave her to understand the difference, if not in their circumstances, which had been made equal by the Revolution, then, in any event, in their destinies. He said to her, "You are a little ship, and I am a big one. And a different course lies before me."

The infatuated young lady agreed with everything, gazed ecstatically at his face, and said that she did not want to bind him in any way, that he was free to do whatever he thought fit.

Reassured to some degree on this score, Michel even began to say that the marriage was a settled thing, but that he did not yet know exactly when it would take place.

They parted, as they had before, more friendly than hostile. And Michel made his way home with tranquil steps, despite the fact that the wound in his soul could not have healed so quickly.

Michel married Simochka M. about six months later, it seems to me in the winter, probably January of 1920.

The impending marriage had a great effect on the health of Michel's mother. She began to complain of the dullness and emptiness of life and pined away and grew feeble before one's very eyes, hardly getting up from her place by the samovar. In those days people's ideas about marriage were rather different from what they are now, and in the opinion of the old women it was a step taken once and for all, decisive and hallowed by mystery.

Aunt Marya was equally shaken. She was somehow offended by this course of events and said more and more often that this was not the place for her, that in the very near future she would go to Petrograd and begin her memoirs and descriptions of people she had met.

Michel, somewhat perplexed by all the goings-on, walked gloomily from room to room muttering that if he had not given his word he would send them all to hell and go wherever his fancy took him. But anyhow, everyone should know that this marriage wasn't tying him down: he was the master of his fate, he wasn't abandoning his plans and, very likely, would follow his aunt in six months or a year.

The marriage was celebrated modestly and simply.

They signed the marriage register in the commissariat and then had a modest wedding service in the Church of the Transfiguration. All the relatives on both sides walked along in a dignified manner, and all looked offended in various ways. Only the Widow M., powdered and painted, floated in her veil through the church and around Michel's apartment, where a wedding reception had been arranged. The widow did the talking for everyone at the table, proposed toasts, made speeches, and showered the old ladies with compliments, trying as best she could to maintain a mood of gaiety among the guests and thus uphold the proprieties of the wedding.

The bride blushed for her mother, both for her pockmarked face and for her penetrating voice, which gave no one any respite, and she sat at her place with her head bowed.

Michel did not lose his composure all evening, but he was nevertheless gnawed by anguish at the thought that, whatever anyone said, he had been led like a sheep to the slaughter. And that that extremely energetic woman had scared him into it, because, in fact, she would hardly have thrown herself out the window.

At the end of the dinner, after the congratulations and good wishes, smiling a crooked smile he asked the widow about it, bending close to her ear: "You wouldn't really have jumped out the window, Elena Borisovna, would you?" he said.

The widow reassured him as well as she could, declaring and swearing solemn oaths that she would certainly have jumped without fail if he hadn't given his consent. But finally, irritated by his crooked little smiles, she said angrily that she had six daughters, and if she had begun to jump out of windows for every one of them, who knows what would be left of her.

Michel looked timorously at her angry, offended face and walked away in confusion.

"It's all lies, egoism, fraud," he muttered, blushingly remembering the details.

Nonetheless, the evening passed decently and without offense to the guests, and everyday life began with its conversations about going away, about a better life, and about the fact that it was impossible to arrange one's life at all properly in this city in view of the revolutionary storm which was becoming more and more violent.

That spring, Aunt Marya Arkadyevna finally got ready and left for Petrograd. Soon she sent from there a despairing letter in which she wrote that she had been robbed on the road; her suitcase containing some of her valuables had been taken.

The letter was incoherent and confused—evidently the shock had strongly affected the elderly lady.

About this time Michel's mother died quietly and suddenly, without even managing to say good-bye to anyone or give her final instructions.

All this had a strong effect on Michel, who became quiet, timid, and even fearful. Tears were shed, but this event was soon overshadowed by another.

Simochka gave birth to a puny but sweet baby, and a new, hitherto unexperienced paternal feeling took hold of Michel.

But this didn't last long: he began to talk again of

going away, now more realistically and decisively.

In the fall, after getting a letter from Aunt Marya which he showed to no one, Michel quickly began to get ready, saying that he would give his wife and child all his movable property, of which he made them full owners.

The young lady, as much in love with her husband as before, or perhaps even more, listened to his words with horror, but didn't dare try to hold him back, saying that he was free to do whatever he wanted.

She loved him as much as ever and, whatever happened, he should know that here in Pskov there would be a person who was true to him, ready to follow him to Petrograd, to exile, or to penal servitude.

Afraid that she might trail after him to Petrograd, Michel changed the subject, but the young lady, sobbing, continued to talk about her love and self-sacrifice.

Yes, she wasn't his equal, she had always known that, but if he was ever old or crippled, or if he ever went blind or was sent to Siberia—then she would gladly answer his call.

Yes, she would even desire trouble and misfortune for him—that would make them more equal in life.

Tormented by pity and cursing himself for his faint-heartedness and for engaging in such conversations, Michel began to hasten his departure.

During this period of explanations and tears, Michel wrote a new poem, "Maiden, Do Not Hold Me Back," and began to pack his suitcases quickly and hurriedly.

He did not taste family happiness for long, and one fine morning, after he had obtained official permission to leave, he departed for Petrograd with two not very large suitcases and a basket.

6

New plans. Aunt Marya's misfortune. Michel gets a job. A new room. A new love. An unexpected catastrophe. Aunt Marya's serious illness.

Michel arrived in Petrograd and settled on Fontanka, at the corner of the Nevsky Prospect.

He temporarily moved into his aunt's room, behind a folding screen. However, he had definitely been promised a separate room as soon as one of the lodgers in the apartment died.*

But Michel wasn't really in very much of a hurry for that. His mind was crowded with other plans and ideas.

He came to Petrograd about a year or two before the NEP. Hunger and destruction, so to speak, had the city firmly in their grip. And it seemed strange that someone would come at this time to look for a better life and a career. But there were reasons for this.

In her letter Aunt Marya had carelessly told Michel that in the coming months the city of Petrograd would very likely be captured by Finland or England and be declared a free city. At that time rumors of this sort were current among the inhabitants, and Michel, excited by this news, had hurried there.

His aunt had informed him further that she had not changed her liberal convictions at all and did not oppose the Revolution, but since the Revolution was lasting so long and this was already the third year they had failed to give back her estate, it was simply disgraceful, and they would therefore have to take decisive steps themselves.

---

* In those days and to a large extent still, old pre-Revolutionary apartments of many rooms were divided up, one family or—for fortunate people—one individual per room. It was extremely difficult to find living space of any kind. *Ed.*

And so, on the strength of this, Michel came to Petrograd and settled on the Fontanka.

He found his aunt extremely changed. He simply didn't recognize her. She was an emaciated old woman with a drooping jaw and a wandering gaze.

His aunt informed him that during this time she had twice been cleaned out by thieves: first in the train and then here in the apartment. Under pretense of making an official search, some crooks had simply walked in and, showing a fake order, carried away nearly all her remaining valuables.

The formerly gay and lively lady had become a quiet, withered, and incurious old woman. She now lay on her bed most of the time and entered unwillingly into conversation, even with Michel. And if she did begin to speak, she turned the conversation mainly to her robberies, getting upset about them and talking the most utter nonsense.

However, Aunt Marya was not in actual need. On her neck was a wonderful, massive chain with a gold lorgnette. There were various rings on her fingers, and there were more than enough possessions in the room.

From time to time she sold something or other at the bazaar and lived fairly decently, also helping Michel, who had nothing and no prospect of anything.

The rumors about a free city remained unfounded. Because of this it became necessary to think about a more settled life and about one's future destiny.

Michel signed up at the labor exchange and was soon given a job.

He was assigned to the Department of Labor. And because he had no specialty and in fact didn't know how to do anything, he was given some menial, pointless work in the information bureau.

Naturally, this kind of work could not satisfy Michel's intellectual and poetic requirements. Moreover, he was a bit embarrassed and even hurt by having to do such work, which was more suitable for a frivolous young girl. Giving information and directions about where a certain room was located or where a certain comrade worked—it was simply ridiculous, not to be taken seriously, and even somewhat insulting to his masculine dignity.

Still, at that time one couldn't be too choosy, and Michel fulfilled his obligations, vaguely hoping for some kind of change and improvement. At that time he got a room in the apartment which had unexpectedly been left vacant, thanks to the departure from the country of a certain famous poet. It was a wonderful, rather small room with a view of the Fontanka and the Nevsky.

This circumstance raised Michel's spirits, and the poet even made a few rough drafts of verses, refreshing his dwindling creativity in this way.

Since he got his board and a certain amount of financial help from his aunt, he already felt quite respectable and began to go visiting, having found some former friends and comrades of his in the city.

That winter he got two short letters from Simochka.

These letters upset Michel, but, tormented by his pity for her, he couldn't quite make up his mind to answer them, finding it better not to trouble the young woman or give her indefinite hopes.

So he continued his life, finding new sources of pleasure in it.

About that time he began an affair with an extremely beautiful woman who was, it is true, rather too free in her movements and behavior.

This lady was a certain Isabella Yefremovna Kriukov, a very lovely, elegant woman of uncertain occupation, who probably didn't even belong to a labor union.

This relationship gave Michel many new worries and causes for alarm.

Not having the means to live decently, he tried to

get all he could out of his aunt, who every day grew
more morose and curt and unwilling to let Michel into
her room. She always watched his movements worriedly
while he was visiting her, evidently afraid that he might
swipe some of her belongings.

She would give him petty handouts, and Michel had
to plead, shout, and even scold his aunt, calling her a
tightwad and a bully.

This kind of disturbed existence went on for nearly
a year.

The beautiful beloved would come to Michel's on
her French heels and constantly demand more and
more new expenditures. The poet had to squirm and
rack his brains to find new sources of income.

Michel kept his job but took it more and more casu-
ally and negligently. He now gave information unwillingly, shouted at visitors, and a few times even stamped
his feet at them in irritation, sending the more im-
portunate ones to hell and beyond.

He especially disliked the dirty and clumsy peasants
who came for information: they mixed things up, con-
fusing words and expressing their thoughts inaccurately.

He would yell rudely at them, calling them uncouth
blockheads, and would frown at the smell of poverty,
the ugly faces, and the rough clothing.

Of course, things couldn't go on this way for very
long, and after several complaints Michel lost his job,
and with it his monthly ration and some income.

To tell the truth, it was a serious blow and even a
catastrophe, but the infatuated poet did not notice that
clouds were gathering over his head.

Isabella Yefremovna would come to him almost
every day, and sing various gypsy love songs in a low
throaty voice, tapping her feet in time and accompany-
ing herself on a guitar.

She was a charming young lady, born for a better
fate and a carefree existence. She despised poverty and

want and dreamed of going abroad. She tried to induce Michel to take her, dreaming of crossing the Persian frontier with him.

Because of this Michel did not look for work, and lived in hope of some kind of unforeseen circumstances. And these circumstances soon materialized.

One overcast morning when Michel went to his aunt's room to ask her for some money he needed, and had prepared himself for a quarrel, he was astonished to see the room in disorder and things moved from their places. Aunt Marya was sitting in an armchair, sorting bottles, flasks, and little boxes.

She became agitated when Michel entered the room and, hiding her phials under a handkerchief, began screeching and throwing whatever she could get her hands on at Michel.

Michel stood stupefied by the door, not daring to go any further and not understanding exactly what was going on. After a few seconds Aunt Marya, forgetting about Michel, began to spin around the room singing chansonnettes and kicking up her legs. Then Michel understood that Aunt Marya had gone out of her mind. Frightened of her and agitated, he shut the door and began to watch the mad old woman through a crack.

Her movements suddenly became quite extraordinarily youthful. Her immobility of the past year was transformed into a kind of turbulent gaiety, motion, and bustling activity.

Aunt Marya literally fluttered about the room and, running to the mirror, grimaced and made faces, throwing kisses to someone or other.

Michel stood stunned behind the door, wondering what steps to take and what to do and, as a matter of fact, what profit he could get from the whole thing.

Then, shutting the door securely, he dashed to the man in charge of the apartment to tell him about the misfortune.

7

*Aunt Marya is sent to the hospital. The insane asylum.
A merry life. A visit to Aunt Marya. The final sale of
her property.*

The apartment in which Michel was living was a communal one. It had ten rooms and thirty-odd occupants.
Michel had nothing to do with these people and even
shunned them and avoided becoming acquainted with
anyone.

Here among others lived the tailor Yolkin with his
wife, who was a factory worker, R., a bookkeeper in the
State Office for Non-Ferrous Metals, and the postal
clerk N.S., who was in charge of the apartment.

It was Sunday and all the lodgers were in their rooms.

Trying not to make any noise and talking in an excited whisper, Michel warned the superintendent of his
aunt's violent insanity.

They decided to call an ambulance and send the old
woman to the insane asylum as soon as possible, since
the situation involved a definite possibility of danger
to the tenants.

Michel dashed, gasping, to the apartment below and
telephoned for an ambulance, which arrived without
delay.

Two men in white coats went into the old woman's
room, accompanied by Michel.

Aunt Marya, who was huddled in a corner, wouldn't
let anyone come near her; she threw things and cursed
like a man.

Behind the opened doors crowded the tenants, offering advice and plans for how to catch the old woman.

Everyone spoke in whispers and watched the mad
old woman's actions with wild, unconcealed curiosity.

The white-robed male nurses, being more experienced, simultaneously strode over to the sick woman and, seizing her by the arms, clasped her tightly. The old woman tried to bite their hands but, as always happens, her violent energy gave way to calmness and even lifeless apathy.

She let them dress her in a raincoat. They put a kerchief over her head and, shoved from behind by Michel, she was successfully carried downstairs by the arms and seated in an automobile. Michel also got in, glancing with terror at his insane relative.

During the ride Aunt Marya showed hardly any signs of life, and only when the automobile arrived at the Priazhka* and stopped in front of the insane asylum did she once more become violent, refusing for a long time to get out of the car and cursing obscenely again. However, they managed to get her out and led her by the arms through the garden to the entrance.

The watchman at the gate, who was accustomed to such matters, watched this scene without curiosity and, rising from his bench, silently pointed to where they should go.

They led the old woman through a dark hallway and turned her over to the reception office.

Michel filled out a questionnaire, was given his aunt's valuables—her gold chain and lorgnette, her rings and brooch—and left the reception room in an agitated state.

He went through the garden and, finding himself suddenly on the street, stopped in indecision. For a long time he walked up and down the street and with fear and even horror kept glancing at the insane asylum and listening to the shouts and wails which reached him through the open windows.

He was on the point of going home, but, stopping on

---

* A small river in Leningrad. A psychiatric hospital is actually located on it. *Ed.*

the wooden bridge over the Priazhka, he turned around.

The insane asylum with its peeling, dirty stucco was now in full view. Behind the barred windows flitted white figures. Some of them stood motionless by the windows and gazed at the street. Others clutched the bars, trying to loosen them.

On the street below, on the bank of the Priazhka, stood normal people who gazed at the madmen with undisguised curiosity, craning their necks.

Michel went home quickly, without looking back, carrying his aunt's valuables in his hands.

The first days of shock passed, everything calmed down, and life went on as usual.

Having no job and not looking for one, Michel continued to lead a carefree existence and meet with his beloved, living off his aunt's property which had so unexpectedly passed to him.

At that time the NEP was in full swing. Stores, theaters, and movie houses were open again. Cabs and fast drivers appeared. And Michel and his lady plunged into the whirlpool of life.

They appeared arm in arm in all the restaurants and taverns. They danced the foxtrot and, exhausted and almost happy, returned home by cab, to fall sound asleep and begin the same gay, carefree existence in the morning. But at times, remembering his aunt and how he was spending her property, Michel felt pangs of conscience and promised himself each time to visit the sick woman and bring her candy and little gifts and so make her a party to the expenditures.

But the days went by, and he kept putting off his visit.

During this winter of merriment and dancing, Michel heard from the former owner and present lessee of the house in Pskov where he had lived, that his wife, having lost her child and remarried, had moved out of the apartment owing him a considerable sum. She had left some furniture, which the lessee would consider his unless Michel sent money within a month.

Reading this letter the morning after a drinking bout, Michel angrily crumpled it up and threw it under the bed, so as not to remember his former colorless life.

In this way the winter passed, and one day in February, after the last valuables had been sold, Michel set out to visit his aunt.

He bought various things to eat and, with a heavy heart and a vague feeling of terror, set out for the Priazhka.

They led Aunt Marya into a reception room and left her with Michel.

Her violent insanity had given way to quiet melancholy, and now Aunt Marya, in a white linen blouse, stood before Michel and looked at him strangely and craftily, not recognizing her nephew.

He said a few vague words and began to make energetic gestures, understandable to the insane, with his hands. Then he bowed silently and left the premises, intending never to return.

He went home light-heartedly, and now began to dispose of his inheritance with a clear conscience.

Isabella Yefremovna zealously helped him do this, urging him not to stand on ceremony or be overscrupulous about selling the entire property.

8

An unexpected misfortune. A terrible scene. Michel's nervous illness. A quarrel with his beloved. Downfall.

In April of 1925 the weather was exceptionally fair and pleasant.

Michel, wearing a light coat, and with Isabella Yefremovna on his arm, was coming out of his room, intending to take a walk along the water front and watch the ice drifting.

Locking the door and singing "Bananas, Bananas," he kept glancing at his lady.

She was showing off right there in the hallway, executing various steps with her shapely feet and dancing the Charleston.

She looked marvelously beautiful in her light-colored spring outfit, with her charming profile and curls peeping out from under her hat.

Michel gazed lovingly at her, delighted with her beauty, youth, and carefree nature.

Of course she wasn't an educated girl, capable of talking freely about Kant or the theory of probability and relativity.

She definitely didn't know anything about these matters and had no inclination for speculative science, preferring an easy, simple life. No lines of thought furrowed her brow.

Michel loved her passionately and was horrified when he compared her in his mind with his former Simochka: how could he have fallen so low as to marry such a little country chicken?

And so they went down the hall dancing the Charleston, fooling around and holding hands, and when they got to the vestibule, they stepped aside to let an entering couple pass.

It was a messenger with a book and beside him an old woman wrapped up in a winter raincoat and with a woolen kerchief tied around her head.

She was none other than Aunt Marya.

The messenger asked in a rude and jocular tone whether it was here that the now recovered Citizeness A. had lived, and if it was here, would they care to take charge of said individual.

Everything blurred before Michel's eyes. His feet were rooted to the floor, and terror deprived him of the gift of speech.

Somehow managing to make a small curlicue in the messenger's book, Michel turned his gaze to his aunt who, smiling with embarrassment, was stretching out her hand to greet her nephew.

Michel began to babble incomprehensible words and, backing toward the door, tried to block the entrance, not wanting to let his aunt go any further.

Aunt Marya stepped over to him and began to explain matters quite coherently, saying that she had been very ill, but that she was almost well now and needed only complete peace and quiet in the future.

Realizing the seriousness of the matter and not wishing to interfere in the explanations between the relatives, Isabella Yefremovna said that she would drop by tomorrow, fluttered out onto the stairs like a bird, and vanished.

Aunt Marya, accompanied by Michel, went down the hall in the direction of her door.

Michel took his aunt by the arm and, trying not to let her into the room, in which only some pitiful junk was left, pulled her toward his room saying that well, this was fine and splendid and now they'd sit down on the sofa in Michel's room and have a little cup of tea.

His aunt, however, didn't want any tea and walked stubbornly toward her own room, having firmly retained the arrangement of the rooms in her unstable mind.

She entered the room and stopped, stunned and enraged.

The author, sparing the reader's nerves, does not consider it possible to continue his description of the row and the dramatic scenes which took place during the first half-hour. The denuded room yawned with its emptiness. In one corner there stood an untouched marble washstand and a few chairs which had not been sold because they were so worn.

Aunt Marya Arkadyevna immediately grasped what had happened. An awful pallor covered her face. Then her eyes began to sparkle with anger and she furiously flung herself at Michel, once again cursing like a man and yelling out such words that even tenants who had seen a good deal of life were startled.

Her nervous excitement changed to quiet weeping, of which Michel made use. He slipped into his own room and dropped exhausted on the bed.

Toward evening it became apparent that his aunt had again gone out of her mind and was once more leaping and dancing about her room.

Hardly able to drag his legs, Michel made certain of this, completed the necessary arrangements, and went back to his room.

Toward night they took Aunt Marya back to the psychiatric hospital.

The tenants discussed all the uncertainties of fate and spoke of the advisability of bringing Michel to public trial for driving his aunt back out of her mind, with the intention of making use of her last remaining possessions.

However, the next day Michel took to his bed with a nervous fever, and so cut short these discussions.

For three weeks he lay ill, thinking that his day of reckoning had come, but his youth and blooming health saved his life.

Isabella Yefremovna occasionally visited him. Her gaiety had changed to constraint; she hardly talked to the sick man, making spiteful remarks and acting capricious.

Michel's illness produced a marked change in him. All his carefree attitude vanished, and he again became what he had been in Pskov—a melancholy and contemplative fellow.

He was again forced to think about existence and about bare necessities.

M. P. Sinyagin began to bestir himself, and several times went to the employment bureau to sign up and check in.

Not knowing how to do anything and having no spe-

cialty, he did not, of course, have much chance of finding decent work.

It's true that they offered at once to send him to the
peat bogs, saying that since he didn't have a specialty,
he would hardly get something else right away. This offer shocked Michel dreadfully and even frightened him.
What, was he to go someplace-or-other sixty versts away
and dig all kinds of filth and mud with a shovel? He
couldn't come to grips with this idea at all and, angrily
calling the young lady a pig, he went home.

He began to sell the things he had acquired when he
was well-off, and lived fairly decently for six months
without experiencing actual want.

But, of course, things couldn't continue in this way,
and it was necessary to think of something substantial.

Michel realized that he was going downhill but nevertheless tried not to think about it and to put off the decisive moment as long as he could.

At this time he had a fight with Isabella Yefremovna,
who would still drop in to see him sometimes and angrily and querulously ask what he intended to do. He
quarreled with her, calling her a vile creature and a gold
digger. And the rift even eased his existence a little.

Isabella Yefremovna was more than willing to fight
and, slamming the door, fluttered away, but not, of
course, before she had first made a scene and exchanged
strong words with him on various secondary subjects.

Michel realized his critical position, and at times it
seemed to him that life went on everywhere, and that
perhaps it would really be worthwhile for him to go to
the peat bogs. However, after he had lost his temper at
the bureau and torn up his application, he did not have
the courage to go back.

9

A pleasant meeting. New work. Gloomy thoughts. Complete poverty. Peace of mind. Benevolent nature. Help from the author. The theft of a coat with a monkey-fur collar.

Keeping a gray jacket and a fall overcoat for himself, Michel parted with almost all his belongings without regret. But the things he had kept quickly grew threadbare, and this circumstance only hastened his downfall.

When he saw that he could not extricate himself from this situation, he suddenly calmed down and started drifting with the current, worrying little about what was to come.

Once when he chanced to meet an acquaintance who was an NEP businessman and owner of a small soda-water and soft-drink factory, Michel jokingly asked him for some kind of help.

The acquaintance promised to arrange a job for him at his factory, but warned that the work would not be too suitable for a poet and that Michel would hardly accept it. It entailed washing bottles, many of which were returned to the factory in great numbers from all sorts of places, even from garbage heaps, and were restored at the factory to a state of respectability by being rinsed and washed with sand and some other kind of junk.

Michel took this job, and for several months used to walk to the Apraksin market to his job, until his overextended NEP friend went broke.

Michel's tranquillity and placid state of mind did not leave him. It was as if he had lost his old image of himself. When he came home, he would go to sleep, thinking of nothing and remembering nothing. Even when the NEP man went bankrupt and he lost his earnings,

Michel did not consider it a great misfortune.

It's true that at times—though very seldom—a reflective mood would come over him, and then he would run about his room like a wolf, biting and gnawing his nails —a habit he had acquired in the past year.

But these were really the final agitations, after which life flowed evenly, simply, and mindlessly as before.

All the tenants in the apartment already saw and knew how matters stood with Michel and avoided him, afraid that he might somehow start sponging on them.

And without noticing it himself, Michel changed from the possessor of a room to the tenant of a corner, since a certain unemployed fellow, who occasionally walked around selling sunflower seeds, had moved into his room.

In this way almost a whole year passed, and life drew Michel in deeper and deeper.

The tailor, Yegor Yolkin, had several times come into Michel's room and in a drunken voice asked him to look after his baby, since the tailor had to go out and his wife was out wandering no one knew where on account of her good looks and youth.

Michel would go into the tailor's room and uninterestedly watch the half-naked child crawl along the floor, frolicking, playing, and eating cockroaches.

Days followed one another, and Michel still did not undertake anything.

He began to beg now and again. Going out onto the street, he once stopped on the corner of Nevsky Prospect and the Fontanka and stood there calmly waiting for handouts. And, looking at his face and at the suit which had once been respectable, passers-by were not loath to give him a kopeck or two.

When this happened, Michel bowed low, and his face broadened in a courteous smile. While he was bowing, he would keep his eyes on the coin, trying to guess its worth as quickly as possible.

He did not notice the change in himself; his soul was at peace as before, and he was no longer aware of feeling any misery.

The author thinks that it's absolute nonsense when many writers, even famous ones, describe various kinds of heart-rending torments and sufferings of individual citizens who have fallen on bad times, or, let's say, those who lay it on with a trowel when they describe the state of mind of a woman of the streets, crediting her with God knows what, until they themselves are amazed at what they have turned out. The author thinks that, for the most part, nothing like this happens.

Life is arranged—how can I say it?—far more simply, better, and more suitably. There is exceedingly little in it of profit to the writer of *belles-lettres*.

A beggar stops worrying the moment he becomes a beggar. In the same way the millionaire, accustomed to his millions, doesn't think about the fact that he is a millionaire. And a rat, in the author's opinion, does not suffer excessively from the fact that it is a rat.

Well, it's possible that the author has talked out of turn on the subject of the millionaire. The author doesn't feel sure of what he said on the subject of the millionaire, the more so that, for the author, a millionaire's life passes as if in a mist.

But this doesn't alter the matter, and life's majestic picture is still in force.

At this point there comes to mind that fact which the author has already had the pleasure of communicating in his Introduction. Man is excellently made, and eagerly lives the kind of life that is being lived.

The author does not, of course, wish to say that man —in this case, M. P. Sinyagin—has turned into wood and stopped having feelings, desires, a love of good food, and so on.

No, he did have all these, but they were already in a different form and, so to speak, on a different scale, on a level with his opportunities. He didn't suffer because of it. Even his former disappointments, it seemed, were greater and more severe.

The author's emotions at the greatness of nature beggar description!

The author must say further that during those years he himself was in considerable need, and his aid to his relative was negligible. However, many times he gave him as much as he could.

But once, in the author's absence, Michel removed from the coat rack someone else's coat with a monkey-fur collar and sold it, literally for a few kopecks; after which he completely stopped coming to see the author and even stopped greeting him.

Of course, the author understood his miserable situation and didn't say a single word about the theft, but Michel, conscious of his guilt, would simply turn away from the author and didn't want to enter into any conversation with him.

The author is forced to mention this with extreme, so to speak, embarrassment and even with an awareness of a certain fault on his own part, although, actually, he was not in any way to blame.

10

Life begins tomorrow. A day's take. The flophouse. Forty years. Unexpected thoughts. A new decision.

The author deems it necessary to forewarn the reader that our story has a happy ending and that good fortune finally brushes our friend Michel Sinyagin with its wings once more.

But in the meantime we will have to touch on some unpleasant experiences for a little while longer.

Months and years passed. Michel Sinyagin worked as

a beggar, and almost every day he set out for this work of his, either to the Gostiny Dvor or to the Passage.*

He would lean against a wall and stand erect and motionless, without stretching out his hand, but bowing whenever suitable candidates passed by. He would collect about three rubles a day and sometimes even more, and led a tolerable and even well-fed life, at times eating sausage, headcheese, white bread, and so on. However, he was in arrears on his apartment, not having paid his rent for almost two years, and this debt now hung over him like Damocles' sword.

People began to come to his room and openly ask when he was leaving. Michel would say something indefinite and give vague promises and time limits.

But one evening, not wanting to go through any new explanations or be subjected to further demands, he did not return home, but went to spend the night in a hostel, or, as some people say, in a flophouse, on Liteyny Prospect.

At that time, on Liteyny Prospect, not far from Kirochnaya, there was a hostel where for twenty-five kopecks one could get a separate bunk, a mug of tea, and soap for washing. Michel spent the night there a few times and finally moved there completely with his few belongings.

Then began a completely well-ordered and tranquil life without the expectation of any miracles or opportunities.

Of course, collecting money wasn't a very easy job. You had to stand on the street and constantly take off your cap in all kinds of weather, chilling your head. But so far there was nothing else, and Michel didn't look for another way out.

---

* Gostiny Dvor—an imposing eighteenth-century building on Nevsky Prospect in Leningrad, built to accommodate great numbers of small shops and now containing a department store. The Passage (*Passazh*) is a similar building nearby, built in 1848. *Ed.*

The hostel, with its coarse occupants and unceremonious ways, however, significantly changed Michel's retiring character.

Here a quiet and retiring character was of no value and even—how shall I say it?—worthless.

The rude and strident voices, the cursing, the thefts, and the fisticuffs either forced such people to leave or compelled them to make suitable changes in their behavior. And Michel changed in a short time. He started saying coarse phrases in his hoarse voice, and, defending himself from the curses and laughter, attacked in his own turn, cursing shamelessly and even getting into fights.

In the mornings he would clean up his bunk, drink tea and, often not bothering to wash, go hurriedly to work, sometimes taking with him a tattered canvas brief case which somehow marked him as a member of the intellectual class and showed his background and lost opportunities. His bad habit of recent years—chewing his fingernails—became completely unbreakable, and he bit his nails until they bled, without noticing it or trying to break the habit.

Another year passed in this way, making it almost nine years since the day he came to Petrograd. Michel was forty-two years old, but his puffy face, long, graying hair, and the torn rags on his back gave him an even older and more down-at-the-heels appearance.

In May of 1929, while he was sitting on a bench in the Summer Garden and warming himself in the spring sunshine, without noticing it, and to his own surprise—somehow hastily and with a kind of fear—Michel began to think about his former life: Pskov, his wife Simochka, and those former days which now seemed to him astonishing and even fantastic.

He began to think about them for the first time in several years, and as he thought, he felt that old nervous chill and agitation which had long ago left him, and

which he had always felt when he wrote poetry and
thought about elevated subjects.

And that life which had once seemed degrading to
his dignity now shone with a kind of uncommon purity
of its own. That life which he had left behind now
seemed to him the very best part of his existence. Moreover, his former life now appeared to him as a sort of
ineffable wonderland.

Terribly agitated, Michel began to dart around the
garden, waving his arms and running along the paths.

And suddenly a clear and comprehensible thought
made his whole body tremble.

Yes, right away, today, he'd go to Pskov to see his
former wife, his loving Simochka with her dear little
freckles. He would meet his wife and spend the rest of
his life with her in complete accord, love, and tender
friendship. How strange that he hadn't thought of this
before. There, in Pskov, remained a person who loved
him, who would simply be happy that he had returned.

Thinking of this, he suddenly burst into tears from
all the many emotions and raptures which had seized
him.

And, remembering those pathetic and yet happy
words she had said to him nine years before, Michel
wondered in amazement how he could have scorned
her and how he could have acted so basely as to abandon a sweet, loving woman who was ready to give up
her life for him.

He remembered now every word she had said. Yes, it
was she who had said it to him; she had implored fate
to make him sick, old, and lame, supposing that he
would then return to her. And now that had happened.
He was sick, old, tired. He was a beggar and a vagabond,
and had lost everything in life. Now he would return to
her and, kneeling, ask forgiveness for everything he had
done to her. Why she, his Simochka, had said that she
would follow him to prison and to penal servitude.

Even more excited by these thoughts, Michel started to run, not knowing where he was going.

The fast walking quieted his agitation somewhat and then, hurrying and not wanting to waste a single minute, he set out for the station and, once there, began to inquire when and from what platform the train left.

But remembering that he didn't have more than one ruble, he fearfully asked the price of a ticket.

A ticket to Pskov cost more, so he bought a ticket to Luga, deciding that he would somehow manage to get from there to his fairy-tale city where his happiness had once been cut short.

He arrived in Luga at night and fell sound asleep on a heap of ties piled up by the track.

As soon as it was light, trembling all over from the morning chill and his excitement, Michel leaped up, ate some bread, and started walking in the direction of Pskov.

11

The return. Native ground. Michel's meeting with his wife. Dinner. New friends. A job. New dreams. An unexpected illness.

Michel followed a path along the railroad tracks, at first moving with a certain hesitancy and lack of confidence. Then he lengthened his pace and walked for several hours without stopping or thinking about anything.

His agitation and joy of the day before had changed to dull indifference and even apathy. And now he walked along, moving simply out of inertia, without any will or especial desire.

It was a beautiful May morning. The birds twittered, flying loudly out of the bushes Michel passed.

The sun grew hotter and hotter on his shoulders. His

feet, wrapped in strips of cloth and shod in galoshes, grew blistered and tired from the unaccustomed walking.

At noon, exhausted, he sat down on the edge of a ditch and, hugging his knees, stayed there a long time without moving or changing his position.

The motionless white clouds on the horizon, the young leaves on the trees, the first yellow dandelions reminded Michel of his best days and made him grow momentarily excited again about the opportunities he was on his way to encounter.

But this joy was tempered. It wasn't the joy and ecstasy that had taken hold of him in the days of his youth. No, he was a different person with a different heart and different thoughts.

The author doesn't know whether it is true, but a girl who had finished a course in stenography the previous year told him that in Africa there are certain animals like lizards which, when attacked by a larger creature, cast off some of their innards and run away. They then find a safe place where they can collapse and lie in the sun until they grow themselves new organs. And the attacking animal stops chasing them, satisfied with what he has been given.

If this is so, then the author's delight at this phenomenon of nature fills him with new trembling and thirst for life.

Michel did not resemble this kind of lizard: he himself had sometimes been the attacker; he had seized his enemies by the scruff of the neck, but in the scuffle he seemingly also lost part of himself and now sat, empty and almost indifferent, not knowing why he had set out and whether he had done the right thing. He was now even vexed at having started on such a long journey without having found out anything about Sima or exchanging letters with her. Why, perhaps she wasn't even alive.

In two days, resting almost every hour and spending the nights in the bushes, Michel came to Pskov, the sight of which made his heart beat faster.

He walked through the familiar streets and suddenly found himself at his house, looking sadly through the windows and clenching his hands until they hurt.

And then agitation took hold of Michel once more.

Opening the gate with his shoulder, he went into the garden—into that small, shady garden in which he had once written verses and Aunt Marya, Mama, and Simochka had sat.

Everything was the same as it had been nine years ago, except that the garden paths were neglected and overgrown with grass.

The same two tall pine trees grew by the back porch, and the same doghouse with no dog in it stood near the shed.

For a few minutes, Michel stood motionless, like a statue, contemplating these old and dear sights. His heart beat anxiously and rapidly. But suddenly someone's voice brought him back to reality. An old woman, wearing a white kerchief and looking worriedly at him, asked why he had come here and what he wanted.

Fumbling for words and fearfully mentioning some names, Michel began to ask about the former tenants, the lessee and his former wife, Serafima Pavlovna.

The old woman, who had moved there not long before, could not satisfy his curiosity, but told him Simochka's present address.

In half an hour Michel, trying to restrain his pounding heart, stood before a house on Basmannaya Street.

He knocked and, without waiting for a reply, opened the door and stepped over the threshold into the kitchen.

A woman in an apron was standing near the stove, holding a plate in one hand; with her other hand, which held a fork, she was removing some cooked meat from a boiling pot.

The woman looked angrily at the person who had come in and, frowning, was ready to shout at him, but the words suddenly froze on her lips.

She was Serafima Pavlovna, she was Simochka, very much changed and aged.

Oh, she had become very thin. Her formerly plump little body and round face were unrecognizable and unfamiliar. She had a yellowish, withered face and short, cropped hair.

"Serafima Pavlovna," Michel said quietly, and went over to her.

She gave a terrible cry, the metal plate fell from her hands and rolled along the floor with a clang and a clatter. The cooked meat fell back into the pot, splashing the boiling soup.

"My God," she said, not knowing what to do or what to say.

She picked up the plate and, muttering, "Right away . . . just let me tell my husband . . ." disappeared behind a door.

In a moment she came back to the kitchen and, timidly stretching out her hand, asked Michel to sit down.

Not daring to go over to her and terrified about his appearance, Michel sat down on a stool and said that here he was at last, that this was the kind of unhappy and terrible condition he was in.

He spoke softly and, waving his hands, kept sighing and getting confused.

"My God, my God," muttered the young woman, wringing her hands in anguish.

She looked at his puffy face and the dirty rags of his suit and wept soundlessly, not knowing what to do.

But just then Serafima Pavlovna's husband came out of a room and, apparently knowing already what had happened, silently shook Michel's hand, went off to one side, and sat down on another stool near the window.

He was citizen N., the manager of a co-operative, a

middle-aged or even elderly man, rather stout and pale. He understood at once what was going on and, immediately sizing up the situation and his unexpected rival, he began to speak in a ponderous and edifying manner, advising Serafima Pavlovna to look after Michel and help him out.

He suggested that Michel settle temporarily in their house, in a summer room on the top floor, since it was already warm enough.

The three of them dined together at the table and, eating boiled meat with horseradish, now and then exchanged a few words about what further steps to take.

Serafima Pavlovna's husband said that it was very easy to find work at present, that there were fewer and fewer unemployed people at the labor bureau, so he didn't envision any difficulty on that score. And this state of affairs would very likely make it possible for Michel to choose among several job offers. In any event, he didn't have to worry about that. He'd live with them temporarily, and then they'd see about the future.

Michel, not daring to raise his eyes to look at Simochka, thanked him and greedily devoured meat and bread, cramming big pieces into his mouth.

Simochka didn't dare look at him either and only glanced at him occasionally and from time to time muttered, "My God, my God."

They fixed up the room on the top floor for Michel, moving in a canvas cot and a small dressing table.

Michel was given some shirts and underwear and an old wool-and-sateen jacket, and, after he had washed and shaved, he joyfully arrayed himself in clean clothes and joyfully gazed in the mirror for a long time, thanking his benefactor every minute.

His violent agitation and the journey on foot had exhausted him terribly and he slept like a log in his upstairs room.

At about eleven at night, understanding nothing and

not knowing where he was, Michel woke up and leaped from his bed.

Then, when he remembered what had happened, he sat down by the window and began to recall all the words that had been said that day.

Well, it seemed as though everything was all right. It seemed as though peace and happiness would begin again. And, thinking this, he suddenly felt hungry.

Remembering the satisfying, nourishing dinner which he had swallowed greedily and undiscriminatingly, Michel went quietly and stealthily downstairs to the kitchen to rummage around there for something to restore his strength.

He walked carefully into the kitchen over the creaking floor boards and, without turning on the light, began to fumble around at the stove with his hand, looking for something to eat.

Serafima Pavlovna came out into the kitchen, her whole body trembling, thinking that Michel had come to talk with her, to have it out and say the things that hadn't yet been said. She went over to him, took his hand, and began to stammer something in an excited whisper.

At first very much frightened, Michel grasped what had happened and, holding a piece of bread in his hand, silently listened to the words of his former beloved.

She told him that everything was changed, that everything was over, that when she thought about him, to be sure, she still loved him, but that it now seemed to her unnecessary and superfluous to take any new steps or make any changes. She had found her quiet refuge and sought nothing more.

In the simplicity of his heart, Michel failed to hear in her words the half-formed question, the note of yearning and anxiety, and he answered, not without joy, that he too expected no changes, but that he would be happy and content if she would let him live in their house for the time being.

Chewing his bread, he gratefully pressed her hands, asking her not to bother or worry too much about him.

After they had conversed in this way for about an hour, they parted, he calm and almost joyful, she disturbed, shaken, and even shattered. She had vaguely counted on something. And she had expected to hear something different.

Going back to her room, she cried a long time over her past and her whole life and over the fact that everything passes except death.

In a few days, when he had eaten his fill and made himself presentable, Michel found a job in the administration of co-operatives.

His extinguished life returned, and at dinner he would share his impressions of the day and make various plans about future possibilities, saying that now he had begun a new life and that now he understood all his mistakes and all his naïve fantasies, and that he wanted to work, struggle, and make a new life.

Serafima Pavlovna and her husband chatted with him in a friendly way, sincerely happy about his success and his regeneration.

Days and months passed in this way, and nothing darkened Michel's life.

But in February 1930, he suddenly fell ill with influenza which was complicated by pneumonia, and he died in the arms of his friends and benefactors.

Simochka cried terribly and for a long time was terribly upset, blaming herself for not having told Michel everything she had thought and wanted to tell him.

Michel was buried in the cemetery of a former monastery. His grave is decorated with fresh flowers even today.

September, 1930

NERVOUS PEOPLE

Not long ago, a fight took place in our communal apartment. Not just a fight, but an out-and-out battle. On the corner of Glazova and Borova.*

Of course, they put their hearts into the fight. The veteran Gavrilich almost had his last remaining shank hacked off.

The main reason is—folks are very nervous. They get upset over mere trifles. They get all hot and bothered. And because of that they fight crudely, as if they were in a fog.

As for that, of course, they say that after a civil war people's nerves always get shaken up. Maybe so, but from that theory the veteran Gavrilich's noggin won't heal up any faster.

For example, a certain tenant, Marya Vasilyevna Shchiptsova, comes into the kitchen at nine in the evening and lights her primus stove. She always lights her primus about that time, you know. She drinks tea and applies hot compresses.

So she comes into the kitchen. She sets her primus stove in front of her and lights it. But, damn it all, it doesn't light.

She thinks, "Why shouldn't it light, the devil? It might have got clogged with soot, damn it."

And she takes a wire brush in her left hand and is about to clean it, when another lady tenant, Darya Pet-

* Slang for Glazovskaya and Borovaya, two Leningrad streets. The former has been renamed Konstantin Zaslonov Street. *Ed.*

rovna Kobylina, whose brush it is, looks to see what she took, and remarks, "By the way, dear Marya Vasilyevna, you can put the brush back where it came from."

Shchiptsova, of course, flares up at these words and answers, "Please," she says, "Darya Petrovna, go and choke to death on your brush. It disgusts me even to touch your brush, let alone pick it up."

Now, of course, Darya Petrovna Kobylina flared up at these words. They began a real conversation. They made a lot of noise, racket, and clatter.

A husband, Ivan Stepanich Kobylin, whose brush it is, appears at the noise. A big, healthy kind of man, even a bit paunchy, but, in his own way, nervous.

So this Ivan Stepanich appears and says, "I," says he, "I now work exactly like an elephant for thirty-two rubles and a few kopecks in the co-operative store. I smile at the customers," says he, "and weigh out baloney for them, and out of that," says he, "out of my hard-earned pittance I buy myself wire brushes, and I don't care for, that is, I won't permit any extraneous personnel to make use of these brushes."

And here a noisy discussion arose once more over the brush. All the tenants, of course, shoved their way into the kitchen. They bustle about. The retired soldier Gavrilich shows up too.

"What's all this noise," he says, "and no fight?"

Immediately after these words a fight was certified. It began.

But our kitchen, you know, is a narrow one. Not fit for fighting. It's a tight squeeze. There are pots and primus stoves all around. And now twelve people have shoved their way in. For instance, you want to smack one guy in the puss, and you land on three at once. Then, it's obvious, you keep stumbling over everything and falling. Even if you had three legs you wouldn't have a chance of standing up on that floor, let alone if you're a one-legged veteran.

But the retired soldier, old scrapper that he was, shoved his way into the thick of things anyhow. Ivan Stepanich, whose brush it is, shouts at him, "Keep out of this trouble, Gavrilich. Watch out, or they'll tear off your remaining leg."

Gavrilich says, "So I'll lose my leg!" says he. "But I just can't," says he, "go away this minute. They've just smashed my fighter's pride till it bled."

And really, just at that minute someone gave him one across the mug. Even then he doesn't go away, he jumps on him. And at the same time someone hits the veteran over the dome with a pot.

The retired soldier falls—bam!—on the floor and lies there. All by his lonesome.

At this point some parasite rushed out for the militia.

A cop appears. He shouts, "Get your coffins ready, you devils, I'm going to shoot right away!"

Only after these fateful words did the people come to themselves a bit. They dashed to their rooms.

There's a pretty kettle of fish for you, they thought. Why did we, esteemed citizens, get into such a scrap?

The people dashed to their rooms, and only the retired soldier Gavrilich did not dash. He's lying on the floor, you know, all by his lonesome. And blood is dripping from his skull.

The trial took place two weeks after this event.

And the People's Judge turned out to be a nervous kind of man too—he gave us another walloping.

1925

THE LADY ARISTOCRAT

Fellows, I don't like dames who wear hats. If a woman wears a hat, if her stockings are fuzzy, if she has a lapdog in her arms, or if she has a gold tooth, such a lady aristocrat, to my mind, is not a woman, but just a void.

But there was a time when I felt the attractions of an aristocratic lady. When I went out walking with one and took her to the theater. It was in the theater that it all happened. There, in the theater, she unfurled her ideology to its full length.

I first saw her in the yard of our building. At a meeting. I saw such a stuck-up number standing there. Stockings on her feet. A gold tooth.

"Where are you from, citizeness?" I asked. "What's the number of your room?"

"I live in Number Seven," she said.

"Please," I said, "just go on living."

Immediately I took a terrible liking to her. Began calling on her in Number Seven. At times I would visit her in my official capacity. "How is it with the obstruction in the water pipe and the toilet?" I would say. "Do they work?"

"Yes," she would reply, "they work."

And she wrapped herself in a flannel shawl, and not another murmur. Only slashed me with her eyes. And flashed the gold tooth in her mouth.

I kept going to her for a month—she got used to me. Began answering in more detail. That the water pipe worked all right, and thank you, Grigory Ivanovich.

As time went on, we began taking walks along the street. We would go out into the street and she would order me to offer her my arm. I would take her on my arm and drag myself along like a pike swimming. I couldn't think of anything to say. I didn't know, and felt ashamed in front of people.

Well, once she said to me, "Why do you keep dragging me through the streets? My head's dizzy. Now, as my escort and as a man of position, you ought to take me somewhere, to the theater, for instance."

"That can be done," I said.

The very next day the Communist Party cell sent some tickets for the opera. I got one ticket, and Vaska, the locksmith, offered to give me his.

I didn't look at the tickets, but they were different kinds. Mine was for the orchestra and Vaska's up in the highest gallery.

So we went. Sat down in the theater. She sat in my seat and I in Vaska's. I sat up in the crow's nest and I couldn't see a damned thing. But if I leaned forward over the rail I could see her. Not very well, though.

I got more and more bored and then went downstairs. It was intermission. And during intermissions she takes a stroll.

"Hello," I said.

"Hello."

"I wonder whether the water pipes work here," I said.

"I don't know," she answered.

And traipsed off in the direction of the buffet. I followed her. She walked around the buffet and looked at the counter. There was a plate on the counter, and cakes on the plate.

I, like a goose, or an unclipped bourgeois, fussed around her and proposed: "If you wish to eat a cake, don't be bashful. I'll pay."

"*Merci.*"

She slithered right up to the plate, with her sexy walk,

and zup! grabbed a cream puff and started munching away.

And I had next to no money at all on me. At the most enough to pay for three cakes. She ate and I groped uneasily in my pockets, counting with my hand how much money I had. Not enough to put in your eye.

She ate up the cream puff and zup! grabbed another. I almost screamed. Restrained myself. Such bourgeois bashfulness overcame me. Here was I, a lady's escort, and no money!

I walked around her like a rooster. She laughed and angled for compliments.

I said, "Isn't it time to go back to our seats? Maybe the bell has rung."

She answered, "No."

I said, "On an empty stomach—isn't that too much? They might make you sick."

"No," she replied, "I'm used to them."

And took a fourth.

Then the blood rushed to my head. "Put it back!" I cried.

She was scared. Opened her mouth. In her mouth the golden tooth shone.

By this time I was sore as hell. I don't give a damn, I thought; I won't be taking walks with her any more anyway.

"Put it back," I said, "you lousy bitch!"

She put it back.

And I said to the proprietor, "How much for the three cakes she's eaten?"

The proprietor acted nonchalant; he was playing it cool. "For the four cakes she's eaten," he said, "you owe so and so much."

"What do you mean, four?" I asked. "The fourth one is there on the plate."

"No," he replied. "It may be on the plate, but there's a tooth mark on it and it's been crushed by her fingers."

"What tooth mark?" I said. "Come on, now. That's all your imagination."

The proprietor was still playing it cool, circling his hands in front of his face.

Some people, of course, gathered around. Experts. Some said there was a tooth mark, others—not.

I turned my pockets inside out—all sorts of junk fell out on the floor—the bystanders guffawed. But it wasn't funny to me. I counted the money.

When I had counted it, I found there was enough for four cakes, right on the nail!

By God, I had started all this argument for nothing!

I paid and then addressed myself to the lady. "Finish eating it, citizeness, it's paid for."

The lady didn't move. She was too bashful to go on eating.

At this point some old fellow butted in. "Let me have it," he said. "I'll finish eating it."

And he did, the son of a bitch. And on my money!

We went back to our places. Saw the opera to the end. Then home.

And when we got home she said to me, "That's all the lousy tricks I'll stand from you. People who haven't any money don't go out with ladies."

And I replied, "Happiness doesn't lie in money, citizeness, excuse the expression."

That's how we parted.

I don't like lady aristocrats.

1923

THE BATHHOUSE

THEY say, citizens, that the public baths in America are excellent. There, for instance, a citizen goes to the bathhouse, takes off his clothes, puts them in a special box and goes happily off to wash. He has nothing to worry about—there'll be no loss or theft, he won't even take a check for his things.

Perhaps some uneasy American will say to the bath attendant, "*Gutbye*, please look after my things."

And that's all.

This American will wash, then return to the dressing room and his clean underclothes are handed to him—all washed and ironed. His undershirt, believe me, is whiter than snow. His drawers are repaired and patched! What a life!

Our baths aren't so bad, either. But worse. However, you can get washed in them.

The only trouble with our baths is the checks. I went to the bathhouse last Saturday (after all, I can't go to America for a bath). They handed me two checks. One for my underwear, the other for my coat and hat.

But where is a naked man to put those checks? Honestly, there's no place for them. You have no pockets. All you have is a belly and legs. What a nuisance those checks are! You can't tie them to your beard.

Well, I tied a check to each leg so as not to lose them right off. And went into the bath.

Now the checks flop around my feet. It's uncomfortable to walk with them. But walk you must. Then you must find yourself a bucket. How can you wash without a bucket? Can't be done.

I look for a pail. I notice a citizen who's washing himself in three buckets. He stands in one, soaps his head in another, and holds onto the third with his left hand so no one will swipe it.

I pulled the third pail toward me, trying to appropriate it, but the citizen wouldn't let go of it.

"What's the idea," he said, "stealing other people's buckets? If I smack you between the eyes with this bucket you won't like it."

I said, "This isn't the czarist regime, that you can go around bashing people with buckets. What selfishness!" I said. "Other people want to get washed, too. This isn't a theater."

But he turned his back to me and went on washing.

What's the use of standing over his soul? I thought. He'll be washing for three days on purpose.

I went further on.

An hour later I noticed a gaffer who had looked away and taken his hand off his bucket. Maybe he had bent down for his soap, or just gone off into a daydream—I don't know. Only I got his bucket.

Now I had a pail, but there was no place to sit down. And to wash standing up, what kind of a wash is that? It's no good at all.

Well, all right, I had to stand there and wash, holding my bucket in my hand.

And all around me—Heaven help us—there was a regular laundry. One fellow was washing his pants, another scrubbing his drawers, a third wringing out something else. And there was such a din from all that laundering that you don't feel like washing. You can't even hear where you're rubbing the soap! It's a mess!

To hell with them! I thought. I'll finish washing at home.

I went back to the dressing room. They handed me

my clothes in exchange for the check. Everything is mine, I see, except the pants.

"Citizens," I said, "mine had a hole right here, and look where it is on these."

"We're not here to watch over holes. This isn't a theater," the attendant replied.

Well, all right. I put on the trousers and go to get my coat. They give me the coat . . . they demand the check. And I've left the check on my leg. Have to undress again. I take off the trousers . . . look for the check . . . it's gone. The string is there on my leg, but the paper is gone. Washed away.

I offer the string to the attendant. He won't take it.

"I can't hand out coats for string," he says. "Any citizen can cut up string. There wouldn't be enough coats to go around. Wait until the customers have gone," he says. "I'll give you what's left."

"My dear friend," I say, "what if they leave me a piece of junk? This isn't a theater," I say. "Give me the coat that fits this description. One pocket is torn, the other is missing. As for buttons, the upper one is there, and no one expects any lower ones to be left."

He gave it to me after all. Didn't even take the string. Suddenly I remembered: I had forgotten my soap.

I went back in. They wouldn't let me enter the washroom in my coat.

"Undress," they say.

"Citizens, I can't undress a third time. This isn't a theater. At least let me have the price of the soap."

They won't.

All right, they won't. I leave without the soap.

The reader, perhaps, may be wondering what sort of bathhouse I am describing. Where is it? What's the address?

What bathhouse? The usual sort, where the price of admission is ten kopecks.

1925

DOG SCENT

MERCHANT Jeremiah Babkin's fur coat had been stolen. Merchant Jeremiah Babkin raised a howl. He was sorry to lose that coat. "The coat, citizens," he said, "was a very good one. It's a pity. I won't spare money to find the criminal. I'll spit in his face."

So Jeremiah Babkin sent for a bloodhound. A man in a visor cap and knickers appeared, and with him a dog. A great big dog, brown, and with a pointed nose and an unfriendly look.

The man pushed the dog toward the footprints beside the door, said "P-s-s-t," and stepped back.

The dog smelled the air, took in the crowd with his eyes (a mob, of course, had gathered), and suddenly stepped up to Fekla, the woman from Number Five, and began smelling her hem. The wench tried to hide in the crowd. The dog held onto her skirt. The woman twisted aside, the dog after her. He held onto the woman's skirt and wouldn't let her go.

Here the wench flopped down onto her knees in front of the detective. "Yes," she cried, "I'm caught. I won't deny it. Five pails of yeast. That's right," she said. "And the apparatus is there, too. It's all correct. You'll find it in the bathroom. Take me to the militia."

The people, of course, gasped. "And the fur coat?" they asked.

"About the fur coat," she said, "I know nothing. I have no knowledge whatsoever. But the rest, it's the truth. Take me away. Execute me."

Well, they took the woman away.

Again the detective took hold of his dog, pushed him toward the footprints, said "P-s-s-t," and stepped aside.

The dog cast his eye around, took a whiff of empty air, and stepped up to another citizen, the chief of the house committee.

The chief blanched and fell on his face. "Tie me up, good people," he said. "Respectable citizens, I've been collecting the money for the water, and that money I've spent on my own whims."

The tenants, naturally, fell upon the chief and began tying him up. But the dog in the meantime approached a citizen from Number Seven and tugged at his trousers.

The citizen turned pale and collapsed in front of the people. "I'm guilty," he said. "Guilty. I tampered with the birth date in my labor book. I am of military age and should be serving in the army and defending the fatherland. But here I am living in Number Seven and making use of electrical energy and other communal services. Seize me."

The people were dazed. What an extraordinary dog, they thought.

Merchant Jeremiah Babkin blinked, looked around, took out some money, and handed it to the detective. "Take this dog of yours back to the swine he came from," he exclaimed. "Let my fur coat go, the son of a bitch."

But the dog was right there, standing in front of Babkin and wagging his tail. Jeremiah Babkin became confused. He stepped to one side. The dog followed, went up to him and began to smell his galoshes.

Babkin began to stammer and turned pale. "Well," he said, "it seems God's found out the truth; I'm a son of a bitch and a crook. And the fur coat, citizens, wasn't mine at all. I snitched it from my brother. I weep and sob."

At this point the people took off pell-mell in all directions. The dog hadn't time to sniff the air any more. He grabbed two or three who happened to be close and held them. They all confessed. One had lost some government money at the card table, another had clonked his wife with a flatiron, the third told about something that can't even be reported.

The people dispersed. The yard was empty. Only the detective and the dog remained. The dog came up to the detective, wagging his tail. The detective went pale and fell down before the dog. "Kindly bite me, citizen," he said. "I'm paid three rubles for your food and I keep two for myself."

What happened after that I don't know. I took a powder so as to stay out of trouble.

1924

THE CRISIS

THE other day, citizens, a load of bricks was carted through the streets. Honest to God!

My heart began beating with joy. We're building, citizens! Those bricks weren't being carted for nothing. A house is being built somewhere. It's begun—abracadabra, let's keep the evil eye off it!

In twenty years, perhaps, or even sooner, each citizen may have a whole room to himself. And if the population doesn't increase too rapidly—if, for instance, abortions are authorized for everybody—then even two rooms. Maybe even three per head. With a bathroom.

Then we will really live, citizens! In one room, say, we'll sleep, in another receive guests, in the third— something else . . . We'll find lots of things to do living such a free life!

But in the meanwhile things aren't so good with living space. It's pretty skimpy because of the crisis.

I've lived in Moscow, my friends. Only recently returned from there. I've experienced the crisis myself.

I arrived in Moscow. Walked through the streets with my bundles. And there was simply no place to go. Not only no place to stay, but I couldn't even leave my bundles anywhere.

For two weeks I walked the streets with my bundles. I grew a beard and gradually lost all my things. Then kept on walking without my things, traveling light. Still looking for a room.

At last, in one house, I met a little man going down the stairs.

"For thirty rubles," he said, "I can fix you up in a bathroom. The apartment used to be a gentleman's . . . with three toilets and a separate bathroom. You can live in the bathroom. It has no windows, of course, but it does have a door. And water is handy. You can fill yourself a whole tubful of water and dive in it all day if you wish."

"I'm no fish, comrade," I replied. "I have no need to dive. I would like to live on dry land. Reduce the price because of the dampness."

He answered, "I can't, comrade. I'd be glad to do it, but I can't. It isn't my responsibility. It's a communal apartment. And a fixed price has been set for the bathroom."

What could I do? I said, "All right. Take your lousy thirty rubles and let me move in quickly. For three weeks I've been tramping the sidewalks," I said. "I'm afraid I might get tired."

Well, they let me move in. I began living.

It really was a gentleman's bathroom. Wherever you step, a marble tub, hot-water tanks, brass fixtures. But no place to sit down. The only place is on the edge of the tub, but you'd be likely to slip and fall in.

I built myself a cover of boards for the tub and went on living there.

A month later, by the way, I got married. I found a good-natured young spouse. But she had no room of her own.

I was afraid she might turn me down on account of the bathroom, and I might never see family happiness and coziness. But it was all right, she didn't refuse. She just frowned a little and said, "Lots of nice people live in bathrooms. Besides, you can put up a partition. This side," she said, "might be our boudoir and the other our dining room."

"We could put up partitions, of course," I replied, "but the other tenants, the devils, won't permit it. They've decreed: no subdividing."

Well, all right. We lived as is.

Less than a year later a little child was born to me and my wife. We named him Volodka and went on living. We bathed him right there in the tub—and lived on.

And you know, it worked out quite well. The child got bathed every day and didn't catch cold.

There was only one inconvenience—in the evenings the communal tenants would troop into the bathroom to have their baths.

On these occasions we had to move our whole family out into the hall.

I begged the tenants, "Wash on Saturdays, citizens. After all, you can't take a bath every day. When are we going to have time to live? Please think of our position."

There were thirty-two of these scoundrelly tenants. And they all cursed terribly. Even threatened to bash my face in.

So there was nothing that we could do. We lived as best we could.

After a while my wife's mother arrived from the provinces—into our bathroom. She settled down behind the hot-water tank.

"I've been dreaming for a long time," she said, "of rocking a grandchild. You cannot refuse me that diversion."

"I won't refuse," I answered. "Go on, old lady, rock away. Rock yourself straight to hell. You can fill the tub with water," I said, "and dive in with your grandson."

And I said to my wife, "Perhaps, citizeness, you're expecting more relatives? Just tell me, don't keep me in suspense."

"My little brother might just come for Christmas vacation . . ."

I didn't wait for the brother to arrive; I took off from Moscow. I am sending money to my family by mail.

1925

POVERTY

WHAT is the most up-to-date word these days, fellows, huh?

These days the most absolutely up-to-date word is, of course, electrification.

To light up Soviet Russia with light—that is a business of enormous importance, I don't deny it.

But even so, for the time being it has its dark sides. I don't say, comrades, that it costs too much. It doesn't cost much. It doesn't cost much more than money. I'm not talking about that.

But about this:

I lived, comrades, in an enormous building. The whole house was lighted with kerosene. Some people had a mere wick in a can of oil, others a small lamp, and still others, the poorest ones, would light their abode with a church candle. It was terrible!

And then they started putting in the electric light. Soon after the Revolution.

The first to put it in was the director of the building. Well, so he put it in and that was that.

He's a quiet man—doesn't let on what he's thinking. But he started walking about looking strange and kept blowing his nose thoughtfully. But he still didn't let on what he felt.

Then our dear landlady, Elizaveta Ignatyevna Prokhorova, one day announced that she wanted to bring light into our half-dark flat.*

* It should be remembered that large pre-Revolutionary flats

"Everyone," she said, "is doing it. The building director himself has put it in. Why should we lag behind? Besides," she said, "it's economical. It's cheaper than kerosene."

All right! We, too, put in the light . . .

We put in the light, lit up the place, and—ye gods! —what dirt, what filth all around!

Before, you went to work in the morning, came home at night, drank your tea—and to bed. You couldn't see much by the kerosene light. But now that we're all lit up, what do we see? Over there, someone's torn slipper lying around; in another place the wallpaper is ripped off and hangs in tatters; here a bedbug races along, running away from the light; or you see some indescribable rag, a gob of spittle, a cigarette butt, and a flea capers about . . .

Ye gods! It's enough to make you cry. It's downright sad to look at such a spectacle.

In our room, for instance, we had a couch! I used to think it wasn't such a bad couch, even a pretty good one. I often sat on it in the evenings. But today I turned on the electric light—ye gods! Ouch! What a couch! Pieces hanging down, pieces sticking up; pieces coming out from inside. I can't sit on such a couch— my soul protests.

"I'm not so rich after all," I thought. I felt like running out of the house. It hurt me to look at such things. I didn't have the heart to work.

And the landlady, Elizaveta Ignatyevna, I noticed, was also walking about sadly, rattling about in the kitchen, tidying it up.

"Why are you puttering about?" I asked her.

She threw up her hand. "My dear man," she said, "I didn't have any idea that my life was so ugly."

I took a look at the landlady's chattels—really, I thought, it's pretty miserable. Her furniture was awful.

---

had been divided up, usually one family to a room, all sharing the kitchen and bath. *Ed.*

And everything in a mess, debris, garbage, and rubbish. All of it lit up in bright light, you couldn't help seeing it.

I started coming home at night in a pretty poor mood. I would come in, turn on the light, admire the lamp, and climb into bed.

Afterwards I changed my mind, got my pay, bought some whitewash, and set to work. I tore off the wall-paper, drove out the bedbugs, wiped off the cobwebs, fixed up the couch, painted up and bespangled every-thing—and my heart sang and rejoiced.

In general the results were good and even excellent. I felt wonderful.

But our landlady Elizaveta Ignatyevna took a some-what different way out. She cut the wires in her room.

"My dear man," she said, "I have no desire to live in the light. I don't want to light up such modest furni-ture for the bedbugs to laugh at."

I argued with her and begged her, but it was no use. She kept repeating: "I don't want to live in the light. I haven't got the money to fix things up here."

I told her, "But I'll do the fixing for you almost for nothing!"

But she wouldn't do it. "With that bright light of yours," she said, "I'd have to spend the whole day from morning to night cleaning and straightening up. I'll get along without light the way I did before."

The building director also argued with her. And even swore at her. He called her a degenerate petty-bour-geois. But she didn't give in. She just refused.

Well, let her have it her own way.

Personally, I am living by electric light and am end-lessly pleased.

I think the light will sweep out all our trash and rub-bish.

1925

PATIENTS

Man is a pretty queer sort of animal. No, it really can't be true that he is descended from the apes. Old man Darwin must have gone a little haywire on that one.

Because human actions, if I can put it that way, are so utterly and purely human. There's not the least resemblance to the animal world.

If some animals were talking in whatever language it is they talk, they would hardly have such a conversation as I recently heard.

It was at a clinic. Outpatient reception room. Once a week I get treated there for internal illnesses. By Dr. Opushkin. He's quite a good guy and an understanding doctor. He's been treating me for five years. And everything's fine, my illness isn't any worse.

So I come into the clinic. They mark me number seven. No help for it, I have to wait.

So I sit down on a couch in the corridor and wait.

And I hear the other patients waiting there talking to one another. It's a quiet enough sort of conversation; voices are low, and no fighting.

There was one meaty-faced fellow sitting there in a short overcoat who said to his neighbor, "Listen, pal, that isn't much of a sickness you have—a hernia. It's a spit-and-wipe-it-off sort of sickness, that's all. Don't mind the fact that I'm a bit fat in the face. All the same, I'm a very sick man. I've got a kidney disease."

The neighbor said in a slightly offended tone, "It's not only a hernia I've got. I have weak lungs. Besides that I've got a fatty tumor by my ear."

The fat-faced man said, "That's not much. How can you compare such troubles with kidneys?"

Suddenly a lady in a flannel kerchief waiting there said, "So you've got kidney trouble. I have a niece who had kidney trouble and she's all right. She could sew and even iron. With a face like yours your illness can't be very dangerous. You couldn't die from an illness like that."

The fat-faced man said, "Couldn't die! Did you all hear? She says I couldn't die from this disease. A lot you know about it, citizen. And still you stick your nose into medical discussions."

The citizeness said, "I'm not belittling your illness, comrade. It's a genuine illness. I recognize that. But I am telling you that maybe I've got an illness a little more serious than those kidneys of yours. I've got cancer."

The fat-faced man said, "Well, so it's cancer. It all depends on what kind of cancer. Some kinds of cancer are completely harmless. You can get over them in six months."

At this undeserved insult the lady citizen turned quite pale and began to tremble. Then she waved her arms and said, "Cancer in six months! Did you ever hear the like? I don't know what kind of cancer you've seen. You've grown yourself quite a face on that illness of yours."

The fat-faced citizen wanted to reply to this insult in some appropriate way, but he waved his hand and turned away.

At this point another citizen waiting there gave a laugh and said, "Really now, citizens, what sort of things are you bragging about here?"

The patients looked at him and began to wait their turns in silence.

LYALKA FIFTY

Who was the fool who said that life is hard in Petrograd? Life is marvelous there. Nowhere is there such gaiety as in Petrograd. As long as you have some money. Without money, however . . . You'll have to admit, without money it's no go. And when will that wonderful time come when everything will be handed out free?

In the evenings people walk along the Nevsky Prospect. They don't just walk; they stop at corners, take a look at the girls, prance about with spring-like airs, feet dancing, and back to the corner again . . . And every time you need some money. Every time it takes financing.

"Hey, come on over, you lucky boy, come over here. Give a girl a cigarette . . ."

Maxim doesn't move. Maxim has a job on his mind. He is straightening out the details in his head, just how it will be. Maxim has a very remarkable job in the offing. A dangerous one. He won't get caught . . . the very idea makes a cold shiver run over him . . . he'll come out on top. He'll become terribly rich. And take Lyalka Fifty for himself. Just like that. He'll take her.

A wonderful girl is Lyalka Fifty. If she worships money Maxim will give her money. He won't grudge it. She needs lots of it, that's true. A girl like that costs quite a bit. A rug, if you please, on the wall, another great big one on the floor, and in a white cage a tropical bird—a parrot. With sugar to eat . . . Ha . . . ha . . .

Naturally you have to have money, that is, until such time as everything will be gratis.

And speaking of Lyalka Fifty, here she is herself. Coming up the street, her heels clicking on the sidewalk.

"Hello there, Lyalka Fifty . . . and how are you? Don't you recognize me, darling?"

She recognizes him all right. Why shouldn't she know him?—he's a well-known hoodlum. But there's no profit in talk. Lyalka is on her way to the Nevsky; Maxim may be going in another direction.

Lyalka is not very nice today. She doesn't feel like polite conversation. There's no need for it.

Maxim went up close to her and looked into her beautiful bright eyes. "I'll come to see you," he said, "tonight. With big money. Wait for me. Be sure."

Lyalka smiled, Lyalka laughed. But she didn't believe him. Just telling lies, the crook. And why should he lie? No good reason.

But while saying good-bye she held onto his hand just in case.

Maxim went to Nikolayevskaya and stood there by the building he wanted, mulling over the tiniest details of his plan. "Let me have ten rubles' worth of groceries," he will say to Granny Avdotya. The old girl will hand over the stuff, and after that it's in the bag. There won't be any hitch. And if there's no hitch, Maxim will go to Lyalka Fifty. He will lay out the money. "Take it," he'll say. "Please. I don't give a damn for the stuff. Here's a wad for a kiss . . ."

In the meantime Lyalka came out onto the Nevsky, stood on the corner, swung her hips, did a little dance, and immediately annexed a Chinese plutocrat.

Funny, of course, to take up with a Chink. But it might even be interesting. And the Chinaman speaks marvelous Russian. "I'm coming to your place, my pretty one," he says.

2

Chalked on the door: TAILOR. Only no tailor lives there. And never has lived there. The person who lives there is Granny Avdotya, the black marketeer. She has a small secret store. It was she who wrote the inscription on the door to deceive passers-by.

To this Granny Avdotya went Maxim. He gave the right knock on the door, marked TAILOR in chalk. When the door was opened, all of Maxim's plans went awry. It was not Avdotya herself, but her husband who stood before Maxim.

Maxim stepped over the doorsill, muttering something unintelligible. He kept thinking hard—what was to be done? His whole plan was wrecked, damn it all. What a time for this lousy husband to appear . . .

Maxim uttered some silly words: "Granny Avdotya, let me have ten rubles' worth . . ."

Granny's husband snickered and stepped back into the room. Maxim followed him.

While Granny's husband fixed the weights on the scales, Maxim kept trying to figure out what to do. Now that his plan had failed, it was not easy to find a way out of the fix.

Granny's husband inquired, "What sort of goods would you like, pretty boy?"

"Give me all kinds of things."

"Something on the sour side, perhaps?" he queried. "Sauerkraut?"

"Something sour, Granny Avdotya."

Granny's husband began dipping out the kraut from the barrel and Maxim took a quick look around. Maxim grabbed a weight, a three-pound weight, and smashed the husband on the head.

Granny's husband fell right there by the barrel. He

still held the fork in his hand, with kraut on it.

Maxim rushed to the counter. On it stood a cash box. He rummaged with trembling fingers. He pulled out the money. There wasn't much of it. Where the hell was the money?

He searched the room. No money anywhere. All sorts of unwanted things kept coming through his hands, a comb, for instance, or a plate.

Where the devil could that money be?

Someone at the outside door gave the signal knock.

Maxim covered Granny's husband with a piece of sacking and went to the door. He listened. Should he open it or not? I'll open. He calmed his heart and opened the door.

A tiny little old man came in and said in a thin voice, "I want to see Granny Avdotya . . ."

Maxim replied, "Granny Avdotya isn't here. So long now . . . Go away . . . Do me the favor . . ."

He said it and then noticed that the three-pound weight was still in his hands. He was afraid that the man might have noticed the weight. He shoved it into his pocket to hide it. The old geezer, meanwhile, squeezed his way sideways into the room.

"I'll wait here," he said, "for Granny Avdotya. She has such splendid potatoes . . . Oh, and her sauerkraut must be splendid, too. Yes, by God, marvelous sauerkraut."

The old boy turned out to be a big talker, and full of book learning. Maxim would have liked to collect his thoughts, but the old man went on, "Well, they say everything will be free. I agree. Only, according to my scientific view—take communal feeding, for instance. Excuse me, but it's absolute nonsense, nothing but lies. I agree with everything, but . . . on this point . . . I'll come to Granny Avdotya. Can't help it. Excuse me . . . Let's say I have to work with my head . . . Then I need fish. There's phosphorus in fish . . .

And you, if you have to talk a lot, you need a milk diet
. . . And then they tell me—communal feeding. Out
of one trough . . . Yes, young man, I agree with everything, but leave me Granny Avdotya. It's all lies . . ."

"I won't argue with you." Maxim became uneasy.

He stepped out into the hall . . . down the stairs
three steps and into the street . . . He felt for the
money . . . it was in his pocket.

Too little money! Where was the rest of it?

He walked off with a swaying gait.

3

"Come over here, you lucky boy. Come on over!"

"Give me a cigarette."

Maxim was not interested in the girls. He stopped on
a corner and leaned against a window.

Maybe he hadn't killed the man. He hadn't hit him
too hard on the head with the weight. But he might
have hurt him, and Maxim felt sorry . . .

Maxim stood there and turned over his thoughts.
And his thoughts began taking a happy turn.

He looked around him like a king. He searched for
Lyalka Fifty. Lyalka wasn't there.

A little blond stood on the corner, pulling on a cigarette and smiling at Maxim. She had on high boots, up
to the knees, and a silk frou-frou skirt . . . Every time
she turned around the silk rustled. Every time she
laughed it rustled . . .

Rustling, she came up to Maxim and took him gently by the hand.

Suddenly there was a lot of noise all around, people
running.

"It's a raid, girls!" cried blondie, and darted away
from Maxim into an iron gateway.

Maxim followed after the blond, but a man caught

up with him. A man in spurs. He clicked his spurs and rattled his saber and in his hand he held a five-shooter.

Maxim shivered and took flight. His heart pounded. He ran across the Ligovka.

There was a fence in his way. Maxim jumped the fence; his feet landed in a rubbish pile. He jumped over the rubbish. He ran for a ways and then fell in the mud. But he didn't fall of his own accord.

"Somebody tripped me," said Maxim and groped for his money.

Suddenly Blackie was sitting on him. Not just sitting, but choking him.

"Let me go!" gurgled Maxim. "Let me go! I can't breathe!"

Blackie eased his grip.

Blackie sat on him and began a conversation: "I see a man running across rubbish piles. Wait a minute, I think. There must be a reason. That's right. Either a thief or running from a thief. . . . Hand over the money?"

He searched in all Maxim's pockets. "Oh, there goes a packet . . . Oh, he's found another . . . Oh . . ." Again the bastard choked him.

"And what is this?"

"A weight," said Maxim and remembered Granny's husband.

"A weight," snickered Blackie, and hit Maxim on the head with it. "Run now, and don't look around. Run, you crook, I tell you . . . Wait a minute . . . You forgot your weight . . . Here, take it."

Maxim took the weight and ran. He ran with it for a little while and sat down on a rubbish heap.

But why hit a man on the head?

4

Maxim sat on the heap for a while, quieted his beating heart, and then went back to town. He should have been going home, but his feet took him to the Goncharnaya, to Lyalka Fifty. Maxim went to the Goncharnaya. The streets were empty . . . And his heart was empty . . .

There stood Lyalka's white house.

Hello there, Lyalka's dear house!

Maxim went up the stairs, knocked and went into Lyalka's room.

There was a rug on the wall, another great big one on the floor, and in a white cage a parrot.

Lyalka was sitting on a Chinaman's knees, playing with a Chinese mustache with her pretty hand.

"Did you bring it?" asked Lyalka and went up to Maxim.

"I did," said Maxim quietly. "Only send that Chinese character away. It hurts me to look at him . . ."

The Chinaman understood Russian marvelously. He took offense and stood up. Then he spilled a cup of coffee onto the rug.

"Why," he asked, "should I endure such a resolution? I'll go away and I won't pay."

The Chinaman left and slammed the door. Maxim stepped up to Lyalka. He bent over Lyalka and kissed her cheek.

"I don't have any money, Lyalka Fifty."

"Ah!" Lyalka screamed. "You don't have any money?"

"No money. Have a pity on me, Lyalka. It's hard for me. Take me without money. Say you feel sorry for me."

Lyalka screeched, "And my Chinese losses? Who will make up for them?"

"Have you got a heart?" asked Maxim, and sat down on the rug, embracing Lyalka's legs. "Have you got a heart, I ask you. Are you sorry for your bird? Are you sorry for your parrot?"

Lyalka hit Maxim with all her strength. Everything went black before Maxim's eyes.

Maxim groaned. He groaned and got up from the floor.

He felt the weight in his pocket. He took out the weight. He wanted to hit Lyalka on the head with it —but he didn't. His hand didn't dare.

Maxim took a swing and smashed the bird cage.

The parrot screeched terribly and Lyalka screamed thinly. Maxim threw down the weight and again sat down on the rug. "Say you feel sorry for me, Lyalka Fifty."

1922

PELAGEYA

PELAGEYA was an illiterate woman. She couldn't even write her name.

Pelageya's husband, however, was a responsible Soviet official. Although he had once been a simple peasant, five years of living in the city had taught him an awful lot. Not only how to write his name but a hell of a lot besides.

And he was very much embarrassed to have an illiterate wife.

"You, Pelageyushka, ought at least to learn how to write your name," he used to say to Pelageya. "My last name is an easy one. Two syllables—Kuch-kin. And still you can't write it. It's awkward."

Pelageya used to wave it aside. "There's no use in me trying to learn it now, Ivan Nikolaevich," she would answer. "I'm getting on in years. My fingers are getting stiff. Why should I try to learn to make those letters now? Let the young pioneers learn it. I'll make it to my old age just as I am."

Pelageya's husband was a terribly busy man and couldn't waste much time on his wife. He wagged his head as if to say, "Oh, Pelageya, Pelageya!" But he kept his mouth shut.

But one day Ivan Nikolaevich did bring home a special little book.

"Here, Polya," he said, "is the latest teach-yourself primer, based on the most up-to-date methods. I am going to show you how myself."

Pelageya gave a quiet laugh, took the primer in her hands, turned it over, and hid it in the dresser, as if to say, "Let it lie there. Maybe our grandchildren will have some use for it."

But then one day Pelageya sat down to work. She had to mend a jacket for Ivan Nikolaevich. The sleeve had worn through.

So Pelageya sat down at the table. Took up her needle. Put her hand under the jacket and heard something rustling.

Maybe there's money in there, Pelageya thought.

She looked and found a letter. A nice clean one, with a neat envelope, precise little handwriting, and paper that smelled of perfume or eau de Cologne. Pelageya's heart gave a leap.

Can Ivan Nikolaevich be deceiving me? she thought. Can he be exchanging love letters with well-educated ladies and making fun of his poor, dumb, illiterate wife?

Pelageya looked at the envelope, took out the letter and unfolded it, but since she was illiterate she couldn't make out a word.

For the first time in her life Pelageya was sorry that she couldn't read.

Even though it's somebody else's letter, she thought, I've got to know what's in it. Maybe it will change my whole life, and I'd better go back to the country and work as a peasant.

Pelageya started to cry and began thinking that Ivan Nikolaevich seemed to have changed lately—he seemed to be taking more care of his mustache and washing his hands more often. Pelageya sat looking at the letter and squealing like a stuck pig. But read the letter she couldn't. And to show it to someone else would be embarrassing.

Pelageya hid the letter in the dresser, finished sewing the jacket, and waited for Ivan Nikolaevich to come home. But when he came Pelageya didn't let on that anything had happened. On the contrary, in calm and even tones she talked to her husband and even hinted that she had nothing against doing a little studying and that she was fed-up with being a dark and illiterate peasant.

Ivan Nikolaevich was overjoyed to hear it. "That's just fine," he said. "I'll show you how myself."

"All right, go ahead," said Pelageya.

And she stared fixedly at Ivan Nikolaevich's neat, clipped little mustache.

For two solid months Pelageya studied her reading every day. She patiently pieced together the words from the syllables, learned to form the letters, and memorized sentences. And every evening she took the treasured letter out of the dresser and tried to decipher its secret meaning.

But it was no easy job.

It was the third month before Pelageya mastered the art.

One morning when Ivan Nikolaevich had gone off to work, Pelageya took the letter out of the dresser and started reading it.

It was hard for her to decipher the small handwriting, but the scarcely perceptible scent of perfume from the paper spurred her on.

The letter was addressed to Ivan Nikolaevich. Pelageya read:

Dear Comrade Kuchkin:

I am sending you the primer I promised. I think that your wife should be able to master this vast erudition in two or three months. Promise me, old boy, that you'll make her do it. Explain to her; make her feel how disgusting it is to be an illiterate peasant woman.

To celebrate the anniversary of the Revolution, we are liquidating illiteracy throughout the whole Republic by all possible means; but for some reason we forget about those closest to us.

Be sure to do this, Ivan Nikolaevich.

    With Communist greetings,

                            Maria Blokhina

Pelageya read this letter through twice. Then, pressing her lips together sorrowfully and feeling somehow
secretly insulted, she burst into tears.

LUCKY

Sometimes you feel like going up to somebody you don't know and asking, "What kind of a life have you had, old boy? Are you satisfied with it? Have you been lucky in your life? Come on, take a look at what you've lived through!"

Since I came down with catarrh of the stomach, I've been asking a lot of people these questions. Some of them get out of it with a joke. "I'm alive," they say, "and chewing my bread." Others start to fib. "I've got a marvelous life," they say. "I don't ask for anything better. I get the number six salary and I'm pleased with my family."

Only one man ever answered the question seriously and in detail. That was my dear friend Ivan Fomich Testov. By profession he's a glazier. No ordinary man. With a big beard.

"Lucky?" he asked me. "Of course I've been lucky."

"Well," I asked. "How big a stroke of luck was it? A real big one?"

"I don't know whether it was a big one or a little one. But I've remembered it all my life."

Ivan Fomich smoked two cigarettes, collected his thoughts, for some reason winked at me, and began to tell his story.

"My dear friend, it was twenty or maybe twenty-five years ago. I was young and good-looking then, wore a bristly mustache, and was very pleased with myself. And you know, I kept waiting for my luck to strike. In the meantime the years passed and nothing special happened. I hardly noticed how I got married, how I fought with my wife's relatives at the wedding, and how after that my wife had a kid. Or how later on my wife died. Everything went quietly and smoothly. There wasn't anything specially lucky about it.

"But once, on November 27, I went off to work and after work, toward evening, I went into a pothouse and asked for some tea.

"I was sitting there drinking out of the saucer. And thinking, Well, the years are passing and I haven't had much in the way of luck.

"And I hadn't thought very long before I heard a lot of shouting. I turned around and saw the owner waving his arms and the bus boy waving his arms and in front of them a soldier of the Czar, trying to sit down at a table. The owner was pulling him away from the table and not letting him sit down.

" 'No, no,' he was shouting. 'You soldiers are not allowed to sit down at tables in taverns. If I let you I'll have to pay a fine. So get along with you, that's a good fellow.'

"But the soldier was drunk and kept on trying to sit down. And the boss kept pushing him away. The soldier started talking about his parents.

" 'I'm as good a man as you are,' he shouted. 'I want to sit at a table.'

"Well, some of the customers lent a hand and tossed the soldier out. But the soldier picked up a paving stone from the road and slammed it through the plate-glass window. Good-bye, window!

"And it was real plate glass, four yards by three, and terribly expensive.

"The owner's arms and legs drooped. He sat down on his heels, wagged his head back and forth, and was afraid to look at the window.

" 'Look at it, citizens,' he shouted. 'That soldier has

ruined me. Today is Saturday, tomorrow is Sunday—two days without glass. You can't find a glazier just like that, and without glass my customers will take offense.'

"And his customers really did take offense. 'There's a draft,' they said, 'coming through the hole he broke. We came here to sit in a nice warm place, and now look at that great big hole!'

"Suddenly I put my saucer down on the table, put my cap on the teapot to keep it from getting cold, and walked carelessly up to the owner.

" 'Honored man of business,' I said, 'I am a glazier.'

"He was overjoyed, counted the money in the cash drawer, and asked, 'What is this joy ride going to cost me? Can't you paste the pieces back together again?'

" 'No, dear man of business,' I said. 'You can't do anything with the pieces. You need a new three-by-four piece of glass. And the price of such a piece of plate glass is seventy-five rubles. The broken pieces I take. The price, dear man of business, is right, no padding and no bargaining.'

" 'What's wrong with you?' said the owner. 'Have you stuffed yourself silly? Sit down there at your table and drink your tea. If it's that expensive I'd better stuff a quilt into the hole instead.'

"And so he told his wife to run up to their apartment and get a featherbed.

"So they take the featherbed and stick it in the hole. But the featherbed keeps falling out, first on the inside and then on the outside, and makes the customers laugh. But some of them even get annoyed and say that it's dark and not pleasant to drink tea like that.

"Finally, one of them got up and said, 'Featherbeds I can look at at home. What do I need yours for?'

"In the end the owner came up to me and asked me to go for the glass right away and gave me the money.

"I didn't even finish my tea but clutched the money in my hand and ran off.

"When I got to the glass store they were closing. But I pleaded with them and they let me in.

"Everything worked out just as I had thought or even better. The glass cost thirty-five rubles for a three-by-four piece, and five more to have it hauled over there, forty in all. And so I installed the glass.

"I finished my tea with sugar, asked for a plate of chowder and afterwards some hundred proof. I ate it all up and left the pothouse a bit unsteady on my feet. But I had thirty rubles clear profit in my hands. If I wanted I could blow them and if I wanted I could do anything I wanted.

"Boy, did I do a lot of drinking then. I spent two months at it. Besides that I bought a silver ring and some warm shoe linings. I also wanted to buy some trousers and a blouse, but I ran out of money.

"So, my dear friend, as you see, I did have a great big stroke of luck in my life. But only once. All the rest of my life has passed smoothly, without much luck coming my way."

Ivan Fomich fell silent and once again winked at me for some unknown reason.

I looked enviously at my dear friend. I never had any luck like that in my life.

But maybe I just didn't notice it.

A SUMMER BREATHER

You'll agree that to have a separate apartment of your own is after all a pretty bourgeois thing to do.

People ought to live together, in a collective family, and not lock themselves up in some private fortress.

People should live in communal apartments. Where there are plenty of people around. Someone to talk to, consult with, fight with.

Of course, communal apartments have some faults too. For instance, the electricity causes inconveniences.

It's a problem how to settle the bill. How much each person should pay.

Of course in the future, when our industry gets into full swing, every resident in every corner will be able to have two meters to himself. Then the meters themselves will measure how much electricity has been consumed. And then, of course, life in our apartments will shine forth like the sun.

But in the meantime we have quite a bit of inconvenience.

For example, we have nine families in our apartment. One power line. One meter. At the end of the month something has to be done about the bill. And then, naturally, there are some pretty big disagreements and sometimes fist fights.

All right, you will say, charge everybody so much per light bulb.

All right, by the light bulb. But perhaps some dutiful resident turns on his light only for five minutes to get undressed or to catch a flea. While some other resident sits there with the light on chewing on something until twelve o'clock at night. And doesn't want to turn off the electricity. Even though he's no artistic designer.

And there is sure to be another fellow, an intellectual, of course, who will literally sit staring at some book until one in the morning or later, without caring about the people around him. And maybe he'll even put in a more powerful light bulb. And read his algebra, as if it were daylight.

An intellectual like that might shut himself up in his lair and boil water or cook spaghetti on an electric plate. You've got to understand that!

One of our tenants was a stevedore and he really went off his rocker over all this. He stopped sleeping and kept watch to find out which tenants were reading algebra at night and warming food on electric plates. And they finally took him away. He was batty.

And after he went nuts, his room was taken by a relative. That's when things really began to go wild.

Every month the meter used to show that we owed something like twelve rubles. Even in the most decrepit sort of month it wouldn't be more than thirteen. That, of course, was under the supervision of the tenant who went crazy. His inspection system was very well organized. As I told you, he literally didn't sleep for nights on end and was on the alert every moment, darting here and there and threatening to chop you up with an axe if he found you using too much current. The surprising thing is that more of the tenants didn't go out of their minds from living like that.

And so we never used to owe more than twelve rubles a month.

And now suddenly we owe sixteen! Ouch! What had happened? Who was the dog who had burnt up so much juice? It was either a hot plate or an electric heater or something like that.

People argued and swore, but in the end they paid.

A month later it was sixteen again. The honest ones among the tenants said straight out, "It's no good living here. Here we poor bastards have been economizing on current while some other people have been using as much as they like. So we are going to do the same thing. We too are going to burn electric plates and cook spaghetti."

The next month the meter showed we owed nineteen rubles.

The tenants gasped, but nevertheless they paid the bill and then they really began to turn on the heat. Nobody ever put out the lights. They read novels. And burned their hot plates.

The next month the bill was twenty-six rubles.

Then the orgy really began. To make a long story short, when they ran the bill up to thirty-eight rubles, the power had to be turned off. Everyone refused to pay. One intellectual pleaded with us and clung to the power line, but we paid no attention to him. The power was cut off.

Of course, this was only done temporarily. No one is opposed to electrification. We had a communal meeting at which it was officially stated that no one was against it and that in the future we would petition to be hooked onto the power line again. But in the meantime things are all right as they are. Besides, it's getting on toward spring. It's light. And then it will be summer. Little birds singing. No worries about light. No artistic designs to draw. And as for the next winter, we'll see. Maybe in the winter we'll have the current turned on again. Either we'll work out an inspection system or something else.

But in the meantime we need a summer's rest. We're tired out from all this apartment business.

THE MERRY-GO-ROUND

My friends, I think we're going to have to wait a while before we make everything free. We can't do it yet.

Let's suppose everything is free. But we have no sense of proportion. We think if things are free, Come on, boys, let's grab everything wholesale.

Once during the May Day celebrations they put up a merry-go-round in our town square. Well, of course, people crowded around. And a certain young fellow happened to be there. Looked like a country boy.

"What is this," the young fellow asked. "You can ride free?"

"Free!"

So the fellow got on the merry-go-round, climbed onto a wooden horse, and rode until he almost died.

They took him off the merry-go-round and laid him down on the ground. Nothing wrong—after he caught his breath he came to, all right.

"Well, is it still spinning?" he asked.

"Still spinning."

"I think I'll take another little ride," he said. "Seeing as it's free."

Five minutes later they took him off the horse again.

Again they laid him on the ground.

He was puking like pouring from a bucket.

So you see, fellows, we're going to have to wait a while.

THE WATCHMAN

A FELLOW I know told me this amusing story. Unfortunately I've forgotten the name of the village where these events took place. It was something like Krivyuchi or Krivushi. In short, it was somewhere near Pskov.

So in this village there was a church named "St. Nicholas by the Gravestones." That's what they called it. I can't explain why.

And so the church named "St. Nicholas by the Gravestones" had a watchman named Morozov.

And people in Pskov found out that this watchman was being exploited in the cruelest way. He was employed without insurance, without regular wages, and without days off. Maybe they might give him a measly three rubles a month like throwing it to a dog, and tell him to shift for himself.

But the watchman himself never complained. To cap it all he was a religious old fellow and felt some sort of calling to take this job in the church. Maybe he just liked being a church watchman. Maybe it gave him some religious satisfaction. But still, this didn't alter the fact that he was being exploited.

And so to this village of Krivushi was dispatched a detachment of Young Communists. Three Komsomol lads were assigned to investigate the situation and find out whether it was true that the watchman wasn't getting paid.

So the lads arrived in the village and took that watchman in hand. "How are things," they asked him. "Apparently you're not being paid wages, since you are not insured. And if that's true, you can claim back pay for all the time you have worked there."

The old fellow got very excited when he heard this. "Let me see," he said. "How am I to understand what you say? You mean I can claim money from them?"

"Yes," they told him, "you can claim the difference. For instance, if you got five rubles a month, you can claim the difference between that and the minimum wage."

"How much is the minimum wage?"

"It must be something like twenty or eighteen."

"And I can get that for three years?"

"Yes," they said, "you can. How much did they pay you?"

At this point the watchman's psychology really split in two. On the one hand, he wanted very much to latch onto that cash. On the other hand, it seemed a bit awkward to strike such a blow at the church. But all he had to do was to say that they had only paid him a three-spot and immediately an unheard-of sum would appear in his pocket. On the other hand, it was awkward and shameful and his religious feelings suffered. In general it would be an irreparable blow to the church.

So the old geezer got very upset and worried and began chewing on his beard with his teeth. He started muttering something and turning his pocket inside out.

Later on the money won out after all.

"Yes," he said. "You can't deny it. What sort of pay did I get from them? They tossed me a lousy three rubles and I was supposed to eat shit for the rest of the month. They're always on the lookout to skin somebody alive."

The Komsomols said, "Marvelous! We'll draw up a petition and start the case moving up the ladder."

"That would be a great favor," the old man said.

"Let the money be pried out of them. For three years I've guarded this church for nothing. It's just not nice at all."

So the Komsomols went home and soon after that brought suit against the priest for two hundred and eighty rubles.

No pen could describe what happened then. There were scenes, excitement, shouts, and utter confusion.

But there was no way out. The watchman had to be insured, and little by little he had to be paid off.

I should add that this happened just before Easter.

It was a time when all sorts of services were being held, the church bells were ringing, and confessions and that sort of religious fol-de-rol were going on. And along with them such an uproar.

And so the last week in Lent, during the confessions, Watchman Morozov came to the priest with a troubled soul to make his confession. He modestly took his place in line along with the other parishioners.

Of course the priest saw him and came out from behind the screen. "Morozov, I'm not going to confess you. You've bankrupted my church, and there won't be either confession or absolution for you."

"Father," the watchman said. "That was a civil matter according to Soviet law, but confession is part of religion and you can't refuse it to me, since Church and State are now separated."

"Get out," the priest said. "I'm not going to confess you. If you will take back your insolent demands, then we can talk differently."

They both got very excited and started accusing each other.

"All right," said the watchman. "If you don't want to, don't. To hell with you! This isn't the only church in the world. I can go to the next parish. But I can't do without confession. My sins are tormenting me."

So he took a horse and rode sixteen versts.

Now the picture is like this. Watchman Morozov still works in this church. But he doesn't allow himself any religion there. He doesn't even cross himself and demonstratively walks around inside the church with his cap on.

But for praying and other minor religious matters he goes to the next parish. And so the dear man manages without giving up his religion. Let him.

THE CZAR'S BOOTS

This year there was a sale at the Winter Palace of various objects that had belonged to the czar. The Museum Fund or some such was conducting the auction. I might be wrong about that, though.

I went there with Katerina Feodorovna Kolenkorov. She needed a samovar that would serve ten people.

We found no samovar, however. Either the czar drank out of the teakettle, or they carried the tea to him from the kitchen in some sort of crystal glass—I don't know. Only there were no samovars on sale.

But there were lots of other things. They really were all very gorgeous. Different imperial drapes, ornamental borders, various wineglasses, spittoons, chemises, and many other imperial knickknacks. Your eyes ran wild. You didn't know what to choose, what to buy.

So with what money she had to spare, instead of a samovar Katerina Feodorovna bought four shirts of the finest broadcloth. They were gorgeous shirts. Imperial shirts.

I found a pair of boots on the list—Russian boots, price eighteen rubles.

I asked the auctioneer at once, "What sort of boots are these, my dear friend?"

He said, "The usual kind—imperial boots."

"How can you guarantee that they're imperial boots? Some theater usher might have worn them and you're passing them off as the czar's. That would be wrong, you know. Unethical."

He answered, "Everything here is the property of the royal family. We don't sell counterfeits."

"Let's see the stuff," I demanded.

I looked at the boots. I really fell for them, and the size seemed to be right. They were so fine and narrow and neat. They had toecaps and heels. They were real honest-to-goodness boots. And very little worn. The czar probably only wore them three days. Not even the soles were peeling off.

"Just imagine, Katerina Feodorovna," I said, "could you have dreamed, formerly, of wearing imperial footwear? Or of walking about the streets in imperial boots? Lord, how history changes, Katerina Feodorovna."

I paid eighteen rubles for them without lamenting. That was not at all a high price for imperial boots.

I counted out the eighteen rubles and took the imperial boots home with me.

It was quite a job to pull them on. You could barely stretch them over an ordinary sock, not to speak of foot wrappers.

Just the same, I thought, I'll wear them.

I wore them three days. On the fourth the sole came off, not only the sole but the whole lower story, with the heel, fell off. Even my foot came through into the open.

That miserable business happened to me on the street, on the Boulevard of the Unions, near the Palace of Labor. From there I had to walk home to Vassily Island without a sole.

I was sorriest about the money. Eighteen rubles is something. And there was no one I could complain to. Had they been shoes from the "Walkfast" factory or some other factory it would have been different. You could have begun an investigation or even had a red director fired for such technical carelessness. But mine were imperial boots.

Of course, I went back to the Museum Fund head·

quarters the next day. But the sale was finished and the place was closed.

I thought of going to the Hermitage Museum or some such place, but finally I gave up. Katerina Feodorovna discouraged me.

"Not only imperial boots," she said, "but any kingly boot will rot after so many years. After all, it's more than ten years since the Revolution. The threads may have rotted through in that time. You must realize that."

And it's true, my friends, ten years have passed. It's no joke. Even their goods have begun falling to pieces.

Although she had tried to calm me down, when her own imperial chemises fell to pieces after the first wash, Katerina Feodorovna swore terribly at the czar's regime.

But you should remember that ten years have passed —it's ridiculous to take offense. How time flies, my friends!

1928

THE QUALITY OF
PRODUCTION

A GERMAN from Berlin was living with my friends the Gusevs.

He rented a room from them. Lived there almost two months.

He wasn't some sort of Baltic specimen or some other national minority, but a real German from Berlin. He didn't speak a word of Russian. He communicated to his landlords with his hands and his head.

This German, of course, dressed splendidly. His underwear was clean. His trousers neat. Nothing too much. He was as pretty as a picture.

When that German went away he left a lot of things for his landlords. A great big pile of foreign goods. Various little bottles, collars, boxes. Besides almost two whole pairs of drawers. And a sweater that was almost not torn. As well as that, there were trifles too numerous to count—both for men's and ladies' use. All of it left in a heap in the corner by the washbasin.

The landlady, Madame Gusev, an honest lady—nothing can be said against her—hinted to the German just before his departure, "*Bitte, dritte,* haven't you, in your haste, left behind some foreign goods?"

The German shook his head, as if to say, "*Bitte, dritte,* please help yourself—it's not worth talking about."

The landlord and landlady threw themselves on the

products he had left behind. Gusev even made out a detailed inventory of the things. And, naturally, he immediately put on the sweater and appropriated the drawers for himself.

For two weeks he walked around carrying the drawers in his hands. He showed them to everybody, feeling immensely proud and praising German quality.

The things, although they were worn and, generally speaking, barely held together, were real foreign goods and very pleasant to look at.

Among other things there was a flask—well, perhaps not a flask, but a sort of flattish jar—of powder. The powder was sort of pink and very fine. And the smell of it was rather pleasant, something like oregano or rose.

After the first days of joy and transports the Gusevs began guessing what the powder might be. They smelled it, chewed it, threw it in the fire, but could not guess what it was.

They carried it through the whole building, showed it to high-school students and other intellectuals, but couldn't find the answer.

Many said it was face-powder; some pronounced it a fine German talc for dusting newborn babies.

Gusev said, "I can't use any fine German talc. I have no newborn babies. Let's decide it's face-powder. I'll sprinkle it on my face every day after shaving. You have to live in a civilized manner at least once in your life."

He began shaving and powdering himself. After every shave he walked around, pink, blooming, and exuding perfume.

Others, of course, met him with envy and questions.

And Gusev defended the excellence of German production. He praised German wares loudly and warmly.

"For many years," he said, "have I maimed my personality with various Russian rubbish, but now at last

I have the right thing! When this powder gives out I simply won't know what to do. I'll have to send for another jar. It's too marvelous a product!"

A month later, when the powder was running low, a friend of Gusev's, an intellectual, came to visit him. Over the evening tea he read the inscription on the jar. It turned out that it was a German preparation to prevent the propagation of fleas.

Some less enthusiastic person might have been deeply crushed by this discovery. And the face of a less enthusiastic person might have become covered with pimples and warts from undue vexation. But not such was Gusev.

"That," said he, "I understand. That is real quality of production! That's a real achievement. You can't spit on such goods. If you wish, powder your mug with it . . . or scatter it to the fleas. It's good for anything. And what sort of stuff have we got?"

Gusev, once more praising German production, went on, "That's why I've been wondering . . . a whole month I've been powdering myself, and not one flea has bitten me. They bite my wife, Madame Gusev. My sons, too, keep scratching themselves desperately all day long. Even the dog, Ninka, scratches. And I don't feel a thing. They may be insects, the rascals, but they know what real production is. That, indeed, is something . . ."

Gusev's powder has come to an end. The fleas probably are biting him again.

1930

A CLEVER LITTLE TRICK

I DON'T know how it is in Moscow, but here in Leningrad they sell only powerful electric light bulbs. Something like one hundred and fifty, two hundred, or four hundred candle power.

And as for consumers who dream of obtaining a light bulb of ten or maybe fifteen candle power, theirs prove to be truly senseless dreams.* Such light bulbs are not on sale.

Well, I thought, they send these small bulbs to the provinces for use in the villages. And that calmed me down.

Now my old bulbs had burned out. I got three new ones of four hundred candle power each and basked in this bright light. Of course, it's annoying. It's very bright. The main thing is, I'm not a draftsman. It's so ridiculously bright in the hall and the bathroom that you just start to feel bad. But I stood it.

But this month the meter reader came. Started to check how much electricity I had burned up.

"Oho!" he says. "Your bill gets higher every month. What are you doing, frying potatoes in the electricity?"

I say, "No, I've got powerful bulbs. And I just don't know what to do. It's a hopeless situation."

Well, I got to talking with the meter reader. A lot of chit-chat. He had a glass of tea with me. Ate a roll. And

* The phrase "senseless dreams" had become a household word since the Emperor Nicholas II, in a famous statement at the beginning of his reign, used it to refer to the parliamentary aspirations of the Russian liberals. *Ed.*

then he says, "You know why there aren't any small bulbs? Shall I tell you?"

I say, "Tell me, but it'll hardly make me feel any better."

He says, "There's a big trick being played with the small bulbs. The whole thing has to do with the financial-industrial plan."

"I'm afraid I don't quite get you," I said.

He says, "The factory had to fulfill its plan. Well, so they went and fulfilled it."

"No," I say, "ever since so much light has been beating down on me in this apartment, my bean doesn't work so well. I don't understand you."

"What is there," he says, "to understand? Well, let's suppose that according to the plan they had to fulfill a production quota of a million candle power. Well, now just imagine—are they going to start producing this million in small bulbs? They wouldn't make it in two years, the devils. So they decided to get there with big bulbs. Whether you make small bulbs or big ones, the work is the same. But you don't need nearly so many. And so, those devils have settled on big bulbs. They're turning them out like pancakes."

I said, "But that's a filthy trick! And also it's no joy to us that the government is wasting a lot of valuable electric power. Take me—I have four hundred candle power in the toilet. I really feel guilty about going in there."

He said, "Be grateful that they didn't settle on the biggest bulbs of all. Next year they'll probably start turning out bulbs with a thousand candle power."

At this point I suddenly got mad.

"Instead of shooting off your mouth to me," I said, "you should tell me where I can get some small bulbs."

He said, "Even though I work for the electric service, I haven't laid eyes on any small bulbs for two years now."

With these words he said good-bye and departed. And I turned off the lights in the room, lay down on the bed, and in the darkness started thinking about what tricks people resort to in order to balance their office accounts.

THE BOTTLE

A LITTLE while ago some young fellow broke a bottle on the street.

He was carrying something or other. What, I don't know. Kerosene or gasoline. Or perhaps lemonade. In short, some cooling beverage. It's hot this time of year. You get thirsty.

And so this fellow was walking along and, in a moment of absent-mindedness, plunked the bottle down on the sidewalk.

And, you know, people are so undeveloped. He doesn't know enough to sweep the pieces off the sidewalk with his foot. No! He just broke it, damn him, and went on his way. And so the other passers-by have to walk on the broken glass. Very nice.

Then I purposely sat down on the curb near the gate to see what would happen.

What do I see? I see people walk on the glass. They curse, but they still walk. What lack of culture! There's not a single person who will fulfill his social obligations.

Now what would it cost them? Well, someone could stop for a couple of seconds and brush the broken glass off the sidewalk with his cap. But no, they go on by.

No, my friends! I think. We do not yet understand our social responsibilities. We traipse along over broken glass.

At this point I see a gang of boys gather.

"Aw," they say, "too bad there are so few barefooted

people these days. Otherwise," they say, "someone could get himself nicely sliced up."

And suddenly a man comes along.

An absolutely plain, proletarian-looking man.

This man stops by the broken bottle. He shakes his kind head. Grunting, he bends down and sweeps aside the glass with a piece of newspaper.

"Well done!" I think. "I grieved for nothing. Social consciousness has not died out in the masses."

And suddenly a militiaman walks up to this commonplace, simple man and bawls him out: "What do you think you're doing, you featherbrain? I ordered you to take away the broken glass, and you just scatter it off to one side! Since you're the janitor of this building, it's up to you to liberate your district from broken glass."

The janitor, muttering something under his breath, went back into the yard and in a moment appeared again with a broom and a tin dustpan. And began to sweep up.

I sat on the curb for a long time afterwards, until they chased me away, and thought about all kinds of nonsense.

And, you know, the most remarkable thing in this story is the fact that the militiaman ordered the glass to be swept up.

THE NURSEMAID

A SHOCKING thing happened here in Leningrad recently.

A certain couple, the Farforovs, had a nursemaid. They hired her even before their baby was born. They could not provide their baby with care and tenderness themselves because the two of them had jobs in industry.

Seryoga Farforov himself worked, and his wife worked. He earned a respectable salary. And she earned quite a bit.

In such circumstances their baby was born.

They had a real, honest-to-goodness baby and, of course, were obliged to hire a nursemaid for him. Otherwise, of course, they wouldn't have hired one. The more so that they had never been in the habit of hiring nursemaids. They didn't understand such aristocratic customs. But now it was more economical to have a nursemaid than for Madame Farforov herself to quit her job in industry.

And so, of course, a nursemaid offered them her services.

She was neither so very old nor so very young. In a word, she was middle-aged and fairly terrifying to look at. But beneath her ugly exterior the Farforovs soon espied a kind heart. And they could not have dreamed what a viper they had taken to their bosom.

They, of course, had purposely hired such an ugly woman, one who would have no personal happiness and would have eyes for no one but their baby.

They had hired her with good recommendations. They were told that she was a completely sober, elderly, ugly old lady. And that she loved children and could hardly keep her hands off them. And that though she was an old woman, she was an old woman completely worthy of entering the new, classless society.

That's what they were told. But they still hadn't arrived at their own opinion.

So they hired this nursemaid and realized that it was true—she was a treasure, not a nursemaid. Especially as she fell in love with the child at once. She walked with him all the time, hardly put him down, and kept him outdoors until nightfall.

And the Farforovs, being advanced people, did nothing to prevent this. They knew that fresh air and outings would strengthen their baby's organism, and they thought, Go right ahead. Let her walk with him. Besides, we won't have to look at her so much.

Then the following incident took place.

In the morning the parents would be off to the factory, and the nursemaid would take the baby and a bottle of cow's milk and go walking about the streets of Leningrad.

But one day a member of the administration named Tsaplin was walking along the street. He was on the house committee.

He was walking along the street thinking, perhaps, about his own personal affairs, when suddenly he saw a rather bedraggled citizeness standing on the corner. She was standing there, just like that, and holding a baby. And she was begging money for the baby.

Semyon Mikhailovich Tsaplin didn't want to give her anything—he simply took a look at her. And he realized that the face was familiar: it was none other than the nursemaid with the Farforov baby.

S. M. Tsaplin, member of the house committee, didn't say anything to her about it and didn't give her anything, but turned around and went back home.

We don't know how he spent the rest of the day, but in the evening he said to Farforov himself: "I am exceedingly astonished, esteemed comrade, that either you're not paying your domestic anything, or I don't know what's the matter with her. But I'll tell you right now: if you're sending her out to beg with the baby on purpose, then you constitute a definitely alien stratum in our proletarian house."

Farforov, of course, said, "Excuse me, but what are you talking about?"

Then the member of the administration told him what he had seen and what he had felt on witnessing a street spectacle of that sort.

At this point various scenes took place. There were shouts and smiles, and everything became clear.

Then they called the nursemaid. They said to her, "How could you behave like that? Have you lost your wits? Maybe not everyone's home upstairs."

The nursemaid said, "There's nothing wrong with it. What's the difference whether I just stand there, or whether sympathetic passers-by give me a handout. I," she said, "just can't understand why you're offended. It doesn't hurt the baby. And maybe it even amuses him to see so many people bustling around him."

Farforov said, "Yes, but I don't want my child to be exposed to such attitudes from his earliest years. I will not permit you to do such things. I won't allow you to go begging with my child. Besides, we pay you a decent salary, you have everything, you're perfectly well fed and shod."

The nursemaid said, "Yes, but I wanted to make a little extra."

Madame Farforov, pressing her child to her breast, said, "This is offensive to us in the highest degree. You are discharged from your position."

Tsaplin said, "As a member of the administration I

shall say this: you are completely right to fire this crazy nursemaid, inasmuch as she, and not you, is the alien stratum in our proletarian house."

The old woman said, "Goodness, how you do frighten me! Nursemaids are scarce now. I'll probably be snapped up right away. I hardly made three rubles begging with your brat, and got showered with reproaches into the bargain. I'll leave of my own free will, since you're heartless scoundrels and not employers."

On hearing these words Farforov got angry and yelled at her. He even wanted to shake her aged soul out of her frail body, but the member of the administration did not let him do this, and even made a brief speech on the subject. He told Farforov and his spouse the following: "Take a look at this nursemaid of yours. With all her roots she goes back to the distant past when gentry and subordinate slaves got along together. She became reconciled to that life and doesn't see anything shameful in being a beggar or taking handouts. That is the reason why she did the disgusting thing that offended you. However, don't touch her physically but simply dismiss her from her job."

The Farforovs did just that—they dismissed the nursemaid in disgrace.

The latter left without asking for references and no one knows where she went. But she's probably looking after a child somewhere and using him to beg herself a pretty good income.

1931

DON'T SPECULATE

WHILE we are solving all sorts of responsible problems about collective farms and the Promfinplan* together, life continues in its own way. People arrange their destinies, take wives or husbands, pursue their personal happiness, and even, some of them, swindle and speculate. Of course, it's rather difficult to speculate nowadays. But all the same, there are citizens who manage to think up something fresh in this department.

And it's about one such case of speculation that I want to tell you. Besides, the incident is a fairly amusing one. And besides, it really happened. One of my relatives arrived from the provinces and passed this story on to me.

In Simferopol a certain woman dentist named O., by origin a widow, decided to get married.

But it's not so easy to find a husband these days. The more so if a woman is an intellectual and wants to have a similarly intellectual, congenial fellow around.

In our, so to speak, proletarian country the question of intellectuals is a pretty touchy one at present. The problem of cadres has not been solved in a positive sense and especially, excuse the expression, in the case of potential husbands. It's plain that there aren't many eligible intellectual men nowadays. That is, there are some, of course, but there's something wrong with all of them—either they're married already, or they have

* The financial and production plan for an industry or industrial enterprise. *Ed.*

two or three families, or they're of bourgeois origin, which last, of course, doesn't do much to sweeten conjugal life.

So this was the situation in which the Simferopol widow, who had lost her husband the previous year, found herself. The husband had died of tuberculosis.

Well, so her husband died. She probably treated this event lightly at first. Eh, she thinks, a trifle. And then she sees—no, it's far from being a trifle. There are precious few eligible men running around. And, of course, she began to grieve. And so she grieves for nearly a year and tells the milkwoman about her grief. She had a milkwoman who delivered milk. Since her husband had died of tuberculosis, she started taking good care of herself, eating a nourishing diet.

And so she drank milk for almost a year, got healthier, and, by the way, had everyday, woman-to-woman talks with her milkwoman.

I don't know how it came up between them. She probably came into the kitchen and started chatting. "Well, food prices are going up. The milk," she says, "is kind of thin, and there aren't any eligible men at all."

The milkwoman says, "You're absolutely right. Some things are plentiful, but that commodity is a rare one."

The dentist says, "I earn good money. I have everything—an apartment, furniture, cash. And I'm not such a sight myself. And now look—I literally can't manage to get married again. I'm almost ready to put an ad in the newspaper."

The milkwoman says, "Well, an ad in the newspaper isn't the thing. But we'll have to think of something, of course."

The dentist answers, "As a last resort I wouldn't even mind paying money. I'd pay a woman who introduced me to someone with matrimonial intent."

The milkwoman asks, "And would you pay much?"

"Yes," says the dentist, "depending on what kind of

man she dug up. If, of course, he's an intellectual and will marry me, I'll give three ten-spots without batting an eyelash."

The milkwoman says, "Three isn't much. Give me fifty rubles and I'll fix things up for you. I've got a suitable man in mind."

"Yes, but maybe he's not an intellectual," says the dentist. "Maybe he's a stevedore."

"No," says the milkwoman. "Why a stevedore? He's very intelligent. He's an electrician."

"Then introduce me to him. For the time being, here's a ten-spot for your trouble."

And with this they part.

And, I must reveal, the man the milkwoman had in mind was none other than her own spouse. But the substantial sum excited her, and she began to turn over in her mind how she could best get the money out of the dentist.

And so she comes home and says to her spouse, "Listen to this, Nikolasha. You can pick up fifty rubles," she says, "without lifting a finger, for nothing."

So she tells him the point of the thing. Really, why shouldn't she introduce him to that rich dentist, if that woman will be fool enough to slip her fifty rubles for it?

"And as a last resort," she says, "if she insists, you can even register with her. That isn't hard these days. Today you sign up, and tomorrow or the day after—reverse engines."

The milkwoman's husband, a fairly handsome son-of-a-bitch with a little mustache, agreed: "Magnificent. All right! I'll do it gladly. I'm always," he says, "definitely happy to get fifty rubles for nothing. Other people work a whole month for a sum like that, and here it's such a trifle—getting married."

And so in a couple of days the milkwoman introduces her husband to the dentist.

The dentist's happiness is heartfelt, and without any

superfluous discussion she pays the milkwoman in full.

And now here is the situation that develops.

The milkwoman's husband, that notorious good-for-nothing with the little mustache, immediately registers with the dentist, moves to her establishment temporarily, and starts to live there.

He lives there five days, then a week, then ten days.

Then the milkwoman arrives.

"Well," she says, "what's going on?"

The electrician says, "Well, I've changed my mind about coming back. I'm going to stay and live with this dentist," he says. "Somehow it's turning out to be more interesting here for me."

At this point, it's true, he got a smack in the face for his disgraceful conduct, but he did not change his mind. He stayed with the dentist. And when the dentist found out about everything, she laughed very hard and said that since no one had forced him and he had freely chosen to stay, the incident was closed.

It's true that the milkwoman did come to the apartment a couple of times more and made terrible scenes, demanding the return of her spouse, but no good came of it. Furthermore, she was dismissed from her job and forbidden to deliver milk any longer for fear of future scenes and dramatic episodes.

And so for fifty rubles the greedy and miserly milkwoman lost her handsome, intelligent spouse.

1931

THE AFFIDAVIT

A VERY odd thing happened recently.

It's all the more interesting because it's true. There's none of your, well, make-believe or pure fantasy. Just the opposite; it's all taken, so to speak, from the wellspring of life.

And it's even more intriguing because there's a love interest involved. On the strength of this, many people will be quite amused to take a look at what sort of thing is going on at present on this rather important and up-to-date front.

Well, so two years ago in the city of Saratov the following event took place. A certain rather empty-headed young man named Seryozha Khrenov, who was a government employee or, more precisely, worked in the receiving and inspection department of a certain office, began courting a young lady, or rather, let's say, a working girl. Or else she began courting him. Since it was such a long time ago, there is no possibility of clearing up this question. We only know that they began to be seen together on the streets of Saratov.

They began to take walks and go out together. They even began strolling arm in arm. They began to utter all kinds of fond words. And so on. And so forth. And more of the same.

And this young dandy of a goods inspector once remarked to his lady friend, "I'll tell you what, Citizeness Anna Lytkina. Now," he said, "you and I are taking a stroll, and walking together, and we really," he said, "can't foresee what may happen and come of this. And," he said, "please be kind enough to give me an affidavit just in case, if a child should occur, you will make no claims on the party mentioned. And when I," he said, "am in possession of such a statement, I'll be nicer to you. In the opposite case, however," he said, "I would sooner renounce our mutual love than worry in the future about my actions and pay money for the support of progeny."

Either she was violently in love with him, or the little dandy had addled her brains in his morass of empty-headedness, but in any case she didn't spend too much time uselessly arguing with him, but went and signed the statement. It said that and so forth and so on and as a result I have no claims on him and will not demand money from him.

She signed this paper for him but, of course, said a few words beforehand.

"This," she said, "is rather strange on your part. I've never given affidavits like this to anyone before. And it's even exceedingly insulting that your love should take such curious forms. But," she said, "since you insist, I can, of course, sign the paper for you."

The goods inspector said, "Please be so kind. I," he says, "have been observing our country for ten years and I know what can happen in these cases."

In short, she signed the paper. And, not being a fool, he had the signature written by her charming hand certified in the building manager's office and hid this priceless document close to his heart.

To make a long story short, a year and a half later the little dears were standing before a people's judge and testifying to him about their now extinct love.

She stood there wearing a white tricot kerchief and rocking a baby.

"Yes," she says, "it's true that I was foolish enough to sign the statement, but then I had this above-mentioned baby, and the baby's father ought to do his bit. Besides, I'm out of work now."

And he, that is, the young ex-father, stands there fresh as a daisy and smirks into his little mustache.

His expression seemed to say, What's all the talk about? What's going on here, huh? Whatever it is, I can't understand it, when everything is so clear and plain to see. And, if you please, he's got a document with him.

He triumphantly flings open his jacket, gropes a moment in his pocket, and gets his much cherished paper.

He gets his much cherished paper and, laughing softly, puts it on the judge's desk.

The people's judge glanced at the affidavit, looked at the signature and the seal, gave a laugh, and said, "It's a proper document, without a doubt!"

The goods inspector said, "Why, yes, completely, so to speak, proper, if you'll pardon me. And in general it leaves absolutely no room for doubt. It fulfills all requirements and is without any infraction."

The people's judge says, "The document is undoubtedly in order. But the following consideration appears relevant: Soviet law is on the side of the child and protects his interests particularly. And in this case, according to law the child must not be made to answer for it or suffer if, by chance, he happened to land a pretty sharp son-of-a-bitch for a father. And on the strength of the aforesaid," he says, "your affidavit is worthless and has only sentimental value. Here," he says, "take it back, quickly, and hide it next to your heart."

In short, the ex-father has already been paying money for six months.

WEAK PACKAGING

Nowadays they don't take bribes. In the old days you couldn't take a step without either giving or getting something.

But nowadays people's characters have improved a great deal. They really don't take bribes.

A while ago, we sent off a shipment from the freight depot.

Our aunt died of the grippe and in her will directed that some sheets and other petty-bourgeois articles of hers be sent off to the provinces, to her relatives on my wife's side.

So we're standing in the station, and here's the picture we see, in the style of Raphael.

A booth for the receipt of outgoing shipments. There is a line, of course. A metric scale according to the decimal system. Behind it, a weighmaster. The weighmaster, a fine example of a public servant, is rapidly citing figures, writing them down, adjusting the counterweights, pasting on labels, and giving explanations.

You hear only his pleasant voice: "Forty. A hundred and twenty. Fifty. Lift it off. Take it. Step aside . . . Don't stand over there, you fool, stand on this side."

What a pleasant picture of hard work and rapid tempos.

But suddenly we notice that amid all the beauty of his work the weighmaster is a real stickler for the rules. He keeps awfully close watch over the interests of the citizens and the state. Well, not every time, but every second or third time, he categorically refuses to accept a parcel. If the packaging is the least bit flimsy, he won't take it. Although you can see that he sympathizes.

The people whose packaging is flimsy moan and groan, of course.

The weighmaster says, "Instead of standing there and moaning, fix up your packaging. There's a man with nails hanging around here somewhere. Let him fix it for you. Tell him to hammer in a couple of nails and put a wire around the whole thing. And then come to the head of the line, and I'll take it."

And it was really true: a man was standing behind the booth. He was holding some nails and a hammer. Toiling by the sweat of his brow, he reinforces flimsy packaging for those who wish it. And those whose packages have been refused look at him beseechingly and offer him their friendship and money for doing just that.

But now it's the turn of a certain citizen. He's a tow-headed fellow, wearing glasses. He's not an intellectual, but he's near-sighted. He looks as if he has trachoma. So he put on glasses so people couldn't see him as well. Or maybe he works in an optical goods factory, and they give out free glasses there.

He puts his six crates on the metric decimal scale.

The weighmaster looks over the six crates and says, "The packaging's weak. It won't go. Take it back."

When he hears these words, the fellow in glasses loses heart completely. But before losing heart, he gets so mad at the weighmaster that he almost gives him a sock in the teeth. The fellow in glasses yells, "What are you doing to me, you dog! These are not my own crates I'm shipping. I am shipping government crates from an optical goods factory. Where am I going to go with the crates now? Where can I get a wagon? Where am I going to get the hundred rubles to have them carted back? Answer me, you dog, or I'll make mince-meat out of you."

The weighmaster says, "How should I know?" And

at the same time he gestures to one side.

The other, because of his near-sightedness and the fact that his glasses are steamed up, mistakes this gesture for something else. He sputters, remembers something long forgotten, digs in his pockets, and pulls out about eight rubles, all in one-ruble notes. And tries to give them to the weighmaster.

The weighmaster turns purple at the spectacle of this money. He shouts, "How am I to understand that? Can you be trying to bribe me, you bespectacled mare!"

The fellow in glasses immediately, of course, realizes the full disgrace of his position.

"No," he said, "I just took out the money. I just wanted you to hold it while I took the crates off the scale."

He gets completely befuddled, talks absolute nonsense, starts to apologize, and even looks as if he'd agree to being punched in the nose.

The weighmaster says, "You should be ashamed. We don't take bribes here. Get your six crates off the scale —they literally chill my soul. But, since those are government crates, go over to that worker and he'll reinforce the weak packaging for you. As for the money, you can thank your lucky stars that I don't have time to bother with you."

Nonetheless, he calls over another employee and says to him in an offended voice, "You know, someone just tried to bribe me. Can you imagine, how ridiculous! I'm sorry I was in a hurry and didn't pretend to take the money, because now it would be hard to prove it."

The other employee answers, "Yes, that's a pity. You should have raised a row. We don't want people to think that our hands are sticky the way they used to be."

The fellow with glasses, all in a sweat, is fussing with his crates. They fix them for him, get them into decent shape, and drag them back on the scales.

Then I begin to think that my packaging is weak too.

And since it isn't my turn yet, I go over to the worker and ask him, just in case, to fix up my dubious packaging. He asks me to pay eight rubles.

I say, "Have you gone out of your mind, asking eight rubles for three nails?"

He says to me in subdued tones, "That's right, for you I'd do it for a three-spot. But," he says, "consider my ticklish position—I've got to split with that crocodile."

Now I begin to understand how it all works. "Then," I say, "you divvy up with the weighmaster?"

At this point he gets a little embarrassed that he has blurted out everything, talks all kinds of stuff and nonsense, mutters about his low salary and high prices, gives me a big discount, and sets to work.

Then my turn comes. I put my crate on the scale and admire the strong packaging.

The weighmaster says, "The packaging's a bit weak. It won't go."

I say, "Really? I just had it fixed. That fellow over there with the pliers reinforced it."

The weighmaster answers, "Oh, *pardon, pardon.* I apologize. Your packaging is all right now, but it was weak before. I have an eye for that sort of thing. If it's *pardon*, then *pardon*."

He takes my crate and writes a shipping ticket.

I read the ticket, and on it is written, "Weak packaging."

"What," I say, "are you robbers doing? With that kind of label they'll steal everything out of the crate on the road. And the label won't allow me to claim damages. Now I see through your crooked finagling."

The weighmaster says, "If it's *pardon*, then *pardon*. I apologize."

He crosses out the label and I go home, meditating along the way on the complicated mental structure of my fellow citizens, on the rebuilding of character, on craftiness, and on the unwillingness with which my esteemed fellow citizens give up their long-established positions.

If it's *pardon*, then *pardon*.

THE STORY OF A MAN
WHO WAS PURGED FROM
THE PARTY

BACK in the time of the first purge, they expelled a certain character from the Party.

He was something in the line of a disabled soldier turned barber.

And they purged him for a mundane reason—he drank too much. In general, he had something of a dock hand's nature. He'd pour anything down his throat. And he wasn't always steady on his legs.

So that since he was a barber and not an office clerk he could have inflicted physical mutilations on any of his clients. Not to mention spoiling his patients' world outlook and so on.

So I think he was probably purged in accordance with the slogan, "A rotten apple spoils the barrel."

With these words they expelled him.

He wasn't aware of any other things against him. He believed that he had always lived up to the rules. He had worked energetically, wasn't mixed up in anything in particular, and in general was quite surprised to be purged and puzzled about the reason.

Somehow he got very upset. He thought, How many years I held myself back and restrained the outbursts of my nature. How many years, he thinks, I didn't allow myself anything in particular. Behaved properly and didn't permit any excesses. And suddenly—go and shave yourself. And as for drinking, what's wrong with it?

He didn't say anything to the purge committee, but thought, Oh, so that's how it is.

So he went home, got good and drunk, royally stewed, you might say, gave his wife a little thrashing, broke the windows in the porter's lodge, and disappeared for a couple of days.

Where he was mooching around, nobody knew. But he came back with his face all battered, his clothes torn, and no coat.

And he said to the other tenants, "I'm not a bit sorry I was purged. Just the opposite. I'm glad I won't have to run into unnecessary discipline any more. How many years," he says, "I controlled myself and ruined my disposition with all kinds of restrictions. This isn't allowed, and that's not right, and don't hit your wife. But now that's all over with. Amen. My profession is good under any regime. So I can spit on all of you put together."

The tenants were amazed at what he said. But he thought he was doing the right thing. And he got plastered again and broke the new window they had just put in at the porter's lodge.

And in the Tenants' Co-operative Association he tore all the slogans and health posters off the walls. He even hit the chairman with one poster, which said, "Young Pioneers don't drink or smoke—let this guide the grown-up folk."

And really, in three days he let himself go to such an extent that everyone in the house was amazed that such a thing could happen.

Suddenly he found out somewhere, or someone told him, that even though they had purged him, he had now (supposedly) been reinstated.

It's impossible to describe what happened.

In a flash he sobered up and got himself in shape. He

got the tenants together and said, "Things happen, my friends. I beg you to forget what you have seen these past few days. Strange as it seems, I think I have been reinstated."

And he runs to the proper place and says, "Some trick you played on me. First it's this way, and then about-face. Anyone could get confused about how to behave. I didn't know," he says, "and in the interim I did a lot of things I shouldn't have. And now if you get a couple of reports about me, it's not my fault—it's the circumstances."

They tell him, "Why are you getting upset, Comrade? You haven't been reinstated. It's true, one of the comrades said about you, 'I don't think there's anything wrong with him, he just drinks a little. So you,' he says, 'were wrong to purge him.' But now we can have no more doubts with such a picture before us."

He says, "But I didn't know."

They answer, "That means you're not a pure-blooded proletarian. Another one would have stayed pure as the driven snow under all circumstances. But you showed your swinish snout at once. Good day."

So they didn't take him back.

And now he sits quietly in his room and doesn't drink. He keeps thinking that they'll call him in very soon and say, "We see you're living up to the rules. You are reinstated."

But they don't call him in. Since they know him well now.

AN INCIDENT ON
THE VOLGA

To begin with, we'll tell you about a certain amusing little mishap.

This mishap led to a group of vacationers' receiving a moral jolt as a result of a certain misunderstanding.

This is how it happened. The story is true.

During the early years of the Revolution, when life had become more settled and wonderful steamships with first-class cabins and hot meals served to the passengers had begun to sail up and down the Volga, a group of vacationing citizens—six office workers, of whom I was one—set out for a holiday on the Volga.

Everyone had advised us to take a cruise on the Volga. It was a wonderful place for a rest. Nature. The banks. The water, the food, and the cabins.

And so the group of office workers, tired out, so to speak, by the revolutionary turmoil, set out to take a rest.

We got on a wonderful first-class ship called the *Comrade Penkin*.

We got interested in who this Penkin might have been. They told us they thought he worked in the water transport division.

Actually, it was all the same to us, and of course we set sail on this unknown comrade.

We came to Samara.

Our group disembarked and went to look over the

city. We're looking around. Suddenly we hear some kind of whistle.

Someone says, "Schedules aren't very exact nowadays. Our *Penkin* might just up and leave. Let's go back."

And so, having more or less looked the city over, we went back.

We came to the dock and saw that our ship wasn't there. It had left.

Shouts and cries arose.

One of us shouts, "I left my papers in my pants on board." Others shout, "What about us? We've lost our baggage and our money. What shall we do? It's awful!"

I said, "Let's get on this other boat that happens to be here and go back."

We look and see that there is a Volga steamship called the *Storm* tied up at the dock.

In plaintive voices we ask the bystanders whether it's been a long time since the *Penkin* sailed. Perhaps we could catch up with it by land.

The bystanders say, "Why catch up with it? There's the *Penkin*. But now it's called the *Storm*. It's the former *Penkin*. The name has been painted over."

We were really overjoyed at this news. We dashed aboard this boat of ours and all the way to Saratov we didn't set foot on shore. We were afraid.

And incidentally, we asked the captain the reason for this amusing event and the dispatch with which it was carried out.

The captain says, "You see, the ship got that name partly by mistake. Penkin works in the water transport division, but he didn't quite live up to his obligations. At present he is under arrest for having exceeded his authority. We got a telegram to paint out his name. So we called her the *Storm*."

Then we said, "Oh, so that's it!" and laughed nonchalantly.

We arrived at Saratov and our group disembarked to see the city.

We didn't hang around there for very long either. We went to a booth and bought some cigarettes. And we looked over a couple of buildings.

We go back—and again find our ship, the *Storm*, missing. And we see another ship there in its place.

Of course, we weren't as scared as we had been in Samara. We figured there was still a chance. Maybe they painted over the name again. But nevertheless, some of us got very frightened.

We run up closer and ask the bystanders, "Where's the *Storm?*"

The bystanders say, "This is the *Storm* right here. Formerly the *Penkin*. And now, starting at Saratov, they're calling it the *Korolenko*."

We say, "How come they're so generous with their paint?"

The bystanders say, "We don't know. Ask the boatswain."

The boatswain says, "We've had a hot time with these names. They named her *Penkin* by mistake. As for *Storm*, that was a name with little current significance. To some extent it was lacking in principle. A storm is simply a phenomenon of nature. It conveys nothing to the mind or the heart. The captain got a dressing-down for it. That's why they painted it over."

We were overjoyed again and said, "Oh, so that's it!" and boarded the ship *Korolenko*. And sailed off.

But the boatswain said to us, "Be sure you don't get scared in Astrakhan if you come back and find another name."

But we said, "No, that wouldn't be too likely. Since Korolenko is a famous writer."

In fact, we got to Astrakhan safely. And from there we traveled on dry land.

So that we never knew the subsequent fate of the ship.

But you can be sure that the name stayed the way it was. For ever and ever. The more so since Korolenko was dead. Whereas Penkin was alive. And this was the basic shortcoming which led to his name's being replaced.

So it appears that being alive, so to speak, can even be a shortcoming in people. No, *pardon*, it's really impossible to understand what the essence of the shortcoming is. On the one hand, sometimes it would seem more advantageous for us not to be alive. But on the other hand, so to speak, no, thank you very much. It's a doubtful sort of advantage. We'd rather not. But still, being alive also seems in that sense to be a relative shortcoming.

So that a person is beset by unpleasantnesses, so to speak, on both sides.

This is why we included this little misunderstanding, this trifle, in our series of tales of misfortune.

However, great misfortune takes place not only on the Volga, but also in public baths.

We offer for your attention a story about that kind of misfortune.

BATHS AND PEOPLE

At one time I wrote a thing or two about public baths. I called attention to certain dangers. For instance, a naked man has no place to put the check for his clothing and so on.

Since then a few years have passed.

The problem I had referred to evoked heated discussion among members of the Bath and Laundry Trust. As a result, in some public baths special lockers have been installed where each customer can put whatever clothing he may have. After which the locker is locked and the customer, with joyous heart, hurries off to wash. And there he ties the key to his bucket. Or as a last resort he can keep it in his hand. And somehow manage to wash.

To make a long story short, here is what took place despite all this in one of our Leningrad baths.

A certain technician finished washing and then, of course, wanted to get dressed. Suddenly he notices with horror that his entire wardrobe has been stolen. Only the thief, being a kindly sort, had left him his vest, his cap, and his belt.

He simply gasped, this technician. There he stands by his locker with nothing on—and seems to have no outlook on the future. He stands by the locker in his birthday suit and helplessly waves his arms. He is stunned.

He is a technician. Not without education. And he just can't imagine how he's going to get home now. He can hardly stand on his feet.

But then he angrily puts on his vest and cap, takes his belt in his hand, and in this, one might say, quite abstract aspect, walks around the locker room in a daze.

Some of the people say, "Things are being purloined in this bath every day."

Our technician, whose head is spinning, starts to talk in the manner of the old regime, using the word "gentlemen." In his agitation he had probably forgotten some of the elements of his new personality.

He said, "The thing that interests me most, gentlemen, is how I'm going to get home now."

One of the people who had not yet bathed said, "Call the manager. He'll have to think of something."

The technician replied in a weak voice, "Gentlemen, call the manager for me."

A bath attendant clad only in trunks dashes to the exit and quickly reappears with the manager. Then all those present notice suddenly that the manager is a woman. The technician, taking off his cap, thoughtfully asks, "Gentlemen, what is this? One thing worse than the next. We all were yearning to see a man right now, when suddenly, just imagine, a woman comes in. To have such managers in a men's bath," he says, "why, it's like the anomaly of Kursk."*

And, screening himself with his cap, he sits down on the couch in a state of collapse.

The other men say, "It really is the anomaly of Kursk to have a woman manager."

The manager says, "To you I may be the anomaly of Kursk. But over there across the court I have a women's section. And there," she says, "I'm far from being any kind of anomaly of Kursk."

Our technician, huddling in his vest, says, "We, madame, did not wish to offend you. Don't get your dan-

* The phrase "Kursk magnetic anomaly" occurs in Russian physics textbooks because heavy deposits of iron ore near the town of Kursk cause wild compass fluctuations. Here, of course, it is nonsense. *Ed.*

der up. You'd better," he says, "think up something
for me to wear now."

The manager says, "Of course, before I came the managers here were men. And in your section they were
very good at their jobs, but in the women's section
they all went a little out of their minds. They kept pop-
ping in there too often. And now this job is rarely assigned to men. It is given more and more to women.
As for me, I come in here when it's necessary or when
somebody has swiped something, and it doesn't faze
me. But since I am always running up against some insult here on your side and every bather without fail
calls me the anomaly of Kursk, I'm warning everyone
that from now on I'll have whoever insults me at my
post taken to the militia station . . . What happened
to you?"

The technician says, "Gentlemen, why is she so hot
and bothered? Well, the hell with her. I don't see how
I'm going to get home without my pants, and she won't
allow me to call her the anomaly of Kursk. And she
threatens to turn me over to the police. No, it would
be better if the manager were a man. At least he could
lend me his spare pair of trousers. But here the manager is a woman—and that finishes me off once and for
all. Gentlemen, I am now positive that I won't leave
this bathhouse for several days—just you wait and see."

The onlookers say to the manager, "Listen, madame,
maybe you've got a husband here in the bathhouse. And
maybe he's got an extra pair of pants. Then, really, give
them to this guy to wear for a while. Because he's terribly upset, and he doesn't know how he'll get home."

The manager says, "In the women's section I've got
peace and quiet, but in this half it's just like a volcano
erupting every day. No, gentlemen, I refuse to be a
manager here. My husband works in Vyatka, and, of
course, there is no question of my lending you any
pants. Besides, this is the second theft reported today.

It's a good thing they didn't take anything important the first time. Or else they would have pestered me about trousers then. And so, gentlemen, I'll tell you what: If anyone has any extra pants, give them to him, it makes me tired just to look at him. I'm beginning to develop a headache from all this excitement."

The bath attendant says, "All right, I'll give my extra pants again. But they'll really have to make up a pair of government pants. Things are stolen here frequently, and this month they've just worn out my pants. First one takes them, then another. And they are my own."

So the bath attendant gives our technician a pair of chintz trousers, and one of the bathers gives him a jacket and a pair of house slippers. And soon our friend, holding back his sobs with difficulty, arrays himself in this quaint attire. And in this absurd aspect he leaves the bathhouse, utterly dazed.

After his departure somebody cries suddenly, "Look, here's an extra vest and a sock lying around."

Then all the people present surround the newly discovered objects.

One says, "The thief probably dropped them. Look the vest over carefully and see if there's anything in the pockets. Lots of people keep their papers in their vests."

They turn the pockets inside out and discover a certificate. It's a pass in the name of Selifanov, a worker in the central tailoring shop. At this everyone realizes that they are already hot on the trail of the thief.

The manager boldly phones the police and in two hours a search is carried out in Selifanov's room.

Selifanov is terribly surprised and says, "Have you gone crazy, gentlemen? I myself had some things stolen in that bathhouse today. And I even put in a report about it. As for this vest of mine, the thief probably dropped it."

Then everyone apologizes to Selifanov and says, "It was a misunderstanding."

But suddenly the manager of the tailoring shop where Selifanov worked says, "Yes, I'm sure that in the bathhouse you really were the victim. But tell me this: where did you get that piece of heavy cloth lying in the trunk? That cloth comes from our workshop. We have a shortage of it. And you probably took it. It's a good thing I came along with the search party out of curiosity."

Selifanov begins to stammer all kinds of things and soon confesses that he stole the cloth.

He is immediately arrested. And on this my bathhouse story ends and other matters begin. So I will stop here in order not to mix up two different subjects.

In general, both the public baths and the people who bathe there could, I think, in recent years have pulled themselves together so as to make a better show of it. At the bathhouses they could have thought up something special to this end, and people could have refrained from stealing property in such important places.

So, in comparison with other institutions, bathhouses are still bringing up the rear.

And that's a great pity.

1935

A FORGE OF HEALTH

THE Crimea is an absolute pearl. When you see people who have just come back from there, you can't help being astounded. That is, some decrepit little intellectual will take off for the Crimea, and when he comes back you won't recognize him. It's like a photographic enlargement. In general, a tremendous lot of self-assurance and *Weltanschauung*.

In short, the Crimea is a veritable forge of health.

A comrade who lives on our courtyard—Seryoga Pestrikov his name is—went to the Crimea.

He had a pretty washed-out personality. People who knew Seryoga before will all confirm this. That is, there was no smoldering fire or *Weltanschauung* in him.

The other citizens in the house at least have fun on holidays. They play catch, drink, and play games. In general, they live life to the full. That's why they're healthy, the devils.

But that bookworm would come home from work, for example, lie on his belly on the window seat, and stick his nose in a book. He wouldn't even go out for a walk. His system, you see, would be worn out in a day, and he couldn't walk.

And, of course, he didn't drink or smoke or take an interest in female personnel. In a word, he would just lie on the window seat and rest.

That's how unhealthy the man was!

His relatives saw that something was wrong with the fellow. They tried to arrange a trip to the Crimea for him. He couldn't have done that for himself. And they succeeded in fixing it up.

The fellow pulled a long face for a while, but he went.

They kept him there a month and a half. They made him go swimming and squirted some kind of stuff into his leg.

At last he returned. Came back. You could just gasp from amazement. His face, of course, was black, truly. Bursting with health. His eyes were full of fire. And all his melancholy was gone.

Before, this man wouldn't have hurt a fly. But now he'd barely got back, the very first day, when he pushed in the janitor Fedka's mug. Because he hadn't kept an eye on the woodshed—someone had stolen the fire-wood.

He also wanted to shoot the house manager with a re-volver for some trifle or other, and sent all the tenants scattering who tried to take the manager's part.

Well, we saw that you couldn't recognize the guy any more. He had been cured completely. The man had been fixed. A capital repair job. His superabun-dant health even made him start drinking. He didn't let a single girl get past him. There were more rows with him than you could count.

The Crimea is an absolute pearl, the way it renews a person!

One bad thing, though, is that Seryoga Pestrikov is go-ing to be fired from his job. Because he's started going on benders.

It's a great thing, health!

A TRAGICOMEDY

Of course, the kind of story where a man wins, let's say, a hundred thousand, and after that something or other happens to him—such stories, you know, are found in literature in great numbers.

But the one we are going to tell you surpasses in comedy everything heretofore written on this subject.

And we would like to note that it's all the naked truth.

Well, picture a morning. Foggy Leningrad. The toiling masses are just about to set out for their jobs. Now they'll just have another drink of tea and go forth in proud ranks.

And what happens? Somebody, forgive the expression, lets out a yell.

A cry, stamping, a crack and various shouts resound in our communal apartment.

The tenants rush to the scene, and this is what they see. The tenant Borka Fomin is meandering around his room in pink underpants. His lower jaw is trembling. His face is the color of clay. In one hand he holds a newspaper. In the other a post card . . . In a third hand, his spouse holds a lottery ticket and exclaims, "Hey, get out of the room, all of you. Nothing is certain yet. Personally, I can't believe that Borka and I have won five thousand."

Borka Fomin, whose nose is running from excitement, says, "I get a post card from the savings bank.

What is it? *Pardon!* I've won some money . . ." *

His wife says, "My whole life has gone by in the twilight. It's impossible that anything out of the ordinary should happen. If Borka has won that kind of money," she says, "then I know for sure that something or other will happen, thanks to which I will most likely never see the money."

One tenant says, "It often happens that they print something without reading over the figures carefully. Or else their zeros pop out of place and get put in wrong. The toiling masses gasp, but afterwards, of course, they don't win what they thought they had . . ."

At this point seven newspapers are brought in from various rooms. Everyone looks and checks, and they see that there's no doubt about it. Borka Fomin, a fellow with no pretensions to being anyone special, has won five thousand, and no one knows what he's going to do with the money.

Borka has a nephew, a seventeen-year-old boy named Vovka Chuchelov, who lives here too. He still has to pass the examination for the high calling of automobile driver, and so he has not yet got used to running over people. He says to Boris Andreyevich, "Why shout for nothing, Uncle? Run down to the savings bank. If they give you the money, that means you really won."

At this point everyone begins yelling and telling Boris Andreyevich to run to the bank.

With her feminine mistrustfulness, his wife exclaims at this, "He'll go right out and pour himself under a trolley car, the scoundrel, or get snagged by a bus. It simply doesn't happen that I should win five thousand just like that."

So Borka dresses at once, runs out, and quickly returns—as white as clay.

* In Russia, as in many other countries, state lotteries are conducted with savings bond registration numbers. *Ed.*

He speaks to those present in the weakened voice of a man who has just made a flight into the stratosphere.

"Yes," he says, "I've won five thousand. They told me to come for the money the day after tomorrow. They said, 'This happens in our parts once in a hundred years.'"

Then everyone congratulates Boris Andreyevich and orders him to lie down awhile on the sofa, so as not to disrupt the workings of his organism before receiving the money.

His wife shouts, "Oh, everybody get out of the room. I want to think hard about what might happen to keep us from getting the money."

And so a whole day passes, and the next morning a cry, stamping, and rude exclamations are heard once more.

All the tenants rush to the scene, and here is what they see.

Boris Andreyevich is lying on the sofa in his pink underpants. His lower jaw is quivering and his nose is running.

His wife says, "It's a good thing they didn't let that scoundrel of mine into the Party. Then he really would have put one over on me."

The tenants say, "What do you mean?"

"How can you ask?" she says. "It turns out that two weeks ago, without waiting to win the money, he started going around like a child, asking for recommendations from all sorts of important people. It's a good thing they didn't give them to him. He wanted to join up, you see. If he had succeeded, I think he would most likely have had to give up half his money for the fight against this and that, and to the MOPR and all those things." *

* During the early 1930's an effort was made to induce citizens, especially those who won large sums in lotteries, to donate money to the five-year plans. Pressure on Party members to do so

One lodger says, "You don't necessarily have to give it away, but, of course, some people decide to keep around six rubles for cigarettes and give all the rest for construction."

The wife says, "It's a good thing they don't let fools into the Party—that would have been a fine how-do-you-do!"

Borka yells, "Why do you have to talk about it, since it didn't happen? In life everything happens for the best."

The wife says, "Oh, get out of the room, everyone. I want to think about what else might happen."

On the third day Borka received the money in full. With a sigh he contributed a twenty-spot toward a dirigible, and brought the rest home. And locked himself in his room.

On the morning of the fourth day cries, grumbling, wails, stamping, and coarse oaths are heard.

It is Boris Andreyevich. He has had a fight with his wife and is getting a divorce. Now he is taking up with a certain young woman named Fenichka who lives at the other end of the hall. With very light hair, eyebrows, and eyelashes. A Finn, I think. But such an amazingly cute little darling. Slender as a poet's dream.

He has packed his things and is moving in with her. He exclaims about his wife, "I'm leaving her because I have seen through her petty-bourgeois character. She urged me not to make an application to the Party in these heroic times and I'll never forgive her for that and will certainly suffer and grieve every time I see her. But I don't want to leave her without anything. I'll give her a hundred rubles in cash and she'd better keep out of my love life, the devil."

---

was, of course, much greater than on ordinary citizens. The MOPR was an organization for aid to revolutionary activities abroad. *Ed.*

The wife says, "So that's the way it is! Didn't I tell you so?"

Then in a jiffy Vovka the nephew and Boris Andreyevich move his things to Fenichka's room and celebrate all evening with a sumptuous party.

On the sixth day shouts, outcries, and feminine tears are once more resounding in the apartment.

"What is it? *Pardon.* Excuse me, what happened?"

"Oh, you know, someone stole all Boris Andreyevich's money during the night."

A terrible scene of horror and turmoil unfolds.

Boris Andreyevich is lying on the bed with a countenance as pale as clay. He whispers words of astonishment and spreads his arms out, in this way showing the depth of his mental anguish.

Next to him Fenichka lies unconscious on the carpet. Her shoes and coat have been stolen.

At this point it is discovered that Borka's nephew Chuchelov, who has not yet passed his driver's examination, has disappeared, no one knows where. A picture of the lowest form of thievery on the part of this mad relative emerges.

Then Fenichka's brother, or God knows who, suddenly appears. Also, I think, of Finnish origin. With a badge marked GTO.*

He says almost nothing, and only shoves superfluous occupants out of the room with his feet.

Last of all, he kicks out Borka Fomin and gives him a punch in the face for ruining a woman's life and for a pair of shoes and a coat into the bargain.

Borka, with cries of agony, rushes up and down the hall with his cheek swollen the size of a meat pie.

Then his former wife takes him under her protection and permits him to locate himself in her living space once more.

* *Gotov k trudu i oborone* (Ready for Labor and Defense) — slogan for a big propaganda campaign in the 1930's. *Ed.*

Borka lies down on the floor in her room, suffering so terribly that even the militiaman who comes in—a man accustomed to seeing just about everything, can't stand to look at him.

Borka says to his wife, "Oh, I myself can't understand how I could have left you. Only your love has always lightened my incredible sufferings. As if in a fever I lived for three days with that blond Finn, who thoroughly deserved to have her plush slippers and coat stolen, and whose brother is I don't know what kind of scoundrel and killer of living creatures. Oh, my mind simply blacked out as a result of the whole business. In the presence of the comrade militiaman, I convey to you my heartfelt apologies for all these phenomena."

The militiaman says, "Oh, stop your whining. Your words are literally breaking my heart. Please be quiet and tell what happened, not how things used to be. I," he says, "am making a report, not writing epic poems about the lives of ragamuffins."

Borka says, "Then listen. Fenichka was sleeping during the night and I went to the bathroom for a minute, I don't remember what for. Vovka Chuchelov probably saw all this and took the money and things from the room."

The militiaman writes this down and leaves.

The husband and wife make up and live together in extraordinary love and harmony.

Borka and Fenichka no longer speak to one another. And she struts around in some new shoes, acquired from an unknown source.

Fenichka's sister Sima, with whom Borka fell into conversation, told him that the blond man who had hit him was not her brother at all, but her lover. And this explained everything.

Borka's sufferings are ended. He goes to work and there makes various bold promises.

His wife says, "Well, all right, what can I do? If you

want to, go and ask someone for a recommendation. You reach out for everything, like a child."

Suddenly, after two weeks, Borka is called to the police station. And there they inform him that in Gagry, in the Caucasus, his nephew, Vovka Chuchelov, has been caught. He had spent four hundred rubles, but Borka can have the rest of the money back at once.

With a face as pale as clay, Borka returns home. He has the money in his hands. He sits down on the sofa, looks reluctantly at everyone, and doesn't quite understand what has happened.

His wife says, "Oh, get out of the room, everyone. It's still not certain what will happen."

This uncertainty continues for three days.

After which Boris Andreyevich all of a sudden up and marries Fenichka's sister, Sima.

From happiness he stayed home from work three days, and for that was suspended for six months. But he didn't give a damn about that. He put his money in a savings bank. And now he carries the bankbook next to his chest, strung around his neck on the very thickest kind of cord.

Fenichka said it was all the same to her. And his ex-wife said, "Isn't that something!" and unexpectedly married an acquaintance of hers, a former Pole, who moved into her living space, as one who didn't have any such himself.

And now it will be interesting to see what will happen when Boris Andreyevich has run through all his money.

1934-1935

AN AMUSING ADVENTURE

A CERTAIN white-collar worker's wife, a fairly young and very fascinating woman, who had come from a petty-bourgeois family, fell in love with an actor.

He was a performer of serious drama and comedy. And she up and fell in love with him.

Perhaps she had seen him behind the footlights, and he overwhelmed her with his splendid acting, or perhaps, on the contrary, she had never seen him act and was simply attracted by his histrionic appearance; but in any case, she fell pretty powerfully in love with him. For a while she didn't even know what to do: leave her husband and go to the actor, or not leave her husband and simply enjoy herself with the actor without rearranging her life.

But then, when she discovered that the Thespian didn't seem to have a thing to his name—no position and nothing much else—she decided not to leave her husband. Besides, the actor himself was not burning with desire to marry her, since he was already a man burdened with a large family.

But since they were in love with one another, they still managed to get together from time to time.

He used to call her on the telephone, and she would drop in at a rehearsal to have a look at how dashingly he acted his roles. Because of this she fell even more deeply in love with him and yearned to make their rendezvous more frequent.

But since they had absolutely no place to meet, they

began, just like Romeo and Juliet, to meet on the street or at the movies, or drop into a café to exchange sweet nothings.

Brief meetings of this kind did not, of course, afford them much satisfaction, and they mourned constantly that their lives were turning out unhappily and that they did not even have a place where they could discuss their mad love.

She could not, of course, visit his home, since the actor was a family man.

And as far as stopping in at her place went, she frequently asked him over when her husband was at the office. But after dropping in a couple of times, he categorically refused to do it any more.

Being a nervous man and endowed besides with a morbid artistic imagination, he was simply afraid to be in her apartment, thinking that any minute her husband might come in, and the result might be a big discussion accompanied by shooting and so on.

And because of such thoughts, the actor visited her in, so to speak, an abnormal state of mind and really half dead with fright.

Then she, of course, stopped inviting him, since she saw that the man was simply in a state of mental illness and was scarcely fit for this world.

And so one day she said to him, "Look, here's what! If you want to see me, come to my girl friend's place on your next day off."

The Thespian said, "Well, that's splendid! Otherwise, you know, my profession demands refined nerves and I," he said, "can't help feeling timid when I'm at your apartment."

She had a best friend named Sonechka. A very nice person, not without some education. She was a ballet dancer, I think. Our heroine's husband completely approved of this acquaintance, saying that a better friend for his wife he couldn't wish for himself.

After some impassioned pleading, our ballet dancer gave her friend permission to use her room for negotiations with the beloved actor.

And so, on the morning of his day off, our actor got himself all dolled up and sallied forth to his rendezvous.

But we must relate that in the trolley car he had a little altercation, a conflict with his neighbor. Just a little argument, some shouting, and so on. As a result of which the actor, as a man with a little less self-control than was desirable, lost his temper. And when, after the argument, the neighbor got off the trolley car the actor couldn't restrain himself and spat at him. He was very glad when the trolley car quickly started up again and his insulted neighbor couldn't catch up with him, however much he wanted to.

However, this clash did not dampen our actor's spirits. He met the lady of his heart, and together they went to her girl friend's place, to which they now had the key—a rather small but cosy room in a communal apartment.

They went into the room and sat down on the couch to discuss their future life, when suddenly someone knocked at the door.

The young woman signaled the actor to keep quiet, but the artist had already frozen into silence of his own accord.

A voice was heard on the other side of the door: "Will she be back soon, do you know?"

As our heroine heard the voice, she grew terribly pale and whispered to the actor that it was her husband's. And that he must have seen them on the street and tracked them down here.

When the Thespian heard of this terrible turn of events, he started shaking and trembling and then, breathing cautiously, he lay down on the couch, looking in anguish at his heartthrob.

The voice behind the door said, "Then I'll leave a note. Say that I was here."

So our heroine's husband (for it was really he), wrote a note, stuck it under the door, and departed.

Our heroine, very much surprised, like lightning snatched up the note and began to read it. After which she began sobbing loudly, and wailing, and fell on the couch.

The Thespian, recovering himself somewhat at the sound of a female voice, also read the note with considerable surprise. It said: "Sonechka, sweetheart, I happened to get out of work early and ran over to see you, but—alas!—you were out. I'll come at three. A big kiss. Nikolay."

Through her tears and sobs our heroine said to the actor, "What could this mean? What do you think?"

The actor said, "Most likely your husband is having a romance with your girl friend. And he dropped in here for no other reason than to take a rest from family life. Now your conscience needn't bother you. Let me kiss your pretty hand."

Just as he was about to raise her hand to his chapped lips, there came a furious knock at the door. Behind the door they heard the excited voice of the girl friend.

"Open the door quickly, it's me. Did someone come here while I was out?"

When she heard these words, our heroine immediately burst into sobs and, opening the door, tearfully handed her girl friend the note that had been left for her.

After reading the note, the latter, somewhat nonplused, said, "There's nothing surprising about it. And since you know everything, I won't try to cover up. Besides, I'd like you to leave instantly, since some people are coming to see me."

Our heroine says, "What do you mean, 'some people'? It's obvious from the note that it's my husband

who is coming to see you right now. A pretty business to go away at such a moment. And maybe I'd like
to watch that scoundrel cross the threshold of this den
of iniquity."

The young man, who had been completely unnerved
by all this fuss, wanted to make himself scarce, but
our heroine in the heat of her irritation ordered him
not to go.

She said, "My husband will arrive in a minute, and
then we'll cut through this whole tangled knot."

Hearing words associated with the vocabulary of military life, the actor found his hat and began saying good-
bye even more energetically, and trying to leave. But at
this point an argument broke out between the girl
friends concerning him, as to whether he ought to go.

At first, both women wanted to keep him there as
material evidence until the husband came, the wife in
order to show her husband what sort of a character the
girl friend was, letting them use her room; the other to
show him what sort of a wife he had.

But then they changed their minds. The friend suddenly decided she didn't want to compromise herself
and the wife did not want to lose her husband's esteem. So, having agreed on this, they ordered our actor to get out of there pronto.

And no sooner did the latter, pleased with this turn
of events, begin saying good-bye, than there was another knock at the door. And the husband's voice said,
"Sonya, darling, it's me! Open the door!"

At this there was a certain amount of panic and confusion in the room.

The Thespian immediately became downcast and, in
terrible misery, was about to lie down on the couch and
pretend he was sick or dying, when it occurred to him
just in time that in a horizontal position like that they
would most likely open fire on him as a frivolous
lounger on sofas.

So he started dashing around the room, tripping over everything and making a terrible noise and racket.

The newly arrived husband, standing behind the door, was thoroughly astonished at the delay and the uproar, and he began pounding on the door even more vigorously, thinking that something odd was going on in the room.

Then the girl friend said to the actor, "This door leads to my neighbor's room. I'll open it for you right away. Go through there, and you'll find the door to the hall and the stairs. Best of luck!"

She hurriedly unlatched the door and told the actor to go as fast as he could, especially as the husband, hearing the noise in the room, had started tearing the door from its hinges in order to get in. Our actor ran like a shot into the next room and was trying to get out into the hall when he suddenly noticed that the door to the hall was locked from the outside, apparently with a padlock.

He was about to dash back to tell the two ladies that his situation was critical—the door was locked and he couldn't get out—but it was too late.

The husband had been admitted to the room, and a discussion had arisen during which the appearance of the actor would have been highly undesirable.

The actor, being a somewhat unbalanced man, suddenly grew weak from the multitude of events and, experiencing extreme physical debility and dizziness, he lay down on the bed, supposing that he was completely safe there.

So he lay there on the bed and thought various despairing thoughts—about this and that and sometimes about the absurdity of falling in love. Suddenly he heard someone rattling the lock in the hall. Someone or other, in fact, was fiddling with the door and would probably come into the room any moment.

Then the door really did open, and there appeared

on the threshold a man holding a basket of pastries and a bottle of wine.

When he saw a man lying on his bed, the new arrival gaped in astonishment and, scarcely knowing what he was doing, was about to slam the door behind him.

The actor began to apologize and stammer various things, when he saw to his horror that the tenant who had come in was none other than the man with whom he had quarreled that morning, and at whom he had spat from the platform of the trolley car.

Unable to count on his legs to get him out of there, our actor once more lay down on the bed like a small child, thinking that maybe it was all only a dream that would soon be over, and then a splendid life would begin, without any unpleasantness and quarrels.

The new arrival, whose astonishment had overcome his anger, said in a plaintive voice, "What's going on, ladies and gentlemen? A lady friend is coming to see me any minute and here, just look, some kind of plug-ugly has made himself at home in my room. How on earth did he get in? Through a locked door?"

Seeing that no one was breaking his arms or punching him in the snoot, the actor said with heartfelt enthusiasm, "Oh, *pardon!* I'll be off this minute. I just lay down to rest for a teeny second . . . I didn't know this was your bed . . . I got dizzy from a lot of things that happened . . ."

At this point the tenant, whose rage had overcome his astonishment, started to shout, "But this is disgraceful! Look, he sprawls on my bed, feet and all! It happens I don't even let my acquaintances lie there with their feet up. What's the big idea? What a scoundrel!"

And he ran up to the actor, grabbed him by the shoulders, and literally shook him off the bed. But then he noticed that the actor's countenance was already familiar to him from the morning's incident.

There was a short pause.

The tenant, utterly dazed, said, "So that's where I ran into you before, you fish-eye!" And he made as if to grab him by the throat.

But at that moment a gentle knock at the door was heard. The tenant says, "Well, thank your lucky stars that the lady I've been waiting for has arrived. Or else I'd have made mincemeat out of you."

Seizing the actor by the collar, he dragged him to the door so he could throw him out into the hall like a rag, to which the actor had no objections. He even felt grateful.

But just then the door opened, and on the threshold appeared the rather attractive lady who had come to visit the tenant and who had proved to be something of a lifesaver for our illustrious actor.

When he saw the lady, however, our actor stepped backwards in amazement and even staggered, since the lady who had come in was his wife.

As coincidences go, this really was something remarkable.

Our actor, who had been extremely taciturn for the past two hours, now began to bellow and raise the roof, demanding that his wife explain the meaning of this secret visit.

The wife began to cry and sob and said the man worked in the same office with her and that she really did visit him sometimes to drink tea and eat pastries.

Her abashed colleague said that, since they were now quits, they could make it up and all three have some tea, to which the actor replied with such furious cursing and shouting that his wife became hysterical. Her co-worker squared off again for a fight, once more feeling the insult of having been spat upon.

All the neighbors came running to see what was going on and among the onlookers were our heroine with her husband and her girl friend.

When they found out all that had happened, all

six of them got together in the room and began to confer about what they should do.

The ballet dancer said to her girl friend, "It's very simple! I'll marry Nikolay, the actor can marry you, and these two co-workers will make a happy couple too, since they work in the same office. That's what we should do."

The co-worker who had been visited by the actor's wife said, "That's a fine how-do-you-do! She's got a whole bunch of kids, and I should marry her? You think you've found some kind of a sucker."

The Thespian said, "I beg you not to insult my wife. Besides, I don't intend to marry her off to the first passer-by."

The actor's wife said, "But I wouldn't move in with him anyway. Take a look at what kind of room he has! Could I live here with three children?"

The co-worker says, "And I wouldn't let you into this room with your children if they shot a cannon at me. She's got such a scoundrel of a husband, and on top of that she wants to take over my room. I've already seen one character lying on my bed."

Sonechka, the ballet dancer, said in a conciliatory tone, "Then let's do it this way: I'll marry Nikolay, the actor and his wife will stay together as they are, and we'll marry Nikolay's wife to this fool of a co-worker."

The co-worker said, "Isn't that just fine and dandy! Nothing could be simpler. I'll go and register with her right away. Not on your life! Why, this is the first time I've set eyes on her mangy figure. Besides, she might be a female pickpocket."

The actor said, "Kindly refrain from insulting our ladies. I think that's the right solution."

Our heroine said, "Well, you know, I don't think so. I have no intention of moving out of our apartment. We have three rooms and a bath. I'm just not going to go meandering around any communal apartments."

Sonechka said, "Just because of three trouble-makers, all our couples are falling apart. Otherwise it would have been fine. I'd marry Nikolay, she could marry that one, and those two could stay together."

At this point a rude argument with accusations of this and that broke out between the ladies, after which the husbands, with heavy hearts, decided that everything should go on as before. And on this they parted.

However, not everything did go on exactly as before. Before long Sonechka got married to her neighbor, the co-worker of the actor's wife. And from time to time she used to receive visits from our actor, who appealed to her because of his soft, defenseless character.

And our heroine, disappointed in the actor's philistine character, fell in love with a certain physiologist. And as for Nikolay, he doesn't seem to be having any love affairs at the moment and is completely engrossed in his work. But incidentally, he does meet Sonechka occasionally and quite often takes trips to the country with her on his days off.

1935

A WATER BALLET

A CERTAIN Moscow motion-picture man came to Leningrad on business and he stayed at the Hotel Europa. He had a wonderful cosy room. Two beds. A bath. Rugs. Pictures. All this, so to speak, put our visitor in the mood to see people and have a good time.

His friends and acquaintances started dropping in and, as always happens, some of these acquaintances would take a bath when they came. After all, lots of people live in apartments without baths. Not everyone likes to go to the public bath, and people even forget about this bit of life's routine. And here such a convenient occasion presented itself: you drop in to see your friend, chat a while, philosophize a bit, and wash as well. Besides, there's hot water here. A free towel, and so on. For this reason many people are glad when their friends come to town.

In short, after about five days our visiting Muscovite got a little tired of the seemingly endless line of his friends. But, of course, he controlled himself, until finally a catastrophe took place.

One evening six friends arrived at his room almost simultaneously.

There was plenty of chitchat, but right away a short line of guests formed in front of the bathroom.

Three of them washed quickly, had some tea, and left.

But the fourth was an old lady. A relative of the visitor. She took an extraordinarily long time washing. She even seemed to be doing some laundry in there.

She carried on so long that the Muscovite and the people waiting their turn began to feel glum. She didn't come out of the bathroom for an hour and a quarter.

But since she really was our Muscovite's aunt, he didn't allow his friends to take any liberties in addressing her. In short, it was already long after midnight when she came out.

One of the friends hadn't cared to wait any longer and had left. But the other, who was amazingly persistent and brazen, was determined to have a bath that day no matter what, so he could be clean for something-or-other the next day.

So he waited until the aunt emerged. He washed the tub. He let the hot water run. And he lay down on a couch to wait for the tub to fill.

But then somehow he happened to fall asleep from exhaustion. And on top of that the Muscovite dozed off on the sofa.

The water filled the tub and overflowed, quickly flooding the room and leaking through to the floor below. But since there was an empty lounge underneath, the catastrophe was not noticed immediately.

To make a long story short, our two acquaintances awoke from the intense heat and the steam. The Muscovite, as he later recounted, had been dreaming that he was in Gagry.*

When he awoke he saw that the room was filled with water upon which slippers, newspapers, and various wooden articles were floating.

The hot water did not, of course, permit them to stop the flood at once, since they couldn't screw up their courage to run to the tub and turn off the faucet. Sitting on their couches, they didn't want to take the chance of putting their feet in the steaming water.

* Gagry—a resort town in Abkhazia, on the southeast coast of the Black Sea. *Ed.*

But then, by somehow moving some chairs about and jumping from one chair to the next, the Muscovite's terrified chum got to the tub and turned off the faucet.

No sooner had they turned off the faucet and noticed the water beginning to run off somewhere than the management ran into the room.

After inspecting the bathtub and the floor below, the management began to consult about something with an engineer who had come in.

Meanwhile our friends got into a serious argument: whose fault was it, and who was to pay the damages?

The Muscovite's friend, hardly breathing from terror, said that he could somehow put up forty rubles, but that anything above that should be paid by the occupant of the room, who had thoughtlessly permitted outsiders to bathe there.

At this point they got into an argument that could have ended unhappily if the management hadn't been right there.

In a trembling voice the Muscovite asked the management, "Tell me, how much will the damages amount to?"

The director answered obligingly, "You see, some plaster-of-Paris decorations in the lounge below were washed away: one large antique figure and three cherubim. So that greatly increases the expense."

The Muscovite's friend literally began to tremble when he heard about the plaster-of-Paris decorations and the cherubim.

The Muscovite, looking at the management in anguish, whispered, "And how much were these dissolved cherubim worth?"

The engineer said, "We figure we'll have to spend around seven or eight thousand on repairs and redecoration."

This sum completely unnerved the Muscovite, and

he lay down on the sofa, understanding little of what was going on.

His acquaintance revealed an ugly side of his character. He acted like a scoundrel, trying to sneak away and hide. He was, however, detained by the weak but honest hand of the visitor.

The visiting Muscovite, hardly able to wiggle his tongue, asked the director, "Couldn't you make it two thousand? At least I shouldn't have to restore those cherubim. These are no times to have things like that in hotels."

The director said, "But you're getting excited and bargaining for nothing. I don't think we've asked you to pay any damages."

Upon hearing these words, the Muscovite's friend closed his eyes, thinking he was dreaming.

But then the director said, "We are not blaming you at all. It was a technical oversight of ours. We calculated the water outflow poorly, and that's our technical inadequacy."

Here the engineer gave a scientific explanation. He said, pointing to the bathtub, "You see, there's a hole here at the top of the tub through which the water is supposed to flow when the tub is filled to the brim. And according to correct scientific calculation, the water has no right to flow over the edge. But in this case we were somewhat at fault and the hole, as you can see, was unable to ingest the flowing liquid. And so we beg your pardon for the resulting inconvenience. This won't happen again. We will fix it. These are technical flaws which have no business existing in our splendid times."

When he heard these words, the Muscovite's friend wanted to fall on his knees to give thanks both to the management and to fate, but the visitor did not allow him to do this.

He said to the director, "Of course, it couldn't be

otherwise. But tell me, who will make good my losses? My bedroom slippers are ruined, my suitcase is soaked, and perhaps something else was spoiled too, thanks to your technical inadequacy."

The director said, "Make out a claim—we'll pay damages."

The next day the Muscovite received forty-six rubles for his water-soaked suitcase.

The Muscovite's friend also wanted to take advantage of the situation and collect a small sum at the expense of contemporary technology, but he didn't get to do this, since he had no right to be in someone else's room at night. And for this reason he used his own funds to have his wet suit pressed at a tailor's.

Wearing this pressed suit, he arrived at the hotel again the following day and took a bath there, notwithstanding the fact that the Muscovite was extremely displeased about it and even got angry.

1935

MUCH ADO ABOUT NOTHING

HERE's an incident that happened in Arzamas. As it now turns out, there's a felt factory there.

I don't take it upon myself to say just what this factory manufactures. But we must assume that it's not mere felt insoles for boots, but something in the highest degree exceptional, and beneficial to all in a civic sense. Like waterproof felt overshoes and so forth.

But that's not the point.

Here's what happened in that factory.

During their lunch hour five girls got together and started fooling around and babbling all kinds of stuff and nonsense. Well, naturally—that's the way young girls are. They have just finished working. Now they're having a break. And, of course, they feel like joking a little, laughing, and flirting.

Besides, they are not professors, dried-up pedants, interested only in things like integrals and so on. They are simply the most ordinary kind of girls, from eighteen to twenty years old.

So that their conversation was rather of a frivolous nature than possessing a scientific foundation.

In short, they were discussing the boys they liked and which one each of them would like to marry.

There's nothing bad about that. Why not talk about it? The more so that it was their lunch hour. And even more so that it was a splendid spring day. The end of February. The first, so to speak, awakening of nature. Sunshine. Madness in the air. Birds chirp-chirping. You feel light-hearted and joyous.

So these five girls are sitting around having a nice chat together.

And one of these girls was, as they say nowadays, exceptionally full of pep. When the conversation turned toward marriage she took paper and pencil and, laughing gaily, said, "I've decided to write down minutes of everything we're talking about here. And I'll make a record right now of which boy each one of us likes, and maybe something a little more tangible will come out of all this fortune telling."

They all began to laugh and giggle, and they started joking with absolute inspiration. Then in the heat of inspiration they up and wrote some ludicrous minutes of their discussion. As we say: first debate and then decision. They decreed that this girl would marry that man. And that man was bound to propose to this girl. And so on. All in that spirit.

Of course, it was all a joke. Kidding around. Nonsense in every respect. A foolish business, unworthy of attention.

As a matter of fact, we don't even know how these crazy minutes ever got to the management. Most likely, some odd character, probably suffering from diabetes and exophthalmus, put the paper on the director's desk. Maybe he even went to the director's office in person, on his own hind legs, and, sighing, handed him the minutes, saying, "Here, take a look at what sort of tricks our girls are playing."

Kistanov, the director, pulled a long face, read the minutes, and went into an indescribable state of irritation.

He fired two of the girls from the factory, as it was literally stated in his directive, "for dissension-breeding activity, manifested in the organization of an official section possessing its own minutes, which had as its aim the cultivation of a petty-bourgeois spirit in young men."

To another girl he gave a severe reprimand and a threat of dismissal. The other two received warnings.

Maybe they cried a little, we don't know; only, after they had finished crying, they decided to lodge a protest about their unjust dismissal.

Here began a long song and dance which is still going on.

The injured parties presented a petition to the Grievance Commission.

The Factory Grievance Commission, under the same director's chairmanship, confirmed the dismissals.

Then the girls presented their petition to the union.

People there were attentive to feminine woe.

The inspector of the Central Committee of the Union of Woolen Workers issued the following completely correct resolution:

> The fact that minutes were recorded which attached certain girls to certain fellows with the purpose of marrying them cannot serve as grounds for their dismissal. For this reason the decision of the Factory Grievance Commission must be reversed as incorrect.

This resolution, however, had no effect on the director's unfeeling soul, so the inspector advised the girls to take their case to the people's court.

The people's court ordered the dismissals to be rescinded and the girls to be paid for their period of enforced idleness.

It would seem that everything had turned out fine and dandy, and that feminine conversations about love and marriage could begin again. Nothing of the sort.

After receiving the communication from the people's court, the director decided to undertake the proper education of these young persons.

With the very best intentions, he wrote the following directive concerning these unlucky girls:

> The affair which they organized could not do any real harm. But Comrades V. and G., as organizers of this

completely unnecessary group for corrupting young men, have received moral punishment. All this should teach Comrades V. and G. that in the future, as organizers, they must learn to distinguish the wholesome from the harmful and useless . . .

Perhaps at some future time people's courts will pass sentences for such a style and for such turns of phrase, but until then we will have to make our peace with them.

Further on, the directive stated:

Taking into consideration the fact that V. and G. have already been morally and socially punished, the directive will be changed with reference to releasing them from their work, but will retain the same formulation in the description of their act.

In short, the directive, as one can see, left the girls tagged with a humiliating and ridiculous label: "Organizers of a section for the corruption of young men."

And no matter how the girls struggled and protested, nothing came of it.

We do not doubt that the Central Committee of the Union will come to their aid and that the good name of the five girls (whose ages, all together, add up to ninety-five) will be restored to its former luster. But it disturbs us that the business has dragged on so long.

This affair has been going on for six months, and it can hardly be having a beneficial effect on the health and appearance of all the participants in the matter.

Even the director himself has probably grown faded and completely ceased to be attractive to women.

But more likely he was never attractive to them. And this can, in part, be sensed from his character.

All in all, the lance of our realistic satire is aimed straight at every sort of dried-up fellow and pedant who neither loves nor understands laughter and gaiety.

Well, so the girls had themselves a laugh. Imagine,

what a terrible misfortune! What earthly harm could it do? Absolutely none.

The main thing, it's amusing to note, is that the director felt called upon to defend the young men. As if they were poor, helpless things on the verge of being corrupted in "a petty-bourgeois spirit." While in fact they were in long pants themselves, as the saying goes, and could have got along quite well without his self-appointed support.

A stupid and trivial affair. But how much shouting, noise, and hurt feelings it caused!

A TRUE INCIDENT

LATELY, all sorts of thrilling things are being accomplished everywhere.

Aviators are setting world records. Construction is increasing. Trade is flourishing. A certain group of citizens unexpectedly went up onto Mount Kazbek* and apparently got to the top of one of its glorious peaks. Another group of citizens is, just imagine, sailing to Kazan in skiffs. Others, on the contrary, stay home and by their personal presence do what they can to help things along according to their abilities.

On top of that, many people have greatly matured. Others strive to spend their time in a cultured manner. They bathe frequently. And so on.

So that in view of such a turn of events, one doesn't even want to see something unworthy, any kind of petty thievery or swindling. Somehow it's irritating to see such things against such a bright background or to find oneself among them.

But last month when we were exchanging apartments, we ran into just such things. And now we want to expose them in print for the edification of our fellow citizens, so that certain individuals won't get away with throwing dust in people's eyes.

The people who exchanged rooms with us pretended at first to be people of principle.

"We have no intention," they said, "of deceiving you. We want to warn you that our room is in an apart-

* One of the highest peaks in the Caucasus, 16,541 feet. *Ed.*

ment which is above a shooting gallery. People shoot at targets there, and therefore you can sometimes hear shots. But you don't have to pay attention to them, and then it will be possible to live in that apartment."

My wife and I were touched by the honesty of these people, and, in our turn, we said frankly to them, "As far as our apartment goes, its faults, in comparison with yours, are not great. And we even wonder why we're trading. It's a wonderful, warm apartment, below which for five years there was a bakery, so that our fellow tenants got out of the habit of buying firewood. But about nine years ago the bakery closed and a repair man moved in. He fixes primus stoves and children's sleds there."

The people we were trading with said to us, "So it turns out there's a repair shop below you. There must be an infernal noise and racket."

And to tell the truth, there was such a racket you couldn't hear yourself think. Furthermore, there was a strong smell of burning, so that my wife, a southern girl, was always feeling half faint, and the doctor categorically forbade her to live there. Because of that we decided to move.

But now, when the conversation got down to brass tacks, we openly admitted that, of course, we did have noise, but then, they had shooting, which was also, as they say, worth something.

The man who wanted to trade with us said, "Yes, but what kind of fool am I, to move here and listen to this racket? Why, in that case, I'd be better off listening to shots. Shooting, at any rate, helps strengthen our military might and develops one's aim. And what, pardon me, will I hear at your place? Primus stoves and pots. No, thanks, I won't go along with you without a little extra payment, you know."

In short, we gave him a little extra and he traded with us. The fact that there weren't any children here tempted him. He gave a debit rating to children's cry-ing. He didn't like it. Of course, he didn't catch on that here in our apartment there were already three ladies under suspicion. One of whom was awaiting imminent developments. But I didn't feel like talking to him about that. After all, why upset a man ahead of time?

Thus we exchanged abodes. And we soon ascertained that we had been dealing with a crook.

Besides the shooting gallery, he stuck us with a *Wunderkind*. This was a teen-age boy who had received a commendation for his violin-playing at a musical competition, and therefore this artist of tender years sawed away continually on his instrument, so that my wife here too went into her half faint.

Besides that, there was a mental defective living here in this apartment. He lived with his brother and his mother.

True, he was a comparatively quiet defective, and it was even amusing to watch him at first. But all the same, as they say, why should we be in such select com-pany? It's unpleasant, and could frighten us at night.

On top of that, when we decided to trade rooms again, the presence of a crazy man played a negative role in the process of exchange. We couldn't even trade, since everyone was afraid to move here. Whereas, when we had traded, this defective was living in the country, and we didn't have any idea he existed.

Every time the doorbell rang, he would run out into the corridor in his underwear, and you couldn't do a thing with him.

At first, my wife and I would shut him in the bath-room. But this didn't do any good, since the people who wanted to trade with us would always look in there too every time, as if on purpose, to see what kind of facilities we had there. And he, naturally, would run out of there like a crazy man all the same, scaring the visitors so that they up and fainted.

It turned out, then, that we couldn't trade for the time being. We even wanted to sue the man who had done this to us and himself taken our quarters. But we were soothed by the thought that he might be left without any room at all, because we heard there was a plan to tear down that whole building in order to widen the street. It's an old house, and it sticks out too far in front of the other houses.

They wanted to move it, as they do in America, back about five meters. They had even started to dig in the cellar already to find out where they could put the machines, in case they needed to. But even before the machines got there, some kind of crack appeared, and in view of the decrepitude of the house, they decided to tear it down and to hell with it, so they could build something worthier of this epoch.

So that swindler who stuck us with his den is now put in a difficult position himself.

He thought that he had hooked us, as they say, with his trickery. But he had another think coming. You can't live by trickery. And now let that be a lesson to him and to everyone.

THE GALOSH

OF course, it's not difficult to lose a galosh in a trolley car. Especially if there's a crush and some hooligan steps on the back of it from behind—there you are without a galosh.

Losing a galosh is the merest trifle.

I got stripped of a galosh in a jiffy. You could say I didn't even have time to gasp.

I got on the trolley car—both galoshes were in place, as I now remember. I even felt with my hand as I was climbing on, to see if they were there.

But when I got off the trolley car—I looked: one galosh is there, but the other was gone. My boot is there. And, I see, my sock is there. And my drawers are in place. But one galosh is gone.

And, of course, there's no running after a trolley car . . .

I took off the galosh that was left, wrapped it in newspaper, and went off like that. After work, I think, I'll go hunt it up. An article like that can't drop out of sight. I'll dig it up somewhere.

After work I went to look for it. First off, I consulted with a certain streetcar conductor I know.

He cheered me up right away. "Thank your lucky stars," he says, "that you lost it on a trolley car. You were very lucky that it was a trolley car where you lost it. In another public place I wouldn't guarantee anything, but lose it on a trolley car and it's as good as found. We've got such a lost-and-found department! Come and get it. As good as found!"

"Well," I say, "thank you. It's a load off my mind. The main thing is that the galosh is nearly new. This is only the third season I've been wearing it."

The next day I go to the lost-and-found department.

"Can I," I say, "get a galosh of mine back, pals? They took it off me in the trolley car."

"You can," they say. "What kind of galosh?"

"A galosh," I say, "an ordinary galosh. Size twelve."

"We," they say, "may very well have twelve thousand size twelves. Describe its characteristics."

"Its characteristics," I say, "are ordinary ones: the back is, of course, a bit mangled, there's no lining inside—it's worn out."

"We," they say, "have got maybe over a thousand galoshes like that. Aren't there any special characteristics?"

"There are," I say, "some special characteristics. The toe is almost torn right off—it barely holds. And," I say, "there's hardly any heel. The heel wore out. But the sides," I say, "are still all right—so far they've held out."

"Stay here," they say. "We'll look right away."

Suddenly they bring out my galosh.

Well, I was awfully glad. I was really moved.

Look, I think, how wonderfully our system works. And, I think, what idealistic people, to have taken so much trouble over one galosh.

I say to them, "Thank you, friends," I say, "from the bottom of my heart. Give it to me quick. I'll put it right on. I thank you."

"No," they say, "dear comrade, we can't give it to you. We," they say, "don't know, maybe it wasn't you that lost it."

"It *was* me," I say, "that lost it. Have you gone off your rocker?"

They say, "We believe you, and we fully sympathize, and it's very likely that you lost just this galosh. But we can't give it to you. Bring an affidavit that you really lost a galosh. Let the management of your apartment house certify this fact, and then we'll give back what you legally lost without any extra fuss."

"Pals," I say, "honest comrades, they don't even know of this fact in my apartment house. Maybe they won't give me a paper like that."

"They'll give it to you," they say, "it's their business to give it. What are they there for?"

I took another look at the galosh and left.

The next day I went to the manager of our building.

"Give me," I say, "a paper. My galosh is lost."

"But did you really," he says, "lose it? Or are you making it up? Maybe you want to grab yourself an extra piece of consumer goods?"

"I swear to God," I say, "I lost it."

He says, "Of course, I can't just take your word for it. Now, if you had brought a statement from the trolley-car terminal that you had lost a galosh—then I would give you the paper. But this way I can't."

I say, "But *they* sent me to you."

He says, "Then at least write me a statement."

I say, "What should I write?"

He says, "Write: 'On such and such a date my galosh was lost. And so forth. I hereby,' you can write, 'state I will not move out until the matter is cleared up in full.' "

I wrote the statement. And the next day I received a formal affidavit.

I went to the lost-and-found department with this affidavit. And there, just imagine, they gave me my galosh without any fuss or red tape.

Only when I put on the galosh did I feel touched to the heart. People, I thought, certainly do work! Where on earth would people have bothered with my galosh for such a long time? They would have tossed it out of the trolley car, and that's that. And here it only took me a week's finagling and they gave it back.

The only thing that bothers me is that during the week I was working on it I lost my other galosh.

I was carrying it wrapped up under my arm the whole time, and I don't remember where I left it. The main thing is, it wasn't in a trolley car. That's the saddest part, that it wasn't in a trolley car. Well, where am I going to look for it?

But, anyhow, I have the other galosh. I put it on my dresser. Whenever I feel sad I take a look at my galosh and feel happy and unresentful. Look, I think, how well our system works.

I've told you this story and now I'm afraid that the trolley people might take offense at it. But why should they take offense? They've probably corrected these shortcomings of theirs already, and they probably give out galoshes even more simply. The more so that this happened back in 1930. Since then I haven't lost anything. So that I can't satisfy your curiosity.

And really, the heart of this matter doesn't have to do with trolley cars, but with upside-down psychology. And since a struggle against this psychology is going on and the whole system is getting straightened out, this *feuilleton* of ours may be read simply as an artistic reminiscence or a kind of memoir on a lost galosh.

A HEART OF STONE

Not long ago a man came to see me and told me his sad story. He asked me to write a *feuilleton* on the subject of what he related to me.

But his story disturbed me, and at first I even refused to do anything, because it was impossible to write without checking the facts. And, as you will soon see, it seemed impossible to check these particular facts.

But I found a way out. I will tell this story without mentioning names. And if it is true, then let the guilty party in this matter morally choke, so to speak, on my *feuilleton*.

So this is how it was.

The director of a certain fairly small government office told his business manager on the day before their regular day off that he was moving to his country place with his family the following day and for this reason he needed a truck to transport his belongings.

The business manager answered delicately that it was certainly an unusual occurrence when he couldn't comply with a request from the director. Two trucks were in the shop for major repairs, one had been mobilized for road-building, and as for the fourth, that had been promised since the beginning of May to bookkeeper M., who was also moving to the country the next day.

Others were present during this conversation, and the director in no way betrayed his irritation. But when the outsiders had left his office, he turned on the business manager and bawled him out in coarse terms, saying that a word from the director was not a request but an order, and that if there were no truck tomorrow he could damn well find himself another job. And he said that, in general, if you came right down to it, he was sick and tired of his independent tone, the way he leaned his elbows on tables and chairs, and his complete lack of that respectfulness which it was high time to inculcate in underlings, as had been done in other offices.

The business manager showed himself to be a man of some boldness. He answered the director in this way, "I have no lack of respectfulness. As for leaning my elbows on tables and chairs, I agree completely with you that it was probably superfluous on my part. But your coarse abuse and your threats are also carrying things pretty far, as they say. Now, if you were a product of the old order, an attitude like that toward your subordinate would be understandable, but you're a man out of the proletarian batch, and where you got a general's tone like that I simply can't understand. I have always carried out all your orders without a murmur. Your honored spouse, if we come right down to it, literally never gets out of our limousine. But I don't say anything about that to you, I don't think. Because I don't allow myself to make any remarks to my superior or his wife which would injure their dignity. But as for the truck which I'm supposed to take away from the bookkeeper to give to you—I won't agree to that as a matter of principle, and I won't do it even if you have them shoot at me from a cannon."

These words infuriated the director. He shouted, "You're forgetting where you are and what you are, you boor! You have the nerve to talk to me as if you were my superior and I your subordinate. I really will fire you. And then you'll understand the difference between us."

"I'd like to see just how you're going to fire me," said

the business manager. "I haven't committed any crimes and my conscience is clear. And it won't be quite so easy to have me dismissed, since your motive for this will not raise you in people's esteem."

"Don't you worry about how easy it will be," said the director. "You'll fly out of here so fast you won't recognize your own mother."

So ten days pass, and then, out of a clear sky, the director in a written order gives the business manager a severe reprimand for bad management and squandering of property.

Then two more weeks go by, and the business manager, who had still not recovered from the first blow, is dismissed from his duties with the explanation in the directive that he had caused the work of the enterprise to break down.

The stunned business manager begins running from the office union committee to the union itself, and from the union to the people's court. And he tries to prove to everyone that there had been no breakdown on the job and no bad management either, but rather the reverse—he had bent over backwards to get the business on a sound footing. And for this he had been censured for squandering property. He had, he said, sold the carriage and horse in order to acquire things that were of more use to the office. And that, finally, the whole business was the manager's personal revenge.

But all these timid words were drowned in the whirlpool of all the records and documents produced by the director.

Moreover, the indignant director testified to the union that he felt no personal animosity at all, and that if he had once shouted at the business manager it was because of his unsatisfactory work.

And at this point the director, after rummaging through some documents, produced some bills according to which it turned out that the business manager had twice purchased tires from a private source. And although the business manager cried that this had been done in an emergency and only with the director's consent, this fact played a decisive role.* And the director's order remained in force, although, to be sure, with the slight modification that the victim could find himself some minor job.

When the business manager came in for the pay that was due him, the director accidentally met him in the hall and smilingly asked, "Well, did you take a bit of a beating?"

The business manager was on the point of assaulting the director, but he restrained himself and, giving him a contemptuous look, went out.

Then he came to me and requested that I write a *feuilleton.*

And here is the *feuilleton* before you.

Here is, so to speak, a sort of "pinnacle of bureaucracy." The director did everything very subtly and with such thorough knowledge of human nature that it was impossible to prove anything. That dyed-in-the-wool bureaucrat, with his moss-covered heart, will shrug his shoulders and deny everything.

Only public opinion and comradely support could begin to fight against this.

And so, if the truth has been told about this director, then let's hope he chokes a bit on my *feuilleton.*

---

* By the mid-1930's, when this story was written, it was quite irregular for a government office to buy anything from a private source; but it was often impossible to obtain things through official channels. *Ed.*

MORE ON
THE ANTI-NOISE CAMPAIGN

AND so the campaign against noise continues energetically. But if we're going to talk about this campaign, I'd like first of all to mention the radio.

For sheer strength of sound the radio takes first place. Maybe only gunshots make a louder noise. But there is, as they say, a special science against gunshots—ballistics. But against the radio scientific thought seems to be blind.

The main thing is, it's irritating that the anti-noise campaign did not start with this discovery. For some reason scientific thought at first followed, so to speak, the trolley line.

But the noiseless trolley car—that, in the final analysis, is technical knowledge plus, perhaps, ordinary rubber or, to use scientific terminology, gutta-percha.

What that same rubber can do against the radio—that is still an unexplored question.

Personally, I'm still in good shape as regards the radio. Some people, when they are in their apartments, can hear the radio from the street, and from the floors above and below, not to mention the neighbors on either side.

A certain relative of mine notes down for scientific purposes every sound from the entire building which can be heard in his apartment. And, if he's not lying, he can hear sixteen radios in his place.

Of course, I don't hear so many, but I'll tell you frankly that two radios really get me down.

Now one of my neighbors has a set, but I don't care much about him. You couldn't call him a great lover of radio. He comes home from work and listens to the children's hour. And then you don't hear any more from him. Unless, when he's under the influence, he turns on some kind of singing for five minutes more. That's all his radio listening for you. He is a gentle, humane person. Not much of a drinker. He has other things on his mind.

But my other neighbor—he's something exceptional. He purposely leaves the radio on for long periods. And even, for example, when he goes to the public bath, he leaves the radio playing.

What was our astonishment, agitation, and rage when he went on vacation and left his radio going full blast! He didn't turn it off. And he locked his room with an American padlock while he himself, as they say, calmly sailed off to the Crimea for a month. He went there to get a sun tan. To the south shore of the Crimea. And we, as they say, had to put up with the noise from his room.

The first two days we didn't even recognize the degree of absent-mindedness we were faced with. But then we hear it playing completely outside the regular times. Suddenly we realize: his radio is playing around the clock.

Then I run to the building management and ask them to cut off the aforementioned noise.

The chairman says, "Yes, there's an anti-noise campaign going on, I don't deny it. And, of course, it isn't nice on a tenant's part to produce noise during his vacation. But I don't dare break down the door to get in without his permission."

Then his other neighbor and I chip in and send a telegram to him in the Crimea saying, "You Judas, you forgot to turn off your radio. Send immediate permission to break down the door."

But since at the last moment, out of nervous irritation, I added a few more caustic words to the telegram, he didn't answer it.

I tried to get used to the constant sound from his room somehow. And I did begin little by little to get used to the music, but when some young lady from the weather bureau started reading off what temperature it was in what town, I couldn't stand it any more and dashed out of my room to do something about it.

One tenant says to me, "Go up on the roof and cut down his antenna. Hardly any radio can play without an antenna. In this way you will find peace of mind."

Then I, who had never been on the roof and did not even know how to get up there, climbed up at the risk of my life and broke off an enormous antenna like a boat hook right above his window.

But what was my surprise when I got down and heard the sound again!

Then the tenant said, "He must have a very powerful radio, since it can play without an antenna. If you like," he says, "I'll send a teen-ager I know to you this evening—he knows radio mechanics very well."

So that evening he sent over the teen-ager.

The teen-ager looked over everything pertinent and said, "You," he says, "have broken off someone else's antenna. For that you can expect some unpleasantness. As for your neighbor, he doesn't need any antenna, since all he's got is an outlet connected to a central receiver—that is, he's just got wires and a loud-speaker hooked up to them. If you like, I'll cut those wires in the hall and it'll stop playing."

So he did, and the music ceased at once. A blessed silence ensued. And I enjoyed it for about twenty minutes, to my complete pleasure.

Then my other neighbor turned on his radio for no

reason at all, and the devilish noise and howling started again. On top of that someone came to my room to discuss the broken antenna, and then began noise and shouting of a different order, which vex the spirit and weaken the blood even more.

They really should think up something to do about the radio first off, and then tackle the trolleys with new energy. The more so that tests revealed that the newly produced noiseless trolley really makes a considerable amount of noise, whatever they want to call it.

Perhaps some kind of governor for radio outlets could be invented?

I won't say anything. Radio is a great discovery but—how shall I say it?—I'm pretty fed up with it.

THE DICTAPHONE

Say what you will, these Americans are pretty sharp characters! How many amazing discoveries, how many great inventions they have made! Steam, Gillette safety razors, the earth's rotation on its axis—all these were discovered and thought up by Americans and, in some cases, Englishmen.

And now, if you please: mankind has once more benefited. The Americans have given the world an exceptional machine—the dictaphone.

Of course, this machine may have been invented somewhat earlier, but just now they sent one to us.

It was a triumphant and remarkable day when we got this little machine.

A crowd of people gathered to have a look at the marvel.

Our widely esteemed Konstantin Ivanovich Derevyashkin took the cover off the machine and reverently wiped it with a rag. At that moment our eyes told us what a great genius had invented it. Really: a great number of little screws, rollers, and cunning knobs were exposed to view. It was even amazing to think how this little machine, so delicate and fragile to look at, could work and fulfill its purpose.

Oh, America, America—what a great nation that is!

When everyone had looked over the machine, our widely esteemed Comrade Derevyashkin, after some complimentary remarks about the Americans, said a few introductory words about the usefulness of brilliant inventions. Then we proceeded to practical experiments.

"Which of you," said Konstantin Ivanovich, "would like to say a few words into this ingenious apparatus?"

Upon which our esteemed comrade Tykin, Vasily, stepped forward. A thin, long sort of fellow, who gets a salary of the sixth class plus overtime.

"Permit me," he says, "to try it out."

They let him.

He went up to the machine, not without a certain agitation, and thought a long time about what he should say, but he couldn't think of anything and with a wave of his hand walked away from the machine, sincerely regretting his low level of literacy.

Then someone else went up. Without thinking for very long, this fellow yelled into the open mouthpiece, "Hey, you damn fool!"

At once they took off the lid, took out the roll, put it where it was supposed to go—and what do you know?—the roll played back to all those present the exact same words mentioned above.

Then the delighted onlookers elbowed their way up to the microphone, trying to say all sorts of phrases and slogans. The machine obediently produced faithful recordings of everything.

At this point Vasily Tykin, who gets a salary of the sixth class plus overtime, stepped up again, and asked someone in the crowd to curse obscenely into the microphone.

Our esteemed Konstantin Ivanovich Derevyashkin at first categorically forbade cursing into the microphone and even stamped his foot, but then, after some wavering, he got carried away by the idea and told them to fetch from a neighboring house a former Black Sea sailor—a terrible curser and brawler.

The Black Sea sailor didn't make them wait long. He presented himself.

"Where," he asks, "am I to curse? Into what aperture?"

Well, they showed him, of course. And how he bent their ears back—even esteemed Comrade Derevyashkin himself flung his arms wide, as if to say, That's telling 'em; this is no America.

Then, just as soon as they could pry the Black Sea sailor away from the microphone, they put on the roll. And really, the machine had willingly and accurately noted it all down.

Everyone began to come up again, to take his turn cursing into the aperture in every style and dialect. They began to make various sounds: they clapped their hands, tap danced, clicked their tongues—and the machine worked without a stop.

Now everyone really saw just how great and ingenious this invention was.

The only trouble was that the machine turned out to be a bit fragile and unaccustomed to shrill noises. For instance, Konstantin Ivanovich shot a revolver, not, of course into the microphone but, so to speak, to one side in order to record on the roll for history the sound of a shot—and what do you think—it turned out that the machine got spoiled; it broke down.

From this point of view the laurels of the American inventors and speculators fade and diminish somewhat in importance.

However, their merit remains great and significant in the eyes of humanity.

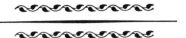

THE HISTORY OF
AN ILLNESS

FRANKLY, I prefer to be ill at home.

Of course, it goes without saying that the hospital may be brighter and more civilized. And, perhaps, the caloric value of the food is more carefully supervised there. But, as they say, there's no place like home.

I was taken to the hospital suffering from typhus. The members of my household thought this would alleviate my incredible sufferings.

But they did not accomplish their purpose, since I happened to get into some special kind of hospital where not everything pleased me.

Anyhow, no sooner do they bring in a patient and register him than suddenly he sees a notice on the wall: "Delivery of corpses from 3:00 to 4:00."

I don't know about other patients, but I just got weak in the knees when I read that announcement. The main thing was that I had a high fever and really, my constitution might have been barely hanging onto life, maybe just by a hair—and all of a sudden I had to read words like that.

I said to the man who was registering me, "Why, Comrade Medical Assistant," I say, "do you hang up such vulgar notices? Somehow," I say, "it's not so interesting for patients to read that."

The medical assistant, or what do you call him—med-aide?—was surprised that I talked to him like that, and he says, "Will you look at that: a sick man, he can hardly walk, he's got such a fever he almost breathes out steam, and still he's throwing the criticism around. If," he says, "you get better, which is unlikely, then go ahead and criticize, otherwise we'll really deliver you between three and four in the form it says here, and then you'll know."

I wanted to have it out with this medical aide, but since I had a high temperature, 39.8,* I didn't feel like arguing with him. I just said to him, "You look here, stethoscope, when I get better you'll have to answer for your insolence. Should sick people have to listen to that kind of talk? It morally undermines their strength."

The assistant was astonished that a seriously ill patient was arguing with him so freely, and cut short the conversation at once. At this point a little nurse trotted up. "Come along, patient," she says, "to the washing-down station."

But I was also a little taken aback by these words.

"It would be better," I say, "to call it a bath instead of a washing-down station. That is a nicer expression and uplifts the patient. I'm not a horse that I should be washed down."

The nurse says, "It's not enough that he's sick, he's got to notice all kinds of fine points too. You probably won't get well, so why do you have to stick your nose in everything?"

Then she led me to a bath and ordered me to undress.

So I started undressing, and suddenly I see that there is already some kind of head sticking out of the water in the tub. And then I realize that it looks like an old woman, probably one of the patients, is sitting in the tub.

I say to the nurse, "Where have you dogs brought me

* 103.6° Fahrenheit. *Ed.*

—to the women's bath? There's already someone taking a bath here."

The nurse says, "Oh, that's a sick old lady sitting there. Don't you pay any attention to her. She has a high temperature and doesn't react to anything. So go ahead and undress without embarrassment. And meanwhile we'll get the old lady out of the tub and hunt up some fresh water for you."

I say, "The old lady doesn't react, but maybe I still do. And it's definitely unpleasant for me to look at what you've got swimming in the tub."

Just then the assistant came back.

"I," he says, "have never seen such a fussy patient. "He doesn't like this, that, and the other thing, the smart aleck. A dying old lady is taking her bath and he has to complain. She's probably got a temperature of close to 40, and she doesn't care about anything and sees everything as if she were looking through a sieve. In any event, the sight of you won't hold her in this world an extra five minutes. No, I like it better when patients come to us unconscious. Then, at least, everything is to their taste, they're pleased with everything and don't enter into scientific disputes with us."

At this point the old lady in the bath spoke up: "Take me out of the water," she says, "or I'll get out myself and let you all have it."

So they busied themselves with the old lady and ordered me to undress.

While I was undressing they instantly filled the tub with hot water and told me to get in. And, knowing my character, they didn't attempt to argue with me any more, but tried to humor me in everything. Only, after my bath, they gave me some enormous underwear, not at all my size. I thought they had tossed me an outsized set like that on purpose, out of spite, but then I saw that this was the normal procedure with them. There seemed to be a rule that small patients wore large nightshirts, and big patients, small ones.

My set even turned out to be better than some others. On my shirt the hospital label was on the sleeve and did not spoil the general appearance, whereas some of the other patients had it on the back and some on the chest, and this lowered their human dignity.

But since my temperature kept going up, I didn't try to argue about these details.

They put me in a smallish ward where there were nearly thirty patients of various kinds. Some of them, to look at, were gravely ill. But others, on the contrary, were getting better. Some of them were whistling. Others were playing checkers. Still others were sauntering around the wards and spelling out what was written over the head of each bed.

I say to the nurse, "Maybe I've landed in a mental hospital. In that case, say so. I've been in hospitals every year, and I've never seen anything like this. There is silence and order everywhere else, but here you've got some kind of bazaar."

She says, "Perhaps you would care to be put in a private ward with a sentry to chase away the flies and fleas?"

I set up a hue and cry for the chief doctor, but instead of him that same assistant appeared. I was in a weakened condition, and at the sight of him I lost consciousness altogether.

I came to only after about three days, I think.

The little nurse says to me, "Well," she says, "you must have as many lives as a cat. You have gone through everything. We even left you near an open window by accident, and even so you unexpectedly started to get better. And now, if you don't catch anything from the other patients, then you can be sincerely congratulated on your recovery."

However, my constitution did not succumb to any

more illnesses. The only thing was that, just before I left, I caught a childish disease—whooping cough.

The nurse says, "You probably caught the infection from the next wing. That's our children's section. And, probably, you carelessly used the same eating utensils as a child with whooping cough. That's why you got sick."

Well, soon my constitution asserted itself, and I began to get better again. But when the time came to release me, here too, as they say, I got my fill of troubles. I got sick again, this time with a nervous disorder. From nervous causes my skin broke out in little pimples, like a rash. The doctor said, "Stop being so nervous, and in time it will go away."

But I was nervous only because they didn't release me. Either they'd forget, or there was something missing, or someone hadn't shown up, and they couldn't make it official. So, finally, a movement started among the patients' wives, and the whole staff was run ragged. The assistant says, "We're so overcrowded that we haven't got time to release any patients. On top of that, you're only eight days overdue, and you're raising a rumpus. Why, we have some recovered patients who still haven't been released after three weeks, and they're still waiting quietly."

However, soon they released me, and I returned home.

My wife says, "You know, Petya, a week ago we thought you had passed on to the next world, since a notice came from the hospital which said, 'Upon receipt of this, come at once for the body of your husband.' "

It turned out that my wife had run to the hospital, but there they apologized for the mistake, which had been made in the bookkeeping department. It was someone else who had died, and for some reason they thought it was me, although by that time I was healthy, and I was only covered with those pimples of nervous origin. This incident made me feel bad, for some reason, and I wanted to run to the hospital and bawl out somebody, but when I remembered what sort of things happen there, well, you know, I didn't go after all.

And now I stay home when I'm sick.

1936

BIG-CITY LIGHTS

THE father of one of the tenants in our communal apartment house arrived from the country.

Actually, he arrived at the time of his son's illness. If that hadn't happened, he would probably have lived out his days without seeing Leningrad. But since his son had got sick, here he was.

His son was our lodger. He was a waiter in a certain restaurant. He handed out the servings there, and was well thought of.

Perhaps, after working still harder, he got overheated from his nocturnal labors one evening, dashed out on the street to go home, and thus naturally caught cold —while serving, so to speak, at his culinary post. First he developed a head cold and sneezed for seven days. Then the cold went down into his chest and his temperature went up to 40.*

On top of that, wanting to spend one of his days off in a cultural manner, he went to Pavlovsk to look at the palaces,† and there strained himself slightly while helping his wife into the train.

So that all this taken together produced a melancholy picture of a man struck down by illness in the full flower of his vigor.

And, since he was by nature a hypochondriac, our

---

* 104° Fahrenheit. *Ed.*

† Pavlovsk—a town and large park some 20 miles from Leningrad, formerly one of the Imperial summer residences. *Ed.*

poor waiter was certain that he would not recover and would never again, as we say, enter upon the fulfillment of his direct responsibilities.

And so on account of this he asked his father to come to Leningrad so that he could bid him farewell for the last time.

It wasn't that he loved his father so deeply and now, at the sunset of his life, wanted to see him no matter what; just the opposite—he had not inquired about him in the course of forty years, and treated the fact of his existence with the utmost indifference. But when his spouse saw that her husband was running such an impossibly high temperature, rather out of vanity—as if to say, We're doing everything as it should be done— she sent papa a telegram, saying, "Come to Leningrad, your son is ill."

And when the son had already begun to recover, his papa, much to everyone's astonishment, arrived in Leningrad from very distant parts, wearing bast shoes, with a sack on his back, and carrying a walking stick. It's true that the old man later turned out to have a pair of boots in the sack, but he refused to wear them on principle, saying on the subject, "A rich man cares for his chest, the poor man for his vest."

Of course, everyone including the son had supposed that there would arrive a self-effacing, even religious old chap of about seventy, who would utter pious remarks and be afraid of everything. But it turned out, as we say, just the opposite.

It turned out that the old geezer was a rare one for being quarrelsome, and also something of an expert at making scenes, a boor, and a loudmouth. And on top of that, if he wasn't exactly a counterrevolutionary, he did display astonishing backwardness in political matters.

As soon as he got into the yard of the apartment house, he lit into the janitor, and pulled by the ears a certain youth who had come to visit his uncle, a tenant in the house for twelve years.

Then he had such a sharp exchange with the chairman of the tenants' office that the chairman was amazed at the kind of attitudes toward the contemporary world that existed and even wanted to send a report on this to the father's place of residence.

To top it all off, the newly arrived father terrified his son when right off the bat he submitted an official inquiry about whether he could be assigned living space for permanent residence in Leningrad.

Of course, the old man was probably comparatively nice if you left him alone, but from the day of his arrival almost all the tenants here turned out not to be on the highest plane in terms of polite behavior. They all began to tease him, joke about him as if he were a fool, and laugh at his provincial, yokelish ways. And everyone tried to say something nonsensical to him, like the janitor, who said in a voice like a rooster's every time he met him, "From what collective farm have you arrived, young man?"

And his son, the waiter Gavrilov, joined, of course, in the general gaiety, and one time, choking with laughter, looked purposely at the newspaper and said to the old man, "Don't go out on the street today, papa— today they're going to round up everybody with gray or red hair."

Of course, all this was done rather amiably and without malice, but nevertheless, as we say, it was probably not entirely pleasant for the newly arrived old man, who had lived for seventy-two years and was probably smarter than all of them put together. But they thought he was a simpleton, a fool, and a hayseed, and that's how they treated him.

And this, as one might expect, had a negative effect on his behavior.

From the time he arrived there was at least one

uproar a day. There were shouts, coarse scenes, and so on.

On top of everything, on the seventh day of his stay he got soused in a beer parlor and started acting up there. They even wanted to hand him over to the militia. But he hid from everyone and went gallivanting through the streets.

So there he was, walking along the street, singing a song. He was a little old man, gray-haired and wearing extremely simple country garb. He was going along the street, and suddenly he realized he was lost.

Of course, it was absurd to get lost here. Especially since he knew the address. But in his tipsy state he got scared and even sobered up.

He asked a passer-by which way to go. But the passer-by did not know and told him to apply to the militia.

Of course, our old man was afraid to go right up to the militiaman standing on duty, and walked on a couple of blocks out of agitation. But then he cautiously approached a militiaman, thinking that the latter would blow his whistle and shout at him.

However, the militiaman, in accordance with his training, saluted the old man, raising his white-gloved hand to the peak of his cap.

Ready for a scene and accustomed to them, the old man got a bit confused from the unexpectedness of the act and stammered a few words having nothing to do with the matter. The militiaman, asking him what street he was looking for, showed him where to go and, saluting once more, returned to his duties.

But that little gesture of respect and courtesy, intended at one time for generals and barons, made an extraordinary impression on our elderly visitor. The old man began to tremble when the militiaman saluted him the second time and in this way showed that there had been no mistake, that it was the accepted thing.

Then the old man, as it later turned out, went up to another militiaman and again received a salute, which left an even deeper imprint on his impressionable mind.

Of course, I don't know whether it's possible for such a thing to have immediate influence on a person's character, but everyone noticed that when the old geezer came back, his manner was exceedingly restrained, and he did not engage in the usual heated exchange when he passed the janitor, but saluted him in silence and went in.

I don't know whether it's possible for such a trivial incident and such a really negligible occurrence to play a certain part in the reshaping of character, but everyone noticed that something new and extremely original was going on with Papa Gavrilov.

Some observed him going up to the militiaman on the corner near the house and chatting politely with him, and many people with somewhat crude minds ascribed the change they noticed to the terror which the old man had experienced when they wanted to hand him over to the militia. But others explained it differently.

A certain intellectual from our apartment, who was a diabetic, said concerning the incident, "I've always been of the opinion that respect for individuals, praise, and esteem produce exceptional results. Many personalities unfold because of this, just like roses at daybreak."

The majority did not agree with him, and an inconclusive discussion even took place in our apartment.

About three days later, Papa Gavrilov informed his son that pressing business demanded his return to the country.

Some of the people from our apartment, wishing to smooth over their awkward jokes with the old man, saw him off at the station, and when the train started, Papa, standing on the rear platform, saluted them all. They all burst out laughing, and Papa laughed and rode away to his native soil.

There he will probably introduce a new cordiality

into his relations with people. And because of this, life will become brighter and pleasanter for him.

1936

CLOUDS

A short time ago I was riding on a trolley car. I was standing on the platform, of course, since I'm no lover of riding inside.

I'm standing on the platform and admiring the panorama which surrounds me.

We're crossing the Trinity Bridge. Everything around it looks stunningly beautiful. The Peter and Paul Fortress with its golden spire. The Neva with its mighty flow.* And just now the sun is setting. It is, as we say, very magnificent.

And so I'm standing on the platform; and my soul is rapturously drinking in every color, every rustle, every separate moment.

All sorts of exalted thoughts come to me. All sorts of humane phrases crowd into my head. All sorts of poems come into my mind. My memory dredges up something-or-other from Pushkin: "Papa, Papa, look! Our fish nets hauled a dead man to the shore . . ."

Suddenly the conductress shatters my exalted mood by starting to argue with one of the passengers.

And at this point, as we say, I descended from the clouds, to this mundane world, with its narrow interests and petty passions.

The young, attractive conductress is saying to the passenger in ugly tones, "What do you think? That I'm

* Famous Leningrad sights. The "mighty flow" is a quotation from Pushkin's famous poem "The Bronze Horseman." *Ed.*

going to give you a free ride? In short, pay or get off my car."

And the words she is uttering are to a modestly dressed man. This man is standing there with a gloomy countenance and, in fact, not paying his fare. He's trying to get around paying. First he digs down into his pockets and doesn't find anything, then he says ingratiatingly, "Such a cute little conductress with such pretty little lips, and she's getting herself so upset and spoiling her appearance . . . Well, I haven't got any money . . . I'll get off right away, I'll just ride one stop . . ."

"I won't let you ride any stops for free," says the conductress. "But if you don't have any money, smarty, what did you push yourself on the trolley for? That's what I can't understand."

The passenger says, "Well, walking—maybe I've got blisters on my feet. How unfeeling people are these days. They haven't any sympathy for a person. Everything is money, money, money. You just can't protect yourself from it. Just gimme, gimme, gimme . . ."

My heart fills with humane emotions. I feel sorry for this man who is too broke even to ride the trolley.

I take out some money and say to the conductress, "Take enough for that fellow with the gloomy face. I'll pay for him."

The conductress says, "I don't permit any side payments."

"How is that?" I say. "How can you not permit it? That's a fine how-do-you-do!"

"I just," she says, "don't permit it. And if he doesn't have any money, let him take the shoe-leather express. In my sector of work I won't let anyone encourage the very things we're fighting against. If a person has no money—that means, he hasn't earned any."

"Excuse me," I say, "but that's not humane. You have to treat a person humanely when he's in bad shape, and not the opposite. You have to pity and help a human being when something happens to him, not when everything is going splendidly. Besides, maybe he's my relative, and I want to help him because of family feelings."

"I'm going to send your relative to a certain place right now," says the conductress, and, leaning out of the trolley, she begins to blow her whistle.

The passenger with the gloomy countenance says, sighing, "What a mean little dame it turned out to be this time. Well, stop blowing your whistle and let's go on: I'll pay right away."

He takes a wallet out of his pocket, pulls out three ten-ruble notes, and says with a sigh, "I didn't want to change such big bills for nothing in the trolley. But since this female is going out of her mind and won't allow the passengers to contribute, well, take it—if, of course, you have change, which isn't very likely."

The conductress says, "Why are you sticking such big bills under my nose? I don't have change. Can anyone change this?"

I wanted to change it, but seeing the passenger's surly glance, I changed my mind.

"Well, that's it," says the passenger. "That's why I didn't use the bill, because I knew that it would have been futile—that they wouldn't be able to change it on the trolley."

"What a long-drawn-out business with this fellow," says the conductress. "I'm going to stop the car right here and put him off, to hell with him. He's putting the brakes on my work."

And she reaches for the bell and is about to ring it.

The passenger, heaving a sigh, says, "This conductress is something exceptional. That is, it's the first time I've seen such behavior. Hey, don't be in such a hurry to ring: I'll pay right away. Really, what a nasty person turned up . . ."

He digs down in his pocket and takes out two kopecks.

The conductress says, "Well, why didn't you give me that before, you parasite? I suppose you wanted to wangle a free ride?"

"There's never enough of anything to go around. Take the money and stop up the fountain of your eloquence . . . Rattling one's tongue for an hour over such trifles. I'm sick and tired of it."

"Although these are trifles," says the conductress, turning to the people, "they hinder the smooth working of the apparatus of government. And because of all this I've let in a lot of passengers without tickets."

After two stops, the ill-starred passenger with his petty, quarrelsome soul got off the trolley. And as he was getting off, he even cursed in coarse and unprintable language.

Then the conductress said, "What good-for-nothing people there are!"

One of the passengers observed, "Yes, some folks are niggling and worthless. If it weren't for that, everything would be splendid, no clouds in the sky."

I recollect some verses appropriate to the moment:

> Since the more fair and crystal is the sky,
> The uglier seem the clouds that in it fly.

But at this point we again arrived at some bridge, and once more I became absorbed in nature's pictures, forgetting the trivia of life.

1936

THE PUSHKIN CENTENNIAL

FIRST SPEECH ABOUT PUSHKIN

I WOULD like to point out with a feeling of pride that our building is not lagging behind in the march of current events.

In the first place, we have obtained for six rubles and fifty kopecks a one-volume edition of Pushkin for general use. In the second place, a plaster-of-Paris bust of the great poet has been placed in the tenants' co-operative office, which fact, in turn, should remind negligent bill-payers about arrears in their rent payments.

In addition, before the gateway to the building we have hung an artistic portrait of Pushkin, wreathed in pine branches.

And, finally, the present gathering speaks for itself.

Of course, perhaps this isn't very much but, to tell the truth, our tenants' association didn't expect that there would be such a to-do. We thought, Well, as usual, there will be articles in the press: they'll say, "A poet of genius, he lived during the cruel epoch of Nicholas I." And there, on the platform, they'll begin all sorts of artistic readings of excerpts, or they'll sing something from *Evgeny Onegin.*

But the things that are being done these days, to tell the truth, force our tenants' association to put itself on its guard and review its position in the realm of *belles-lettres,* lest we be accused later of undervaluing poetry and so on.

And you know, it's a good thing that in the matter of poets God, as the saying goes, has spared our house. It's true we do have one tenant, Tsaplin, who writes verses, but besides that he's a bookkeeper and, in addition, such a smart aleck, that I just don't know how I'm going to talk about him on these Pushkin Centennial days. The day before yesterday he comes to the office, threatens, and so on. "You long-tailed devil," he shouts, "I'll see you in your coffin if you don't move my stove before the Pushkin Centennial. I'm burning up from it," he says, "and can't write verses." I say, "With all due respect for poets, I can't move your stove at present, because our stove man has gone on a spree." So he goes right on yelling. He took off after me.

Let's just be thankful that we don't have in our complement of tenants all sorts of literary personnel and such. Or else they would certainly have pestered the life out of me, like this Tsaplin.

Well, so what if he can write verses. Excuse me, but my seven-year-old Kolyunka could make such demands at the tenants' office: he writes too. He's got some little poems that are not at all bad:

> We children love that time when the bird is in
> its cage.
> We love not those who against the five-year-
> plan rage.

The little tyke is seven years old, and look how boldly he writes. But that doesn't mean that I want to compare him with Pushkin. Pushkin is one thing, and the burned-up tenant Tsaplin is another. What a good-for-nothing! The main thing is, my wife was coming to meet me, and he takes off after me. "I'll stick your head in my stove right away," he yells. Well, what kind of thing is that? The Pushkin Centennial is taking place right now, and he makes me so nervous.

Pushkin writes in such a way that each of his lines is the height of perfection. For such a genius of a tenant we would already have moved his stove last fall. But to move Tsaplin's—that I refuse to do.

A hundred years have passed, and Pushkin's verses still astonish us. But, excuse me, what's a Tsaplin after a hundred years? That boor! Or if that same Tsaplin had lived a hundred years ago—I can imagine what would have happened to him then, and in what shape he would have come down to us!

To tell the truth, if I had been in D'Anthès' place I would have drilled him full of holes straight off.* The second would have said, "Take one shot at him," and I would have let fly all five bullets at him, because I don't like smart alecks.

Great poets of genius die before their time, and this Tsaplin stays around as if he'd never heard of this law. And just you wait, he'll squeeze the blood out of us yet.

However, I think we'll have to move his stove for him anyhow, so that in a hundred years we won't be accused of lack of literary appreciation.

SECOND SPEECH ABOUT PUSHKIN

Of course, dear comrades, I am not a literary historian. I shall allow myself to approach this great date simply, as the saying goes, in a human way.

A simple and heartfelt approach like this, I think, will do even more to bring the great poet's image closer to us.

A hundred years separate us from him! Time really does fly!

The German war, as we all know, began twenty-three years ago. That is, when it began, it wasn't a hundred years after Pushkin's death, but only seventy-seven.

And I was born, just imagine, in 1879. So I was even

---

* D'Anthès—the French officer who killed Pushkin in a duel. *Ed.*

closer to the great poet. Not close enough so that I could have seen him but, as the saying goes, we were separated only by about forty years.

But my grandmother, an even more striking case, was born in 1836. That is, Pushkin could have seen her and even picked her up. He could have dandled her on his knee, and she, I'm afraid, could have cried, not realizing who it was who had picked her up.

Of course, Pushkin couldn't really have dandled her, especially since she lived in Kaluga and I don't think he was ever there, but all the same we can entertain the exciting possibility, especially since he may very probably have taken a trip to Kaluga to see some acquaintances.

Now my father was born in 1850. But, alas, Pushkin was no longer alive then, otherwise he might have dandled my father as well.

But he could definitely have held my great-grandmother on his lap. Just imagine, she was born in 1763, so that the great poet could simply have gone to her parents and demanded that they let him hold and dandle her . . . Though, by the way, in 1837 she was, if you please, sixty and a little bit, so to tell the truth, I don't quite know how things were with them and how they managed . . . Maybe she even dandled him . . . But these matters, which for us are shrouded in the mists of uncertainty, probably didn't give them any trouble at all, and they must have easily figured out who should be dandled and who should rock whom. And if the old lady was really over sixty at that time, it's funny even to think that someone might have dandled her. That means that it was she who did the dandling.

Perhaps, without knowing it herself, she awoke poetic emotions in him as she rocked him and sang lyrical little songs, and perhaps, together with his renowned nurse, Arina Rodionovna, she inspired the composition of several specific poems.

As for Gogol and Turgenev, they could have been dandled by almost all my relatives, since an even shorter time separated them from others.

All in all, I'll say this: children are the adornment of our lives, and a happy childhood is, as the saying goes, a problem of no little importance which has been resolved in our time. Crèches, nursery schools, mothers' and babies' rooms at railway stations—all are significant aspects of one and the same effort . . . Yes, now what was I saying? Oh, yes, about Pushkin! As I was saying—Pushkin . . . the Centennial date. And soon other famous jubilees will sound forth—Turgenev, Lermontov, Tolstoy, Maykov, and so on and so forth. It goes on and on. And it's fair, if it's been earned.

But all in all, and just between ourselves, you even start to wonder sometimes why we have this attitude toward poets. For example, I won't say that we have a low regard for singers, but we don't carry on as much about them as about these fellows. Yet they too, as we say, have talent. They pluck at your heartstrings. And they stir up your emotions. And many other things. Then too, some of them perform without pay at benefit concerts, which also, as we say, gives you a picture of our artists' idealistic side. And in so doing they make a worthy contribution to the development of art, the influence of which on society is enormous and undisputed . . . But allow me, what were we talking about? Oh yes, about Pushkin . . .

So, as I was saying: Pushkin's artistic influence on us is enormous and undisputed. He was a great poet of genius, and we must regret that he is not alive at present, together with us. We would carry him in our arms and arrange a fabulous life for the poet, if, of course, we knew he would turn out to be Pushkin. Otherwise, it sometimes happens that contemporaries have high hopes for one of their own and arrange a decent life for him, giving him cars and apartments, and then it turns out that he's not the thing at all. But then, as the saying goes, you can't get blood from a stone . . . Altogether, it's a dark profession, but God be with it. Somehow, singers please one even more. They start singing—and you see right away what kind of voices they have.

Well, in concluding my talk on the poet of genius, I would like to point out that after the ceremonies there will be an artistic concert.

Loud applause. Everyone rises and goes to the buffet.

1937

THE CANVAS BRIEF CASE

I BEG you to excuse me, dear readers, for detaining you with such a trifle, such an insignificant incident, which is, perhaps, unworthy of your enlightened attention, focused as it is on other matters. But I really heard a very amusing case in the people's court.

Imagine this. A certain engineer used to work overtime at night exceedingly often. So, at least, he explained to his wife. But really there was no overtime at all; he simply went to visit a certain little woman from back home in Rostov.

Once upon a time, in Rostov, they had been passionately in love, and now they met again, not without interest. They would go to the movies, the theater, and so on.

But at home he would, of course, say that he had extra work, take a brief case for appearance' sake, and go to see his girl friend.

He probably acted in this way because he did not, as we say, wish to darken his family's horizons with personal matters. Besides, he had a wife and a little son of about ten.

And so, one evening after he had come home from work and had had dinner, he told his wife that he had to go to an extra session that evening.

His wife began to gasp and say that they were piling a little too much business on him, that because of this he was never home, that she'd never heard of anything like it, and that if it went on for long she would write to Comrade Mikoyan himself, or to one of the big men in the economy, telling them what was going on.

Extricating himself with difficulty from this family discussion, our husband put on his coat, took his brief case, and started for the door.

But he had hardly got out on the stairs when a meter reader from the electric office suddenly came into the apartment.

Our husband, wanting to see how much electricity he had burned up, waited a moment in the entrance hall. When he learned the amount, he took his wallet out of his pocket and gave the money to his wife, asking her to pay the bill then and there. He himself left as quickly as possible, lest another discussion arise.

But it happened that in his haste and worry over being late, he took the meter reader's brief case instead of his own and hurriedly left with it.

It was an ordinary, cheap, canvas brief case. In it were various official forms, documents, cards, and so on.

But our engineer, whose thoughts were elsewhere, simply did not notice what he was carrying.

Now we must reveal that in his own brief case, as luck would have it, there were some chocolates which he wanted to present to his friend, a lady's silk scarf, and a pretty little portfolio for letter writing.

And so that ill-starred brief case containing the presents remained on a chair in the entrance hall, and our engineer arrived at his girl friend's with the piece of canvas junk.

But either because he was late or I don't know why, she was unable to receive him. That is, she came out into the entrance hall and explained sweetly that some uncle of hers on her mother's side, who had just arrived from the provinces, was visiting her now and that, thinking the engineer was not coming, she had already agreed to go somewhere with her uncle.

Feeling very much aggrieved, our engineer did not,

of course, leave at once, but hung around a long time in the entrance hall, complaining that he had come only five minutes late and that it was a shame his evening was ruined. Then she promised to meet him the following day.

So our engineer, feeling extremely upset, began to say good night to his girl friend. And he was ready to go when he suddenly noticed a sort of canvas thing in his hands, some kind of dog-eared brief case which did not belong to him.

Completely sure then that he had taken it by mistake, he put it on the table in the entrance hall and began to look for his own brief case.

And under a chair in the entrance hall was a brief case. When he found it, our engineer was somewhat astonished and began trying to remember when he could have managed to stick his brief case under the chair.

But since his Rostov girl friend began hurriedly bidding him good night again and seeing him out, he didn't think about the matter any longer but pulled the brief case out from under the chair, and, deciding he would present his gifts the following day, kissed his friend's hand once more and left with another man's property. She didn't say anything to him, since she too probably didn't know the brief case was her uncle's. Besides, the entrance hall was very dimly lit.

And so, going out on the street, our engineer went slowly home, swinging the brief case.

But we must reveal that there had already been a complete upheaval in his home.

After receiving his money, the meter reader couldn't find his brief case and raised a fuss. Thinking that the little boy had been playing with it and had dragged it off into some other room, he began to look everywhere and turned the whole apartment upside down.

The wife busily helped look for the government

documents too, but, finding her husband's brief case, she was surprised that he had not taken it. And from pure feminine curiosity she took a look inside to see what was there. When she found things that were rather odd for overtime work, she got upset and went to her room to think over what it all could mean.

The engineer's son, the ten-year-old boy, saw the contents of the brief case, dug out the box of chocolates, and, as we say, paid the confectioner's trade its due.

Arriving at the conclusion that her husband had lied to her about his overtime work, the wife began to cry. But then the telephone rang and a rude male voice said that if her husband hadn't come home yet, she should tell him that he had left his brief case containing some stupid papers where he had just been and taken someone else's instead. And he'd better return it as soon as he came back, since they were about to have supper and the brief case contained things to eat.

Through her tears the wife promised that she would give her husband the message and, hanging up, she began to sob, understanding in part where her husband had been spending his time.

All in all, the house was in a state of pandemonium when our ill-starred spouse appeared once more on the family horizon.

The meter reader from the electric office, who was now turning the kitchen upside down, collared the engineer as he came in and demanded that his brief case, which contained the electric accounts for the whole neighborhood, be returned at once.

Not yet realizing what was going on, the husband heard his spouse's sobbing and hurried to her room. And there such a storm broke out that the meter reader did not dare go in, but sat down on a chair in the corridor with a martyred air and waited to see how it would all end.

At this point the engineer's little boy saw the new brief case and began to wonder what else papa had brought. And although his grandmother had forbidden him to touch that brief case, the boy dug out of it a second box of chocolates and some relish, pressed caviar, and sardines in tomato sauce.

When he no longer had much of an appetite for candy, the boy put the box in the china closet. His grandmother, not being informed about the course of events, thought that the food had been brought for the household and put the pickles, caviar, and sardines outside on the window sill. While she did this, she tasted the caviar and dug into it more than she should have, so that, to tell the truth, only an exceedingly small amount ever got to the window sill.

During these household proceedings and at the height of the screams in the bedroom, the telephone rang again, and the husband, in embarrassment, began to explain into the receiver that it had simply been a mistake and that the brief case would be returned at once.

With these words the engineer went into the corridor, found the meter reader, apologized to him, gave him an address and a ruble for the bus, and asked him to take the portfolio lying in the entrance hall to that address and exchange it for his own, which had been mistakenly carried there.

The meter reader, happy that his brief case containing government papers had been found at last, didn't dilate on the matter too much, and, after giving the absent-minded intellectual a small piece of his mind, he departed, taking with him to be exchanged the brief case which had been emptied by grandmother and grandson.

But hardly had quiet settled on the apartment and the exhausted spouses lain down to rest after the storm, when the telephone rang again, and a rude male voice informed the wife that her spouse, apparently, was simply a crook if he would extract from someone else's brief case everything that had been in it. And if it came to that, he could keep the sardines in tomato sauce, but he'd better return the caviar and relish right away or things would go badly for him. And that even his lady friend sent the message that he was a scoundrel.

The husband, sensing that a scandalous conversation was taking place, tore the receiver from his wife's hand and began to shout that he hadn't taken anything out of the brief case and hadn't even opened it, and they could all go to hell. And that he couldn't answer for the man he had sent, and if that person had taken something out of the brief case, then let them deal with him.

Then the rude male voice grew softer and said that the man who had been sent hadn't left yet and that he'd shake the daylights out of him, but he'd make him give back the caviar and relish.

Finally everything quieted down. Husband and wife, united in a common military front, were even somewhat reconciled. And the wife made him promise solemnly that there would be no further episodes of this sort.

However, in about an hour an extremely pale and harrowed-looking meter reader appeared in the apartment and made an unbelievable scene, demanding the return of some kind of groceries. But since neither husband nor wife knew anything about these groceries, and the grandmother was already sleeping the sleep of the just, the infuriated engineer ordered the meter reader to leave at once. The meter reader said he had never seen such scoundrels in his life and that he would lodge a complaint in the people's court against the engineer and against that man who had just shaken the daylights out of him. Besides, he had not only wasted a working day, but had also been shaken up emotionally and physically and, on top of that, had not yet got back his brief case containing government papers, which that fellow was holding for ransom.

And the meter reader really did go to court. And in court the whole chain of events was untangled.

The public was immensely amused when the witnesses on the stand explained how it had all happened. But their laughter reached its highest pitch when the grandmother began to describe how she had eaten the caviar.

The judge of the people's court, a woman, noted in her opinion that the petty-bourgeois mode of life, with its adulterous episodes, lying, and similar nonsense, was still a factor in our lives, and that this led to unhappy results. For example, the meter reader who had suffered while on duty was, in a way, the victim in this case.

The accused man, who, by the way, turned out to be not the uncle of the engineer's girl friend, but instead a former suitor who had arrived from Rostov, apologized to the meter reader. The engineer too apologized eagerly.

The court decreed public censure for the engineer, and because the uncle from Rostov had battered the meter reader a bit, justly sentenced him to hard labor for two months.

The public received this sentence with complete satisfaction.

What will happen in the future we cannot tell you, but since the uncle will not appear on the horizon for two months, it is possible that the engineer and his girl friend will make up. And then some kind of nonsense may again appear on the domestic front.

1937

THE FUNERAL FEAST

Not long ago, a certain nice man died.

Of course, he was only an obscure worker. But when, as we say, his earthly race had been run, a lot of people began to talk about him, since he had been a very pleasant person and a wonderful worker in his field.

He received a great deal of praise and attention after his death. Everyone began to remember how neatly and tastefully he had dressed. And in what good order he had kept his lathe: he used to blow the dust off it and wipe every little screw with cotton.

In addition, he always maintained his high principles.

This summer, for example, he fell ill. He began to feel bad when he was in the vegetable garden.* He had gone to his vegetable garden on his day off and was working there, looking after the vegetables and fruit. Suddenly he began to feel bad. He got dizzy and fell.

Another man in his place would have cried, "Get me some valerian drops!" or "Call a specialist!" But he didn't bother about his health, and when he fell down he said, "Oh, my, I fell on the carrot bed and squashed the carrots."

People wanted to run for a doctor, but he did not permit laboring hands to be taken from their work.

Nevertheless, they carried him home, and there he

* Russian city-dwellers often have little garden plots on the outskirts of town where they raise vegetables. *Ed.*

lay ill for two months, attended by the best doctors.

Of course, they gave him a wonderful funeral. Funeral waltzes were played. Many of his co-workers accompanied the coffin to the cemetery.

Extremely solemn speeches were made. They praised him and expressed astonishment that such wonderful people were found on this earth.

Toward the end, one of his close friends, who was standing next to the widow, said, "The widow invites those who wish to honor the memory of their friend and comrade to her apartment, where tea will be served."

Among the mourners was a co-worker of the deceased, a certain M. This M. had not known the departed particularly well, but he had seen him a couple of times at work.

And now, when the widow was inviting people to drop in, he up and went too. He went, as we say, simply out of the goodness of his heart. He did not go to the funeral spread in order to eat. Besides, these days you can't impress anyone with food.* He went simply on principle. "This was a nice man," he thought. "I'll just drop in and listen to his relatives reminisce about him, and sit in a warm place for a while."

So he went along with one of the groups.

Everyone arrived at the apartment. The table, of course, was set. There was food. This, that, and the other thing.

The guests took off their coats. And our M. also took off his cap and coat. He wandered among the grieving relatives, listening to their reminiscences.

Suddenly three men came up to him in the dining room.

"The close relatives have gathered here," they said,

* By 1937, when this story was written, the food situation in the Russian cities had improved somewhat, after the "hunger years" of the early 1930's. *Ed.*

"and you'll be out of place among them. The widow considers your presence in this apartment an act of pure gall. Put on your coat and relieve the premises of your presence."

These words, of course, made him feel extremely uncomfortable, and he began explaining things to them: he came here, he said, for no other reason than the call of his heart.

One of the three said, "We know all about your heart—you came here to stuff your face, and in so doing you offended the memory of the departed. You'd better scram out of here as fast as you can, because at such a moment you're putting the friends and relatives in a bad mood."

With these words, he took M.'s coat and flung it over his shoulders, and the other acquaintance grabbed his cap and shoved it on his head with both hands so hard that his ears bent.

Well, they didn't really manhandle him, of course; none of them even took a swing at him. In that sense everything was done in a well-behaved manner. But they took him by the arms and led him out into the anteroom, and in the anteroom the relatives on the widow's side pressed him along a bit, and one of them even gave him a little push with his knee. This was more painful to him morally than physically.

Finally, understanding little of what was going on, he suddenly emerged onto the stairs with hurt and resentment in his heart.

He couldn't calm down for three days.

And so he came to see me yesterday evening and asked me to analyze this incident of his. He was upset, and his chin trembled and his eyes watered from his hurt feelings.

He told me the story and asked me what I thought about it.

After thinking it over, I said, "As concerns you, dear

friend, you made a little mistake. You went there because your heart called you. And I believe that. But the widow had in mind only relatives and people who knew her spouse well. Now, if the factory had invited you to a gathering in his memory, and then they smoked you out of there and called you a stranger—that would really be surprising. You should always try to understand these subtleties. But as far as they are concerned, they behaved rudely, untactfully and, I would say, boorishly. The one who shoved your cap on your head is simply a swine."

Here my visitor M. brightened a little. He said, "Now I understand in what sense they called me a stranger, and all the rest of it doesn't disturb me any longer."

Then I shook his hand, and gave him a book as a present. We parted the best of friends.

After he had gone away, it occurred to me that the same people who so rudely threw him out probably treat their machines very gently. They probably take excellent care of them and coddle them. Or, anyway, they don't toss them out onto the stairs, but when they have to send them someplace they write on the crate, "Do Not Drop!" or "Handle with Care!"

Then it occurred to me that it wouldn't be a bad idea to write something in chalk on a person too. Some attention-getting word: "China!" or "Fragile!" Since a person is a person and a machine serves him, he is, therefore, to some degree, no less worthy than the machine.

After thinking over these matters, I decided to write this educational *feuilleton*. And here it is before you.

1937

ROSA-MARIA

An inhabitant of the village of F., a certain comrade Lebedev, took it into his head to have his baby christened.

Until then he had been against religion. He didn't go to church. He didn't do anything churchy. Just the opposite—having progressive views, he had at one time belonged to an atheist group.

But his wife had a little girl, and he took it into his head to have her christened.

More accurately, his wife, that faint-hearted mother, drove him to it. And not so much even the wife as her short-sighted parents were the ones who set the tone for the whole matter. Because they began to chatter that it wasn't nice not to christen her. All of a sudden she might grow up or, on the contrary, die, and wouldn't be christened, and then what?

You know the frivolous discussions of politically backward people.

Now Lebedev really didn't want his little girl christened in the least. But he couldn't stand it when they kept nagging him. And since he too had inner conflicts about the matter, he gave his consent. He said to them, "All right. Christen her. But I don't want a lot of noise over this matter. There's no doubt that I'm master of my own beliefs. If I want to, I'll christen her, if not, just the opposite—I won't. But a whole hullabaloo of talk will start anyhow; they'll say, 'He christened her after all, the dog; he turned to the services of the church'; and they'll say, 'It's not for nothing that in peacetime his uncle was the landlord's head janitor.' "

To this his wife said that if he himself didn't raise a row at his daughter's christening, there wouldn't be any kind of noise over the matter.

And so the parents arranged with the priest to have their daughter christened. And for five rubles the priest agreed to do it and set the day and the hour.

In the meantime the parents registered their baby in the Office of Vital Statistics under the name of Rosa and received a certificate there. Then they appeared in church on the appointed day to have the christening performed.

On that day another baby was being christened, and our family, while waiting their turn, stood and watched to see how the thing was done.

But Lebedev, opposed as he was to religion, and having, so to speak, a critical view of everything connected with the church, absolutely could not keep quiet. He kept taunting the priest with sharp remarks.

Whatever the priest did, Lebedev would smile ironically, or mutter something to him behind his hand. "Well, you said that through your nose," he says. Or else, "Just look what he's thought up now . . ." Or, looking at the priest's reddish hair, he says suddenly, "None of the saints had red hair . . . but this fellow's redheaded."

This last remark aroused some laughter among the relatives. The priest even interrupted the christening for a moment and looked angrily at everyone.

But when he got to Lebedev's baby, Lebedev lost some of his sense of restraint and began openly to needle the priest with insinuating comments.

He even said, jokingly, it's true, "Well, beardy, make sure my baby doesn't get a chill thanks to your christening, or I'll go right out and set fire to your church."

The priest's hands began to tremble when he heard this.

He said to Lebedev, "Listen, I don't understand you.

If you came here to annoy me, I'm surprised at you. Have you considered what the result will be? At the moment when I'm holding your little girl in my arms, instead of a purifying prayer, anger and obscenities flare up against you in my heart. And that's the kind of send-off into life my thoughts give your little girl. Now maybe she'll get feverish spells all her life, or become a deaf mute."

Lebedev says, "Well, if you ruin my baby, I'll tear out all your curls by the roots. Bear that in mind."

The priest says, "You know what? You'd better wrap up your whelp in the blanket and clear out of the church. I'll give back your five rubles and we'll part friends. Why should I listen to such insolence all the time?"

At this point the relatives began to hush up Lebedev, telling him, "Come on now, shut up. Wait a while; when you're out of the church you can let loose. Don't pick on the priest, or he might very well drop the baby on the floor. Look, his hands are trembling and his knees are shaky."

And although Lebedev was being torn by inner conflicts, he restrained himself and didn't say too much more to the priest.

He just said, "Well, all right, all right, I won't say any more. Just make it a high-class christening, long-whiskers."

So the priest began to repeat the words of the service. Then, turning to Lebedev, he said, "What name shall I give her? What have you named your little girl?"

Lebedev says, "We've named her Rosa."

The priest says, "My, what a lot of trouble your presence has created for me. You not only kept baiting me, but now it turns out you haven't given your baby a proper name. Rosa is a Jewish name, and I refuse to christen her with that name. Wrap her up in the blanket and leave the church."

Utterly perplexed, Lebedev says, "One thing worse than the next. First he wishes spells of fever on the child, then he completely refuses to christen her. But the name comes from the word 'rose,' that is, a plant, a flower. Now Rosalia Semyonovna, for example, the cashier at the co-operative—that's a different matter. In that case I won't argue: it's a Jewish name. But here you can't refuse to christen her with that name."

The priest says, "Wrap your baby in its blanket. I won't christen it at all. There's no such name in my calendar of saints."

The relatives say to the priest, "Listen, we registered her in the Office of Vital Statistics under that name. What are you kicking up such a fuss about, for heaven's sake?"

Lebedev says, "I told you so. Look what kind of priest he is. He goes against the Office of Vital Statistics. Now everyone can see what an insolent political world view he has."

Seeing that the relatives were not leaving and not taking away the baby, the priest began to remove his vestments. He took off his brocade cassock, and then everyone saw that he was wearing trousers and high boots.

In this blasphemous attire he goes up to the icons and puts out the candles. And he is about to pour out the water from the baptismal font.

In the church, meantime, there was a certain newly arrived individual. This individual had come to town on business, to inspect the co-operative, and now, having nothing in particular to do, he had purposely come into the church to see what things were like there now.

This individual enters the conversation and says, "Although I'm against rituals and am even surprised at the backwardness of the local citizens, I think that since they've already unwrapped the baby and the parents are burning with eagerness to have it christened, it must be done, come what may. And as a way out of the situation that has been created, I suggest that you give your baby a double name. For example, you call her Rosa, and here, for example, she could be called Maria. Together that makes Rosa-Maria. There's even an operetta by that name, which signifies that such a name exists in Europe."

The priest says, "There are no double names in my calendar of saints. And I'm surprised that you would even try to confuse me that way. If you like, I'll call her Maria. But Rosa—I wouldn't even say the name in my thoughts."

Lebedev says, "Well, the hell with him. Let him call her Maria then. We'll straighten it all out afterwards."

The priest put his cassock back on and rapidly, in five minutes, performed the whole ecclesiastical operation.

Lebedev was chatting with the stranger, and therefore didn't insert any remarks concerning the priest's performance. So everything went smoothly.

But Lebedev's hope that there would be no great stir over the matter was not realized. As you see, the whole story has even got into print. And there's a moral to it. Don't spend your time in churches if your philosophy is against them. And in case you do happen to enter a church, behave respectfully, and don't annoy the priest with stupid remarks.

A JOLLY GAME

A SHORT time ago I had dinner in a restaurant and then looked in at a poolroom. I felt like seeing, as they say, how the balls were rolling.

There's no question that it's an interesting game. It's absorbing, and can distract a man from any kind of misfortune. Some even find that the game of billiards develops courage, a sharp and steady eye, and good aim, and doctors assert that this game is extremely beneficial to unbalanced men.

I don't know. I don't think so. Some unbalanced man might fill himself so full of beer while playing billiards that he could hardly crawl home after the game. So I doubt that this would be beneficial to the nervous and distraught. And as for its giving you a sharp eye, that all depends. A fellow from our house got both his eyes blacked with the cue when his partner was taking aim, and even though he wasn't blinded, he did go slightly blind in one eye. There's your development of a sharp eye for you. If someone should give him a workout in the other eye now, the man will be completely deprived of any vision at all, let alone aim.

So that in the sense of usefulness, it's all, as they say, old wives' tales.

But the game is certainly amusing. Especially when they're playing "for keeps"—very absorbing to watch.

Of course, they rarely play for money nowadays. But they think up something original instead. Some of them make the loser crawl under the table. Others make him buy a round of beer. Or have him pay for the game.

When I went to the poolroom this time, I saw a very mirth-provoking scene.

A winner was ordering his bewhiskered partner to crawl under the table carrying all the balls. He stuffed some balls in his pockets, put a ball in each hand, and on top of that tucked one under his chin. And in this state the loser crawled under the table to the accompaniment of general laughter.

After the next game the winner once again loaded down the bewhiskered fellow with balls and on top of that made him carry the cue between his teeth. And the poor fellow crawled again, to the Homeric laughter of the assembled company.

For the next game, they had trouble thinking up anything.

The bewhiskered one says, "Let's make it something easier, you've done me in as it is."

And really, even his mustache was drooping, he was so dragged out.

The winner says, "Don't be a fool—with such penalties I'll give you a marvelous lesson in how to play billiards."

An acquaintance of the winner's was there. He said, "I've thought of something. If he loses, let's do this: have him crawl under the table loaded down with the balls and we'll tie a case of beer to his foot. Let him crawl through like that."

The winner, laughing, says, "Bravo! That'll really be some trick!"

The bewhiskered one said in a hurt way, "If there's going to be beer in the case, I won't play. It'll be hard enough to crawl with an empty case."

In a word, he lost, and amid general laughter they again loaded him down with the balls, put the cue between his teeth, and tied a case to his foot. The winner's friend also started poking him with a cue to hasten his journey under the billiard table.

The winner laughed so hard that he fell into a chair and grunted from exhaustion.

The bewhiskered one emerged from under the table in a state of stupefaction. He gazed dully at the company and did not move for a while. Then he dug the balls out of his pockets and began untying the case of beer from his foot, saying that he wasn't playing any more.

The winner was laughing so hard he shed tears. He said, "Come on, Egorov, old pal, let's play one more game. I've thought up another funny trick."

The other says, "Well, what else have you thought up?"

The winner, choking with laughter, says, "Let's play for your mustache, Egorov! That fluffy mustache of yours has bothered me for a long time. If I win, I'll cut off your mustache. Okay?"

The bewhiskered one says, "No, for my mustache I won't play, not unless you give me a forty-point handicap."

In a word, he lost again. And before anyone could catch his breath, the winner grabbed a table knife and began sawing off one side of his unlucky partner's fluffy mustache.

Everyone in the room was dying of laughter.

Suddenly one of those present goes over to the winner and says to him, "Your partner must be a fool, agreeing to such forfeits. And you take advantage of this and make fun of a man in a public place."

The winner's friend says, "What damn business is it of yours? After all, he agreed of his own free will."

The winner says to his partner in a tired voice, "Egorov, come here. Tell the assembled multitudes that you agreed to all the forfeits of your own free will."

The partner, supporting his half-severed mustache with his hand, says, "Obviously it was of my own free will, Ivan Borisovich."

The winner says, turning to the company, "Some

people make their chauffeur wait in the freezing cold for three hours. But I treat people humanely. This is the chauffeur from our office, and I always bring him inside where it's warm. I don't patronize him, but play a friendly game of billiards with him. I teach him, and I punish him a little. And why they're picking on me now, I just can't understand."

The chauffeur says, "Perhaps there's a barber in the house. I'd like my mustache evened off."

A man comes out of the crowd and says, taking a pair of scissors from his pocket, "I will be sincerely happy to even off your mustache. If you like, I'll make you one like Charlie Chaplin's."

While the barber was fussing with the chauffeur, I went up to the winner and said to him, "I didn't know that was your chauffeur. I thought it was your friend. I wouldn't have let you pull such tricks."

The winner, a bit shaken, says, "And what sort of a bird are you?"

I say, "I'll write an article about you."

The winner, really frightened, says, "But I won't tell you my name."

I say, "I'll just describe the actual event and add that it was a fairly stout reddish-haired man named Ivan Borisovich. Of course, you may even get away with it, but if you do I hope your rotten soul will tremble before the lines of print."

The winner's friend, hearing something about an article, instantly made himself scarce and disappeared from the premises.

The winner drank beer and talked big for a long time, shouting that he didn't give a damn for anyone.

They trimmed the chauffeur's whiskers, and he became somewhat younger-looking and handsomer. So that I even decided to tone down my *feuilleton*.

After I came home, as you see, I wrote it up. And now you're reading it and probably feeling amazed that

such passionate gamblers exist and that you can run
into such unattractive reddish-haired men.

1938

A FINAL UNPLEASANTNESS

This time let me tell you a dramatic episode from the life of some people now dead.

Since it is factual, we will not allow ourselves to include in our exposition too much laughter or too many jests, so as not to offend those remaining among the living.

But since this story is comic to a certain degree and laughter, as the saying goes, can burst out by itself, we beg our readers' pardon in advance for any unwitting tactlessness on our part with regard to the living and the dead.

Of course, the situation itself had nothing comic about it at first. On the contrary, a man died, an insignificant worker who went unnoticed in the general brilliance of our time.

And, as happens frequently, resounding words were uttered after his death. People said, "He perished at his post; ah, what a man have we lost; now there was a real man; what a pity, friends, that he has been taken from us."

Now it's clear, of course, that during his lifetime no one said anything of the kind to him, and he set out on his final journey without suspecting what a figure he cut in the imagination of his acquaintances. Of course, if he hadn't died, it's not certain what turn their imagination would have taken. Most likely, that same circle of acquaintances would, as the saying goes, have pinned his ears back for him.

But since he died without a murmur, he got the funeral treatment of a god.

On the one hand, friends, to die is splendid, but on the other hand—*merci*, I'd rather not. I'll manage somehow without your touching expressions of gratitude.

In short, a meeting took place after hours in the office where he had worked, and in the course of this meeting many touching episodes from the life of the deceased were recalled.

Then our manager himself made a speech, and by the power of his forensic art he raised the talk to such an emotional pitch that he himself shed a few tears. Through his tears he eulogized the deceased beyond all measure.

At this point emotions broke loose completely. Each speaker vied with the next in trying to prove that he had lost a true friend, a father, a brother, a son, and so on.

Just then someone in the audience cried out that an impressive funeral ought to be arranged, so that other workers would strive to earn just such a funeral.

Everyone said, "That's right," and the manager announced that the funeral would be carried as a state expense.

Then still another person arose and said that, really, such wonderful people ought to be buried with music and not drawn in silence through the empty streets.

Then, wiping his eyes, there arose from his place a relative of the deceased, his nephew, whose name was Kolyesnikov. He spoke thus: "My God, for how many years I lived in the same apartment with my uncle! I won't say that I actually quarreled with him often, but all the same we didn't get along too well, since I didn't realize what sort of uncle I had. And now, when you tell me about this, your every word falls on my heart like molten metal. Oh, why didn't I arrange a decent life for my uncle! Now it will torment me for the rest of my life. No, I won't shirk the trouble of going down to Zelyenin Street, where I know there is a fine brass band consisting of six horns and a drum. And we will invite this band to play something special for my uncle."

And everyone agreed, "That's right, invite the band, and by so doing you will in part make up for your boorish behavior toward your uncle."

In short, the funeral took place in two days. There were many wreaths and a great number of people. The musicians didn't play at all badly and attracted the attention of passers-by, who kept asking, "Who are they burying?"

The uncle's nephew himself went up to the manager on the way and said softly to him, "I invited the band, but they made a condition—they want to be paid right after the funeral, because they're leaving soon for a guest performance in Staraya Russa.* How can we pay them without too much fuss?"

The manager asked, "Aren't you going to pay for the band?"

The nephew was astonished and even frightened. He said, "You yourself said that the funeral would be held at government expense. I only went down to invite the band."

The manager said, "Be that as it may, but we didn't include the band in our estimate. As a matter of fact, it was a petty, insignificant person who died and we up and hired a band for him! No, I can't go along with that; the union would have my hide for it."

The people who were walking with the manager also said, "After all, the office can't pay for everyone who dies. Be thankful that they paid for the hearse and the other funeral paraphernalia. But pay for the band yourself, since it's your uncle."

---

* Staraya Russa—an ancient Russian town, some thirty-five miles south of Novgorod. *Ed.*

The nephew said, "Are you crazy—where am I going to get two hundred rubles?"

The manager said, "Then get together with your relatives and get out of it somehow."

The nephew, beside himself, ran to the widow and explained to her what was going on.

The widow sobbed even louder and refused to pay anything.

Kolyesnikov pushed his way through the crowd to the band and told them to stop blowing their horns, since there had been a mix-up and it was now uncertain who would pay them.

There was some confusion among the band members, who were marching in step. Their leader said, "We won't stop the music, we'll play to the end and then we'll sue the person who engaged us." And, brandishing his cymbals once more, he cut short the discussion.

Then Kolyesnikov pushed through once again to the manager, but the latter, foreseeing unpleasantness, got into his car and quietly departed.

The running around and bustle evoked surprise in the ranks of the marchers. The manager's departure and the loud moaning of the widow amazed those present even more. Remarks, questions, and whispers began making the rounds, the more so that someone started a rumor that the manager had been called away at once to discuss a general cut in salaries.

All in all, they arrived at the cemetery in complete disorder. The burial itself took place at an extremely rapid tempo and without speeches, and everyone parted rather displeased. Some heatedly criticized the deceased, remembering first one thing and then another from his humble life.

The following day the deceased uncle's nephew put so much pressure on the manager that the latter promised to take the question up with the union. But at the same time he said that the thing would hardly go through, since it was the union's business to look after the living, not to waste time on the dead.

One way or another, Kolyesnikov in the meantime sold his heavy coat in order to get rid of the bandsmen, who really would have stopped at nothing to get their "clean cash."

He sold his heavy coat for two hundred sixty rubles, and after paying the band, he had sixty rubles left. With this money the nephew of his uncle has been drinking for three days now. This circumstance signifies to us that that office, including its manager, did not quite measure up to standards.

After getting drunk, this uncle's nephew came to me and, wiping his tears, told me about this petty unpleasantness of his, which was probably far from being his last.

But for the uncle this petty unpleasantness was his last. And that's a good thing.

1939

BEES AND PEOPLE

A RED Army soldier arrived at a certain collective farm on a visit, and he brought a jar of flower honey as a present for his relatives.

Everyone liked this honey so much that the collective farmers decided to begin keeping bees.

But there weren't any beekeepers in the area, and the farmers had to start from scratch—making hives and moving bees from the woods into these new apartments.

Realizing that this would be a long process, the collective farmers got discouraged. "That'll take forever," they said. "By the time we do this, that, and the other thing, the summer will be over, and we won't see any honey till next year. But we need it now."

Among the members of the *kolkhoz* there was a splendid person, a certain Ivan Panfilich, who was an elderly man of about seventy-two. In his youth he had been a beekeeper.

And so he said, "If we want to drink tea with honey this year, we'll have to go some place where they keep bees and buy the object of our dreams from them."

The farmers said, "Our collective is worth a million. We won't let expense stand in its way. Let's buy a stock of bees in full swing, with the bees already in the hives. Otherwise, if we get bees from the woods they may turn out to be no good. They might start making some kind of terrible honey like linden-tree honey. And we want flower honey."

So they gave Ivan Panfilich some money and sent him to the town of Tambov.

He arrived in Tambov, and there they told him, "You did well to come to us. Three of our villages have been resettled in the Far East, and we have an extra apiary left over. We can give you this apiary for almost nothing. Only, how you are going to transport the bees —that's a question for us to think about. The merchandise is, you might say, easily scattered—winged. The least little thing and it'll fly away in all directions. We're afraid that you'll arrive at your destination with only the little beehives and the larvae."

Panfilich said, "I'll get them there somehow. I know bees. I've been around bees all my life."

And so he brought sixteen beehives to the station on two carts. At the station he wangled a flatcar. He put his beehives on the car and covered them with a tarpaulin.

In a little while the freight train started moving. And our flatcar started rolling.

Panfilich stood solemnly on the flatcar and conversed with his bees . . . "It's all right, little fellows," he told them. "We'll get there! Just be patient in the dark a little while, and then I'll let you out in the flowers again. And there, I think, you'll get what you want. The main thing is not to get upset that I'm transporting you in the dark. I put the tarpaulin over you on purpose, so you wouldn't get silly and fly out while the train was moving. In that case, I don't think you'd manage to hop back on the train."

The train traveled on for a day. And it traveled for another day.

On the third day Panfilich began to get a little worried. The train was going slowly. It stopped at every station. It stood a long time. And it wasn't clear when it would arrive at his destination.

At the station "Polya" Panfilich got down from his

car and addressed the stationmaster. He asked, "Tell me, honored sir, will the train be stopping long at your station?"

The stationmaster answered, "To tell you the truth, I don't know. It might even stop till evening."

Panfilich said, "If it's till evening, I'll take off the tarpaulin and let my little bees out in your fields. Why, they're exhausted from traveling. It's the third day they've been sitting under the tarpaulin. They're starving. They haven't eaten or drunk, and they're not feeding the larvae."

The stationmaster said, "Do what you want! What do I care about your winged passengers! I've got enough to do without them. And now I'm supposed to worry about your larvae. What kind of nonsense is that!"

Panfilich returned to his platform and removed the tarpaulin.

The weather was splendid. A blue sky. The July sun shining. Fields all around. Flowers growing. A chestnut grove in bloom.

So Panfilich took the tarpaulin off the flatcar, and at once a whole army of bees rose skyward. The bees circled, looked around, and set out for the fields and woods.

Passengers crowded around the car. Panfilich stood on it and delivered them a lecture on the usefulness of bees. But during the lecture the stationmaster came out on the platform and began signaling the engineer to start the train.

Panfilich gasped in horror when he saw these signals. In agitation he said to the stationmaster, "Honored sir, don't start the train. All my bees are out."

The stationmaster said, "You'd better whistle to them to come back in a hurry! I can't hold the train longer than three minutes."

Panfilich said, "I beg you, hold the train till sunset!

At sunset the bees will return to their places. At least uncouple my flatcar! I can't leave without my bees. There are only a thousand left here; fifteen thousand are in the fields. Understand my situation! Don't be indifferent to a misfortune like this!"

The stationmaster said, "This isn't a health resort for bees, it's a railroad. Just imagine, his bees flew away! On the next train they'll say the flies flew away. Or the fleas, they'll say, jumped out of the sleeping car. So do I have to hold up the train for that? Don't make me laugh!"

At this point the stationmaster again signaled to the engineer.

And so the train began to move.

Panfilich, white as a sheet, stood on his flatcar. He threw up his hands, looked on all sides, and trembled from outraged feelings.

And the train moved along.

Well, a certain number of bees did manage to hop on after the train was in motion. But the majority remained in the fields and groves.

The train disappeared from sight.

The stationmaster returned to the station and got down to work. He was writing something in his records and drinking tea with lemon.

Suddenly he heard a kind of noise in the station.

He opened the window to see what had happened, and he saw that the waiting passengers were in an uproar, running and bustling about.

The stationmaster asked, "What happened?"

They answered, "Some bees have stung three passengers. And now they're attacking the rest. There are so many of them that they darken the sky."

Then the stationmaster saw that a whole cloud of bees was swirling around his station.

Naturally, they were looking for their flatcar. But the car wasn't there. It had gone. And so they were attacking people and everything else around.

The stationmaster was just about to move away from the window to go out into the station when a swarm of enraged bees flew in through the window. He grabbed a towel and started waving it around to chase the bees out of the room.

But apparently this was his downfall.

Two bees stung him on the neck. A third, on the ear. And a fourth stung him on the forehead.

Wrapping the towel around him, the stationmaster lay down on the sofa and began to emit piteous groans.

Soon his assistant ran in and said, "You're not the only one. The bees have stung the telegrapher on duty on the cheek, and now he refuses to work."

The stationmaster, lying on the sofa, said, "Oh, what shall we do?"

Then another employee ran in and told the stationmaster, "The ticket seller, that is, your wife, Klavdia Ivanovna, got stung on the nose just this minute. Now her looks are completely spoiled."

The stationmaster groaned more loudly and said, "We'll have to get back that flatcar with the crazy beekeeper as soon as we can."

He leaped from the sofa and called on the telephone. And from the next station they answered, "All right. We'll uncouple the flatcar right away. But we don't have an engine to deliver it to you with."

The stationmaster shouted, "We'll send an engine. Hurry up and uncouple the flatcar. The bees have already stung my spouse. My station, 'Polya,' is empty. All the passengers are hiding in a barn. There are only bees flying around here. And I refuse to go out; I don't care if there's a wreck!"

And so the flatcar was quickly returned. Everyone sighed with relief when they saw the flatcar with Panfilich standing on it.

Panfilich ordered them to put the flatcar in the same place where it had been standing before. And when they saw the flatcar, the bees instantly flew over to it.

There were so many bees and they were in such a hurry to get to their places that there was a terrible crush. Such a rumbling and buzzing sound arose among them that a dog began to howl and some pigeons flew skyward.

Panfilich stood on the platform, saying, "Calmly, little fellows, don't hurry! There's time. Take your places according to your tickets!"

In ten minutes everything was quiet.

Having assured himself that everything was in order, Panfilich climbed down from his car.

The people at the station applauded him, and Panfilich, like an actor, began bowing to them. He said, "Turn your collars back down. Unveil your faces! And stop trembling for your fate—no further beestings will take place."

After saying this, Panfilich went to the stationmaster.

The stationmaster, swathed in a towel, was still lying on the sofa. He was gasping and groaning. But he groaned even harder when Panfilich entered the room.

Panfilich said, "I greatly regret, honored sir, that my bees stung you. But it is your own fault. You can't be so indifferent about things, whether they are great or small. Bees will not stand for that. They'll sting people for that without further ado."

The stationmaster groaned even harder, and Panfilich continued, "Bees absolutely cannot tolerate bureaucracy or indifference to their fate. Why, you treated them the way you probably treat people—and there's your reward."

Panfilich looked out the window and added, "The sun has set. My traveling companions have taken their places. I have the honor to bid you farewell! We're ready to leave."

The stationmaster nodded weakly, as if to say, Leave as soon as possible! And he whispered softly, "Are you sure you caught all the bees? Look sharp you don't leave any of them with us!"

Panfilich said, "Even if two or three bees remain with you, that will be for your own good. They'll remind you of this occurrence with their buzzing."

With these words Panfilich left the premises.

Toward evening of the following day our glorious Panfilich arrived at his destination with his live merchandise.

The collective farmers greeted him with music.

March, 1941

THE BUOY

In the morning, enemy planes began to circle above our ship. The first six bombs fell into the water. The seventh bomb hit the stern, and our ship caught fire.

Then all the passengers began throwing themselves into the water.

I don't remember what I was thinking of when I jumped overboard without knowing how to swim. But I jumped into the water too, and sank to the bottom at once.

I don't know how the laws of chemistry or physics were operating there, but the fact was that despite my complete inability to swim I rose to the surface.

I rose to the surface and at once grabbed hold of some kind of buoy with horns that was sticking out of the water.

I hold onto this buoy and don't let go. I thank heaven that I'm among the living and that horned objects like that are stuck around in the sea to indicate shallow places and so on.

So I'm holding onto this buoy, when suddenly I see someone swimming toward me. I see that it's some kind of civilian, like me. Respectably dressed in a sandy-colored jacket and long trousers. I waved him toward the buoy, and he grabbed hold of it too.

And so we hold onto this buoy. And keep quiet. Because there's nothing to talk about.

I did ask him where he worked, but he didn't answer. He just spat out some water and shrugged. Then I realized the tactlessness of asking this question in the water, and although I had been interested to learn whether he was sailing as part of a staff as I was, or alone, I nonetheless did not inquire about this.

So we hold onto this buoy in silence. We are silent for an hour. For three hours we don't say anything. Finally my fellow conversationalist remarks, "A motorboat is coming . . ."

And we really do see a rescue boat coming and picking up people who are still afloat in the water.

My fellow conversationalist and I started to shout and wave our arms so that the people in the motorboat would notice us. But for some reason they don't notice us. And they don't cruise over to us.

Then I throw off my jacket and shirt and start to wave the shirt, crying, "Here we are, this way. Please be so kind as to come over."

But the motorboat doesn't come over.

With my last remaining strength I wave the shirt, shouting, "Think how we feel . . . We're perishing . . . Save our souls."

Finally someone in the boat sticks his head out and shouts through a megaphone at us, "Hey, you blankety-blank fools, you're holding onto a mine, that's what!"

As soon as he heard these words, my fellow conversationalist immediately plunged off to one side. And I look—he's started swimming toward the motorboat.

I too instinctively let go of the buoy. But as soon as I let go I sank in over my head.

I grabbed the buoy again and didn't let go any more.

They're yelling through a megaphone from the motorboat, "Hey, you blankety-blank, don't touch the mine."

"Fellows, I'm telling you, without the mine it's just like without arms for me. I'll drown right away. Have some feeling for me. Come over here, be magnanimous enough to do that."

They yell into the megaphone, "We can't come over, you chowderhead—we'll explode the mine. Swim over here, you blankety-blank. Or we'll go away this minute."

I think, It's a fine business to swim when you absolutely don't know how. And I hold onto the buoy so tightly that you couldn't tear me away even if you wanted to.

I shout, "Fellow sailors! Esteemed naval comrades! Think up some way to save a precious human life."

Here one of the crew throws me a line. Meanwhile they call, through the megaphone and without it, "Don't wriggle, may you choke to death—you'll explode the mine!"

I think, They themselves are making me nervous with their shouting. It would be better, I think, if I didn't know this was a mine—I would behave more calmly. And now, of course, I jerk—I'm afraid. I'm afraid of the mine, and without the mine I'm even more afraid.

I finally managed to grab the line. I carefully tied it to my belt.

I shout, "Start pulling, damn you . . . They yell and yell until you get sick of it . . ."

They started pulling me. I see that the line doesn't help. I see that, contrary to my wishes, I'm sinking to the bottom, line and all.

I'm already touching bottom with my hands. Suddenly I feel an upward pull, lifting me up.

They pull me up to the surface. They curse me out, but I have no strength left to reply. Not using the megaphone, they yell, "Just because of you we've been stalled here all this time. I hope you croak. You grab onto a mine in wartime . . . On top of that you can't swim . . . You should have exploded on that mine— you'd have made it harmless and yourself to boot."

Of course, I keep quiet. I don't answer them. After all, how could I reply to people who had just saved me? Besides, I myself am aware of my inadequate experience in questions of war, my lack of understanding of technical matters, my inability to distinguish a simple buoy from God knows what.

They pull me on board. I lie there. They surround me.

I see that my fellow conversationalist is here too. And he's cursing me out and yelling at me too. Why, he asks, did I tell him to grab hold of the mine? "You're nothing but a sea-going hooligan," he says. "For that," he says, "people should be sentenced to hard labor under water for from three to five years."

I did not reply to my fellow conversationalist either, since my spirits had fallen when I discovered that I did not have my shirt with me. I had the jacket, but no shirt.

I wanted to ask the captain to circle around in the cutter to see whether my shirt was floating on the water. But when I saw the captain's stern expression, I couldn't make up my mind to ask him to do that.

Most likely I left my shirt on the mine. If that's so, then it's gone for good, of course.

After being rescued I solemnly promised myself to study the art of warfare.

One shouldn't lag behind others in these matters.

1943

THE ADVENTURES
OF A MONKEY

In a certain town in the south there was a zoo. A rather small zoo, which contained one tiger, two crocodiles, three snakes, a zebra, an ostrich, and one monkey, known as "Monk" for short. And, of course, various small fry—birds, fishes, frogs, and other lightweight members of the animal kingdom.

At the beginning of the war, when the fascists were bombing this town, a bomb fell right into the zoo. And there it exploded, with an enormous, deafening crash. To the amazement of all the animals.

The three snakes were killed—all at once, which may not seem like such a heavy loss. And, unfortunately, the ostrich.

The other animals were unharmed. As we say, they got off with only a scare.

Of all the animals, Monk the monkey was the most terrified. His cage was overturned by the blast. It fell from its height. The side wall broke. And our monkey fell out of the cage and right onto one of the zoo paths.

He fell onto the path, but didn't remain lying motionless there like the human beings, who had grown accustomed to the circumstances of war. Just the opposite. He climbed up a tree at once. From there he jumped onto a fence. From the fence into the street. And ran away like a streak.

He ran and probably thought, Huh, I don't go along

with their dropping bombs here. And that meant he ran along the city streets as fast as he could.

He ran through the whole town. He ran out onto the highway. And he ran along this highway straight out of the town. Well, he was a monkey. Not a human being. Didn't know what was what. Didn't see any sense in staying in this town.

He ran and ran until he was tired. Completely exhausted. He climbed a tree. Ate a fly to fortify his energy. Also a couple of worms. And fell asleep on the branch, right where he sat.

Just at that time a military vehicle was coming along the road. The driver saw the monkey in the tree. He was astonished. Very softly he crept up to him. Threw his overcoat over him. And put him in his car. He thought, I'd better give him to someone I know; why should he die here of hunger, cold, and other privations? And so he rode away with the monkey.

He came to the town of Borisov. He went about his official duties. And left Monk in his car. He said to him, "Wait for me here, chum. I'll be right back."

But our Monk didn't wait. He climbed out of the car through a broken window and went gallivanting around the streets.

And now he goes marching along the street like a prince, strutting, taking a walk with his tail in the air. The people, of course, are astonished, and want to catch him. But catching him isn't so very easy. He is lively and agile and runs fast on his four hands. So they didn't catch him, but only wore him out with futile running.

He was tired out and, naturally, felt hungry.

But where could he get something to eat in the town? There was nothing very edible in the streets. And with his tail he couldn't go into a restaurant. Or a co-operative grocery. And besides, he had no money. No reduced rates. He didn't have any ration cards. It was nightmarish.

He went into the co-operative anyway. He sensed that they had something or other in there. And there they were giving out vegetables to the populace: carrots, turnips, and cucumbers.

He popped into the store. And he saw a long line. No, he wasn't going to stand in line. But he didn't start shoving people to get up to the counter. He ran to the salesgirl right along the customers' heads. And jumped onto the counter. He didn't ask how much a kilo of carrots cost. And then, as we say, he was off. He ran out of the store, pleased with his purchase. After all, he was a monkey. He didn't know what was what. Didn't see the sense of remaining without provisions.

Of course, in the store there arose an uproar, hubbub, upheaval. The crowd began to shout. The salesgirl, who was weighing some turnips, almost fainted from the shock. And it's true, you can really get scared if instead of a regular normal customer something kind of furry and with a tail hops in. And, on top of that, doesn't pay.

The crowd dashed into the street after the monkey. And he ran along, chewing on his carrot, having breakfast. He didn't know what was going on.

Some boys ran ahead of everyone. After them came the grownups. A militiaman ran behind them, blowing his whistle.

Suddenly a dog darted out from somewhere. And it too ran after our Monk. It not only yelped and barked, but straight off set about catching the monkey in its teeth.

Our Monk ran faster. He ran and probably thought, Eh, I should never have left that zoo. I could breathe easier in my cage. I'll certainly go back to the zoo the first chance I get.

And he ran as fast as he could, but the dog didn't fall behind and was within a hair's breadth of catching him.

Then our monkey hopped up on some kind of fence. And when the dog jumped up to catch the monkey, by the leg if nothing else, the monkey hit the dog on the nose with the carrot with all his might. And he hit so hard that the dog squealed and ran home with its injured nose. It probably thought, No, citizens, I'd better lie quietly at home instead of catching monkeys for you and undergoing such unpleasantnesses.

In short, the dog ran away, and our monkey jumped into a back yard.

And in the yard at this time, a certain teen-age boy named Alyosha Popov was splitting firewood.

So he was splitting firewood, and suddenly he saw a monkey. He was very fond of monkeys. All his life he had dreamed of having a monkey like this for himself. And suddenly—there was a monkey, if you please!

Alyosha took off his jacket and threw it over Monk, who had backed into a corner of the stairs.

The boy took him home. Fed him. Gave him tea to drink. And the monkey was very pleased. But not completely. Because Alyosha's grandmother took a dislike to him at once. She yelled at Monk and even wanted to slap his paws. All because, while they were drinking tea and the grandmother put a half-eaten piece of candy on her saucer, the monkey had grabbed Grandmother's piece of candy and crammed it into his mouth. Well, he was only a monkey. Not a human being. A human being, if he took something, wouldn't do it right under Grandmother's nose. But the monkey did it right in Grandmother's presence. And, of course, almost made her cry.

Grandmother said, "In general, it's really very unpleasant when some kind of macaque with a tail lives in your apartment. He'll keep scaring me with his inhuman appearance. He'll jump on me in the dark. Eat my candy. No, I categorically refuse to live in the same apartment with a monkey. One of us will have to live at the zoo. Do I really have to be the one to move to the zoo? No, it would be better if he lived there. And I'll go on living in my apartment."

Alyosha said to his grandmother, "No, Grandmother, you don't have to move to the zoo. I guarantee that Monk won't eat anything of yours any more. I'll educate him like a human being. I'll teach him to eat with a spoon. And drink tea from a glass. As far as jumping goes, I can't forbid him to climb on the lamp that hangs from the ceiling. From there, of course, he can jump down on your head. But the important thing is for you not to get scared when that happens. Because he's only a harmless monkey who got used to jumping and leaping in Africa."

The next day Alyosha went off to school. And he asked his grandmother to keep an eye on the monkey. But Grandmother had no intention of keeping an eye on him. She thought, That's all I need, to look after all kinds of monsters. And with these thoughts Grandmother up and fell asleep in her armchair on purpose.

Then our monkey crawled out on the street through an open ventilator in the window. And set off for a walk along the sunny side. It's not clear whether he wanted to take the air, or whether he had decided to stop in at the store again to buy himself something. Not for money, but just like that.

Now at this time a certain old man was walking along the street. The retired soldier Gavrilich. He was going to the public bath. And he was carrying in his arms a small basket, which contained soap and clean underwear.

He saw the monkey and at first didn't believe his eyes that it *was* a monkey. He thought he was seeing things, since he had just had a mug of beer.

He looked at the monkey in astonishment. And the monkey looked at him. Maybe he thought, What kind of a scarecrow carrying a basket is that?

Gavrilich finally realized that it was a real monkey and not an imaginary one. Then he thought, Why don't I just catch him? I'll take him to the market tomorrow and sell him for a hundred rubles. And with that money I'll drink ten mugs of beer in a row.

With these thoughts, he began trying to catch the monkey, saying persuasively, "Here, puss, puss, puss, come here."

Well, he knew that Monk wasn't a cat, but he didn't know in what language to address him. And he realized only later that this was the highest member of the animal kingdom. Then he took a piece of sugar out of his pocket, showed it to the monkey, and said to him, bowing, "Noble Monk, wouldn't you care to partake of a little piece of sugar?"

Monk replied, "Thank you, I would" . . . That is, he really didn't say anything, because he didn't know how to talk. But he came up, grabbed the piece of sugar, and began to eat it.

Gavrilich picked him up and put him in his basket. In the basket it was warm and cosy. Our Monk didn't try to jump out. Perhaps he thought, I'll let this old blockhead carry me along in his basket for a while. It's even interesting.

At first Gavrilich thought he would take him home. But then he didn't feel like going back home, and he went to the public bath with the monkey. He thought, It'll be even better if I take him along to the bath. I'll wash him there. He'll be clean and nice. I'll tie a bow around his neck. And they'll give me more for him at the market.

So he came to the bath with his monkey and began taking a bath with him.

It was very warm and humid in the bathhouse—just like in Africa. Our monkey was very pleased with this warm atmosphere. But not completely. Because Gavrilich soaped him and some soap got in his mouth. Of course, it doesn't taste good, but it's not bad enough to make you cry out, scratch, and refuse to be washed. Anyhow, our monkey tried to spit it out, but then some soap got in his eyes. This drove Monk completely crazy. He bit Gavrilich on the finger, tore himself from his grasp, and dashed like a streak out of the bath.

He leaped out into the room where people were undressing. And there he frightened everyone. Why, no one knew that it was a monkey. They saw something round, white, and covered with soapsuds pop out. First it bounded onto a sofa. Then onto the stove. From the stove to a box. From the box to someone's head. And back to the stove again.

Certain nervous visitors started screaming and began to run out of the bath. Our monkey ran out too. And went down the stairs.

Now downstairs there was a cashier's booth with a little window. The monkey jumped in through that little window, thinking it would be more peaceful in there and, most important, there wouldn't be such bustling and shoving. But in the booth there sat a fat lady cashier who gasped and began to squeal. And rushed out of her booth crying, "Help! I think a bomb has fallen into my booth! Get me some valerian drops!"

Our Monk was tired of all these shouts. He jumped out of the cashier's booth and ran along the street.

There he was, running along the street, all wet, covered with soapsuds, and again people were running after him. The boys in front. Behind them the grownups. Behind the grownups a militiaman. And behind the militiaman our aged Gavrilich with his clothes on every which way and carrying his boots in his hand.

At this point a dog again jumped out from somewhere or other—the same dog which had chased the monkey the day before.

Seeing it, our Monk thought, Well, citizens, now I'm really done for.

But this time the dog didn't chase him. The dog just looked at the running monkey, felt a severe pain in its nose, and didn't start running. It even turned away. It must have thought, Running after monkeys won't leave you any nose for your old age. But although it turned away, it gave an angry bark, as if to say, Go ahead and run, but remember that I'm here.

At this time our boy, Alyosha Popov, came home from school and didn't find his beloved monkey. He felt very bad. His eyes even filled with tears. He thought that now he'd never see his wonderful, beloved little monkey again.

And so, out of sadness and loneliness, he went out on the street. He was walking along the street looking very melancholy. Suddenly he saw people running. No, at first he didn't think they were running after his monkey. He thought they were running on account of an air attack. But then he saw his little monkey—all wet and covered with soap. He ran up to him. He took him in his arms. And he hugged him close to him so as not to let anyone else have him.

All the people stopped running and surrounded the boy.

But then our aged Gavrilich stepped out from the crowd. Showing everyone his bitten finger, he said, "Citizens, don't let this young whippersnapper pick up my monkey, which I want to sell at the market tomorrow. It's my own monkey, which bit me on the finger. Look at this swollen finger of mine, everyone. It proves that I'm telling the truth."

The boy, Alyosha Popov, said, "No, this isn't his monkey, it's my monkey. Look how eagerly he let me pick him up. That proves that I'm telling the truth."

Now another man stepped out of the crowd—the driver who had brought the monkey here in his car. He said, "No it's not your monkey, or yours either. It's my monkey, because I brought him here. But now I'm going back to my outfit, and for that reason I give the monkey to the person who is holding him lovingly in his arms, and not to the hard-hearted person who wants to sell him in the market place for drink. The monkey belongs to the boy."

The entire crowd applauded. And Alyosha Popov, beaming with happiness, hugged the monkey even closer to him. And triumphantly carried him home.

Gavrilich went back to the bathhouse with his bitten finger to finish his bath.

And from that time the monkey lived with the boy, Alyosha Popov. He is still living with him today. I recently took a trip to see the town of Borisov. I purposely stopped in at Alyosha's to see how Monk was getting along. Oh, he is getting along fine! He doesn't run away anywhere. He has become very obedient. He wipes his nose with a handkerchief. And doesn't take other people's candy. So that Grandmother is very pleased now, doesn't get angry at him, and no longer wants to move to the zoo.

When I went into Alyosha's room the monkey was sitting at the table. He sat there looking very important, like a cashier in a movie theater. And he was eating rice cereal with a teaspoon.

Alyosha said to me, 'I have brought him up like a human being, and now he sets a good example for all children and even for some grownups."

1945

AN
EXTRAORDINARY INCIDENT

This past summer I spent my vacation in a rest home.

The director of our rest home directed all his paternal attentions to feeding his guests well, assuming quite rightly that a good table would make up for many defects in his establishment.

He enticed into working for him an exceptionally good chef, who prepared splendid *pirozhki,** amazing salads, and quite tolerable cutlets. The dessert created by this chef's skillful hand always evoked general acclaim.

For this reason, the vacationers were favorably disposed and more than once thanked the director for his exemplary domestic management and for his splendid cuisine.

Wishing to gratify the vacationers even more, the director once said to some people who had come to thank him, "With your permission, I will convey your thanks to our chef, Ivan Fomich, who is doing his best over there at the stove. That will no doubt encourage him. And in this way we will attain even better results."

And really, from the next day on the quality of the meals was even higher. The director, beaming with pleasure, said to the vacationers, "You see what efforts our chef has put forth since receiving your thanks. But oral gratitude is only the narrow edge of the wedge. From my heart I advise you: write a note praising the

* Little pastries stuffed with meat or cabbage. *Ed.*

chef. We'll print it in our wall newspaper. And then we'll see what happens."

The vacationers did just that. They inserted in the wall newspaper a letter with five signatures in which they praised the culinary efforts of the chef, Ivan Fomich, in a grandiloquent style.

A vacationing artist surrounded the letter with a handsome frame, wreathed with ribbons, flowers, and laurels.

The effect surpassed the director's expectations.

The marvelous *pirozhki* prepared by our chef now literally melted in one's mouth. The salads became so delicious that even people who were completely full continued to eat more and more. And from that day forward the dessert evoked general wonder mingled with loud delight.

But especial delight was expressed by one of the vacationers—a young composer who sat next to me at the table. Or, to put it more precisely, he more frequently leaped up than sat. Some hidden spring did not allow his long, thin body to remain at rest.

A doctor of philology and his wife also sat at our table. The philologist was an exceptionally gaunt and taciturn fellow. But his wife more than made up for these shortcomings.

Well, at dinner one day the young composer expressed such extraordinary delight that he seemed on the verge of nervous convulsions. He bestowed unlimited praise upon everything that was brought to the table on that occasion. But when the dessert was brought in, he leaped from his chair and exclaimed, addressing the philologist, "Taste the Bavarian cream at once! It's a marvel of culinary art!"

The doctor of philology tasted the cream, said, "Yes," and nodded his head as a sign of satisfaction.

The philologist's wife began to explain to us why this particular cream was good and why boiled custards were sometimes of indifferent quality.

Without waiting for her to finish, the composer exclaimed once again, "No, no, we haven't fully taken cognizance of our chef's great services! We must encourage this divine gift again and again!"

The philologist's wife suggested that they collect some money from the vacationers and buy the chef a silver cigarette case or a length of plain fabric for a suit. But the composer cried out in irritation, "Oh, that's not the thing at all! We have before us an amazing master of his craft—an artist, a genius! And we must pay him the homage due an artist."

With these words the composer began to applaud.

The diners looked at him in astonishment. Then the composer made a quick circuit of the tables and quietly informed everyone that it had been decided to call out the chef with applause in order to give him an ovation.

Everyone agreed willingly to this. And, at a signal from the composer, friendly applause arose in the dining room.

The kitchen staff did not immediately grasp the significance of the noise. The dishwasher appeared at the threshold of the dining room. And after her popped out the apprentice cook Fedyushka. Smiling, but not understanding, they both gazed at the clapping public.

The waitresses ran in. The director appeared. He immediately joined in the applause and loudly shouted for the chef, "Ivan Fomich! Please come out . . ."

Soon Ivan Fomich appeared. He was a heavy-set fellow with a drooping gray mustache. His high chef's hat gave him a somewhat terrifying appearance.

Of course, Ivan Fomich had already got used to attention and success, but the ovation noticeably stirred and even stunned him by its sheer novelty. For a time the chef stood in silence on the threshold of the dining room and, wiping his perspiring face with his apron, looked askance at the people who were standing and applauding him.

The applause grew louder. The composer dashed to the piano and struck up a fanfare. And then the chef Ivan Fomich came out into the center of the dining room.

Now a whole gamut of emotions shone forth from his suddenly pale face. Simultaneous pride, agitation, delight, and astonishment could be read in his countenance.

The director raised his arms and, when he had obtained silence, addressed a short speech to the chef. Without the slightest hesitation he said, "Dear Ivan Fomich! Your predecessors long tormented the public with their dubious cuisine. And only with your arrival did the management attain that peace of mind which is the key to health. Permit me in the name of all the vacationers to thank you once again for your great skill, which has shone like the sun upon our modest rest home!"

And here, amid a thunder of stormy applause, the director embraced the chef and kissed him three times on his mustache and cheeks.

Now it was the chef's turn to speak in reply. But Ivan Fomich did not turn out to be as expert at this complex art as at cooking. Or perhaps agitation fettered his powers of speech. One way or the other, Ivan Fomich let fall a few niggardly sentences, from which, however, it was possible to judge the noble character of his thoughts. Taking off his white hat and pressing it to his heart, he said, "I tried . . . I attained . . . I promise to take pains for people in the future, too . . . I thank you from my heart for your attentions . . . Thank you . . ."

The meeting between the vacationers and the chef ended with stormy applause, music, and shouts of "bravo." Shyly bowing, Ivan Fomich withdrew to the kitchen.

No, I did not observe the events that followed, but

eyewitnesses described to me with the thoroughness of an official report the things that happened soon afterwards.

At five in the afternoon Ivan Fomich took his nephew Fedyushka and set out for the village to see some fishermen he knew. After getting very drunk there, Ivan Fomich hired a boat and two oarsmen. He decorated this boat with rugs and plants. He had an accordion player he knew sit in the stern. And in this boat, to the sounds of music, he floated along the lake past the village and past countless health resorts and sanitariums.

The chef made the entire water journey standing in the boat with his hand on one of the oarsmen's shoulder. For the entire trip (according to eyewitnesses) Ivan Fomich stood like a monument amid the plants and rugs. And when the accordion player fell silent, the chef's apprentice Fedyushka immediately started twanging his mandolin.

However, the considerable quantity of liquor which the chef had swallowed brought the expedition to an unexpected shipwreck. When the oarsmen turned the boat around sharply for a second circuit, Ivan Fomich could not keep his balance and fell overboard. His corpulent body rocked the frail and rickety craft, which filled with water and overturned.

Fedyushka and the oarsmen swam to the shore themselves. And some fishermen hauled out the chef and the accordion player with his instrument.

Ivan Fomich had swallowed a lot of water and for a long time lay almost motionless on the shore. The villagers wanted to give him artificial respiration, but he wouldn't let them. Together with his sopping wet nephew Fedyushka, he hurried back to his apartment.

And there in his apartment (people assert) Ivan Fomich drank, ate, and even roistered until late at night.

People found out about this extraordinary incident in

our rest home only on the following day, when for breakfast, instead of dainty salads, they were served porridge
with a vulgar cranberry sauce.

At breakfast the doctor of philology remarked to us,
almost smiling, "Yes, I've always thought that extravagant praise demands of people exceptional moral
strength."

The philologist's wife began to decode her husband's
idea for us and, in so doing, took it upon herself to explain in a great many words that it was necessary to
praise people, that it was pedagogically sound and produced splendid results. However, in the case of certain
excesses, she said, strange and unexpected things sometimes happen—like the scandalous incident with our
chef. From which it is apparent that immoderate praise
carries a certain danger for a weak mind.

The young composer exclaimed vehemently, "No, I
don't agree with you! Even the highest praise can't do
any damage. And I am more than certain that when
our chef recovers from his shipwreck he will outdo himself!"

That day we were served a dinner which had been
hurriedly prepared by someone's inept hand. And for
five days more—and for vacationers this is no short time
—the dinners were of extremely dubious quality. But
toward the end of the week the vacationers were once
more unable to refrain from loud raptures on the subject
of our chef Ivan Fomich.

Then the young composer, eating his dessert after
dinner, said excitedly to the philologist's wife, "Just
taste these meringues! Extravagant praise didn't hurt
matters at all. The homage we paid to the chef only
gave wings to his amazing skill!"

The philologist's wife praised the meringues, but did
not change her opinion. She said that extravagant praise
was more dangerous for an inexperienced novice than
for a first-rate master. An inexperienced novice often

ceases to develop after immoderate praise, thinking that there is nowhere further for him to go. Or he loses heart at the first failure, and then he seeks oblivion in liquor.

The young composer jumped up from the table to reply to this, but the philologist's wife continued without a pause, "However, there is a certain danger here even for a first-rate master. Unlimited praise sometimes lulls one's consciousness, gives rise to conceit, and prevents one from taking a critical attitude toward his work. For this reason a first-rate master—let's say, a literary artist—may sometimes lose his divine skill and become a homegrown preacher, a shrill bigot, or a worn-out decadent."

The philologist's wife spoke long and verbosely on this subject, and concluded her speech with the following words: "Of course, such a transformation cannot take place in our chef. The extravagant praise upset his emotional balance for only a short time. Judging by the meringues, the matter has ended fortunately for everyone. And now, apparently, we can praise our chef once again without the risk of running into any unexpected unpleasantness."

The doctor of philology did not take part in this conversation and only toward the end of the discussion remarked in didactic tone to the composer, "Young man, a sturdy moral fiber is absolutely necessary in any profession, including the culinary trade and especially including music, which is so frequently accompanied by applause."

To this the young composer did not reply and, with the unsteady gait of one satiated with honors and applause, left the premises.

1955

BEFORE SUNRISE

A *Tale*

[EXCERPTS*]

II. I AM UNHAPPY AND
DO NOT KNOW WHY

O sorrow! To flee from the light of the sun
And seek solace in prison
By the light of a lamp . . .

WHEN I think about my youth, I am astonished at how much grief, unnecessary anxiety, and anguish I experienced.

The most wonderful years of youth were painted over in black.

As a child I had not experienced anything of the sort.

But my first steps as a young man were darkened by this amazing anguish, which I know nothing to compare with.

I was eager to know people, I delighted in life, I sought friends, love, happy encounters. But I couldn't

* Unfortunately, considerations of space made it impossible to include the whole of this work, or rather the whole of what was published before the censors called a halt. The two published installments are about twice the length of the translation published here. However, all the sections presented here are complete in themselves; there has been no editing or deletion within any section translated. *Ed.*

find relief in any of these things. Everything lost its luster in my hands. Melancholy dogged my every step.

I was unhappy and did not know why.

But I was eighteen, and I found an explanation.

The world is horrible, I thought. People are cheap
and vulgar. Their behavior is comical. I don't run with
the herd.

Over my desk I hung the lines from Sophocles:

> Not to be born is, past all prizing, best; but, when a man
> hath seen the light, this is next best by far, that with all
> speed he should go thither, whence he hath come.*

I knew, of course, that other outlooks existed—joyous,
even ecstatic ones. But I did not respect people who
were able to dance to the coarse and vulgar music of
life. Such people seemed to me on a level with savages
and animals.

Everything I saw around me confirmed this view.

Poets wrote sad verses and prided themselves on their
misery.

"Sorrow has come—my sovereign lady, my gray-haired
mistress." I kept muttering these lines from somewhere;
I don't remember who wrote them.

My favorite philosophers referred to melancholy respectfully. "Melancholics possess a sense of the exalted,"
wrote Kant. And Aristotle believed that "A melancholy
turn of mind aids profound thought and accompanies
genius."

But not only poets and philosophers provided fuel
for my dim fire. Surprisingly enough, in my time sadness was considered the mark of a thinking person. In
my circle the people we admired were thoughtful and
melancholy, those who even seemed to be estranged
from life.†

---

* *Oedipus at Colonus*, R. C. Jebb, trans.
† Not long ago, rereading Valery Briusov's *Diary*, I found the
following lines: "Yaroshenko is fine. A nice man. Alien to life."
Author's note.

In a word, I began to believe that a pessimistic out-look on life was the only possible one for a thoughtful and refined person, born, as I was, a member of the gentry.

That means, I thought, that melancholy is my nor-mal state, and depression and a certain revulsion against life are characteristics of my mind. And, evidently, not of my mind alone. Evidently, of every mind, every con-sciousness, which strives to be higher than the conscious-ness of animals.

It's very sad if this is true. But it probably is. In na-ture the coarser strains are victorious. Coarse feelings and primitive thoughts prevail. Everything that be-comes refined perishes.

So I thought at eighteen. And I won't hide from you the fact that I thought so a good deal later.

But I was mistaken. And I am now happy to tell you about this terrible mistake of mine.

At that time, this mistake almost cost me my life.

I wanted to die, since I could see no other way out.

In the autumn of 1914 the World War began and, leaving the university, I went into the army to die an honorable death at the front for my country, for my na-tive land.

However, during the war I almost stopped feeling de-pressed. I did feel that way at times, but it would go away quickly. During the war for the first time I felt al-most happy.

I thought, Why is this? It occurred to me that I had found wonderful comrades there and had stopped being depressed for this reason. This was logical.

I served in the Mingrelsky regiment of the division of Caucasian grenadiers. We were all good friends; both the soldiers and the officers. Or maybe it just seemed that way to me.

At nineteen I was already a lieutenant.

At twenty I had five decorations and had been recom-mended for promotion to captain.

But this didn't mean that I was a hero. It meant that I had been in the front line for two years.

I took part in many battles and was wounded and gassed. My heart was damaged. Nevertheless, my happy state of mind hardly ever vanished.

When the Revolution began, I returned to Petrograd.

I felt no regrets about the past. On the contrary, I wanted to see a new Russia—a less melancholy one than I had known. I wanted to be surrounded by people who were healthy and vigorous and not, as I was, inclined to depression, melancholy, and sadness. I didn't experience any so-called "social discontents." Nevertheless, I began to feel depressed again.

I tried changing cities and professions. I wanted to run away from this terrible anguish of mine. I felt that it would destroy me.

I went to Archangel. Then to Mezen, on the Arctic Ocean. Then I returned to Petrograd. I went to Novgorod, to Pskov. Then to the province of Smolensk, to the town of Krasny. I returned to Petrograd again.

Depression followed right at my heels.

In three years I lived in twelve cities and had ten professions.

I was a militiaman, a bookkeeper, a cobbler, an instructor in poultry-farming, a telephone operator in the border patrol, a detective, a court secretary, and a chief clerk.

This wasn't determined progress through life, it was madness.

I spent six months at the front again with the Red Army, fighting near Narva and Yamburg.

But my heart had been injured by poison gas, and I had to think of a new profession.

In 1921 I began to write stories.

My life changed a great deal when I became a writer. But my old depression was still there. It even began to afflict me more and more frequently.

Then I consulted doctors. Besides depression I had

something wrong with my heart, my digestion, and my liver.

The doctors energetically set to work on me.

They began to treat my three illnesses with pills and water. Mostly with water—internally and externally.

They decided to direct an all-out attack on my depression—to hit it from all four sides, on the flanks, front, and rear—with journeys, ocean-bathing, Charcot douches, and with the amusements which were so necessary for one of my youthful age.

Twice a year I began going to resorts—Yalta, Kislovodsk, Sochi, and other favored places.

In Sochi I met a man who was considerably more depressed than I was. At least twice a year they would take his head out of the noose into which he had stuck it because he was tormented by causeless depression.

I began to converse with this man with a feeling of the very greatest respect. I expected to find wisdom, a mind filled to overflowing with knowledge, and the mournful smile of a genius forced to live on our transitory earth.

I didn't find anything of the sort.

He was a dull person, uneducated, and without even a shade of enlightenment. He had not read more than two books in his entire life. And he wasn't interested in anything except money, food, and women.

The person before me was the most ordinary sort, with vulgar thoughts and stupid desires.

I didn't realize at once that this was the case. At first it seemed to me that the room was smoky or that the barometer had fallen, indicating a storm. Somehow I felt uneasy when I was talking with him. Then I saw that he was simply a fool. A mere blockhead you couldn't talk to for more than three minutes.

My philosophical system was shattered. I realized that it wasn't only a matter of higher consciousness. But what was it, then? I didn't know.

With the greatest humility I put myself in the hands of the doctors.

In two years I swallowed half a ton of powders and pills.

Without a murmur I drank all kinds of detestable, nauseating stuff.

I allowed myself to be stuck with needles, x-rayed, and put into baths.

However, the treatment was not successful. And soon things even got so bad that my acquaintances stopped recognizing me on the street. I became incredibly thin, nothing but skin and bones. I felt terribly cold all the time. My hands shook. And the yellowness of my skin amazed even the doctors. They began to suspect that I was such a hypochondriac that their procedures were useless. Hypnosis and clinical treatment were necessary.

One of the doctors managed to put me in a trance. When I was asleep he began to suggest to me that my depression was pointless, that everything in the world was wonderful and there were no reasons for being unhappy.

For two days I felt more vigorous; then I got markedly worse than before.

I almost stopped going out of the house. Each new day was a burden.

> *The day came, the day passed*
> *The years went by uncounted*
> *I had lost the memory, it seemed*
> *Of earthly change . . .*

I was hardly able to move along the street, choking from heart seizures and the pains in my liver.

I stopped going to resorts. Or, more correctly, I went, suffered for two or three days, and returned home in an even more terrible state of depression than when I had left.

Then I turned to books. I was a young writer. I was

only twenty-seven. I naturally turned to my great colleagues—writers and musicians. I wanted to find out whether they had experienced something of this sort. Whether they had had depressions like mine; and, if they had, what did they think caused them? And what did they do to prevent them?

I began to note down everything that had to do with depression. I took notes without any particular plan or system. However, I did try to select what was characteristic of a person, things that were repeated during his life and didn't seem to be mere accidents, momentary imaginings or outbursts.

These notes stirred my imagination for several years.

. . . I leave the house, go out into the street, turn melancholy, and return home again. What for? To mope.   *Chopin*, LETTERS, *1830*

I did not know where to go to escape this melancholy. I myself did not know where this melancholy came from . . .   *Gogol to his mother*, *1837*

I have attacks of such severe despondency that I'm afraid I'll throw myself into the sea. Dear friend! It's very sickening . . .   *Nekrasov to Turgenev*, *1857*

I am so *ill*—so terribly, hopelessly *ill* in body and mind that I CANNOT live . . .*
                    Edgar Allan Poe to Annie, *1848*

I am suffering under a depression of spirits such as I have never felt before. I have struggled against the influence of this melancholy . . . I am wretched, and know not why.† *Edgar Allan Poe to Kennedy*, *1835*

Twenty times a day the thought of a pistol comes into my mind. And that thought makes me feel better . . .
                    Nekrasov to Turgenev, *1857*

* Original cited from *Life and Letters of Edgar Allan Poe*, James A. Harrison, ed. (New York, 1902-3). *Trans.*
† Original cited from *The Letters of Edgar Allan Poe*, John Ustrom, ed. (Cambridge, 1948). *Trans.*

Everything has become repugnant to me. It seems to me that I could hang myself right now with pleasure—but pride keeps me from doing it . . .   *Flaubert, 1853*

I live badly and feel terrible. I get up every morning with the thought: wouldn't it be better to shoot myself?
Saltykov-Shchedrin to Panteleyev, 1886

To this was added indescribable anguish. I absolutely did not know what to do with myself, what to lean against . . .   *Gogol to Pogodin, 1840*

Everything in the world is so repugnant, so unbearable . . . It's boring to live, talk, write . . .
L. Andreyev, JOURNAL, 1919

I feel tired and beaten down to such a degree that I can hardly keep from crying from morning till night . . . The faces of friends irritate me . . . Daily conversations, sleeping in the same bed, my own voice, my face, its reflection in the mirror . . .
Maupassant, "Under the Sun," 1881

Hanging myself or drowning seemed to me somehow like a medicine and a relief.
Gogol to Pletnev, 1846

I am tired, tired of all relationships. All people and all wishes have exhausted me. To go away somewhere into the wilderness or to fall into one's "final sleep."
V. Briusov, JOURNAL, 1898

I hide the rope, so as not to hang myself from the cross-beam in my room when I am alone in the evening. I no longer go hunting with a gun lest I succumb to the temptation to shoot myself. It seems to me that my life has been a stupid farce.
L. N. Tolstoy, 1878. L. L. Tolstoy,
THE TRUTH ABOUT MY FATHER

I filled an entire notebook with quotations of this sort. They astonished and even shook me. Why, I had not chosen people who had just experienced some grief, misfortune, or death. I took a state of mind which had recurred again and again. I took people many of whom said that they themselves could not understand where this state of mind came from.

I was shaken, perplexed. What is this suffering to which people are subject? Where does it come from? And how should one fight it, by what means?

Perhaps this suffering stems from the disorders of life, from social discontents, or world problems? Perhaps this provides the basis for such anguish.

Yes, it's true. But I remembered the words of Chernyshevsky, "It's not over world problems that people drown themselves, shoot themselves, and go mad."

These words confused me even further.

I could find no solution. I did not understand.

Perhaps, nevertheless, I thought once more, this is that *Weltschmerz* to which great people are subject because of their higher consciousness.

No! Side by side with the great people I have listed, I found no fewer great people who had experienced no depression at all, although their consciousness was equally high. And there were even considerably more of these.

At a musical evening devoted to Chopin, his "Second Concerto for Piano and Orchestra" was performed.

I was sitting in one of the back rows, exhausted and spent.

But the second concerto dissipated my melancholy. The powerful, masculine sounds filled the hall.

Joy, struggle, extraordinary strength and even exultation rang out in the third part of the concerto.

Where did this weak man, this musician of genius whose sad life I now knew so well get this enormous strength, I wondered. Where did he get such joy, such ecstasy? Did it mean that he had all this? That it was only fettered? By what?

At this point I thought of my stories, which made people laugh. I thought of the laughter which was present in my books but not in my heart.

I won't hide it from you: I was frightened when I suddenly thought that I had to find the reason why my strength was fettered and my life was so unhappy; and the reason why there are people like me, susceptible to melancholy and causeless anguish.

In the autumn of 1926 I forced myself to go to Yalta. I forced myself to remain there four weeks.

I lay in my hotel room for ten days. Then I began to go out for walks. I walked in the hills. And sometimes I would sit by the shore for hours, happy that I was better, that I felt almost well.

I got much better in a month. My spirits grew calm, even happy.

To improve my health still further I decided to prolong my rest. I took a ticket on a boat to Batum. From Batum I intended to go straight to Moscow by train.

I took a private cabin, and I left Yalta in a wonderful mood.

The sea was calm, tranquil. And I sat on deck all day, admiring the Crimean shore and the sea I loved so much and came regularly to Yalta to visit.

In the morning, as soon as it was light, I was on deck again.

A splendid morning was dawning.

I sat on a chaise longue, enjoying my wonderful state of mind. My thoughts were happy, even joyful. I thought about my trip, about Moscow and the friends I would meet there; about the fact that my anguish was gone. Let it remain a riddle, as long as it was gone.

It was very early in the morning. I gazed thoughtfully at the lightly rippling water, the patches of sunlight, and the gulls which kept alighting on the water with repellent cries.

Suddenly, in one moment, I began to feel bad. It wasn't only depression. It was agitation, anxiety, almost terror. I could hardly get up from the chaise longue. I could hardly get back to my cabin. I lay motionless on my berth for two hours. And my anguish came back again, worse than I had ever known it.

I tried to struggle against it. I went out on deck. I began listening to other people's conversations. I wanted to distract myself. But I couldn't do it.

It looked as if I couldn't and shouldn't continue my journey.

I was hardly able to wait until we got to Tuapse. I went ashore, intending to continue my journey in a few days.

I was in a nervous fever. I went as far as the hotel on a carryall. And there I collapsed.

It was only after a week that, by an effort of will, I forced myself to start out again.

The traveling distracted and diverted me. I began to feel better. The terrible anguish was fading.

It was a long trip, and I began to think about this unfortunate illness of mine, which was capable of vanishing as quickly as it arose. Why? And what were the reasons?

Or were there no reasons?

It seemed as if there were no reasons. It was probably just "weakness of the nerves," excessive "sensitivity." Probably my moods would always swing like a pendulum.

I began to wonder: was I born so weak and sensitive, or had something happened in my life that damaged my nerves, injured them, and made me a wretched particle of dust to be blown about by every wind?

And suddenly it seemed to me that I could not have been born so unfortunate and defenseless. I could have been born weak, scrofulous, with one arm, one eye, or lacking an ear. But to be born to feel despondent, and to be despondent for no reason—because the world seems cheap and vulgar! Yet I was not a Martian. I was a child of this earth. And, like every animal, I was made to feel the rapture of existence. To feel happy when all was well. And to struggle if things went badly. But to feel despondent? When even an insect who is granted only four hours to live revels in the sunshine! No, I could not have been born such a monster.

And suddenly it dawned on me that the reason for my misfortunes was hidden in my life. There was no doubt about it—something had happened, something or other had had an oppressive effect on me.

But what? And when had it happened? And how was I to search for this unfortunate occurrence? How was I to discover the reason for my despondency?

Then I thought: I must recall my past life. And I began to recall things feverishly. But I realized at once that nothing would come of this unless I somehow imposed some system upon my recollections.

There's no need to remember everything, I thought. It's enough to remember only the strongest and most vivid things. It's enough to remember the things associated with emotion. The answer to the riddle could lie only there.

So I began to recall the most vivid pictures that remained in my memory. I saw that my memory had preserved them with unusual exactness. Trifles, details, colors, and even odors were preserved.

Emotion, like a flash bulb, illuminated everything that had taken place. These were flash photographs which had remained in my brain like momentos.

In a state of extraordinary perturbation, I began to study these photographs. And I found that they upset me even more than did the wish to find the cause of my misfortune.

III. FALLEN LEAVES

The life of every man repeats one theme
Expressed in other lives before his own,
And if a man explores within the past
There he may learn quite well to prophesy
The march of things to come . . .

And so I decided to recall my life in order to discover the reason for my misfortune.

I decided to find the incident or series of incidents that had affected me adversely and made me an unfortunate particle of dust to be blown about by every gust of wind.

For this purpose I decided to recall only the most vivid scenes of my past life, only those scenes connected with great emotional disturbance, rightly calculating that the answer to the riddle could lie only there.

However, there is no need to remember the years of childhood, I thought. What kind of emotional upheavals can a little boy have? Imagine, such tragedies! He lost three kopecks. The kids beat him up. He ripped his pants. Somebody swiped his stilts. The teacher gave him a zero . . . That's all the upheavals of childhood amount to. It would be better, I thought, to recall scenes from my conscious life. Besides, I fell ill not in my childhood, but after I was already grown. I'll start at the age of sixteen, I thought.

Then I began to recollect the most vivid scenes, beginning at the time I was sixteen.

1912-1915

A Letter

The dining room. Brown wallpaper. A crystal salt-shaker shaped like an inverted pyramid.

My sisters and mother are at the table.

I have been detained at the Gymnasium and come in late, and they have started eating dinner without me.

Exchanging glances, my sisters laugh softly.

I take my seat. At my place there is a letter.

A long, lilac-colored envelope. Unusually fragrant.

I tear open the envelope with trembling hands. I take out an even more fragrant sheet of note paper. The scent of the paper is so strong that my sisters, unable to control themselves, sputter with laughter.

Frowning, I read it. The letters dance before my eyes.

"Oh, how fortunate I am to have met you . . ." I memorize the phrase and repeat it over and over in my mind.

My mother's laughing eyes meet mine.

"Who's it from?" she asks.

"From Nadya," I answer drily and almost angrily.

My sisters' merriment increases.

"I don't understand it," says my older sister. "They live in the same house, see each other every day, and on top of that write letters. It's funny. Silly."

I look menacingly at my sister. Silently I gulp my soup and eat my bread, steeped in the scent of perfume.

Easter Eve

I am hurrying to midnight mass. I stand in front of the mirror in my tightly belted Gymnasium uniform. In my left hand I am holding a pair of white doeskin gloves. With my right hand I am fixing the amazing part in my hair.

I am not very satisfied with my appearance. I look too young.

At sixteen you ought to look a little bit older.

Carelessly throwing my overcoat around my shoulders, I go out on the stairs.

Tata T. is coming up the stairs.

Today she looks surprisingly beautiful, wearing a short fur jacket and carrying a muff.

"Aren't you going to church?" I ask.

"No, we're celebrating at home," she says, smiling. And coming closer to me, she adds, "Christ is risen! . . . Mishenka . . ."*

"It's not midnight yet," I mutter.

Putting her arms around my neck, Tata T. kisses me.

Not the usual three Easter kisses. It's a single kiss which lasts a minute. I begin to realize this is not a Christian kiss.

At first I feel happy, then astonished, and then—I laugh.

"What are you laughing at?" she asks.

"I didn't know that people kissed like that."

"Not people," she says, "but men and women, little stupid!"

She caresses my face with her hand and kisses my eyes. Then, hearing a door slam on her landing, she goes hurriedly up the stairs, beautiful and mysterious, just the kind of woman I would want to love always.

Torture

I am lying on an operating table. Under me there is white, cold oilcloth. In front of me an enormous win-

---

* It was customary for Russians at the stroke of midnight on Easter Eve to kiss one another three times with the words, "Christ is risen. Verily He is risen." *Ed.*

dow. Beyond the window a bright blue sky.

I have swallowed a crystal of mercuric chloride. I used these crystals in photography. Now they are going to pump out my stomach.

A doctor in a white coat is standing motionless by the table.

The nurse hands him a long rubber tube. Then, taking a glass pitcher, she fills it with water. I watch this procedure with revulsion. So they are going to torture me. They should have let me die. At least all my disappointments and vexations would be over.

I got a "1"* in Russian composition. Besides the "1" there was an inscription in red ink on the paper: "Rubbish." True, it was a composition on Turgenev's "Liza Kalitina."† What did I have to do with her? But it was still impossible to endure.

The doctor shoves the rubber hose into my gullet. The repulsive brown tube goes deeper and deeper.

The nurse lifts the pitcher of water. The water pours into me. I choke. I writhe in the doctor's arms. With a groan I wave my arms, begging them to cut short the torture.

"Gently, young man, gently," says the doctor. "Now aren't you ashamed? Such a coward . . . about nothing." The water pours out of me like a fountain.

Was It Worth It for Him to Hang Himself?

The student Mishka F. hanged himself. He left a note, "No one is to blame. The reason is an unhappy love affair."

I knew Mishka slightly. An awkward fellow. Disheveled. Unshaven. Not very intelligent.

The students, however, were well-disposed toward him—he was an easy-going, companionable person.

* The lowest mark. *Ed.*
† Heroine of *A Nest of Gentlefolk. Ed.*

Out of respect for his tragedy, we decided to drink to his eternal rest.

We got together in a tavern on Maly Prospect.

First we sang, "Swift as the Waves Are the Days of Our Lives." Then we began to reminisce about our comrade. However, no one could remember anything special.

Then someone remembered how Mishka F. had at one sitting eaten several dinners in the university dining room. Everyone started to laugh. They began recalling all kinds of trivia and nonsense from Mishka's life. An incredible laugh went up.

Choking with laughter, one of the students said, "One time we were getting ready to go to a dance. I stopped by for Mishka. He didn't feel like washing his hands. He was in a hurry. He stuck his fingers in a powder jar and whitened the dirt under his nails."

There was an explosion of laughter.

Someone said, "Now we know why he had an unhappy love affair."

Laughing, we began to sing "Swift as the Waves" again. One of the students got up every time we came to the words "You'll die and be buried as if you had never lived," and emphatically waved his arm like a conductor.

Then we sang "Gaudeamus," "Evening Bells," and "Dirlim-Bom-Bom."

A Proposal

I am walking through the cars of a train. In my hand I have a ticket punch.

My punch has been clicking away for half a month now.

The elegant branch line from Kislovodsk to Mineralnye Vody* hires students in the summer. That's

* Resort towns in the Caucasus. *Ed.*

why I'm here in the Caucasus. I've come here to earn some money.

Kislovodsk. I go out onto the platform. At the door of the station is an enormous gendarme with medals on his chest. He stands as stiff as a monument.

The cashier comes over to me, smiling and bowing politely.

"Colleague," he says to me, although he is not a student,* "a few words . . . Next time don't punch the tickets, but give them back to me . . ."

He utters these words calmly, smiling, as if he were talking about the weather.

I murmur in bewilderment, "What for? So you can . . . sell them again?"

"Why, yes . . . I have an agreement with almost all of your fellows . . . We split the profits . . ."

"You crook! You're lying!" I mutter. "With all of them?"

The cashier shrugs his shoulders.

"Well, not with all of them," he says, "but with a lot . . . Why are you so surprised? Everyone does it . . . Could I live on thirty-six rubles . . . I don't even consider it a crime. They force us into it . . ."

Turning sharply, I walk away. The cashier catches up with me.

"Colleague," he says, "if you don't want to, you don't have to, I don't insist . . . Only, don't think of telling anyone about this. In the first place, no one will believe you. In the second place, you can't prove it. In the third place, word will get around that you're a liar and a scandalmonger."

I slowly make my way home . . . It's raining . . .

I have never been more astonished in my life.

---

* Russian students used customarily to address one another as "Colleague." *Ed.*

Elvira

The railway stop "Minutka." I have a quiet room with windows facing the garden.

My contentment and quiet don't last long. The circus performer Elvira, who has just arrived from Penza, is moving into the next room. On her passport she is listed as Nastya Gorokhova.

She is a hefty creature, almost illiterate.

In Penza she had a short romance with a general. Now the general and his wife have come to Kislovodsk to take the waters. Elvira has followed them, counting on I don't know what.

From morning to night all of Elvira's thoughts are focused on the unfortunate general.

Showing me her arms, which have supported three men under the circus tent, Elvira says to me, "To tell you the truth, I could kill him very calmly. And they wouldn't give me any more than eight years for it . . . What do you think?"

"But what do you really want from him?" I ask her.

"What do you mean!" says Elvira. "I came here only because of him. I've been living here almost a month and, like a fool, paying for everything myself. I want him at least to pay my fare both ways out of decency. I want to write him a letter about it."

Because of Elvira's illiteracy I write this letter. I write with inspiration. My hand is guided by the hope that when Elvira gets the money she will go back to Penza.

I don't remember what I wrote. I remember only that when I read this letter to Elvira she said, "Yes, that's the cry of a woman's soul . . . And I'll definitely kill him if he doesn't send me anything after this."

My letter touched the general to the very depths of his soul. He sent Elvira five hundred rubles by messenger. This was an enormous and even grandiose sum in those days.

Elvira was stunned.

"With that kind of money," she said, "it would be simply foolish to leave Kislovodsk."

She remained. And remained with the idea that I was the sole cause of her wealth.

Now she hardly left my room.

Luckily, the World War began soon afterward. I left.

1915-1917

Fate treated me more kindly
Than it did many others . . .

Twelve Days

I am traveling from Viatka to Kazan to get reinforcements for my regiment. I am using post horses. There is no other means of transportation. I ride in a covered wagon, wrapped in blankets and fur coats.

The three horses gallop over the snow. The landscape is bare. There is a cruel frost. Next to me is Ensign S. We are going for the reinforcements together.

We have been traveling for two days. Everything has been said. All our reminiscences have been repeated. We are incredibly bored. Pulling his revolver from its holster, Ensign S. shoots at the white insulators on the telegraph poles.

These shots irritate me. I get angry at Ensign S. I rudely tell him, "Cut it out, you idiot!"

I expect a scene, shouts. But instead I hear a plaintive voice in reply. He says, "Sub-lieutenant Zoshchenko . . . don't stop me. Let me do what I want. I'll get to the front and they'll kill me."

I gaze at his snub nose, I look into his piteous bluish eyes. Now, almost thirty years later, I can remember his face. He really was killed the second day after we got to our position.

In that war sub-lieutenants lived, on an average, not more than twelve days.

Sleepy

We go into the ballroom. There are raspberry-colored velvet curtains on the windows. Mirrors in gilt frames hang on the walls between the windows.

A waltz is thundering. A man in full dress is playing it on the piano. He has an aster in his buttonhole. But his face is the face of a murderer.

On sofas and armchairs sit officers and ladies. Several couples are dancing.

A drunken cornet enters. He sings, "The Austrians were not so bright: with Russia they began a fight."

Everyone catches up the tune. They laugh.

I sit down on a sofa. There is a woman next to me. She is about thirty. She is a bit heavy. Dark. Vivacious.

Looking into my eyes, she says, "Shall we dance?"

I sit there gloomy and morose. I shake my head in refusal.

"Sleepy?" she asks. "Then come to my room."

We go to her room. In her room there is a Chinese lantern. Chinese screens. Chinese kimonos. That's amusing. Funny.

We go to bed.

It's already midnight. My eyelids are heavy. But I can't fall asleep. I feel bad. Depressed. Restless. I am upset.

She is bored with me. She tosses and sighs. She touches my shoulder.

"You won't be angry if I go to the ballroom for a little while. They're playing lotto there now. They're dancing."

"Go ahead," I say.

She kisses me gratefully and goes away. I fall asleep immediately. Toward morning she isn't there, and I close my eyes again.

Later she is sleeping tranquilly and I dress quietly and leave.

Nerves

Two soldiers are slaughtering a pig. The pig is squealing unbearably. I come closer.

One soldier is sitting on the pig. The other one, armed with a knife, is skillfully ripping up the pig's belly. An immense expanse of white fat is laid open on both sides.

The squealing is so bad you have to put your fingers in your ears.

"You ought to muffle it with something, fellows," I say. "Why cut it up like that?"

"You can't, your honor," says the soldier sitting on the pig. "The taste won't be the same."

Seeing my silver saber and the monograms on my shoulder boards, the soldier jumps up. The pig tears itself loose.

"Sit still," I say. "Hurry up and finish the job."

"It's not good to do it fast either," says the soldier with the knife. "Hurry spoils the lard."

Glancing at me with pity, the first soldier says, "Your honor, there's a war on! People are suffering. And you feel sorry for a pig."

Making a final gesture with the knife, the second soldier says, "His honor's got nerves."

The conversation is taking on an overly familiar tone. That shouldn't happen. I want to go away, but I don't.

The first soldier says, "In the forest of Augustowo*

---

* A forest to the west of Grodno, now lying between Poland and Byelorussia. There was heavy fighting there between Russian and German forces in February 1915. *Ed.*

the bones in this hand got broken to bits. They put me right on the table. Gave me half a glass of vodka and started to cut. And I was eating sausage."

"And it didn't hurt?"

"Of course it hurt. It hurt an awful lot . . . I ate up the sausage. 'Give me some cheese,' I said. As soon as I finished the cheese, the surgeon said, 'All done. We're sewing it up.' 'Go right ahead,' I said . . . Now you wouldn't have been able to stand that, your honor."

"His honor's got weak nerves," the second soldier says again.

I go away.

An Attack

At midnight sharp we come out of the trenches. It's very dark. I have a revolver in my hand.

"Quiet, quiet," I whisper, "don't rattle your helmets."

But it's impossible to stop the noise.

The Germans are beginning to shoot. That's annoying. It means they've noticed our maneuver.

We run forward amid the whistle and whine of bullets to force the Germans out of their trenches.

A torrent of bullets rains on us. Machine guns and rifles both. And the artillery is beginning to join in.

People are falling all around me. I feel a bullet singe my leg, but I run ahead.

We're already right up to the German barbed-wire entanglements. My grenadiers are cutting the wire.

The furious machine-gun fire puts a stop to our work. It's impossible to lift an arm. We lie motionless.

We lie there for an hour or two.

At last the telephone man hands the receiver over to me. The battalion commander is speaking: "Withdraw to your previous positions."

I pass the order down the line.

We crawl back.

In the morning they are bandaging me in the regimental infirmary. My wound is trifling. It wasn't a bullet, but a piece of shrapnel.

The regimental commander, Prince Makayev, says to me, "I'm very pleased with your company."

"We didn't do anything, Your Grace," I reply in confusion.

"You did what was wanted. Why, that was a feint, not an attack."

"Oh, it was a feint?"

"It was simply a feint. We had to draw the enemy away from the left flank. That was where the attack was."

I feel extraordinary resentment inside, but I try not to show it.

I Came for Nothing

I ride up to the high gates at a fast gallop. The headquarters of our division is here.

I am agitated and excited. The collar of my field jacket is unbuttoned. My cap is on the back of my head.

Jumping off my horse, I go in at the side gate. A staff officer, Lieutenant Zradlovsky, comes rapidly toward me. He mutters through his teeth, "Out of uniform . . . Button your collar . . ."

I button my collar and straighten my cap.

The staff officers are standing near the saddled horses.

I see among them the commander of the division, General Gabayev, and the staff commander, Colonel Shaposhnikov.

I report.

"I know," says the general in irritation.

"What shall I report to my commander, Your Excellency?"

"Report, that . . ."

I sense that the general has some oath on the tip of his tongue, but he controls himself.

The officers exchange glances. The staff commander almost smirks.

"Tell him that . . . Well, what can I tell a man who has lost his regiment? You came for nothing . . ."

I leave in embarrassment.

Again I am galloping along. And suddenly I see my regimental commander. He is tall and thin. He is holding his cap in his hands. The wind tousles his gray sideburns. He is standing in a field and stopping retreating soldiers. These are not soldiers from our regiment. The commander runs up to each one with a shout and an entreaty.

The soldiers go obediently to the edge of the woods. Here I see our reserve battalion and some two-wheeled baggage wagons.

I go over to the officers. The regimental commander comes over too. He mutters, "My fine Mingrelsky regiment is lost."

Throwing his cap on the ground, the commander stamps on it in his rage.

We try to console him. We say that we have five hundred men left. That's quite a lot. We'll have a regiment again.

I Go on Leave

I am holding a suitcase. I am standing on the platform at the Zalesye station. The train will be here in a minute, and then I will return to Petrograd via Minsk and Dno.

The cars roll up. They are all heated freight cars, with one regular passenger car. Everyone dashes toward the train.

Suddenly there are shots. They sound like anti-aircraft guns. German airplanes appear in the sky.

There are three of them. They circle above the station. Soldiers shoot haphazardly at them with their rifles.

Two bombs fall from a plane with an oppressive whine and explode near the station.

We all run out into a field. In the field are vegetable gardens, a hospital with a red cross on its roof, and further off some fences.

I lie down on the ground by a fence.

After circling over the station and dropping one more bomb, the planes turn their course toward the hospital. Three bombs fall near the fences almost simultaneously, hurling up earth. That's pure swinishness. There is an enormous cross on the roof. Impossible not to notice it.

Three more bombs. I see them break loose from the planes. I see the beginning of their fall. Then there is only the whine and the whistling in the air.

Our anti-aircraft guns are firing again. Now pieces of shrapnel and shell cases bestrew the field. I press close to the fence. And suddenly I see through a crack that on the other side of the fence there is an ammunition dump.

Hundreds of cases of artillery shells stand under the open sky.

A watchman is sitting on top of the cases and gaping at the airplanes.

I rise slowly and try to spot a place to go. But there's no place to go. If a single bomb hit those cases everything would be blown up for several kilometers around.

After dropping a few more bombs, the planes depart.

I walk slowly toward the train, inwardly blessing their bad aim. War will become an absurdity, I think, when technology achieves perfect aim. I would have been killed at least forty times this year.

I Am In Love

I ring. Nadya B. opens the door. She cries out in astonishment. And rushes into my arms.

On the threshold are her mother and sisters.

We go out in the street so that we can talk in peace. We sit down on a bench by the *Steregushchy* monument.*

Squeezing my hands, Nadya cries. Through her tears she says, "How stupid. Why didn't you write me anything? Why did you go away so unexpectedly? Why, it's been a year. I'm getting married."

"Do you love him?" I ask, not knowing yet about whom we are speaking.

"No, I don't love him. I love you. I'll never fall in love with anyone again. I'll refuse him."

She is crying again. I kiss her face, wet with tears.

"But how can I refuse him?" says Nadya, interrupting her own thoughts. "We've exchanged rings. And there has been a betrothal ceremony. Today he gave me an estate in the Smolensk district."

"Then don't," I say. "After all, I'll be leaving for the front again. And why should you wait for me? Maybe I'll be killed or wounded."

Nadya says, "I'll think it all over. I'll decide everything myself. Don't say anything to me . . . I'll tell you the day after tomorrow."

The next day I meet Nadya on the street. She is walking arm in arm with her fiancé.

There is nothing unusual about that. It's natural. But I am infuriated.

That evening I send Nadya a note saying that I am

* A statue erected in 1911 to commemorate the heroism of two sailors on the mine layer *Steregushchy* (Guardian) during the Russo-Japanese war of 1904-5. *Ed.*

being called to the front at once. And a day later I leave.

That was the stupidest and most pointless act of my life.

I loved her very much. And I have not stopped loving her to this day.

A *Thief*

I am a battalion commander. I'm worried about the fact that discipline is growing lax.

My grenadiers salute me smilingly. They almost wink at me. It's probably my own fault. I chat with them too much. There are people hanging around outside my mud hut all day. I have to write letters for some of them. Others come for advice.

What kind of advice can I give when I hear them calling me "Sonny Boy" behind my back?

It has got to the point where things have begun to disappear from my mud hut. My pipe has vanished. My shaving mirror. Candy and paper have disappeared.

I'll have to pull them all up short and get tough with them.

We're off duty. I am sleeping in a hut, on a bed.

In my sleep I suddenly feel someone's arm reach across me to the table. I shudder with terror and wake up.

Some wretched soldier dashes headlong out of the hut.

I run after him with my revolver in my hands. I am more furious than ever before in my life. I yell, "Stop!" And if he had not stopped, I would have shot him. But he stopped.

I go up to him. And immediately he falls on his knees. He is holding my safety razor in its nickel-plated box.

"Why did you take it?" I ask him.

"For my tobacco, sir," he mutters.

I realize that I should punish him, have him court-martialed. But I don't have the strength to do it. I see his dejected face, pathetic smile, trembling hands. I am disgusted that I chased after him.

Taking out the razor, I give him the box. And I go away, irritated with myself.

July Twentieth

I stand in the trenches and gaze curiously at the ruins of the little place. This is Smorgon. The right wing of our battalion juts up against the kitchen gardens of Smorgon.

This is a famous place, from which Napoleon fled after handing the command over to Murat.

It's getting dark. I go back to my mud hut.

It's a humid July night. I have taken off my field jacket and am writing letters.

It's already close to one o'clock. Time to go to bed. I want to call the messenger. But then I hear some kind of noise. The noise gets louder. I hear marching feet and the jingling of helmets. But there are no cries. And no shots.

I run out of the mud hut. Suddenly I am seized by a sweet suffocating wave. I shout, "Gas! . . . Masks!" I dash into the mud hut. My gas mask is hanging there on a nail.

My candle went out when I ran headlong into the mud hut. I feel for my gas mask with my hand and begin to put it on. I have forgotten to open the intake. I suffocate. Opening the intake, I run out to the trenches.

All around me soldiers are running, wrapping their faces in gauze masks.

Extracting some matches from my pocket, I set fire

to some brushwood which is lying on front of the trenches. This brushwood was prepared in advance. In case of a gas attack.

Now the fire lights up our positions. I see that all the grenadiers have come out of the trenches and are lying near the bonfires. I lie down near a bonfire too. I feel sick. My head is spinning. I inhaled a lot of gas when I yelled, "Masks!"

Near the bonfire I begin to feel better. Even completely well. The fire raises the gas and it passes over without touching us. I take off my mask.

We lie there for four hours.

It begins to get light. Now the direction in which the gas is drifting is visible. It's not a solid mass. It's a cloud twenty yards wide. It is coming slowly toward us, driven by a light breeze.

We can move to the right or the left, and the gas will pass by without touching us.

Now it's not terrifying. I already hear laughter and jokes here and there. It's the grenadiers shoving one another into wisps of gas. Laughter. Noise.

I look through my binoculars at the Germans. Now I can see them releasing the gas from balloons. It's a repulsive sight. I become furious when I see how methodically and cold-bloodedly they do this.

I order our men to open fire on those vermin. I order them to shoot with all the machine guns and rifles we have, although I realize that we won't do them much harm—the distance is fifteen hundred paces.

The grenadiers shoot lackadaisically. There aren't many riflemen. All at once I see that many soldiers are lying dead. Most of them. Others are groaning and can't rise from behind the fire.

I hear the sound of a bugle in the German trenches. The poisoners are signaling cease-fire. The gas attack is over.

Leaning on a stick, I make my way to the infirmary.

There is blood on my handkerchief from terrible vomiting. I go along the highway. I see yellowed grass and a hundred dead sparrows fallen on the road.

1917-1920

Back to the army he dashed on his steed
And over the nation there blew a new
wind . . .

I Don't Understand Anything

The first days of March. I am riding home from the station in a cab.

I ride past the Winter Palace. I see a red flag on the palace.

It means there's a new life. A new Russia. And I too am new and not what I was. Let everything be in the past—my disappointments, my nerves, my depression, my weak heart.

Ecstatically I go into my own house. And that same day I go around to all my friends. I see Nadya and her husband. I meet Tata T. I drop in on my university comrades.

I see joy and exultation all around me. Everyone is pleased that the Revolution has taken place. Except Nadya, who says to me, "This is terrible. It's dangerous for Russia. I don't expect any good from it."

For two days I feel wonderful. On the third day I am depressed again, have palpitations, gloom, and melancholy.

I don't understand anything. I try vainly to guess where this anguish came from. It shouldn't be!

I probably need to go to work. I should probably dedicate all my strength to people, to my country, to the new life.

I go to the general staff, to a representative of the Provisional Government. I ask him to assign me to the army again.

But I'm unfit for the front lines, and they make me commandant of the main post and telegraph office.

The most unpleasant thing of all has happened to me. I sit in an office and sign papers. This work is repugnant to me in the highest degree. I go back to the general staff and ask to be sent anywhere in the provinces.

They offer me Archangel—adjutant in the home guards. I accept.

I have to go there in a week.

Vava the Fiancée

I arrived in Archangel gloomy and terribly depressed. Nevertheless, or perhaps for that very reason, people set out to find a wife for me.

They had picked out Vava M. as my bride-to-be; she was the daughter of a very wealthy fish merchant.

I had not seen this girl, and she had not seen me. But that kind of matchmaking was accepted there. It occupied the ladies, who had nothing else to do.

They solemnly arranged for me to meet my fiancée in the conservatory of some wealthy house.

Before me was a very young, very quiet girl.

They left us alone together, so that we could talk.

I have always been taciturn. But that evening was simply a catastrophe. I literally could not think of anything to talk about. I pulled words out of myself with pliers to fill the horrifying pauses.

The girl looked fearfully at me and also remained silent.

I could not expect relief from any quarter. Everyone had gone to the farthest rooms and tightly shut the door to the conservatory.

Then I began to recite poetry.

I began reciting verses from V. Inber's fashionable book *Melancholy Wine*.* Then I began to recite Blok and Mayakovsky.

Vava listened to me attentively, without saying a word.

When some people came into the living room I was almost gay. I asked Vava whether she had liked what I recited. She said quietly, "I don't like poetry."

"Then why did you listen to it for a whole hour?" I exclaimed, muttering, "You fool!" under my breath.

"It would have been impolite of me not to listen to what you were saying."

I turned on my heel in almost military fashion and, infuriated, walked away from the girl.

Chamois Gloves

On Tuesdays and Saturdays we go to D.'s. She is a young woman, the widow of a naval officer.

It's always very cheerful at her place. She is witty and flirtatious.

I have no success with her. She likes Midshipman T., a good-natured, broad-shouldered officer.

Evening. We are playing poker at her house. D. is flirting with the midshipman. She touches his hand as if by accident, and gazes into his eyes for long periods. It seems as though she'll invite him to her place not only on Tuesdays and Saturdays.

However, she is cordial to me as well. But not as much. She says that I am too inert, unmanly, and sad. Melancholy is not her ideal.

We leave her place at night. And on the street

---

* Vera Inber (b. 1890), a contemporary Soviet poet who has long since officially outgrown the "decadent" tendencies of her early work, exemplified in the volume mentioned here, *Melancholy Wine* (Paris, 1912). *Ed.*

we tease the midshipman, who smiles enigmatically.

In the morning I can't find my gloves. I'm very sorry to lose them. They are English chamois gloves. I must have left them at D.'s. I telephone D. I hear a prolonged laugh in reply. Through her laughter she says to me, "Oh, are they your gloves? For some reason I was positive they were the midshipman's . . ."

I stop by her place at the appointed time. She doesn't let me leave, and we have tea in her boudoir. After she has finished her tea, she leans her head against my chest. And I leave her three hours later.

In the front hall she gives me my chamois gloves.

"Here are your gloves, you rogue," she says, smiling. "You'll admit that your ruse was a bit naïve—leaving your gloves so you could come to see the lady afterwards."

I mutter an apology. Laughing, she shakes her finger at me. Sighing, she says, "As you see, I appreciated your charming trick. You're an enterprising character, I wouldn't have expected it of you . . ."

"Madame," I say, "I assure you . . . I left my gloves by accident . . . I had no intention . . ."

I was sorry I said it. Her face grew unattractive, yellow, almost old.

"Oh, so that's the way it was," she said, through her teeth. "In that case I'm very sorry . . . Oh, let this be a lesson to me!"

She did not invite me to her house any more.

In her place I would have done the same.

At the Gate

I bound up to the third floor in one breath. My heart is pounding.

I ring at Nadya's door. No one opens it. I knock on the door softly at first, then kick it.

A neighbor's door opens.

"Do you want the V.'s?" asks an old woman. "They've all gone away."

"Where to?"

"I don't know. Ask the janitor."

I stand at the gate. The janitor is before me. He recognizes me. He smiles.

"All the V.'s have gone away," he says, almost gleefully.

"When?"

"Last month. In February."

"Don't you know where they went?"

"Where do you think? To the Whites . . . After all, papa was a general . . . And here they were shooting at your sort something awful . . . Of course they went away . . ."

The janitor sighs sympathetically, probably noticing the dismay on my face.

"Well, which one were you pining over?" he asks. "That's something I can't figure out—was it Nadenka or Katenka?"

"Over Nadenka."

"A very nice young lady," he says. "Her papa is a general, her husband a landowner . . . It's plain . . . She took her baby and went away."

"Did she have a baby?"

"That's what I said—she took her newborn baby and went away."

I go home. The whole world seems colorless.

The Cast-Iron Shadow

The former landowners' manor house "Mankovo" is in the Smolensk district. Now it is a state farm.

I passed with a good grade the examination in poultry farming given by the local executive committee. And now I am in charge of a poultry farm.

I wander among the fowls with books in my hands.

Certain breeds of birds I have seen only in roasted form. And now my textbooks come in handy.

For two weeks I don't leave the birds, almost spending the night with them, trying to learn their character and habits.

The third week I allow myself short walks in the surrounding countryside.

I walk along the side roads. From time to time I meet peasants.

These meetings astound me every time. When he is about fifteen feet away, the peasant will take off his cap and bow low to me.

I politely raise my cap and walk on in confusion.

I think first that these bows are accidental, but then I see that they are repeated every time.

Could they be mistaking me for some big shot?

I ask an old woman who has just bowed down to me almost to the ground, "Granny, why are you bowing to me like that? What's it all about?"

Kissing my hand and saying nothing, the old woman goes away.

Then I go up to a peasant. He is middle-aged. He is wearing bast shoes and wretched, worn-out clothes. I ask him why he pulled off his cap when he was ten paces away from me and bowed to the waist.

Bowing once more, the peasant tries to kiss my hand. I snatch it away.

"How have I displeased you, master?" he asks.

Suddenly in these words and that bow of his, I have seen and heard everything. I have seen the shadow of former habits of life. I have heard the landowner's bellowing and the quiet answer of the slave. I have seen a life about which I had no conception. I am more affected than ever before in my life.

"Father," I say to the peasant, "the workers and peasants have been in power for a year now. And you're trying to lick my hand."

"It hasn't reached us here," says the peasant. "It's true, the masters went away from their houses and live in huts . . . But who knows what's going to happen . . ."

I walk with the peasant to his village. I go into his hut.

At every step I see the cast-iron shadow of the past.

An Old Man Dies

I am standing in a peasant hut. On the table lies a dying old man.

He has lain there for three days and still he does not die.

Today there is a wax candle in his hand. It falls and goes out, but they light it again.

His relatives stand at the head of the table. They gaze steadily at the old man. All around is incredible poverty, dirt, rags, want . . .

The old man is lying with his feet toward the window. His face is dark, strained. His breathing is uneven. At times it seems that he has already died.

Bending toward the old woman—his wife—I say to her softly, "I'll go for a doctor. It isn't right that he should lie here for three days."

The old woman shakes her head, refusing.

"Don't bother him," she says.

The old man opens his eyes and gazes dully at the bystanders. His lips are murmuring something.

One of the women, young and dark-skinned, bends over the old man and listens silently to his muttering.

"What does he want?" asks the old woman.

"He wants titty," the woman answers. And quickly unbuttoning her blouse, she takes the old man's hand and puts it on her uncovered breast.

I see how the old man's face brightens. Something like a smile passes over his lips. He breathes more evenly, more peacefully.

Everyone stands silently without stirring.

Suddenly the old man's body shudders. His hand drops helplessly. His face grows stern and altogether calm. He stops breathing. He is dead.

The old woman at once begins wailing. And everyone wails after her.

I leave the hut.

We Play Cards

On the table is a kerosene lamp with a coquettish pink shade. We are playing "preference."

My partners are a stout lady named Olga Pavlovna, an old man with decayed teeth, and his daughter Veronica, a beautiful young woman.

They are former landowners of the neighboring region. They had not wanted to move far from their estates. So they rented this hut from some peasants and are living here as private citizens.

We have already been sitting at the table for four hours. I am sick to death of the game. I would be delighted to stop. But it's awkward for me. I'm losing, and I'm out a large sum.

My luck is terrible. Olga Pavlovna is the lucky one, and she grows noisier and more joyful every time she wins.

When she takes a trick, she ecstatically smacks the table with the palm of her hand.

"I'm lucky," she cries. "I've always been lucky in everything . . . Two or three months will go by, and then I'm positive I'll get back my estate . . ."

The old man with the decayed teeth begins to laugh.

"Cards are one thing, dear Olga Pavlovna," he says, "and Russia, politics, and revolution are quite another."

"It doesn't make any difference," shouts Olga Pavlovna. "In life we also play cards. One person is lucky, another isn't. And I'm always lucky in everything—both in life and at cards . . . You'll see, I'll get back my 'Quiet Backwater' again . . ."

Dealing the cards, she says, "I'll get my 'Quiet Backwater,' thrash my peasants a bit, and everything will be the way it used to be."

"After such a revolution you'll only thrash them?" asks the old man with the decayed teeth, no longer laughing.

Olga Pavlovna stops dealing and replies, "I'm not so brainless as to put my peasants in jail. I don't intend to be left without workers. Keep that in mind . . ."

"No, most respected Olga Pavlovna," says the old man. "I disagree categorically with you . . . I'm going to oppose your policies . . . Two of them I'll hang—I know who. Five I'll send to hard labor. The rest I'll thrash and fine. Let them work only my land for a year."

I throw down my cards so hard that they bounce on the table and spill onto the floor.

"Oh!" exclaims Olga Pavlovna haughtily.

"Rascals, criminals!" I say quietly. "It's because of you that there's such misery, such backwardness in the countryside, such abysmal ignorance . . ."

I dig some money out of my pockets and toss it on the table.

I'm in a fever.

I dart out into the hall and, feeling for my fur coat, with difficulty get my arms into the sleeves.

The room is quiet. No one is even whispering. I expect Veronica to come out into the hall, but she doesn't.

I go outside. I lead my horse out through the gate. I lie down in the sleigh.

The horse runs smartly—it knows the way by itself.

Overhead is the dark sky, stars. Snowy fields all around. And terrible silence.

Why did I come here? What am I here for, among poultry and jackals? I will leave tomorrow.

At Regimental Headquarters

I am sitting at a table. I am recopying an order for the regiment. I made a draft of the order this morning with the commander and commissar of the regiment.

I am the adjutant of the first model regiment of poor peasants.

Before me is a map of northwestern Russia. The front line is marked with red pencil; it goes from the Gulf of Finland through Narva to Yamburg.

Our regimental headquarters is in Yamburg.

I copy out the order in a beautiful, legible hand.

The commander and the commissar have gone out to our positions. I have a heart ailment. I am not allowed to gallop on horseback. Because of this they seldom take me with them.

Someone is knocking on the window. I see the figure of a civilian in a tattered, dirty overcoat. After knocking on the window, the man bows.

I tell the sentry to let the man in. The sentry does so unwillingly.

"What can I do for you?" I ask. Taking off his hat, the man hangs back near the door.

I see before me a very pathetic person, somehow very unfortunate, beaten down, and hurt. To encourage him, I lead him over to an armchair and, pressing his hand, ask him to have a seat. He sits down unwillingly.

He says, hardly moving his lips, "If the Red Army leaves, should we leave with you or stay?"

"And who might you be?" I ask.

"I've come from the colony at Swift Brooks. Our leper colony is there."

I feel my heart sing. I wipe my hand inconspicuously on my cotton trousers.

"I don't know," I say. "I can't decide that question by myself. Besides, there is little question of our leaving. I don't think the front will move beyond Yamburg."

The man bows to me and leaves. Through the window I see him showing his sores to the sentry.

I go the infirmary and wash my hands with carbolic acid.

I did not fall ill. Our fear of this disease is probably exaggerated.

Bread

I fainted when I left headquarters in the morning to take a little walk in the fresh air.

The sentry and the telephone operator brought me back to consciousness. For some reason they kept rubbing my ears and moving my arms as if I were a drowned man. Nevertheless, I came to.

The commander of the regiment said to me, "Go and take a rest at once. I'll give you two weeks' leave."

I went to Petrograd.

But in Petrograd I did not feel any better.

I went to an army hospital for advice. After listening to my heart, they told me I was unfit for army service. They left me in the hospital until a commission should decide what to do with me.

And now it's the second week that I've been lying in a ward.

Besides feeling ill, I'm also hungry. This is 1919! In the hospital they give you four hundred grams of bread and a bowl of soup per day. That's very little for a man of twenty-three.

Now and then my mother brings me some smoked carp. I feel guilty about taking this fish. We have a big family at home.

Across from me a young fellow is sitting on his bunk in his drawers. They have just brought him two big loaves of bread from the country. He cuts off pieces of bread with a penknife, spreads them with butter, and dispatches them into his mouth. He does this endlessly.

One of the sick men begs him, "Sviderov, give me a little piece."

The other replies, "Let me have my feed first. When I'm finished, I'll give you some."

When he is thoroughly stuffed, he throws pieces to all the bunks. He asks me, "Hey, intellectual, should I give you some?"

I say, "Just don't throw it. Put it on my table."

This annoys him. He would like to throw it. It's more fun that way.

He sits silently, glancing at me. Then he gets up from his bunk and clowns as he puts a piece of bread on my table. He bows theatrically and makes faces as he does this. There is laughter in the ward.

I would very much like to throw this offering on the floor. But I control myself. I turn my face to the wall.

At night, lying on my bunk, I eat the bread.

My thoughts are bitter.

Brie Cheese

Every day I go to the fence, where a copy of *The Red Gazette* is pasted up.

There is a "P. O. Box" in the newspaper. It contains replies to authors.

I have written a little story about country life. I have sent it to the editors. And now, not without anxiety, I am awaiting a reply. I didn't write this little story to make money. I am a telephone operator for the border patrol. I have security. I wrote the story just to write it—it seemed a good idea to write a story about the country. I signed the story with the pseudonym "M. M. Chirkov."

It's drizzling. And cold. I stand in front of the paper and look over the "P. O. Box."

I see: "To M. M. Chirkov. We need black bread, not Brie cheese."

I don't believe my eyes. I am stunned. Perhaps they didn't understand me?

I begin to recall what I wrote.

No, I was sure it was written correctly, neatly, and well. A bit mannered, with embellishments and a Latin quotation . . . My Lord! For whose benefit did I write like that? The Old Russia is gone . . . Before me is a new world, with new people, and a new speech . . .

I go to the railroad station to leave for Strelna,* where I am on duty. I get on the train and ride for an hour.

The devil must have induced me to take up intellectual work again. It's the last time. I won't do any more of that. My motionless, sedentary occupation is at fault. I have too much time to think.

I'll change my occupation.

The Twelfth of January

It's cold. You can see your breath.

The pieces of my desk are lying by the stove. But it is hard to warm up the room.

On the bed lies my mother. She is delirious. The doctor said that she had the "Spanish flu"—a terrible form of influenza from which people are dying all around.

I go up to my mother. She is lying beneath two blankets and two overcoats.

I put my hand on her forehead. Her fever burns my hand. The little kerosene lantern goes out. I fix it. And sit down next to my mother, on her bed.

I sit for a long time, looking into her exhausted face.

* A town near Petrodvorets (Peterhof) in the outskirts of Leningrad. *Ed.*

All is quiet. My sisters are asleep. It's already two in the morning.

"No, no . . . don't do that . . ." mutters my mother.

I put some water to her lips. She takes a few sips. She opens her eyes for a second. I bend over her. No, she's delirious again.

But now her face grows calmer. Her breathing is more even. Could this have been the crisis? She'll get better . . .

I cover her shoulders with the blanket, which has slid off.

It looks to me as if a shadow passes over my mother's face. Afraid to think anything, I slowly raise my hand and touch her forehead. She is dead.

For some reason I have no tears. I sit motionless on the bed. Then I get up and, after waking my sisters, go to my room.

A New Road

In the handcart are a small desk, two armchairs, a rug, and a bookcase.

I'm wheeling these things to a new apartment.

There has been a change in my life.

I could not remain in the apartment where a death had taken place.

A woman who loved me said, "Your mother is dead. Move in with me."

I went to the registration office with this woman. And we registered our marriage. Now she is my wife.

I am carting my things to her apartment, on the Petrograd side.

It's very far. It is hard for me to push my cart.

Ahead of me is the hill leading to the Tuchkov Bridge.

I no longer have the strength to push the cart. My

heart is pounding terribly. I look sorrowfully at the passers-by. Maybe some kind soul will appear and help me make the ascent.

No, the passers-by look me over indifferently and go their way.

To hell with them! I'll have to do it myself . . . If only I don't have a heart attack . . . It would be silly to die while wheeling armchairs and a desk over a bridge.

Almost collapsing, I roll the cart up onto the bridge. Now it's easy.

1 9 2 0 - 1 9 2 6

*If I had been friendly with fortune, I say
I'd not have begun what I'm doing today.*

The House of the Arts

This house is on the corner of the Moyka and Nevsky Prospect.

I am walking up and down the corridor, waiting for a literary evening to begin.

It doesn't mean anything that I'm a detective. I have already published two critical articles and four short stories. And they have all been very well received.

I walk up and down the corridor and look at the literary celebrities.

Here comes A. M. Remizov. He is small and ugly, like a monkey. A male secretary is with him. A cloth tail sticks out from under the secretary's jacket. It is a symbol. Remizov is the father superior of "The Monkey's Free Tribunal." *

There stands E. I. Zamyatin. His face is rather shiny.

* Aleksey Remizov (1877-1957), noted writer, emigrated in 1921.

He is smiling. In his hand is a long cigarette in a long elegant holder.

He is talking to someone in English.*

Shklovsky approaches. He is wearing a fez. He has an intelligent and audacious face. He is arguing furiously with someone. He sees nothing except himself and his opponent.†

I exchange greetings with Zamyatin.

Turning to me, he says, "Blok is here, he came. You wanted to meet him . . ."

Zamyatin and I enter a dimly lit room.

A man is standing by the window. His face is deeply sun-tanned. He has a high forehead and light, wavy, almost curly, hair.

He is surprisingly motionless. He is watching the lights on Nevsky Prospect.

He does not turn around when we enter.

"Aleksandr Aleksandrovich," says Zamyatin.

Slowly turning, Blok looks at us.

I have never seen such vacant, dead eyes. I never thought that such depression and such indifference could be reflected in a person's face.

Blok holds out his hand—it is limp and lifeless.

I feel awkward at having disturbed a man who seems in a sort of trance . . . I mutter an apology.

In a slightly hollow voice Blok asks me, "Will you be reading something this evening?"

"No," I say, "I came to listen to you writers."

Apologizing once more, I leave hurriedly.

Zamyatin remains with Blok.‡

I walk up and down the corridor again. I am op-

* Evgeny Zamyatin (1884-1937), novelist and critic, author of *We. Ed.*

† Viktor Shklovsky (b. 1893), critic, one of the founders of the Formalist school. *Ed.*

‡ Aleksandr Blok (1880-1921), the greatest of the symbolist poets. According to many other accounts, his last years were spent in a state of acute depression, from which he never recovered.

pressed by some sort of emotion. Now I almost see my own fate. I see the finale of my life. I see the depression which will certainly destroy me.

I ask someone, "How old is Blok?" The reply is, "Close to forty."

He is not yet forty! But Byron was thirty when he wrote,

> *Is it that weariness which springs*
> *From all I meet, or hear, or see?*
> *To me no pleasure Beauty brings;*
> *Thine eyes have scarce a charm for me.*

Byron wrote "It is" rather than "Is it?" It is I who mentally ask this question. I wonder—is this really weariness?

The literary evening begins.

An Encounter

I go up and down endless flights of stairs. I am carrying a portfolio of papers and forms. On the forms I enter information concerning tenants. This is the all-Union census.

I took this job so I could see how people live.

I believe only what I see. Like Haroun-al-Raschid, I visit strangers' houses. I go through hallways and kitchens, I enter rooms. I see dim lamps, torn wallpaper, washing hanging on lines, terrible crowding, garbage, rags. Of course, difficult years, hunger, and destruction have just passed . . . But even so, I did not think I would see the things I saw.

I go into a dimly lit room. A man is lying on a bunk with a dirty mattress. He receives me inhospitably, without even turning toward me. He gazes at the ceiling.

"Where do you work?" I ask.

"Donkeys and horses work," he says. "Personally, I don't work, and I'm not planning to, either. Write that

down in your lousy papers . . . You can add—I go to
the club, I play cards . . ."

He is irritated. Perhaps ill. I want to leave so I can
get the information from his neighbors. As I leave, I
look at him. I've seen that face somewhere.

"Alyosha!" I say.

He sits up on his bunk. His face is unshaven, morose.

I see before me Alyosha N., a Gymnasium friend. He
was a class ahead of me. He had been a Little Lord
Fauntleroy, a grind, an A student, a mamma's boy . . .

"What happened, Alyosha?" I mutter.

"Absolutely nothing happened," he says. I see resentment on his face.

"Can I help you in any way?"

"I need absolutely nothing," he says. "But, by the
way, if you have some money, give me a fiver and I'll
go down to the club."

I offer him a lot more, but he takes only five rubles.

In a few minutes I'm sitting on his bunk, and we're
talking the way we used to ten years ago.

"It's essentially the same old story," he says. "My
wife ran off with some good-for-nothing character. I
started to drink. I drank up everything I had. I lost my
job. Started to play cards at the club . . . And now,
you know, I don't feel like going back to things as they
were. I could, but I don't want to. It's all bosh, nonsense, comedy, rubbish, smoke . . ."

I make him promise that he'll come to see me.

At Night

On my pillow lie some letters to the editor of *The Red
Gazette*. They are complaints about mismanagement
in the public baths. These letters were given to me so
that I could write a *feuilleton*.

I look the letters over. They are helpless, comical.
But at the same time they are serious. Very much so.

They discuss a human concern of no little importance —baths.

I draw up an outline and begin writing.

Even the first lines amuse me. I laugh. I laugh louder and louder. I finally guffaw until the pencil and pad drop from my hands.

I write again. And again my body shakes with laughter.

No, later on when I'm recopying the story, I won't laugh like that. But the first draft always amuses me uncommonly.

My stomach hurts from laughing.

My neighbor is knocking on the wall. He is a bookkeeper. He has to get up early tomorrow. I'm keeping him awake. Today he's pounding with his fist. I must have waked him up. It's annoying.

I shout, "Excuse me, Pyotr Alekseyevich . . ."

I turn to my writing pad again. Again I laugh, this time burying my face in a pillow.

In twenty minutes the story is finished. I'm sorry I wrote it so fast.

I go over to my desk and copy the story in a beautiful, even hand. While copying, I go on laughing softly.

But tomorrow, when I read the story aloud in the editor's office, I won't laugh. I'll read it gloomily and even morosely.

It's two in the morning. I go to bed. But I can't fall asleep for a long time. I'm thinking over themes for new stories.

It begins to grow light. I take a bromide to fall asleep.

Rubbish Again

The offices of a literary magazine, *The Contemporary*.

I sent five of my very best little stories to this magazine. And now I've come for a reply.

Before me is one of the editors, the poet M. Kuzmin.* He is elaborately polite. Even overly so. But I see in his face that he intends to tell me something unpleasant.

He has trouble beginning. I help him out.

"I suppose my stories don't quite fit into the program of the magazine?" I say.

He says, "You understand, this is a literary magazine . . . But your stories . . . No, they're very funny, amusing . . . But they're not written . . . After all, they're . . ."

"Rubbish, did you mean to say?" I ask. And in my mind there flares up the inscription on my Gymnasium composition—"Rubbish."

Kuzmin waves his hand.

"God forbid. I don't mean that at all. Just the opposite. Your stories show a great deal of talent . . . But you yourself will agree that they're somewhat in the order of caricatures."

"They aren't caricatures," I say.

"Well, if you take just the language . . ."

"The language isn't caricatured. It's the syntax of the streets, of the people . . . Maybe I exaggerated a little so that it would be satirical, so that it would be critical . . ."

"Let's not argue," he says mildly. "Give us one of your ordinary novellas or stories . . . Believe me, we value your work very highly."

I leave the office. I don't feel the emotions now that I once felt in the Gymnasium. I am not even irritated.

Let him be, I think. I'll get along without the literary magazines. They want something "ordinary." They want something that looks like a classic. That's what impresses them. It's extremely easy to do that. But I have no intention of writing for readers who don't exist.

*Mikhail Kuzmin (1875-1936), a poet and novelist with "decadent" tendencies. *Ed.*

The people have a different idea of literature.

I don't regret it. I know I'm right.

In the Tavern

Broad daylight. Sunshine. I'm walking along the Nevsky. S. Esenin is coming toward me.*

He is wearing a fashionable blue coat with a belt. He is hatless.

His face is pale. There is no light in his eyes. He walks slowly. Mutters something. I go up to him.

He is gloomy and taciturn. There is a dejected air about him.

I want to go away, but he doesn't let me.

"Do you feel bad? Are you ill?" I ask him.

"Why?" he asks anxiously. "Do I look bad?"

And he suddenly laughs. He says, "I'm getting old, dear friend . . . Soon I'll hit thirty . . ."

We come to the "European" Hotel.

Esenin stands by the door for a minute and then says, "Let's stop in across the street. At the tavern. For a minute."

We go into the tavern.

The poet V. Voinov† and some friends are sitting at a table. He comes happily over to greet us. We sit down at his table. Someone pours out mugs of beer.

Esenin says something to the waiter. And the waiter brings him a glass of liqueur.

Esenin closes his eyes and drinks. I see life return to him with each gulp. Color comes into his cheeks. His gestures are more confident. His eyes light up.

He is about to call the waiter again. To distract him, I ask him to recite some poems . . .

He agrees, for some reason readily and even gladly.

---

* Sergey Esenin (1895-1925), a famous poet. *Ed.*
† Vladimir Voinov, a minor Soviet poet. *Ed.*

Rising from his chair, he recites the poem "The Black Man."

People gather around the table. Someone says, "That's Esenin."

Almost everyone in the tavern crowds around us.

Another minute and Esenin is standing on the chair and gesturing as he recites his short poems.

He recites splendidly, and with such feeling and such pain that everyone is shaken.

I have seen many poets perform. I have seen extraordinary successes, ovations, entire halls in ecstasy; but I have never seen people display such feeling and warmth as they do toward Esenin.

Dozens of arms lift him from his chair and carry him to a table. Everyone wants to clink glasses with him. Everyone wants to touch him, embrace him, kiss him.

In a tight ring the crowd surrounds the table where he is now sitting.

I leave the tavern.

It's My Own Fault

Evening. I am walking along the Nevsky with K.

I met her in Kislovodsk.

She is beautiful, witty, vivacious. She has that *joie de vivre* which I lack. Perhaps this is what attracts me to her more than anything else.

We walk tenderly holding hands. We come to the bank of the Neva. We stroll along the dark water front.

K. continually talks of something. But I don't particularly follow what she is saying. I listen to her words as if they were music.

But then I hear a certain displeasure in that music. I pay attention.

"This is the second week that I've been walking through the streets with you," she says. "We've been through all these stupid water fronts and parks. I'd simply like to sit awhile in some hotel with you, to chat and drink tea."

"Let's go into a café," I suggest.

"No, someone will see us there."

Oh yes. I completely forgot. She leads a complicated life. A jealous husband, a very jealous lover. Many enemies who say that they have seen us together.

We stop on the water front. We embrace one another. We kiss. She murmurs, "Oh, how stupid that we're on the street."

We begin walking again and kiss again. She covers her eyes with her hand. These endless kisses have made her dizzy.

We come to the gate of some building. K. tells me, "I've got to stop in here to see my dressmaker. Wait for me here. I'll just try on a dress and come right back."

I walk up and down near the building. I walk for ten minutes, fifteen, then at last she appears. She is happy. She laughs.

"Everything's fine," she says. "The dress is turning out very nicely. It's very simple and unpretentious."

She takes my arm, and I escort her home. I meet her again in five days. She says, "If you like, there's a house we can go to today—my girl friend's place."

We come to a building. I recognize this building. Here, at the gate, I waited twenty minutes for her. This is the house where her dressmaker lives.

We go up to the fourth floor. She opens the door with her key. We go into the room. It's a well-furnished room. It doesn't look like the room of a dressmaker.

From professional habit, I leaf through the book I find on the night table. On the flyleaf I see a familiar name. It's the name of K.'s lover.

She laughs.

"Yes, we're in his room," she says. "But don't worry. He's gone to Kronstadt for two days."

"K.!" I exclaim. "I'm worried about something else.

Does this mean you were with him that time?"

"When?" she asks.

"When I waited for you at the gate for twenty minutes."

She laughs. Closes my mouth with a kiss. Says, "It was your own fault."

September Twenty-third*

The window of my room looks out on the corner of the Moyka† and Nevsky Prospect.

I go over to the window. An extraordinary scene— the river has swollen and grown black. Another half-meter and the water will overflow the banks.

I run out onto the street.

Wind. An inaudible wind is blowing from the sea.

I go along the Nevsky. I am agitated and excited. I come to the Fontanka. The Fontanka is almost up to the pavement. Here and there water laps over the sidewalk.

I jump into a trolley and ride to the Petrograd side. My family lives there—my wife and tiny son. They live with their relatives. I moved to the House of Culture so that the baby's crying wouldn't interfere with my work.

Now I'm hurrying to them. They live on the first floor, on Pushkarskaya Street. Maybe they'll have to go up to the second floor.

The trolley turns into Aleksandrovsky Prospect. We are riding through water. We stop. It's impossible to go further. The wooden paving blocks have floated loose and prevent the trolley from moving.

The passengers jump down into the water. It's not deep here—up to one's knees.

* The flood described here took place in 1924. *Ed.*

† The Moyka and the Fontanka, actually branches of the Neva, are rivers which pass through the central part of Leningrad. The Petrograd side, mentioned below, is on the other side of the Neva. *Ed.*

I go through the water and come to Bolshoi Prospect. There is no water on the avenue yet.

I almost run to Pushkarskaya Street. The water has not reached it.

My relatives are worried and excited. They are very glad that I have come and am now with them.

After changing my clothes, I go out on the street again. I want to see whether the water is coming.

I go out onto Bolshoi Prospect. I buy some bread at a bakery. I come toward Vvedenskaya Street. It's dry.

And suddenly I see an extraordinary spectacle— water is coming out of all the manholes and pouring over the pavement. Again I go home through water.

The water is already at the foot of the stairs.

We move to the second floor with our bundles.

I make chalk marks on the steps to see how much the water is rising.

At five in the afternoon the water is already lapping at the doors.

It's getting dark. I sit by the window and listen to the howling of the wind.

Now almost the whole city is flooded. The water has risen nearly fourteen feet.

There is a red glow in the sky from fires somewhere.

It's getting light. From the window I see the water gradually recede.

I go out on the street. A terrible sight. On the avenue is a barge with firewood. Beams. Boats. A small craft with a mast lies on its side.

Everywhere there is ruin, chaos, destruction.

At the Table

Moscow. I am sitting at a table in some theatrical club. My table is set for two. That's because Mayakovsky is going to have supper with me. He ordered his meal and went to play billiards. He'll be right back.

I hardly know Mayakovsky. We have met only at parties, at the theater, in public.

Now he is coming to the table. He is breathing heavily. He has an unhappy expression. He is gloomy. He wipes his forehead with a handkerchief.

He won the game, but winning did not make him feel any better. He sits down at the table somehow sluggishly, heavily.

We are silent. We hardly talk. I pour him some beer. He takes one gulp, then pushes the glass away.

I too am gloomy. And I don't feel like artificially trying to make conversation. But to me Mayakovsky is a master. I am almost a novice in literature; I've been working only five years. I somehow feel guilty about remaining silent. I begin to mutter something about billiards, about literature.

For some reason I feel remarkably ill-at-ease with him.

I talk incoherently, dully. And I fall silent in the middle of a word. Unexpectedly, Mayakovsky laughs.

"No, listen," he says, "this is just too good. I thought you would be witty, joke, tell stories, and instead you . . . No, this is simply rich! Just astoundingly rich . . ."

"Why should I be witty?"

"Well—a humorist! You're supposed to . . . And instead you . . ."

He gives me a somewhat painful look. He has surprisingly unhappy eyes. There is a kind of gloomy fire in them.

"And why are you . . . like this?" he asks.

"I don't know. I'm trying to find out myself . . ."

"Really?" he asks guardedly. "Do you think there is a reason? Are you ill?"

We begin to talk of illnesses. Mayakovsky lists several ailments he has: something is wrong with his lungs, his digestion, his liver. He can't drink and even wants to give up smoking.

I notice still another ailment of Mayakovsky's: he is even more of a hypochondriac than I am. Twice he wipes off his fork with a napkin. Then he wipes it with some bread. Finally he wipes it with his handkerchief. He also wipes the rim of his glass with his handkerchief.

An actor acquaintance of ours comes over to our table. Our conversation is cut short. Mayakovsky says to me, "I'll call you in Leningrad."

I give him my phone number.

Beasts

I wander along the paths of the Leningrad zoo.

In one cage is a huge, magnificent tiger. Next to him is a small white dog—a fox terrier. She suckled this tiger, and now, by a mother's right, she lives in the same cage with him.

The tiger gazes at her in a friendly way.

It's an amazing sight.

Suddenly I hear the most dreadful cry behind me.

Everyone runs to the cage where the brown bears are kept.

We see a terrible scene. Next to the brown bears is a cage with bear cubs. Besides iron bars, the cages are separated with boards.

A little bear cub has climbed up these boards, but his paw got caught in a crack. And now one of the brown bears is tearing furiously at this little paw.

Trying to tear himself loose and screaming, the cub gets another paw caught in a crack. Now the second bear seizes hold of that paw.

Both bears tear at the cub so dreadfully that someone in the crowd faints.

We try to chase off the bears with rocks and sand, but they become even more furious. One little paw with its black claws has already dropped to the floor of the cage.

I take some kind of long pole and beat one of the bears with it.

The horrible screams and roars of the bears bring guards and managers running.

They tear the cub loose from the boards.

The brown bears pace furiously up and down their cage. Their eyes are bloodshot. Their muzzles are covered with blood.

Roaring, the male mounts the female.

They carry the unfortunate cub to the office. His front paws have been torn off.

He is no longer screaming. They will probably shoot him at once. I begin to understand what beasts are. And in what way they are different from human beings.

Enemies

Sunday. I am walking along the street. Someone cries out, "Misha!"

I see a woman. She is simply dressed and is carrying a shopping bag full of groceries.

"Misha," repeats the woman, and tears begin to flow from her eyes.

The woman before me is Nadya V.'s sister, Katya.

"My God," she mutters. "It's you . . . it's you . . ."

My heart pounds terribly.

"Didn't you go away?" I ask. "And where is Nadya? And your family?"

"Nadya and Marusya are in Paris . . . Let's go to my place. I'll tell you all about it . . . Just don't be surprised—I live very modestly . . . My husband is a very good person . . . He respects and pities me . . . He is a simple workman . . ."

We enter a small room.

A man rises from the table. He is about forty. After greeting us, he immediately puts on his coat and leaves.

"You see how good he is, how tactful," says Katya.

"He understood right away that we had to talk."

We sit down on the couch. Our emotion is choking us. Katya begins to cry. She cries so hard that someone opens the door and asks what has happened.

"Nothing," cries Katya shrilly.

She shakes with sobs again. She is probably crying about the past. She probably sees the past in me. Her youth, her childhood years. I soothe her.

Going over to the washstand, she wipes her tear-stained face and loudly blows her nose.

Then she begins to tell me her story. In 1917 they went to the south, planning to get to the Caucasus and from there out of the country. But in Rostov the father came down with typhus. It was impossible to wait. Only a few days remained.* The sisters drew lots to decide who should stay with their father. Katya remained. She was terribly poor after her father's death. She worked as a charwoman, then as a house servant. Later she managed to go to Leningrad. But there it was no easier for her—she had neither an apartment nor friends.

"Why didn't you come to me?" I ask. "You must have heard about me . . ."

"Yes. But I never thought it was you."

Katya begins to talk about her sisters. The older one writes to her, but Nadya doesn't. She hates everything that remains in Russia.

"What if I wrote to her?" I ask.

Katya says, "You know Kolya M. You remember how much he loved her. He wrote to her. She sent him a post card with four words on it: 'Now we are enemies.' "

I said good-bye to Katya. I promised to come and see her.

---

* I.e., the city would remain in White hands only a few days longer. Ed.

Madness

A man comes into my room. He sits down in an armchair.

He sits silently for a moment, listening. Then he gets up and closes the door tightly.

He goes up to the wall and, putting his ear against it, listens.

I begin to realize that he is mad.

After listening at the wall, he again sits down in the armchair and covers his face with both hands. I see that he is in despair.

"What's the matter?" I ask.

"They're after me," he says. "I was just riding on the trolley and I clearly heard voices: 'There he is . . . take him . . . grab him . . .'"

He covers his face with his hands again. Then he says softly, "You alone can save me . . ."

"In what way?"

"We'll exchange surnames. You'll be Gorshkov, and I, the poet Zoshchenko." (He said just that—"the poet.")

"It's all right with me," I say.

He rushes over to me and shakes my hand.

"Just who is it that's after you?" I ask.

"That I can't say."

"But I'll have to know that when I bear your name."

Wringing his hands, he says, "That's just it, I don't know myself. I only hear their voices. At night I see their hands. They reach out toward me from all sides. I know they'll grab me and strangle me."

His nervous chill communicates itself to me. I feel bad. My head is spinning. There are circles in front of my eyes. If he doesn't leave right away, I'll probably lose consciousness. He is having a fearful effect on me.

Gathering my strength, I murmur, "You can go.

Now you have my name. You can be calm."

His face has brightened, and he leaves.

I go to bed and feel a terrible depression taking hold of me.

In the Hotel

Tuapse.* A small hotel room. For some reason, I am lying on the floor. My arms are outflung. And my fingers are in water.

It is rain water. A thunderstorm has just passed. I didn't feel like getting up to close the window. So rain water streamed into the room.

I close my eyes again and lie in a kind of torpor until evening.

I should probably get up onto the bed. It's more comfortable there. A pillow. But I don't want to get up from the floor.

Without getting up, I stretch my hand out to a suitcase and take out an apple. I have eaten nothing again today.

I take a bite of the apple. I chew it, as if it were straw. I spit it out. It's unpleasant. I lie there until morning.

In the morning someone knocks at the door. The door is locked. I don't open it. It's the maid. She would like to do the room. At least once in three days. I say, "I don't need anything. Go away."

In the afternoon I get up with difficulty. I sit down on a chair.

Anxiety takes hold of me. I realize that things can't go on like this any longer. I'll die in this wretched room if I don't leave here soon.

Opening my suitcase, I feverishly get my things together. Then I call the chambermaid.

---

* A resort town on the eastern shore of the Black Sea, not far from Sochi. Ed.

"I am ill," I tell her. "Someone has to take me to the station and buy me a ticket . . . Quickly . . ."

The chambermaid fetches the management and a doctor. Stroking my hand, the doctor says, "It's nerves . . . only nerves . . . I'll prescribe a bromide for you . . ."

"I have to get away quickly," I mutter.

"You'll go away today," says the hotel manager.

CONCLUSION

And now my reminiscences are finished.

I have come up to the year 1926. To the time when I stopped eating and almost died.

In front of me are sixty-three stories. Sixty-three incidents which at one time disturbed me.

I have re-examined every story. I hoped to find the reason for my depression, my unhappiness, my illness in one of them.

But I didn't see anything in these stories.

To be sure, some of them are gloomy. But not any gloomier than the things people are used to experiencing. Everyone's mother dies. Everyone leaves home sometime. Parts with the girl he loves. Fights at the front . . .

No, not in one of these stories did I find what I was looking for.

Then I put all the stories together. I wanted to see the overall picture, the repeated chord which had perhaps deafened me, like a fish taken from the water and thrown into a boat.

Well, of course, great upheavals took place during my life. Changes of fortune. The destruction of the old world. The birth of a new life, new people, a new nation.

But, after all, I didn't see any catastrophe in this!

Why, I myself tried to see it as the dawn of a new day. And even before these events depression haunted me. That means that they weren't the decisive factor. So they didn't seem to be the reason. On the contrary, they enabled me to take a new look at the world, at my country and the people I had begun to work for . . . There shouldn't be any depression in my heart at all! But there is . . .

I was discouraged. I seemed to have set myself a problem that was beyond me—to discover the reason for my depression, to find the unhappy occurrence which had made me a wretched speck of dust blown about by the winds of life.

Perhaps this incident took place at an earlier age, I thought. Perhaps my childhood years prepared the shaky ground along which I now stumble?

Of course! Why had I dismissed the years of childhood? After all, that is the time of one's first acquaintance with the world, one's first impressions, which are therefore the deepest. How could I have failed to reckon with them?

Here too there is no need to remember everything, I thought. It will be enough to remember the brightest and strongest impressions, only those which were connected with my emotional turmoils.

Then with feverish haste I began to recollect the incidents of my childhood. And I saw that in my childhood too anxiety cast an extraordinary light over the things which had happened.

Again these were flash photographs which had remained in my brain with blinding clarity.

Remembering these childhood occurrences, I saw that they agitated me even more than the events of my adult years. I saw that they disturbed me significantly more than did the desire to find the reason for my unhappiness.

IV. A FEARFUL WORLD

Only in the story does the prodigal son
Return to his father's house

And so I began to recall the most striking scenes from my childhood.

Amid these scenes, which were associated with strong emotion, I hoped to find the unfortunate incident, hoped to find the reason and explanation for my terrible depression.

From what age shall I begin? I wondered.

It's comical to begin at age one. Comical to remember the things that happened at two and three. And even at four. Imagine, what great events take place at that minuscule age! People take away your rattle. You drop your pacifier in the potty. You get scared by a rooster. Mama smacks you on the behind . . . Why should I try to remember these petty happenings about which, by the way, I recall almost nothing.

I ought to start at age five, I thought.

So I began to recollect the things which had happened in my life from my fifth year to my fifteenth.

And, rummaging through the history of these years in my mind, I unexpectedly felt fear and even a certain anxiety. I thought, it means that I'm on the right track. It means the wound is somewhere near. It means that now I'll find the unfortunate incident which has spoiled my life.

FROM FIVE TO FIFTEEN YEARS

*Sooner to throw off the burdensome memory
Of my imaginary hurts . . .*

I Won't Do It Again

On the table is a plate. On the plate are dried figs.

It's interesting to chew these figs. They have a great many seeds. They crunch nicely between the teeth. At dinner they gave us only two of those figs apiece. That's much too little for children.

I climb up on a chair. With a determined gesture I move the plate toward me. I bite into a fig.

Yes, that's the way it was, all right—lots of little seeds. It would be interesting to know if all the figs have the same thing inside.

Going through the figs, I take a little bite out of each one. Yes, they're all alike.

Of course, it's not good, and I'm not supposed to do it. But after all, I'm not eating the whole fig. I'm biting off only a little piece. Almost the whole fig remains at the grownups' disposal.

After biting a piece out of every fig, I get down from the chair and walk around the table.

My father and mother come in.

"I didn't eat the figs," I say to them right away. "I only bit a piece out of each one."

Glancing at the plate, my mother throws up her hands. My father laughs. But he frowns when I look at him.

"Come along, and I'll give you a little spanking," says my mother, "so you'll remember better what you're not supposed to do."

She drags me to the bed. And takes a thin belt.

Weeping and sobbing, I cry out, "I won't do it again."

Goldfish

On the window sill is a jar with goldfish.

In the jar two fish are swimming.

I throw them some crumbs from a dry crust. Let them have something to eat. But the fish swim indifferently by.

They must feel awfully bad if they won't eat. No wonder, spending whole days in the water. Now if they were simply lying on the window sill, maybe they would get an appetite.

Sticking my hand in the jar, I take out the fish and put them on the window sill. No, they don't feel so good there. They flop around. And refuse to eat there too.

I throw the fish back in the water.

But they feel still worse in the water. Look, they even swim with their bellies up now. They must be asking to be taken out of the jar.

I take the fish out again and put them in a cigarette box. A half-hour later I open the box. The fish have turned stiff.

Mama says angrily, "Why did you do that?"

I say, "I wanted them to feel better."

Mama says, "Don't pretend you're a little idiot. Fish are meant to live in water."

I cry bitterly from hurt feelings. I myself know that fish are meant to live in water. But I wanted to release them from this misfortune.

The Storm

I am going through the field and picking flowers with my sister Lelia.

I am picking yellow flowers. Lelia is picking blue ones.

Our little sister Yulia trails behind us. She is picking white flowers.

We're picking them that way on purpose, to make it more interesting.

Suddenly Lelia says, "Ladies and gentlemen, look at that cloud."

We look at the sky. A terrible cloud is moving slowly along. It's so black that everything grows dark around us. It creeps along like some monster, enveloping the whole sky.

Lelia says, "Let's hurry home. There's going to be a terrible thunderstorm right away."

We run for home. But we are running toward the cloud. Straight into the monster's jaws.

A wind blows up unexpectedly. It swirls everything around us.

The dust rises. Dry grass blows about. And bushes and trees are bent.

As fast as our legs can carry us we run toward home.

Big drops of rain are already falling on our heads.

A terrible flash of lightning and an even more terrible thunderclap shake us. I fall on the ground and, jumping up, run again. I run as if a tiger were chasing me.

I'm close to home already.

I glance back. Lelia is pulling Yulia by the hand. Yulia is wailing.

Another hundred steps more and I'm on our porch.

On the porch Lelia scolds me: why did I lose my yellow bouquet? But I didn't lose it, I threw it away.

I say, "In such a storm, what do we need with bouquets?"

Pressing close to one another, we sit on the bed.

Dreadful thunder shakes our cottage.

Rain drums on the windowpanes and on the roof.

Through the torrents of rain you can't see anything.

It's So Simple

We are sitting in a cart. A little reddish peasant horse is trotting jauntily along a dusty road.

The landlord's son Vasyutka is driving. He holds the reins carelessly and from time to time shouts to the horse, "Well, well, come on . . . have you gone to sleep?"

The little horse isn't asleep at all; it's running well. But that's probably what you're supposed to shout.

My hands are burning—I want so badly to hold the reins, to drive and shout at the horse. But I don't dare ask Vasyutka to let me.

Suddenly Vasyutka himself says, "How about holding the reins awhile? I'll have a smoke."

My sister Lelia says to Vasyutka, "No, don't give him the reins. He doesn't know how to drive."

Vasyutka says, "What do you mean, he doesn't know how to drive? There's nothing to know."

Now the reins are in my hands. I hold them in my outstretched hands.

Holding on tightly to the cart, Lelia says, "Well, now something's bound to happen—he'll overturn us for sure."

At that moment the cart bounces over a hummock.

Lelia cries, "Well, you see. He'll overturn us any minute."

I too suspect that the cart will overturn, since the reins are in my inexperienced hands. But no, after bouncing over the hummock the cart rolls smoothly along.

Proud of my success, I slap the horse on its sides with the reins and shout, "You're asleep!"

Just then I see a turn in the road ahead.

I hurriedly ask Vasyutka, "What rein do I pull to make the horse go to the right?"

Vasyutka says calmly, "Pull the right one."

"How many times should I pull the right one?" I ask.

Vasyutka shrugs. "Once."

I tug at the right rein and suddenly, as in a fairy tale, the horse goes to the right.

But for some reason I am disappointed, irritated. It's so simple. I thought it was much harder to drive a horse. I thought there was a whole science to it which one had to study for years. And it turns out to be such nonsense.

I give the reins back to Vasyutka. It's not especially interesting.

Someone Has Drowned

I am making a boat. It's a little board with a smokestack and a mast. I still have to make the rudder and a flag.

Waving her hat, Lelia comes running. She shouts, "Minka, hurry! Let's run. Someone's drowned down there."

I run after Lelia. Running, I cry, "I don't want to run. I'm scared."

Lelia says, "But you're not the one who's drowned. Someone's drowned. Why should you be afraid?"

We run along the shore. There is a crowd at the dock.

Pushing people aside, Lelia makes her way through the crowd. I squeeze through after her.

Someone says, "He didn't know how to swim. The current is swift. And now he's drowned."

A boy lies on the sandy bank. He is about eighteen. He is as white as paper. His eyes are closed. His arms are outspread, and his body is covered with green twigs.

A woman is kneeling next to him. She is gazing fixedly into his dead face. Someone says, "That's his mother. She's not crying because her grief is so great."

I look sideways at the drowned man. I want him to stir, rise, and say, "No, I didn't drown. I was just pretending. On purpose. I was joking."

But he lies motionless. I feel so frightened that I close my eyes.

It's Not My Fault

We're sitting at the table and eating pancakes.

Suddenly my father takes my plate and begins eating my pancakes. I howl.

My father is wearing glasses. He has a serious look. A beard. Nevertheless, he is laughing. He says, "You see how greedy he is. He won't give his father one pancake."

I say, "You're welcome to one pancake, go ahead and eat it. I thought you were going to eat them all."

The soup is brought in.

I say, "Papa, do you want my soup?"

Papa says, "No, I'll wait till they bring the dessert. Now, if you give me your dessert, then you're really a kind boy."

Thinking that dessert is cranberry pudding with milk, I say, "You're welcome to it. You may eat my dessert."

Then they bring in a Bavarian cream to which I am not indifferent.

Pushing my plate of Bavarian cream over to my father, I say, "Go ahead and eat it if you're so greedy."

My father frowns and leaves the table.

My mother says, "Go to your father and ask his forgiveness."

I say, "I won't go. I didn't do anything wrong."

I leave the table without touching my dessert.

At night when I'm lying in bed, my father comes in. He is carrying my plate of Bavarian cream.

My father says, "Well, why didn't you eat your pudding?"

I say, "Papa, let's eat it together. Why should we quarrel over this?

My father kisses me and feeds me the cream with a spoon.

At Grandmother's

We're visiting Grandmother We're sitting at the table. Dinner is being served.

Our Grandmother is sitting next to our Grandfather. Grandfather is fat, heavy. He looks like a lion. And Grandmother looks like a lioness.

The lion and the lioness are sitting at the table.

I gaze fixedly at Grandmother. She is Mama's mama. She has gray hair. And a dark, astonishingly beautiful face. Mama said that she was a remarkable beauty in her youth.

They bring a tureen of soup.

That's uninteresting. I probably won't even eat it.

But now they're bringing in some *pirozhki*. That's not bad at all.

Grandfather serves out the soup himself.

Handing Grandfather my plate, I say, "Only a drop for me."

Grandfather holds the ladle over my bowl. He drops a single drop of soup into my bowl.

I look at the drop in embarrassment.

Everyone laughs.

Grandfather says, "He himself asked for one drop. And I fulfilled his request."

I didn't want the soup, but for some reason I feel hurt. I'm almost in tears.

Grandmother says, "Grandfather was joking. Give me your bowl, and I'll serve you some soup."

I don't give her my bowl and don't touch the *pirozhki*.

Grandfather says to my mother, "He's a bad child. He doesn't understand jokes."

Mother says to me, "Well, smile at Grandfather. Say something to him."

I look angrily at Grandfather. I say to him softly, "I'll never come to visit you again."

I came to visit Grandmother only when Grandfather died. He wasn't my real grandfather. I was not sorry when he died.

Mama Cries

Mama is lying on the sofa and crying. I go over to her. Mama hands me a colored post card. On the post card is a beautiful lady wearing a boa and a hat.

Mama asks, "Don't I look like this lady?"

Wanting to soothe my mother, I say, "Yes, a little like her." Although I don't see any special resemblance.

Mama says, "In that case, go to your father, show him this post card and say, 'Papa, look how much she looks like our Mama.'"

Sulkily I ask, "What for?"

"It's necessary. I can't explain what for. You're too young."

I say, "No, tell me anyway. Or else I won't go."

Mama says, "Well, how shall I explain it to you . . . Papa will look at this post card and say, 'Oh, what a fascinating Mama we have . . .' And he'll be nicer to me . . ."

This explanation does not clarify matters for me. On the contrary, it seems to me that Papa will see the lack of resemblance and will get even angrier at Mama.

Very unwillingly, I go to the room where my father is working.

Papa is an artist. There is an easel in front of him. Papa is painting a portrait of my sister Yulia.

I go over to my father and, holding out the card,

say gloomily, "Doesn't this look a little like Mama?"

Glancing sideways at the post card, my father says, "Don't bother me. Go away . . ."

Well, of course. Nothing came of it. I knew it.

I go back to my mother.

"Well, what did he say?"

I tell her, "He said, 'Don't bother me, go away . . .'"

Covering her face with her hands, Mama cries.

My heart is torn with pity. I am even ready to go to my father a second time with that stupid post card, but my mother doesn't let me.

In the Studio

Papa hasn't been at our place for a long time. My mother dresses me. And we go to my father's studio.

Mama walks hurriedly. She drags me by the hand, so that I can hardly keep up.

We go up to the seventh floor. We knock. Papa opens the door.

When he sees us, he frowns at first. Then, taking me in his arms, he tosses me almost to the ceiling. He laughs and kisses me.

Mama smiles. She sits down on the sofa with Papa, and they begin some kind of secret conversation.

I walk around the studio. There are paintings on the easels. There are paintings on the walls, too. Enormous windows. Disorder.

I inspect the boxes of paints. Brushes. All kinds of little bottles.

I've looked into everything, but my parents are still talking. It's very nice that they're talking so quietly, without shouting and quarreling.

I don't bother them. I make the rounds of the boxes and pictures a second time.

Finally, my father says to my mother, "Well, I'm glad. Everything's all right."

He kisses Mama good-bye. And Mama kisses him. They even hug each other.

We put on our coats and go.

On the way, Mama suddenly begins to scold me. She says, "Oh, why did you insist on tagging along with me . . ."

It's strange to hear this. I didn't insist at all. She herself dragged me off to the studio. And now she's displeased.

Mama says, "Oh, how sorry I am that I took you with me. If you hadn't been there we would have made it up once and for all."

I whimper. But I whimper because I don't know why I am in the wrong. I behaved quietly. I didn't even run around in the studio. And now such unfairness.

My mother says, "No, I'll never take you with me again."

I want to ask what is the matter, what happened. But I keep quiet. I'll grow up to be big, and then I'll find out everything for myself. I'll find out why people are sometimes blamed when they haven't done anything wrong at all.

At the Gate

I stand at the garden gate. I am looking fixedly at the road which leads to the dock.

Mama went to the city. And now she has been away since morning. We have already had dinner. Soon it will be evening. Oh, good heavens, where is she?

I look into the distance again. No! Some people are coming, but she isn't among them. Something must have happened to her.

But what could have happened to her? After all, she isn't a small child. She's a grown-up person. She's thirty years old.

Well, and what of that? All sorts of horrible things

happen to grownups too. Grownups too are threatened by dangers at every step.

Perhaps Mama was riding in a cab. The horse bolted. It's true that cab drivers have gentle horses. They can hardly drag themselves along. It's doubtful that horses like that would bolt. And if they did bolt, one could always jump out of the carriage.

But now if Mama went by boat, one can't jump out of a boat if it's sinking. Of course, there are life preservers. You can grab hold of one of these life preservers and save yourself. But life preservers aren't good for anything if there's a fire; if, for instance, our city apartment caught fire. Although, actually, our house is made of stone and would hardly burst into flame like a match.

Most likely, Mama stopped in at a café and ate something there and got sick. And now a doctor is operating on her.

Oh, no! Here comes our mama!

With a cry, I run to meet her. Mama is wearing an enormous hat. Around her shoulders is a white feather boa. And she has a bow on her belt. I don't like Mama to dress like that. I wouldn't put on those feathers for anything in the world. I'll grow up to be big and ask Mama not to dress like that. This way, it's embarrassing for me to walk with her—everyone turns around.

"You're not glad that I came back, are you?" asks Mama.

"No, I'm glad," I answer indifferently.

A Ton of Iron

I am busy going through my pencil case. I sort the pens and pencils. I admire my little penknife.

The teacher calls on me. He says, "Answer quickly: which is heavier, a ton of feathers or a ton of iron?"

Not seeing any trick in this, I answer without thinking, "A ton of iron."

Laughter.

The teacher says, "Tell your mama to come in and see me tomorrow. I want to have a talk with her."

The next day Mama goes to see the teacher and returns home sad. She says, "The teacher is dissatisfied with you. He says that you're absent-minded, don't listen to anything, don't understand, and sit at your desk as if what happens in the classroom has nothing to do with you."

"And what else did he say?"

Mama's face becomes completely sad.

Pressing me close to her, she says, "I thought you were an intelligent and well-developed boy, but he says that your mental development is inadequate."

"Well, he's talking nonsense," I cry angrily. "I think his mental development is inadequate. He asks the students silly questions. And it's harder to answer silly questions than clever ones."

Kissing me, Mama weeps.

"Oh, it won't be easy for you to live in this world," she says.

"Why?"

"You're a difficult child. You're like your father. I don't believe that you'll be happy."

Mama kisses and hugs me again, but I pull away. I don't like all this slobbering and tears.

A Closed Heart

Grandfather has come. He is my father's father. He came from Poltava.

I had thought that there would arrive a withered little old man with long whiskers, wearing a Ukrainian shirt. And that he would sing, dance, and tell us fairy tales.

Just the opposite. A stern, tall man arrived. Not very old, not very gray. Strikingly handsome. Clean-shaven. Wearing a black frock coat. And he was carrying a small velvet-covered prayer book and a red bone rosary.

I was surprised that we had that kind of grandfather. I wanted to talk with him about something or other. But he didn't talk to us children. He only talked a little with Papa. And to Mother he said angrily, "It's your own fault, madame. You had too many children."

Then Mama began to cry and went to her room.

I was even more astonished that we had the kind of grandfather who was displeased that Mama had had children, one of whom was I.

I wanted terribly to find out what Grandfather did in his room, which he rarely left and allowed no one to enter. He was probably doing something extremely important there.

And so I push open the door and quietly enter the room. My stern grandfather is not doing anything. He is sitting in an armchair and simply doing nothing. He looks fixedly at the wall and smokes a long pipe.

Seeing me, Grandfather asked, "What do you want here? And why did you come in without knocking?"

Then I got angry at my grandfather and said, "After all, this is our apartment, and if you want to know, this is my room, and they moved me in with my sisters. Why should I knock on my own door?"

Grandfather threw his rosary at me and began to shout. Then he went and complained to my father. And my father complained to my mother.

But Mama didn't scold me. She said, "Oh, I wish he would go soon. He doesn't love anyone. He's like your father. He has a closed heart."

"Do I have a closed heart too?" I ask.

"Yes," says my mother, "I think you have a closed heart too."

"Does that mean I'll be just like Grandfather?"

Kissing me, my mother says through her tears, "Yes, you'll probably be like that too. It's a great misfortune —not to love anyone."

A Heart Attack

I quietly open the door and go into Papa's room.

My father is usually sprawled on the bed. But today he is standing motionless by the window.

Tall and sullen, he is standing by the window and thinking about something.

He looks like Peter the Great. Only he has a beard.

I say softly, "Papa, I'm taking your penknife to sharpen a pencil."

Without turning around, my father says, "Go ahead."

I go over to the desk and begin to sharpen the pencil.

In the corner by the window is a small round table. On the table is a carafe of water.

My father pours himself a glass of water. Drinks it. And suddenly falls.

He falls on the floor. And the chair he catches hold of falls too.

I scream in terror. My sisters and mother come running.

Seeing my father on the floor, my mother throws herself upon him with a cry. She pulls at his shoulders, kisses his face.

I run out of the room and lie down on my bed.

Something terrible has happened. But maybe everything will turn out all right. Maybe Papa has fainted.

I go into my father's room again.

My father is lying on the bed. My mother is at the door. The doctor is next to her.

My mother is shouting, "You're mistaken, Doctor!"

The doctor says, "In this matter we don't dare make mistakes, madame. He is dead."

"But why all of a sudden like that? It can't be!"

"His heart ruptured," says the doctor. And he leaves the room.

Lying on my bed, I cry.

Yes, He Is Dead

Oh, how unbearable it is to look at Mama! She cries all the time.

Now she is standing by the table on which my father lies. She has fallen on him with her face to his, and she is weeping.

I stand in the doorway and watch this terrible grief. No, I could never cry like that. I probably do have a closed heart.

I want to console my mother, distract her. I softly ask her, "Mama, how old is our papa?"

Drying her tears, Mama says, "Oh, Mishenka, he's still quite young. He's forty-nine. No, it's impossible that he's dead!"

She tugs at my father's shoulders again and mutters, "Maybe it's a deep faint, a cataleptic state . . ."

My mother unfastens a pin from her blouse. Then she takes my father's hand. And I see—she wants to stick the pin into his hand.

I give a shriek of horror.

"Don't scream," says my mother. "I want to see, perhaps he isn't dead."

She sticks the pin through his hand. I shriek again. My mother pulls out the pin from the pierced palm.

"Look," she says. "There isn't a drop of blood. Yes, he's dead . . ."

Falling on my father's chest, my mother weeps again.

I go out of the room. I am shaking with fever.

At the Cemetery

This is the first time I've been at a cemetery. It's not at all terrifying. Only very unpleasant.

It's so unpleasant that I can hardly stand still in the church. I wish the requiem would end soon. I try not to look at the corpses which are lying on six catafalques. But my eyes can't help looking at them.

They lie pale and motionless, like wax dolls. Two old women in caps. My father. Someone else's father. A young, dead girl. And a paunchy, stout man. So paunchy that it looks as if the coffin will hardly close over such a belly. However, they'll press it down with the cover. They won't stand on ceremony. Anyway, he doesn't feel or see anything now.

I don't know whether I'll be able to go up to my father and kiss him. Everyone is going up and kissing him already.

Holding my breath, I go up. I barely touch his dead hand with my lips. I run out of the church.

The pallbearers are artists—Papa's friends. In front, on a small velvet pillow, someone carries the decoration Papa was awarded for his picture, *Suvorov's Departure.* This picture hangs in the Suvorov Museum. It's a mosaic. In the left corner of the painting there is a little green pine tree. I made the lower branch of this pine. It came out crooked, but Papa was pleased with my work.

The choir is singing. The coffin is lowered into the grave. Mama shrieks.

They fill the grave. It's all over. The closed heart no longer exists. But I exist.

His Days Are Numbered

Mama's brother came down with tuberculosis. They took a room for him outside the city and he began living there.

But the doctor told Mama, "He's in very bad shape. His days are numbered."

I went out to see him one Sunday. I took him some *pirozhki* and sour cream.

Uncle George lay on his bed surrounded with pillows. He was breathing hoarsely and heavily.

I put the things I brought down on a chair and wanted to leave. But he said to me, "I'm alone for whole days at a time. I'm terribly lonely. Let's at least play a game of cards."

Uncle George took a deck of cards from under his pillow and we started to play "sixty-six."

I was terribly lucky. And he wasn't. He lost two hands. And demanded that I play a third.

We began to play a third hand. But he was even unluckier. Then he began to get angry at me. He began to shout and throw cards. He was vexed that he was losing even though we weren't playing for money, but just for fun.

I was surprised that he felt so bad, since his days were numbered and he would soon die.

Now he dealt me the cards. And they were almost all trumps. Seeing this, my uncle shook with anger and began coughing. He began to moan. And he began to feel so ill that he seized an oxygen bag and put it to his mouth. It was hard for him to breathe. He was afraid he would suffocate.

Then, when he felt better, we continued the game.

But I began to discard good cards purposely. I made bad leads. I wanted to lose to him, so he wouldn't suffer.

Then I began to lose. And this cheered up my uncle so much that he began to joke and laugh. And he slapped me on the forehead with the cards, saying that I was still too small to play with grownups.

I didn't play a fourth hand with him, although he very much wanted to.

I went away intending never to come to see him again.

And I really didn't have another chance to visit him. He died the next Sunday.

Chlorophyll

Only two subjects interest me—zoology and botany. The rest don't.

Actually, history interests me too, only not the way it is in the book we're using.

I'm very sorry I'm such a poor student. But I don't know what to do about it.

Even in botany I only got a "3." And that's a subject I know very well. I read a lot of books and even made a herbarium—an album in which I pasted leaves, flowers, and herbs.

The botany teacher tells about something in class. Then he says, "And why are leaves green? Who knows?"

The class is silent.

"I'll give a five to anyone who knows," says the teacher.

I know why leaves are green, but I keep quiet. I don't want to be a show-off. Let the top students answer. Besides, I don't need a five. What good would it do sticking out among my twos and threes? It would be comical.

The teacher calls on the best student. But he doesn't know.

Than I carelessly raise my hand.

"So," says the teacher, "you know. Well, tell us."

"Leaves are green," I say, "because they contain the pigment chlorophyll."

The teacher says, "Before I give you a five, I want to know why you didn't raise your hand at once."

I keep quiet. It's very difficult to answer that.

"Perhaps you didn't remember right away?" asks the teacher.

"No, I did remember right away."

"Perhaps you didn't want to be ahead of the best students?"

I keep quiet. Shaking his head reproachfully, the teacher marks down a five.

It's All Over

The wind is so strong that it's impossible to play croquet.

We sit on the grass behind the house and talk.

Besides my sister on the grass are Tolya, who attends a scientific Gymnasium, and his sister Xenia.

My sisters are teasing me. They think I am not indifferent to Xenia—I look at her all the time and set up good shots for her when I play croquet.

Xenia laughs. She knows that I really do set up good shots for her.

Certain of my feelings, she says, "Could you go to the cemetery at night and pick a flower there for me?"

"What for?" I ask.

"Nothing special. To fulfill my request."

I speak softly, so my sisters won't overhear. "For you I could do that."

Suddenly we see people running behind the fence. We go out of the garden. My God! The water is up to the highway. Elagin Island is already under water. In a little while the water will overflow the road we are walking along.

We run to the yacht club. The wind is so strong we can hardly stand on our feet.

Xenia and I run ahead, holding hands.

Suddenly we hear Mama's voice. "Back! Come home!"

We turn around. Our garden is under water. The water has flooded from the field and submerged everything behind us.

I run to the house. The gutters are full of water. Boards and beams float by.

Wet to the knees, I run up on the porch.

But where are Xenia, my sisters, and Tolya?

They have taken off their shoes and are coming through the garden.

On the porch Xenia says to me, "To run away first . . . abandon us . . . Well, really . . . It's all over between us."

I go silently to my room on the second floor. I lie down on my bed in terrible misery.

CONCLUSION

And now my reminiscences of my childhood are finished.

Before me are thirty-eight stories which at one time upset and troubled me.

I began to re-examine and analyze all these stories. I hoped to find in them the source of my suffering.

However, I did not find anything special in these stories.

Yes, of course some of the scenes are extremely sad. But no sadder than what happens to everyone.

Everyone's father dies. Everyone sees his mother's tears.

Everyone has disappointments in school. Hurt feelings. Worries. Tricks played on him. Everyone is frightened by thunder, floods, and storms.

No, in not a single one of these stories did I find the unfortunate incident which had ruined my life and brought me melancholy and anguish.

Then I put all these stories together. I wanted to see a general picture of my childhood, a common chord which had, perhaps, deafened me, as with faltering, childish steps I walked along the narrow path of my life.

But even in this common chord I didn't see anything exceptional. An ordinary childhood. A somewhat difficult child. Nervous. Easily hurt. Extremely impressionable. More concerned with what was bad than what was good. Perhaps timid for this reason. But not at all feeble—rather strong, in fact.

No, the events of my childhood couldn't have ruined my future life.

I was again discouraged. The task was beyond my powers: to find the reason for my depression. To get rid of it. To be happy. Joyful. Ecstatic. The way an ordinary man with an open heart should be. Only in the story does the prodigal son return to his father's house!

But perhaps I am mistaken. Perhaps the unfortunate event I am seeking did not take place. Or did it perhaps take place at an even earlier age?

And really, why did I exclude the years of infancy? Why, one's first impressions are not acquired at the age of six or seven. One's first acquaintance with the world takes place earlier. The first glimmers of understanding arise at two or three. And even, perhaps, at one year.

Then I began to think: what could have happened at such an insignificant age?

Straining my memory, I began to recall myself as a very small child. But here I became convinced that I remembered almost nothing about this. I could not call up anything unified in my memory. A few fragments, pieces, some separate items which were lost against the gray backdrop.

Then I began to think about these fragments. And, recollecting them, I began to feel even greater terror than that I had felt while thinking about my childhood.

It means I'm on the right track, I thought. It means that the wound is somewhere very near.

V.   BEFORE SUNRISE

Some sort of fearful world that was
Without a sky, or light, or stars.

And so I decided to recall my years of infancy, supposing that the unfortunate event must have taken place at just that age.

However, those years turned out to be difficult to remember. They were enveloped in a sort of dim mist. I tried to remember myself as a three-year-old boy sitting in a high chair or on my mother's lap.

Then, through the deep mist of forgetfulness, I suddenly began to remember some separate moments, torn bits, and fragmentary scenes, illuminated with a strange light.

What could have illuminated these scenes? Could it have been terror? Or a child's emotional agitation? Yes, probably terror and agitation had ripped open the dull fabric which shrouded my infancy.

But they were brief moments, the light was fleeting. And then everything sank back into the mist.

Thus, recalling these moments, I found that they referred to the third and fourth years of my life. And some were connected with my second year.

Then I began to remember the things that had happened to me from two until five.

FROM TWO TO FIVE YEARS

*What seems to us such sweetness on our
tongues
Produces acid down inside our stomachs.*

Open Your Mouth

On the blanket is an empty matchbox. The matches are
in my mouth.

Someone shouts, "Open your mouth!"

I open my mouth. I spit out matches.

Someone's fingers go in my mouth. They take out
some more matches.

Someone is crying. I cry louder, both because they're
bitter and because someone took them away.

By Myself

A bowl of kasha. A spoon approaches my mouth. Someone's hand is holding the spoon.

I take away the spoon. I'm going to eat by myself.

I swallow the kasha. It's hot. I roar. In my anger I
bang the spoon on the dish. The kasha splashes into
my face, my eyes.

An incredible scream. It's me screaming.

The Rooster

The yard. Sunlight. Big flies are flying around.

I'm sitting on the doorstep. I'm eating something.
Probably a roll.

I throw pieces of the roll to the chickens.

A rooster walks up to me. Turning his head, he looks
at me.

I wave my hand to make the rooster go away. But he doesn't go away. He comes closer to me. And suddenly hops up and pecks at my roll.

With a shriek of horror I run away.

Just Playing

I'm standing on the fence. Someone is holding me up from behind.

Suddenly a beggar with a bag comes by.

Someone says to him, "Here, take this boy."

The beggar stretches out his hand.

I cry out in a dreadful voice.

Someone says, "I won't give you away, I won't give you away. I was just playing."

The beggar goes away with his bag.

It's Raining

My mother is carrying me. She is running. I press close to her breast.

Rain is drumming on my head. Streams of water run under my collar. I yell.

My mother covers my head with a kerchief. She runs faster.

Here we are at home already. In my room.

Mother puts me on the bed.

Suddenly there is a flash of lightning. Thunder booms.

I crawl off the bed and yell so loudly that I drown out the thunder.

I'm Scared

Mother is carrying me. We're looking at animals in cages.

Here is a huge elephant. He takes a French roll with his trunk. He swallows it.

I'm scared of elephants. We go away from the cage.

Here is a huge tiger. He tears at some meat with his teeth and claws. He is having lunch.

I'm scared of tigers. I cry.

We leave the zoo.

We're home again. Mama says to my father, "He's scared of animals."

Uncle Sasha Is Dying

I am sitting in a high chair. I am drinking warm milk. I get some skin from the milk in my mouth. I spit. I roar. I smear the skin on the table.

Behind the door someone cries out in a terrible voice.

Mama comes. She is crying. Kissing me, she says, "Uncle Sasha is dying."

After smearing the skin on the table, I began drinking my milk again.

And again there is a terrible cry from behind the door.

At Night

Night. Dark. I've waked up. I cry out.

My mother picks me up.

I scream even louder. I look at the wall. The wall is brown. And on the wall hangs a towel.

My mother soothes me. She says, "Are you afraid of the towel? I'll take it away."

Mother takes down the towel and hides it. She puts me back in bed. I cry out again.

And then they put my little bed next to my mother's bed.

Crying, I fall asleep.

CONCLUSION

And now before me are twelve stories about a little child.

I have examined these stories carefully, but I don't find anything special in them.

Every child sticks into his mouth whatever he gets his hands on.

Almost every child is terrified of wild animals and dogs. Spits when he gets milk skin in his mouth. Burns his tongue. Cries in the dark.

No, it was an ordinary childhood, a small child's normal behavior.

Put together, these stories still did not solve any riddles for me.

It seemed that I had remembered all this childish twaddle for nothing. It seemed that everything I had remembered about my life had been remembered in vain.

All these strong impressions must not have been the cause of my unhappiness. But perhaps they were consequences rather than causes?

Could the unfortunate incident have happened before the age of two? I thought uncertainly.

Of course. Why, one's first acquaintance with things, one's first acquaintance with the surrounding world takes place not at three or four but earlier, at the dawn of life, before sunrise.

It must have been quite a meeting, quite a process of getting acquainted. A little animal, unable to speak and unable to think, encountered life. It was then, and not later, that the unfortunate incident must have taken place.

But how was I to find it? How could I penetrate to that world divested of reason, divested of logic, to that

world about which I could remember absolutely nothing?

BEFORE TWO YEARS

It seemed, as in a grievous dream,
That all was pale and dark and dim . . .

1

Straining my memory, I began to think about the beginning of my life. However, I could not call forth any
scenes from oblivion. I was unable to catch hold of any
distant outlines. The far past merged into a single con-
tinuous and unvaried shadow.

A heavy gray fog muffled the first two years of my
life. It hung before me like a curtain of smoke and kept
my gaze from penetrating to the far-off, secret life of
that small creature.

I did not know how to tear away this fog and see the
drama which had been enacted at the dawn of my life,
before sunrise.

That the drama had taken place at precisely that
time I already had no doubt. If I were stalking that
which had never been, I would not have experienced
such unaccountable dread as I began to experience
when I tried to penetrate that region where people who
have left their childhood behind are forbidden to go.

2

I began to picture myself as a year-old baby with a
nipple in its mouth, a rattle in its hand, and its legs up
in the air.

But these scenes, artfully composed in my mind, did
not stir my memory.

Only once, after intense thought, did some forgotten sights glimmer in my excited mind.

Here are the folds of a blanket. Someone's hand comes out of the wall. A tall, wavering shadow. Another shadow. And another hand. A kind of white foam. And again the long, wavering shadow.

But these were chaotic visions. They reminded me of dreams. They were almost unreal. Through them I had hoped at least to see my mother's shadow, her form, her figure bent over my bed. But no, I was unable to do this. The outlines ran together. The shadows vanished, and after them once again came emptiness, darkness, nothingness . . . As the poet said:

> *All merged into a turbid shade*
> *And it was neither night nor day;*
> *It was obscured, yet shadowless*
> *And an abyss of emptiness*
> *Without extent or boundary,*
> *And forms without a face to see.*
> *Some sort of fearful world that was*
> *Without a sky, or light, or stars.*

This was the world of chaos. It would disappear at the first contact with my rational mind.

I did not manage to penetrate that world.

There is no doubt—that was a different world, a different planet, with different, extraordinary laws which are not controlled by reason.

3

But how can a small creature live in that chaos? I wondered. How can it protect itself from danger without reason and logic?

Or is there no protection? Is everything left to chance and parental care?

After all, even with parents, life in this world of wavering shadows is not without danger.

Then I opened the textbooks and research works of the physiologists, wishing to find out what science had to say about this turbulent period of human life.

I saw that amazing laws were to be found in these books—they had been deduced by scientists from their observations of animals.

They were unusually strict and exact laws which, in their own way, protect the small creature.

It didn't matter that both reason and logic were lacking. They were made up for by a special reaction of the organism—the reflex, which is the organism's own peculiar way of responding to any irritation which is produced in the infant by its environment. This reaction, this reply, constitutes the organism's defense against danger.

What does this reply consist of?

Two basic nervous processes characterize reflex behavior: excitation and inhibition. A combination of these processes produces any given response. But all the variety of this mental activity can be reduced essentially to a very simple function—muscular movement. That is, in response to any stimulus there takes place a muscular movement or combination of such movements which is necessarily purposeful.

The principle of this reflex pertains equally to man, to animals, and to an infant.

So it turns out that not chaos, but the strictest order, established over thousands of years, protects the small creature.

And it turns out that one's first acquaintance with the world takes place according to the principles of this reflex. One's first meetings with things establish the habit of relating to them in one way or another.

6

[At this point Zoshchenko gives an extended outline of the whole Pavlovian theory of conditioned reflexes.]

I wanted to apply to my own life this great discovery—this law of conditioned reflexes, of temporary nervous connections.

I wanted to see this law in action, applied to the events of my infancy.

It seemed to me that my unhappiness could have arisen from the fact that incorrect conditioned connections which were to terrify me in the future, could have been established in my infant brain.

It seemed to me that I was frightened by the hypodermic needle with which the poison had once been injected.

I wanted to destroy these erroneous mechanisms which had grown up in my brain.

But once again I was confronted with an obstacle: I could remember nothing about my life as an infant.

If I could have remembered at least one scene, one event, I could have unraveled the rest. But no, all was swathed in the fog of oblivion.

Then someone told me that if one went to the scene of something forgotten, one might remember that forgotten thing.

I asked my relatives where we had lived when I was a baby, and they told me where I had lived during my first years of life.

There were three such houses, but one building had burned down. I had lived in another when I was two years old. In the third I had spent no less than five years, beginning at the time I was four years old.

There was one more house. That house was in the country, where my parents used to go every summer.

I wrote down the addresses and, in an extraordinary state of agitation, went to inspect these old buildings.

I looked for a long time at the house where I had lived as a three-year-old child. But I could remember absolutely nothing.

Then I went to the building where I had lived for five years.

My heart sank when I went up to the gates.

My God! How familiar everything here was! I recognized the stairs, the little garden, the gate, the yard.

I recognized almost everything. But how little it resembled what was in my memory!

Once the house had seemed like a gigantic monolith, a skyscraper. Now there stood before me a small, shabby, three-story building.

Once the garden had seemed a magic and mysterious place. Now I saw a pathetic little square.

It had seemed that a tall, massive iron fence girdled this little garden. Now I touched some wretched iron stakes no higher than my waist.

How different were my eyes then and now!

I went up to the third floor and found the door to our apartment.

My heart contracted with incomprehensible pain. I began to feel ill. And I convulsively clutched the banisters, not understanding what was happening to me or why I was so upset.

I went downstairs and sat for a long time on a stump in front of the gate. I sat there until the janitor came. Looking at me suspiciously, he told me to go away.

7

I returned home very ill, shattered, not understanding what had upset me.

I returned home in dreadful misery. And now that misery did not leave me day or night.

During the day I paced around my room—I could neither lie down nor sit. And at night terrifying dreams tormented me.

I used not to have dreams. Or, more correctly, I had them but forgot them. They were short and incomprehensible. And I usually dreamed them near morning.

But now they appeared when my eyes were hardly closed.

They weren't even dreams. They were nightmares, dreadful visions from which I awoke in terror.

I began to take bromides to suppress these nightmares, to calm down. But bromides didn't help much.

Then I called a doctor and asked him to give me something that would prevent the nightmares.

When he found out that I was taking bromides, the doctor said, "What are you doing? On the contrary, you need to dream. Your dreams arise from the fact that you are thinking about your childhood. Only by means of these dreams can you hope to understand your illness. Only in dreams will you see those childhood scenes you are seeking. Only through dreams can you penetrate that distant forgotten world."

I told the doctor my most recent dream, and he began to interpret it. But he interpreted it in such a way that I got indignant and did not believe him.

I said that I had dreamed about tigers and an arm coming out of the wall.

The doctor said, "That is more than clear. Your parents took you to the zoo when you were too young. You saw an elephant there. It frightened you with its trunk. The arm in the dream is a trunk. The trunk is a phallus. You have a sexual trauma."

I didn't believe the doctor and became indignant. He was offended, and answered, "I interpreted your dream by Freud's method. I am a disciple of his. And there is no more accurate science which could help you."

So I consulted a few more doctors. Some laughed,

saying that the interpretation of dreams was nonsense. Others, on the contrary, attached great significance to dreams.

Among these doctors was one who was very intelligent. He explained a great deal to me and told me many things. I was very grateful to him. I even wanted to become his disciple. But then I changed my mind about it; it seemed to me that he wasn't right. I didn't believe in his treatment.

He was a violent antagonist of Pavlov. Except for experiments of a zoological nature, he saw nothing in Pavlov's work. He was an orthodox Freudian. He saw sexuality in every act of a child or an adult. He deciphered every dream as if it were the dream of an erotomaniac.

His interpretation did not coincide with what I considered beyond reproach; it did not coincide with Pavlov's method, the principle of conditioned reflexes.

[The author makes some investigations of the role of dreams in the history of medicine, going back to ancient times. He finds that great importance had been attached to them, but the explanations were invariably mixed up with religion and magic.]

9

What, then, is a dream, from the point of view of contemporary science?

First of all, it is a physiological state in which all external manifestations of consciousness are absent. Or, more correctly, all the higher psychic functions are closed off while the lower functions are accessible.

Pavlov believed that at night a person separates himself from the external world. During sleep the pent-up energies, suppressed emotions, and frustrated desires come to life.

This happens because there is an inhibiting action in the mechanism of sleep. But this inhibition is partial: it does not embrace the entire brain; it does not embrace all the areas of the great hemispheres. The inhibition does not extend beyond the centers immediately beneath the outer layer of the brain.

Our brain, in the opinion of physiologists, has, as it were, two stories. The upper story is the outer layer—cortex—of the brain. Here are the centers of control, logic, the critical faculty, the centers of acquired reflexes, and here is one's life experience. The lower story is the source of inherited reflexes, animal habits, and animal forces.

These two stories are linked together by means of the neural connections of which we spoke.

At night the upper story is immersed in sleep. For this reason, consciousness is absent. Control, the critical faculty, and conditioned habits are absent.

The lower story remains awake. However, the absence of control permits its inhabitants to display themselves to a greater or lesser degree.

Let us suppose that logic or developed intelligence has inhibited or repressed some terror which had once arisen in a child's mind. In the absence of control, this terror can arise again. But now it arises in dreams.

Therefore, dreaming is the continuation of mental life, the continuation of a person's psychic activity at a time when control is absent.

Thus, dreaming can explain what sort of forces inhibit a person, what terrifies him, and what he can drive away with the light of logic and reason.*

* Future events revealed that it was possible to discover the reason for pathological inhibition not only through dreams, but in another way. *Author's note.*

10

So, our brain has two stories—an upper and a lower.

Life experience and conditioned habits coexist with hereditary experience, with the habits of our ancestors and of animals.

It is as if two worlds were enclosed in the complex apparatus of our brain—the world of civilization and the animal world.

These two worlds are not infrequently in conflict. The higher forces struggle against the lower ones. They vanquish them, drive them even further down, and sometimes expel them entirely.

It seems that it is this struggle which is the source of many nervous afflictions.

However, the main trouble does not lie here at all.

I don't want to run too far ahead, but I'll say this briefly. Even if we allow that this conflict between higher and lower forces is a cause for nervous afflictions, this cause is still not an all-encompassing one; it is only a partial cause, far from being the most important or the basic one.

This conflict between higher and lower could—let us suppose—lead to certain sexual psychoneuroses. But if science saw in this conflict or struggle the sole cause, it would not proceed further than the discovery of sexual inhibitions.

After all, conflict in this sphere is to a certain extent normal, not pathological.

It seems to me that Freud's system errs at precisely this point.

This error, this mistake, was easily made by one who had not taken into consideration the mechanisms discovered by Pavlov.

Inexactness in primary premises and vagueness in the formulation of the struggle between the higher and lower mind produced an inexact deduction and led Freud to pursue one line of investigation only—the line of sexual deviations. But this did not define the problem. It was only part of a larger whole.

11

In the conflict between higher and lower, in the collision of atavistic impulses with the feelings of a modern civilized person, Freud saw the source of nervous afflictions. He wrote: "Forbidden by the process of civilized life and repressed into the depths of the unconscious, these impulses exist and make themselves known, breaking through into our consciousness in distorted form . . ." And so, in the victory of reason over animal instinct he perceived a cause of tragedy. In other words, higher reason is subject to doubt.

In the history of human thought there are many instances when misfortunes have been attributed to reason, when man's higher consciousness has been subjected to attacks, and thus, at times, people have seen the tragedy of human reason in that higher consciousness, in the struggle of the higher with the lower. They believed that the victory of consciousness over the lower instincts did harm and caused illnesses, nervous afflictions, emotional weakness, and psychoneuroses.

This seemed to them a tragedy, the only way out of which was a return to the past, a return to nature, a departure from civilization. It seemed that the paths of human reason were mistaken, artificial, and unnecessary.

I do not consider this philosophy equivalent to the philosophy of fascism. Fascism has different roots and a different nature, but with regard to reason fascism has borrowed something from this philosophy, distorting and simplifying it, reducing it to the level of dull-witted minds.

The return to barbarism is not a formula invented by fascism merely to meet necessities of war. It is one of the basic premises of the future state of man from the point of view of fascism.

Barbarity, savagery, and animal instincts are better than the further progress of consciousness.

Nonsense!

People artificially thrown back into a state of barbarism would not be at all relieved of the nervous afflictions which disturb them. The world would be populated with scoundrels freed from any responsibility for their vileness. But they would be scoundrels who had not got rid of their previous afflictions. They would be suffering scoundrels, even unhealthier than they had been before.

To return to that harmonious condition of savagery about which people have daydreamed was not considered possible even thousands of years ago. And even if it had been possible, the source of suffering would have remained. For the mechanisms of the brain would have been the same. We haven't the power to destroy them. We can only learn to deal with them. And we must learn to do this with a skill worthy of our higher consciousness.

We must make an exhaustive study of the mechanisms discovered by Pavlov. The ability to deal with them will free us from the enormous suffering which people bear with the meekness of savages.

The tragedy of human reason arises not from the high level of consciousness, but from its inadequacy.

12

Science is incomplete. Truth is a child of time. Other, more exact paths will be found. Meanwhile, with the help of painstaking analysis of dreams, we can look into the far-off world of the infant, that world which is not controlled by reason, that world of oblivion where the sources of our misfortunes sometimes originate.

Thus, dreams can explain the reasons for pathological inhibitions, and the Pavlovian system of conditioned reflexes can remove the painful condition by following the incidents in the dreams. That which has been repressed can be uncovered.

This repression can be removed by the light of logic, the light of higher consciousness, and not by the dim light of barbarism.

After I had thought all this over I realized that I could now try to penetrate the locked world of the infant. The keys were in my hand.

At night the doors of the lower story would open. The watchmen of my consciousness would fall asleep. And then the shades of the past which had been languishing underground would appear in dreams.

I wanted to meet these shades as soon as possible, to see them, so that at last I could understand my tragedy —the mistake I had made at the dawn of my life, before sunrise.

I wanted to recollect one of the many dreams I had had recently. However, I could not remember a single dream in full. I had forgotten them.

I began to ask what kind of dreams I had most frequently, and what these dreams were about.

Then I remembered that I dreamed most frequently about tigers coming into my room, about beggars standing at my door, and about myself bathing in the sea.

VI.　BLACK WATER

Black as lead, the water bore
Oblivion for evermore.

1

By chance I went to the country house where I had spent my childhood.

I had been planning to go there for a long time. And one day as I walked along the water front, I saw a steamer waiting at the dock. I boarded the steamer almost automatically and went to the country.

It was a village called The Sands, on the Neva not far from Schlüsselburg.

I had not been in those parts for over twenty years.

The steamer did not stop at The Sands. There was no dock there now. I crossed the Neva in a boat.

Oh, how agitated I was as I stepped onto the shore! At once I recognized the little round chapel. It was still there. I immediately remembered the huts across the way, the country road, and the steep hill from the bank where the dock used to be.

Everything now seemed pathetic and miniature in comparison to the grandiose world which had remained in my memory.

I walked along the street and everything there was painfully familiar to me. Except the people. I couldn't recognize a single one of the people I saw.

I went into the yard of the house where we had once lived.

A woman, no longer young, stood in the yard. She was holding an oar. She had just chased a calf out of the yard. And now she was standing there angry and heated.

She didn't want to talk to me, but I mentioned several names of local inhabitants I remembered.

No, all those names belonged to people who were already dead.

Then I mentioned my name, my parents' name. And the woman began to smile. She said that she had been a very young girl then, but that she remembered my deceased parents very well. And she mentioned the names of some of our relatives who had lived here and some of our acquaintances. No, all these names too belonged to dead people.

I sadly returned to my boat.

I walked sadly along the village street. Only the street and the houses were the same. The inhabitants were different. The old ones had lived here awhile like guests and gone—vanished never to return. They were dead.

It seemed to me that on that day I understood what life and death are and how one should live.

2

I returned home in great sadness. At home I didn't even feel like thinking about my investigation or my childhood. I no longer cared about anything.

Everything seemed absurd in comparison with the picture of life's shortness I had viewed that day.

Is it worthwhile to think, struggle, seek, protect oneself? Is it worthwhile to behave like a proprietor in a life which rushes past headlong with such insulting and even comic rapidity?

Isn't it better to take life as it comes without complaining, and then give up one's wretched place to some other offshoot of the earth?

Someone laughed in the next room while I was thinking about these things, and it seemed to me strange and barbaric that people could laugh, joke, and even talk when everything was so stupid, senseless, and insulting.

It seemed to me that it was easier and simpler to die than to wait meekly and dully for the lot which awaits us all. Unexpectedly I considered this a courageous decision. How astonished I would have been if someone had told me then what I know now—that it wasn't courageous at all, but the highest degree of infantilism. It had been dictated by infantile terror of the thing I was trying to discover. It was resistance. It was flight.

I decided to cut short my search. And with this decision I fell asleep.

At night I awoke in terror from some dreadful dream. My terror was so great that I continued to tremble even after I had awakened.

I lit the lamp and wrote down my dream so that I could think about it in the morning—out of curiosity, if nothing else.

However, I couldn't fall asleep and began thinking about my dream.

Actually, it was an extremely stupid dream. A dark, stormy river. Turbid, almost black water. Something white is floating on the water—a piece of paper or a rag. I am on the shore. I run away from the shore as fast as I can. I run through a meadow. For some reason the meadow is blue. Someone is running after me. He is just about to grab me by the shoulder. The person's hand is already touching me. Plunging ahead, I run away.

I started to think over the dream, but understood nothing.

Then I began to realize that I had dreamed of water once again. That dark, black water . . . and suddenly I remembered Blok's lines:

> An old, old dream . . . a murky view
> Some lanterns dashing forth—where to?
> Where only blackened water bore
> Oblivion for evermore.

This dream resembled mine.

I was running from the black water, from "oblivion for evermore."

3

I began to recollect dreams associated with water. Now I am bathing in a turbulent sea. I struggle against the waves. I am wading somewhere, up to my knees in water. Now I sit on the sand with water lapping at my feet. Or else I walk along the very edge of the water front. Suddenly the water begins to rise higher and higher. I am seized with terror. I run away.

I remembered still another dream. I am sitting in my room. Water begins to seep from all the cracks in the floor. Another minute, and the room fills with water.

After such dreams I used to wake up feeling oppressed, ill, in low spirits. Usually my depression was worse after dreams like this.

Perhaps the frequent floods in Leningrad had affected my mind. Perhaps there was something else associated with water.

I began to recall the scenes I had written down in my search for the unhappy event which had affected me. I again recalled the story of the drowned man, the story of the flood, the scenes in which my sister and I nearly drowned.

There was no doubt that water was associated with some strong feeling. But which one?

Could I be afraid of water in general? No. Just the opposite. I love water very much. I can admire the sea for hours at a time. I can sit for hours on the bank of a river. I usually take vacation trips only to places by the seashore or a river. I always try to find a room with windows overlooking the water. I always dreamed of living somewhere on the shore, very close to the water, so that the waves would come almost up to my doorstep.

The sea or a river often calmed me when I was suffering the depression which so frequently visited me.

But what if this wasn't love of the water, but fear of it?

What if concealed behind this exaggerated love lies an impressive amount of fear?

Perhaps I am not admiring the water, but rather, keeping an eye on it. Perhaps I admire it when it is calm, when it is not getting ready to swallow me.

Perhaps I am keeping an eye on it from the shore or the windows of my room. Perhaps I settle as close as possible to it in order to be on my guard, not to let it catch me unawares.

Perhaps this is the fear which cannot enter my consciousness, which lies buried in the lower story of my mind, driven there by logic and the control of reason.

I burst out laughing—it was all so comical and, at the same time, seemingly true.

No doubt remained—a fear of water was there in my mind. But it was distorted. It was not in the way we usually know.

4

Then it seemed to me that I understood my dream. Without doubt it referred to my infancy. In order to understand it I needed to discard habitual ideas and think with the images of a baby, see things through his eyes.

Of course, not completely with his images—they had no doubt been too meager. They had changed during his development. But their symbolism had evidently remained the same.

The turbid, stormy river was a bathtub or trough of water. The blue shore was a blanket. The white rag was a diaper which had been left in the bucket. The child had been taken from the water where they had bathed him. The child was "saved." But the danger remained.

I burst out laughing again. It was funny, but credible. It was naïve, but not more naïve than it should be.

But how could it have happened? All infants are bathed. All are immersed in water. No fear remains in them. Why, then, was I terrified?

It means that water wasn't the original cause, I thought. It means that some kind of terrifying things were associated with water.

At this point I remembered the principle of conditioned reflexes.

One stimulus could arouse two centers of excitation, since a conditioned neural connection could have been established between them.

By itself the water in which I had been immersed could not have aroused such agitation as I had experienced. Therefore, there must be a conditioned association between water and something else. My fear was not of water, but rather it was water that evoked my fear, since nervous connections had associated it with some other danger. This was how complex the solution to the problem was. This was why water could terrify me.

However, what was water associated with? What sort of "poison" did it contain? What was the second unfortunate stimulus which had kindled such a violent response?

For the time being I did not try to guess the nature of the second stimulus, the second center of excitation toward which the nerve connections so clearly extended.

Yet that stimulus had already been partially revealed in the same dream. The infant's world is meager; objects are exceedingly limited in number. Stimuli are not numerous. But my inexperience did not permit me to find the second stimulus immediately.

The riddle had not been solved, but I had the keys in my hand.

Later developments showed that I had not been mistaken in my basic ideas. I was mistaken only about the number of centers of excitation. There turned out to be not two, but several. And they were interwoven in a complex network of conditioned reflexes.

It was by different combinations of these new centers of excitation that a given response was produced.

5

The principle of conditioned reflexes states that neural connections have a temporary character. Repeated experiences are necessary before they can appear and become fixed. Without such experiences they weaken or disappear altogether.

Well, what of that? In this case water was indeed a strong and frequent stimulus in the infant's life. There was definitely repetition. I did not yet know the nature of the second stimulus, but I realized how its conditioned association with water could have become established.

Later, however, as the child developed, this association was destined to disappear. After all, repetitions could not go on forever. Why, if neither the child nor the adolescent could break this false, erroneous connection, the grown man could certainly have done so. And the connection was incorrect, mistaken—that was evident.

Mental development certainly struggles against incorrect, false, illogical conceptions. The developing child, however, may encounter other, more logical proofs of the danger of what he fears.

Once again I began to examine my memories that had to do with water.

I met proofs of the danger of water at every step.

In water people drown. I could drown. Water floods the city. People throw themselves into the water in order to die.

What weighty proofs of the danger of water!

There is no doubt that this could frighten a child and

prove to him that his infant notions were correct.

This peculiar kind of "false" proof could have been present throughout my life. And that is, no doubt, what happened. Water retained its terrifying quality and fed my infant fears. The temporary associations with water which had arisen could have failed to disappear and could have become more and more strongly and firmly fixed.

Therefore, a person's mental development does not destroy temporary conditioned associations, but only re-arranges them, raises these false proofs to its own level of development. And, perhaps, the intellect obligingly seeks out these proofs without really testing them, since even without being tested they can take root in the logical mind, falling as they do on infected ground.

These false proofs frequently become intermingled with genuine ones. Water is really dangerous. But the neurotic perceives the danger differently, and his reaction to the danger is not a normal person's reaction.

6

But if this is so, if water was one of the factors which terrified me, one of the stimuli which combined to produce my psychoneurosis, what a melancholy and pathetic picture was revealed to me.

For it was precisely with water that they tried to cure me. Precisely with water that they tried to relieve my depression.

They prescribed water both internally and externally. They put me in bathtubs, wrapped me in wet sheets, prescribed shower baths. They sent me to the seashore to take boat trips and go swimming.

My God! A cure like that could have depressed me all by itself.

This treatment could have intensified the conflict and created a hopeless situation.

And water was only part of the trouble, perhaps even a minor part.

However, the treatment did not produce a hopeless situation. It was possible to avoid treatment. And that is what I did. I stopped going to doctors.

In order to avoid treatment I thought up an absurd theory to the effect that to be in the best of health a man must work uninterruptedly all the time. I stopped going to resorts, considering it an unnecessary luxury.

In this way I avoided treatment.

But I could not avoid constant encounters with what terrified me. My fear continued to exist.

This fear was unconscious. I didn't know of its existence, since it had been crowded down into the lower story of my psyche. The guards of my reason would not permit it to get out. It had the right to come out only at night, when my conscious mind was not in control.

This terror led a nocturnal existence, living in dreams. In the daytime, in encounters with objects of terror, it appeared only in a distorted form—in those inexplicable symptoms which could have puzzled any doctor.

We know what fear is, we know its effects on the functioning of the body. We know the defensive reflexes it causes. Their basis is the attempt to avoid danger.

Fear produces various symptoms. These depend on the strength of the fear. They can be expressed in contraction of the blood vessels, in intestinal spasms, in convulsive muscular contractions, in palpitations of the heart, and so on. An extreme degree of terror can cause complete or partial paralysis.

Just such symptoms were created by the unconscious terror which I experienced. In one degree or another they were expressed in heart palpitations, shortness of breath, spasms, and convulsive jerking of the muscles.

These were primarily symptoms of fear. Their constant occurrence disrupted the normal functioning of my body, caused periodic malfunctioning, and led to chronic disorders.

These symptoms were all originally "purposeful"—they blocked my way to "danger" and readied me for flight.

An animal which cannot escape danger plays dead.

At times I pretended to be dead, ill, weak—when it was impossible to get away from the "danger."

All this was my response to an external stimulus. It was a complex response, since the conditioned neural connections, as we will see, were exceedingly complex.

7

We may concede that a child wishing to avoid "danger" acts in this way. But how does an adult act?

How did I act? Did I really fail to fight against this nonsense? Did I really try to save myself only by flight? Was I really an unfortunate speck of dust blown about by every circumstance?

No, I did fight it, I did try to defend myself against this unconscious danger. And this defense was always in proportion to my mental development.

In my childhood my behavior tended in the main toward flight and in a certain measure to an effort to master water, to "possess" it. I tried to learn to swim. But I didn't learn. Terror held me fast in its arms.

I learned to swim only as an adolescent, when I succeeded in conquering my fear.

That was my first victory and perhaps my only one. I remember how proud I was of it.

Later on, my conscious mind made no attempt to deflect me from this fight. On the contrary, it drew me toward it. I strove each time to meet my powerful adversary as soon as possible, so I could match my strength with his once more.

Here was the contradiction which masked my terror.

I did not avoid ships and boats, I did not avoid being near the sea. Notwithstanding my fear I deliberately sought opportunities to enter the lists. My conscious mind did not want to admit defeat or even cowardice.

I remember an incident at the front. I was leading my battalion to its position. It turned out that there was a river in front of us. For a moment I was shaken. The crossing was not a difficult one, but nonetheless I sent scouts to the right and left to look for easier places to cross. I sent them with the secret hope of finding some dried-up pathway across the river.

It was the beginning of summer, and there couldn't have been such a pathway.

I was shaken for only a moment. I ordered the scouts called back. And I led the battalion across the river.

I remember my agitation when we entered the water. I remember the pounding of my heart, which I could hardly endure.

It turned out that I had acted correctly. The crossings were just the same everywhere. And I was glad that I had not delayed, that I had acted decisively.

It meant I was not a blind implement in the hands of my fear. My behavior at all times was dictated by duty, conscience, and consciousness. But the conflict which arose frequently under these circumstances would make me ill.

The fear acted independently of my reason. My violent response to the stimulus was independent of my consciousness. But the symptoms of illness were all too evident. I did not know their source. Doctors diagnosed them roughly as neuroses brought on by overwork and exhaustion.

Sensing the unequal nature of the fight, I nonetheless continued to struggle against my unconscious terror. But how strangely this battle was waged. What strange paths I took to a doubtful victory.

8

A thirty-year-old man wanted to get rid of his fear by studying water. The battle was waged with the weapons of knowledge and science.

This was remarkable, since the conscious mind took part in the struggle. I do not fully understand how these paths happened to be the ones taken. The mechanisms of my unhappiness were unknown to my conscious mind, and it was perhaps for this reason that a general course was chosen—one which seemed correct, but in the given case was wrong and even comical.

All my notebooks began to be filled with information about water.

I have these notebooks before me now. I look them over with a smile. Here are some notes on the most violent storms and floods the world has known. Here are the most detailed figures on the depth of seas and oceans. Here is information about the more turbulent bodies of water; about steep-cliffed shores which boats cannot approach; about waterfalls.

Here is some information about people who have drowned. About first aid for such people.

Here is a note underlined in red pencil: "71 per cent of the earth's surface is covered by water, and only 29 per cent is dry land."

What a tragic note! There is added in red pencil, "¾ of the globe is water!"

Here are some more tragic notes from which one can learn the percentage of water in the bodies of men, animals, and plants: "Fish—70-80%, jellyfish—96%, potatoes—75%, bones—50% . . ."

What an enormous amount of work I did! And how senseless it was.

Here is a whole notebook filled with information

about winds. The reason is clear: winds are a cause of floods, tempests, storms.

An excerpt from my notes:

"3 meters per second—leaves stir;

"10 meters per second—large branches sway;

"20 meters per second—strong wind;

"30 meters per second—storm;

"35 meters per second—storm, approaching hurricane force;

"40 meters per second—hurricane, capable of destroying houses."

Under the note is the information: " 'ty'—extraordinary, 'phoon'—wind. The typhoon of 1892 (the island of Mauritius—54 meters per second!)."

Here is still another notebook, this one concerned with floods in Leningrad.

Leafing through these notebooks of mine, I smiled at first. Then my smile changed to distress. What a tragic struggle! What an "intellectual" and at the same time barbaric way had my conscious mind found to use its knowledge in order to master the enemy, destroy my fear, and win the victory.

What a tragic way I had found. It corresponded to my intellectual development.

9

The path I took was also reflected in my writing.

But here I must explain. I don't mean at all that this path—my fear and my desire to overcome it—determined my life, my actions, my behavior, my melancholy, or my literary goals.

Not at all. My behavior would have remained exactly the same if my terror had been absent. But my terror complicated the steps I took, aggravated my illnesses, and deepened my melancholy, which could have existed anyway, but for reasons and circumstances which affected all people to an equal degree.

Fear did not determine the paths I took, but it was one of the complex sum of forces which affect a person.

It would be a mistake not to consider this particular factor. But it would be an even greater mistake to take this part for the sum total, for the only thing which affects a person.

The problem could be solved only in all its complexity.

We have seen this complexity in my behavior. The basic moving force was not fear, but a group of other forces—duty, reason, conscience. These forces turned out to be significantly stronger than the lower forces.

My behavior was essentially rational. Fear did not lead me by the hand like a blind man. But it dogged my heels, interfered with the proper functioning of my body, and forced me to avoid "dangers" if no higher feelings or obligations existed.

It exerted constant pressure on me and, most important, affected my physical condition.

My conscious mind wanted to remove it. My intellectual development chose the path of knowledge. The professional habits of the literary man also took part in this struggle. Among the many subjects for stories which interested me those associated with water were prominent. I had a special fondness for such subjects.

I spent six months going over the material from Epron in my research on the sinking of the *Black Prince*.* While working on this book I painstakingly investigated everything that was related to the subject. I went out to where the work had been done, acquainted myself with the business of deep-sea diving,

* The *Black Prince* was a name ascribed in legend to the British ship, the *Prince,* which was sunk by a hurricane off Balaklava in November 1854, at the outset of the Crimean War. It was believed to have carried a large amount of gold, and many fruitless efforts were made in subsequent years to find this treasure. Zoshchenko published an extended account of the *Black Prince* affair in 1936. "Epron" was the name of the Soviet agency engaged in underwater recovery operations in the Black Sea. *Ed.*

and collected literature about all the inventions in this field.

When I had finished writing my book, *The Black Prince*, I immediately began to gather material on the destruction of the submarine 55.* I did not finish this book. The subject had ceased to interest me, since at that time I found more reasonable means of fighting.

And so, by studying water and all its properties, I wanted to free myself from misfortune, from unconscious fear. This fear did not even relate to water. But water aroused the fear, since it was associated with another object of fear.

My struggle against this fear was, I repeat, in proportion to my intellectual development.

What a tragic struggle! What grief and defeats it promised me. What blows were destined for my wretched body.

What misfortunes emanating from our higher consciousness can we speak about?

So far we can speak only about the insufficient knowledge of the rational mind. We can speak about an unfortunate little savage wandering along a narrow mountain path, hardly lit by the first rays of the morning sun.

10

Thus the first steps in the search for the unfortunate incident had been taken.

The unfortunate incident had taken place when I was making my first acquaintance with the world around me. It took place before sunrise, in the twilight before dawn.

* The British submarine *L-55* was lost in the Baltic Sea in 1919. It was refloated by the Russians after lying in the water for nine years, reconditioned, and put into service again in 1931. But it sank again while on trials. Raised once again, it was used for training purposes. *Ed.*

It wasn't even an incident. It was a mistake, an unfortunate occurrence, a striking combination of chance circumstances.

This chance circumstance gave rise to erroneous, unhealthy conceptions about certain things, among them water.

It was a drama in which my guilt was nothing more than suffering.

However, the end of this drama has not yet been revealed.

> *The snake is cut to pieces, but not dead;*
> *The pieces will regrow and live again.*

I had to find the conditioned neural connections which led from water to something as yet unknown, perhaps to something even more frightening. Without this, water would not have been a source of terror.

And so, confident of my powers, I set off further in the search for my unfortunate experience.

(To be continued)